The making of peace

The Making of Peace represents a unique contribution to the study of war: namely, the difficulties that statesmen have confronted in attempting to put back together the pieces after a major conflict. It contains a number of case studies by many leading historians in the United States and the United Kingdom.

Williamson Murray is Senior Fellow at the Institute for Defense Analyses in Washington, DC, and Professor Emeritus of History at the Ohio State University. He is co-editor of *The Past as Prologue* (with Richard Hart Sinnreich), *The Dynamics of Military Revolution, 1300–2050* (with Mac-Gregor Knox), *Military Innovation in the Interwar Period* (with Allan R. Millett), and *The Making of Strategy* (with Alvin Bernstein and MacGregor Knox).

Jim Lacey is an analyst at the Institute for Defense Analyses in Washington, DC, where he has written several studies on the war in Iraq and on the Global War on Terrorism. Lacey was also an embedded journalist with *Time* magazine during the invasion of Iraq, in which he traveled with the 101st Airborne Division. He is the author of *Takedown: The 3rd Infantry Division's 21-Day Assault on Baghdad*.

The making of peace
Rulers, states, and the aftermath of war

Edited by

WILLIAMSON MURRAY
Institute for Defense Analyses

JIM LACEY
Institute for Defense Analyses

CAMBRIDGE
UNIVERSITY PRESS

CAMBRIDGE UNIVERSITY PRESS
Cambridge, New York, Melbourne, Madrid, Cape Town, Singapore, São Paulo, Delhi

Cambridge University Press
32 Avenue of the Americas, New York, NY 10013-2473, USA

www.cambridge.org
Information on this title: www.cambridge.org/9780521731935

First published 2009

Printed in the United States of America

A catalog record for this publication is available from the British Library

Library of Congress Cataloging in Publication data

The making of peace : rulers, states, and the aftermath of war /
edited by Williamson Murray, Jim Lacey.
p.   cm.
Includes bibliographical references and index.
ISBN 978-0-521-51719-5 (hbk.) – ISBN 978-0-521-73193-5 (pbk.)
1. History, Modern.   2. Peace – Case studies.   I. Murray, Williamson.
II. Lacey, Jim, 1958–   III. Title.
D217.M19   2008
327.1'72 – dc22   2008025524

ISBN 978-0-521-51719-5 hardback
ISBN 978-0-521-73193-5 paperback

Contents

v

Preface: concluding peace

SIR MICHAEL HOWARD

There are three basic theories of peace. One is that of Thomas Hobbes: Peace is simply the absence of war. The second is that of St. Augustine: Peace is a 'just order', rendered 'just' by divine decree, or, in more modern times, by popular endorsement. In the former case, sin shatters the natural harmony, in the latter, the devices and interests of the ruling classes. The third theory is that of Immanuel Kant: Peace, though desirable, is not a 'natural' condition but has to be 'established': created and maintained by constant human effort.

For Thomas Hobbes, writing as he did during the turmoil of Europe's Thirty Years' War, the natural, or default, condition of man was war, a war of all against all, during which life was 'nastie, poore, solitarie, brutish, and short'. To escape this fate, men had created civil societies to provide protection but were themselves in a state of constant war with each other. Only brief and periodic truces provided peace. Professor Rahe's chapter underlines that this was the view held by the Greek city-states. The signatories of the Peace of Nicias, the first of which we have any enduring record, considered it to be simply 'a long-term truce, and never imagined that it would be a lasting peace'. Nor did they desire it to be so. For them, war was a necessary bonding activity, as important for social cohesion as for group survival. Those who could not prevail in war did not survive either individually or communally, as the unfortunate inhabitants of Melos found to their great cost. The Athenians massacred the male survivors in defeat and sold their women and children into slavery. In such a world, only hegemony could establish 'peace', as it would be by the Romans; a solution requiring not only military supremacy but the will to maintain it over generations, until it becomes internalised by prescription and cultural indoctrination.

The contents of this book then jump two thousand years from the Peace of Nicias in 431 B.C. to that of Westphalia in 1648 A.D.; understandably, since their authors deal only with formal agreements between established states and between those dates, 'states', as we understand them, did not exist. Rome established its *imperium* in the west over what were basically tribal communities. The Christian Church then underwrote that *imperium* and prolonged it for another millennium, in the shape of the Holy Roman Empire; until, indeed, as Professors Croxton and Parker describe in their chapter, the signatories of the Westphalian settlement ignored papal protests, and international politics became wholly secularised. Until then, wars were legitimised, either to protect Christendom against its heathen adversaries – and even at Westphalia there still lingered the ideal of uniting Christendom against the Turk – or to preserve or restore property rights that were themselves part of a divine hierarchical order constantly broken and having to be forcibly restored; rights that were to outlive their medieval origins and persist, in 'wars of succession', for another two centuries after Westphalia.

But, although hereditary claims survived as a convenient criterion of legitimacy, the Westphalian settlement established a new basis for the establishment of peace: the common interest of the states concerned, or *raison d'état*. The principal strategic interest of the victors in the Thirty Years' War, France and her allies, was the destruction of the hegemony that the Habsburg dynasty had threatened to establish over Western Europe. The possibility that an alternative French hegemony might be equally unwelcome does not seem to have occurred to Cardinal Mazarin. But, such interested short-sightedness apart, it was generally agreed that the common interest of the European states lay in the creation and preservation of a 'balance of power' to deter and, if necessary, to defeat potential aggressors. This principle was to shape European diplomacy until the First World War.

We have now moved into the age of Kant: At Westphalia, peace was not 'restored' but consciously and deliberately 'established'. Further, peace was no longer simply a Hobbesian truce but rather a condition in itself positively desirable. The domination of Europe by monarchs supported by a feudal aristocracy, who had to be kept out of mischief by fighting, was collapsing in the face of the challenge of a rising class of merchants and businessmen who had to pay for war and drew little profit from it. When peace was established, it was with the intention that it should last, and it was in the interest of all European powers to ensure that it did – hence, the institution of the periodic congresses whose activities this volume describes: congresses attended not only by belligerent but by neutral powers, who underwrote settlements intended to be lasting and in the general interest.

It was in this context that a debate emerged among the victorious powers as to how best to treat their defeated adversaries, a debate that was to surface at the conclusion of every major conflict, not excepting the two world wars of the twentieth century. Should the vanquished foe be 'debellated' – that is, so weakened as to be unable to make any more trouble for the foreseeable future? Or should he be conciliated by a settlement in whose preservation he would have as much interest as his conqueror? In his account of the Peace of Paris in 1763, which concluded not only the Seven Years' War but almost twenty-five years of continuous conflict between France and Britain, Professor Anderson describes how the Duke of Bedford (a member of the maverick Russell family whose unorthodox views were repeatedly to surface over many generations) warned the British government against 'imposing such terms on France as we are sure she cannot long acquiesce under, and which, when she has taken breath, she will take the first opportunity of breaking'. A British monopoly of naval power, he warned, 'would be at least as dangerous to the liberties of Europe as those of Louis XIV was, who drew almost all Europe on his back'. Lasting peace could best be won, he argued, not by the debellation but by the appeasement of the adversary. As it happened, the settlement was so favourable to France, restoring as it did most of her lucrative West Indian possessions, that it infuriated public opinion in London ('Like the Peace of God,' its critics complained, 'it passeth all understanding'). Yet, even this moderation did not prevent 'almost all Europe' falling on Britain's back when the unforeseen and unforeseeable consequences of the war led to the revolt of the American colonies. 'The very fact of a decisive victory in war', comments Professor Anderson drily, with his eye no doubt on more recent events, 'can foster the illusion that military power is less limited and contingent than in fact it is'.

Although by the end of the eighteenth century the continental powers of Europe had little left to gain from internecine conflict, the colonial powers, primarily Britain, France and Spain, still had a very great deal. Among them, peace, or at least peace overseas, still consisted of Hobbesian truces, until Napoleon's continental campaigns (themselves largely a by-product of his attempt to counter British naval supremacy) exhausted France, antagonised her European allies, and left Britain globally supreme. No longer facing existential threats, the statesmen at Vienna were then able to conclude an eminently rational settlement in which, as Colonel Sinnreich shows, the need to enlist France as a balancing element in the emerging rivalry between her former enemies mitigated the desire to reduce French power, and the other great powers accepted France as an essential partner in the settlement's making and preservation.

But, if France's military power were no longer a matter for immediate concern, she now posed – or was for a time believed to pose – a different and even more lethal kind of threat: one to the legitimacy of the entire states-system. It was not so much the power of French bayonets that her former adversaries feared as the revolutionary ideas of the French. The French Revolution introduced an era in which the Augustinian concept of peace, as a condition established by divine decree and disturbed only by mortal sin, had now revived in secular form through the intellectual efforts of

Jean-Jacques Rousseau and his followers. For them also, peace was the natural condition of man, but now only the misgovernment of the ruling classes stood between the people and their enjoyment of it. All that one needed was for the rulers to be overthrown and the peoples of the world to establish free republics for them to live in perpetual amity. France herself might represent an exhausted volcano, but the sparks scattered by Napoleon's armies still smouldered beyond the Rhine and south of the Alps – in the latter case, sedulously fanned by Giuseppi Mazzini and his followers. The statesmen of Vienna were at least as much concerned to extinguish them as to preserve the balance of power. Because no great power had an interest in upsetting that balance, and all proved strong enough to suppress further revolution, the settlement they made endured for nearly half a century.

In fact, the legacy of the Revolution was to be very different from that expected by its instigators. The French had shown that in order to act effectively, 'the people' had to be mobilised as a distinct and self-conscious 'nation'; one distinct, however, not only from their oppressive rulers but from other and alien nations. The French Revolutionary armies may have believed that, by invading their neighbours and overthrowing the *ancien regime* on their borders, they were bringing liberty in their wake and so laying the foundation for a perpetual peace based on the natural unity of all mankind. But those neighbours – Germans, Italians and Spaniards – were less conscious of being released from their fetters than of being occupied by armed foreigners with whom they found they had less in common than they had with their own rulers, who, whatever their faults, were also Germans, Italians or Spaniards. Paradoxically, it was to be the conservative monarchs in Piedmont and Prussia who, by harnessing the new nationalism to their traditional dynastic ambitions, would be the ultimate beneficiaries of the Revolution. Events were to prove that nationalism did not automatically lead to democracy any more than democracy automatically led to peace.

The trouble is that 'the people' are not necessarily peace loving – or, rather, that they may want peace only on terms unacceptable to their neighbours, especially when those neighbours hold beliefs or embody a culture incompatible with their own. When the cultures are so mutually incompatible as to lead to hostilities, any peace treaty is likely, at best, only to represent a truce. That truce may afford sufficient breathing space for mutual understanding to develop, as opposing cultures grow more tolerant or find themselves absorbed in one more powerful. But often the war is simply driven underground, as Professor McPherson shows to have been the case after the American Civil War. Appomattox, he points out, 'did not end the cultural and ideological struggle in which the military conflict was embedded'. The same situation was to recur persistently in the tormented history of Ireland and to appear again in Germany after 1918 – with yet more disastrous consequences for the history of mankind.

Thus, there developed during the nineteenth century the dogma that any 'peace' that did not allow for full 'national self-determination' was by definition unjust, and oppressed nationalities had not only the right but the duty to overthrow it. Liberals of the Enlightenment who opposed war in principle joined up enthusiastically in 1914 to fight for the rights of small nations, whether Belgium or Serbia. Unfortunately, after they had won that war, they discovered that the 'rights' of nations, whether great or small, were as incompatible with each other as they were with the balance of power. Professor Murray rightly describes the settlement of 1919 as 'The Peace Without a Chance'. Where the victorious powers enforced national self-determination, as in Eastern Europe, they created a nest of economically unviable, militarily indefensible, and mutually detesting mini-states. Where they abrogated self-determination, as in the case of Germany, they left a major power seething with resentment.

The Treaty of Versailles was indeed the kind of settlement that Bedford had warned against imposing on France in 1763. John Maynard Keynes was not the only prophet who echoed Bedford's description as one 'we are sure (Germany) cannot long acquiesce under and will take the first opportunity of breaking'. And, *pace* President Woodrow Wilson, the creation of 'democracy' in the defeated powers made little difference. Indeed, the more 'democratic' the states concerned, the more they resented the terms imposed on them. Wilson hoped that whatever the imperfections of the actual peace settlement, the creation of the League of Nations would lay the foundation for a just and stable order. But that hope assumed a mutual compatibility of interests that did not exist. As many powers discovered themselves interested in overthrowing the settlement as were interested in maintaining it, and they rapidly developed the capacity to do so.

But, the preservation of peace was no longer simply a question of 'interest', *raison d'état*. By the early twentieth century, there was emerging in Europe a philosophy that questioned whether 'peace' was desirable at all; whether mankind did not *need* war, in order to avoid racial degeneracy and national humiliation. For some, this represented a simple extension of nationalism: Nations *needed* to fight not only for their existence but for their continuing survival in a Darwinian universe, in which only the fittest survived. For others, it was a rejection of the entire culture of the Enlightenment, with all its consequences in urbanisation, secularism and the creation of a bland, boring, bourgeois world. The guru of the discontented young at the dawn of the twentieth century was no longer Rousseau or Mazzini: It was Friedrich Nietzsche, for whom morality was simply the will of the stronger. Many in Germany had seen the First World War as simply a conflict between *Helden und Handler*, as the economist Werner Sombart put it – heroes against shopkeepers. Supposedly, nations conducted such wars not to redress grievances or to right wrongs: Their object was victory and conquest in preparation for yet further wars – the world, in fact, of the ancient Greeks or, more specifically, the Nordic Gods.

It was this element in German thinking that made any peace with her in 1918 highly problematic, and the forcible transition to 'democracy' in 1918 did little to weaken German attitudes toward war. With the collapse of 'bourgeois democracy' in 1929–1931, there emerged leaders whose ultimate objective was not the assertion of rights or the redress of specific grievances but rather the establishment of a warrior hegemony programmed to fight further wars, and the greater the better. The Second World War was thus a true clash of cultures. No settlement was possible until one or the other had been eradicated. For the Western democracies, it was necessary that their military forces occupy both Germany and Japan, overthrow their bellicose elites, and eradicate their militaristic cultures before the Allies could create a new order that held out any promise of lasting peace.

By the end of the summer of 1945, the victorious powers had eliminated both Germany and Japan as actors on the international scene. In his chapter on the economics of the peace settlement, Jim Lacey underlines how the 'Bedford debate' was once more reenacted. This time, the arguments of those who favored the total debellation of the defeated adversary were again defeated: first by the realisation that Germany's prosperity was inseparable from that of Western Europe as a whole, then by the need to restore her economic and military capability – as it had been necessary to preserve that of France in 1815 – in the interests of the balance of power.

For a new cultural and ideological confrontation had taken the place of the old. Neither the Soviet Union nor the Western Allies were 'bellicist', as had been their Fascist adversaries. Neither wanted war. Both aimed at creating an enduring order legitimised by popular consent. But whereas for the West that consent expressed itself through democratic processes, which themselves assumed the existence of market economies, the Soviets believed that mankind could create such an order only after the destruction of 'war-mongering' capitalist economies and their replacement by economies based on the 'peace-loving' proletariat, under the guidance of a Communist party that retained total control of the economy and political life. Whether that confrontation would have been forcibly resolved had not the development of nuclear weapons established constraints on both antagonists, we shall never know. As it was, both sides tacitly accepted an order comparable to that established in Europe by the Westphalian system, that of *cuius regio, eius religio*: Neither party attempted to interfere with the social system of the other by the overt use of force. A tacit agreement to avoid war preserved the peace, and the balance of terror underwrote the balance of power. No one believed this to be a particularly just order, but it was the best available. Each believed that its own order would ultimately prevail and, eventually, one of them did.

The settlement of the issues that had led to the Second World War was thus delayed for half a century. But, by then, they had largely settled themselves. A new docile, democratic, and prosperous Germany, happily released from the divisive constraints imposed by the Cold War, had abandoned her strident nationalism and accepted her territorial losses in Central Europe with equanimity. At the same time, the collapse of the Soviet Union had restored a Russian state with which the rest of the world could do business and which accepted the loss of her hegemony over Central Europe with relatively good grace.

There was little incentive for the Western Powers to weaken or humiliate their former adversary: The total disintegration of the Soviet Union left little more for them to do and, indeed, they treated the new Russian leaders with commendable civility and restraint. But, in hoping that the new Russia would continue indefinitely to be docile and democratic, they were being overly optimistic. Once they had recovered from the trauma of defeat, the Russians inevitably sought to reassert themselves on the international stage and were as likely to unite behind a national leader who promised to restore their national pride as to turn themselves into a bourgeois democracy happy to do the will of their former adversaries.

That brings us to our current discontents. Professor Kagan has suggested in his chapter that because the leadership of the United States in the 1990s was overwhelmed by the simultaneous settlement of both the Second World War and the Cold War, it missed an opportunity to manage the transition to a new global order – much as had the British after the First World War. But, without considering whether in the 1920s a Britain suffering from imperial overstretch, bankrupted by war debts, at issue with both of its former allies (France and the United States) and riddled with domestic strife was ever in a position to do anything of the sort (or whether the world, including the United States, would have been interested in a new order 'managed' by Britain), we may wonder whether seventy years later the United States could really have done any better. Professor Kagan correctly describes her as 'launched into management of an increasingly chaotic world which [she] had no intellectual basis for comprehending'. But, within a few years, an administration did come to power in Washington that believed itself to have such an intellectual basis for 'managing' the world and proceeded to do so.

That basis was the Rousseauite–Wilsonian belief in the natural underlying harmony of democratic societies – societies the United States now possessed the military power to establish, the wisdom to advise on governance, and the economic wealth to sustain. But it bore a close family resemblance to the illusion that had led the French to seek to 'liberate' their neighbours two centuries earlier – only to learn in the process, as their own Robespierre, that ferocious revolutionary, put it: 'No one loves armed missionaries'. What seemed in Washington to be truths self-evident to all humankind appeared to many, especially in the Muslim world, more like arguments for the imposition of a culturally alien hegemony, against which they instinctively revolted. It certainly did not appear as forming the foundations for an acceptable international order.

It may be wiser, therefore, to base a search for international order not on any perceived universal yearning for freedom and democracy but rather on a much more basic general desire simply to *avoid war* – linked with a universal aspiration for an improvement in economic conditions, the more likely to come about the longer the peace can last. Such a desire is not confined to democratic states, nor do democratic states necessarily hold it any more strongly than others. Nor are revisionist states with little interest in preserving the international order necessarily 'evil'. It is certainly not wise to stigmatise them as such because to do so will inevitably make it more difficult to change the context of their attitudes. Moreover, one may need their support next time around.

We may not share the Hobbesian view of war as being the default condition of mankind; but then, neither is harmony, whether decreed by *vox populi* or *vox dei*. We would be wiser to accept the default condition as being *conflict* – perpetual conflicts whose resolution will only precipitate more. But such conflicts need not necessarily be resolved by force, and it is the business of statesmen to ensure that they are not. 'Peace' is no more than an order in which war does not settle conflicts. It has to be 'established' but, once established, it can become a habit. Its only real enemies are those restless spirits who, for whatever reason, prefer the alternative.

Introduction: searching for peace

WILLIAMSON MURRAY

War appears to be as old as mankind, but peace is a modern invention.[1]

The earliest of historians, Herodotus and Thucydides, provided Greek and Western thinkers with the first efforts to record, examine, and analyze human events. As the latter explicitly stated at the beginning of his history of the Peloponnesian War, "It will be enough for me ... if these words of mine are judged useful by those who want to understand clearly the events which happened in the past and which (human nature being what it is) will at some time or other and in much the same ways, be repeated in the future."[2] Herodotus and Thucydides were indeed the "fathers of history" and, like so many who have followed in their footsteps, their histories focused on war – specifically, the origins and course of the two great wars that buffeted the world of fifth-century B.C. Greece. The first involved the epic struggle of the Greek city-states against the Persian Empire (490–479 B.C.); the second, the terrible, debilitating Peloponnesian War between the alliances of Greek city-states led by Athens and Sparta (431–404 B.C.).

Yet, neither historian involved himself much in discussing the peace making that came afterwards, for reasons which in retrospect are understandable: Herodotus, perhaps because the struggle against the Persians continued well after the defeat of the Persian Army at Plataea in 479 B.C.; Thucydides, because death robbed him of the opportunity to complete his history of

---

[1] Sir Henry Maine quoted in Sir Michael Howard, *The Invention of Peace: Reflections on War and the International Order* (New Haven, CT, 2000), p. 1.

[2] Thucydides, *History of the Peloponnesian War*, trans. by Rex Warner (London, 1954), p. 48.

the Peloponnesian War.[3] And, to a considerable extent, what perhaps they could not control – their own fate – set a pattern that virtually all military histories have followed over the succeeding twenty-five hundred years: namely, to describe in great detail the course of military events while leaving the making of peace largely unexamined.[4]

Moreover, most historians of earlier centuries had no expectation that there was any such thing as a lasting peace, or even that such a goal possibly existed. In the world that existed until the nineteenth century, conflict was not only endemic, it was expected. Times of peace were so few and far between that observers of events could hardly examine, much less understand, what peace might look like in the real world, as opposed to the world of theory.

In his description of the great war between the Athenians and the Spartans, Thucydides more than lived up to his promise to write an history that would be deeply relevant to future generations.[5] Yet, what transpired after the defeat of the Athenian fleet at Aegospotami was a theme worthy of Thucydides' analytic abilities: the complete failure of the Spartans to shape anything like a lasting peace or, for that matter, even a temporary cessation of hostilities, and the continued descent of the Greek city-states into the nightmare of endless, internecine warfare that was to last until the Macedonians appeared on the scene. It would have made an even more depressing tale than that of the Peloponnesian War.

There is little in the history of the intervening twenty-five hundred years to suggest that Thucydides' cold, dark view of the arena of international affairs has changed significantly. As the Athenian negotiators at Melos suggest to their opposite numbers,

> So far as the favor of the gods is concerned, we think we have as much right
> to that as you have. Our aims and our actions are perfectly consistent with
> the beliefs men hold about the gods and with the principles which govern their

---

[3] Thucydides' account breaks off in 411 B.C. as the Athenians were desperately attempting to recover from their disastrous defeat in Sicily and as they were confronting, at the same time, revolution throughout their empire and an oligarchic coup at home.

[4] There has been some interest among political scientists and others about the difficulties involved in peace making in areas where civil wars, such as in the Balkans, have created deep rifts between communities. Yet, even the most sophisticated have largely focused on recent events and relatively small conflicts, rather than the great sweep of history. Among others, see Roland Paris, *At War's End: Building Peace after Civil Conflict* (Cambridge, 2004). The great difficulty that most such academic exercises have in their examination of the making of peace is the almost complete absence of a discussion of the nature of war and its impact on the deliberation of the peacemakers. In this regard, see particularly G. John Ikenberry, *After Victory: Institutions, Strategic Restraint, and the Rebuilding of Order after Major Wars* (Princeton, NJ, 2001).

[5] For discussions of what makes history so difficult for officers (and others) to acquire and then use, see Williamson Murray and Richard Hart Sinnreich, eds., *The Past as Prologue: The Importance of History to the Military Profession* (Cambridge, 2006).

own conduct. Our opinion of the gods and our knowledge of men lead us to conclude that it is a general and necessary law of nature to rule wherever one can. This is not a law that we made ourselves, nor were we the first to act upon it when it was made. We found it already in existence, and we shall leave it to exist among those who come after us. We are merely acting in accordance with it, and we know that you or anybody else with the same power as ours would be acting in precisely the same way.[6]

Such a view of the world seems alien to those who live in the comfort of the First World at the onset of the twenty-first century. Yet, is it so foreign to what history suggests about the nature of the world, including much of the world that has existed in our own time? In fact, the relationship between peace and war finds itself entangled to a considerable extent in how the modern world defines peace. The modern belief, at least in most of the First World, appears to be that peace is the normal order of human affairs, a concept that began to emerge in the liberal consciousness of Victorian Britain.[7] This conception has persisted since then in much of the First World, despite the experiences of two world wars and the innumerable conflicts that marked the course of decolonialization during the Cold War, as well as the conflicts among the locals squabbling over the wreckage left by the withdrawal of the European powers.[8] Yet, the irony of such hopeful expectations lies in the fact that within living memory, the catastrophe of the Second World War spread horror, murder, and destruction across the face of the world in a fashion and to an extent that had never occurred before in all of history and that came frighteningly close to achieving Clausewitz's theoretical concept of "total war."[9]

---

[6] Thucydides, *History of the Peloponnesian War*, pp. 404–5.

[7] For a brilliant dissection of this emergence, see Michael Howard, *War and the Liberal Conscience: The George Macaulay Trevelyan Lectures in the University of Cambridge, 1977* (New Brunswick, NJ, 1978).

[8] Among the conflicts in the first category, one might count Malaya, French Indo-China, Korea, and Algeria; among the conflicts in the latter case, one might number the Arab-Israeli Wars of 1947–1948, 1967, 1973, and 1982; the India-Pakistan Wars of 1948–1949 and 1972; and the interminable conflicts throughout Africa. In addition, there were the conflicts that the United States found itself involved in: namely, the Korean War and the Vietnam War – both of which involved conflicts sparked by the collapse of colonial empires (in this case, Japan and France) with an admixture of the ideological.

[9] Moreover, the revealed wisdom of all too many is that the strategic bombing of Germany or the dropping of the atomic bombs on Hiroshima and Nagasaki represented inexcusable acts of barbarism as evil as the terrible acts committed by the Nazis or the Japanese. The historical record of the war, however, underlines that both of those military operations were absolutely essential to bring the Second World War to a successful conclusion by spring–summer 1945. Among others, see Williamson Murray and Allan R. Millett, *A War to Be Won: Fighting the Second World War* (Cambridge, MA, 2000). For a careful examination of why it was necessary to drop the bombs on Japan, see Richard B. Frank, *Downfall: The End of the Imperial Japanese Empire* (New York, 1999); for the implications of a continuance of the war for China and Southeast Asia had the war continued, see Max Hastings, *Nemesis: The Battle for Japan, 1944–1945* (London, 2007).

Perhaps the only change – and it is a major one – that occurred in the period after the Second World War lay in the fact that the members of the First World did not engage in direct conflict with each other but instead conducted political and ideological battles through proxies, many of whom still struggle with the consequences. Nevertheless, as Colin Gray points out in his chapter in this volume, there was a considerable chance throughout that period that the United States and the Soviet Union might have settled matters as had the ideologically opposed powers in the late 1930s and early 1940s. Moreover, the processes of making peace after the innumerable small wars of the Cold War proved as messy and entangled with ideology and other factors as the making of peace after the great world wars.

As Sir Michael Howard has suggested recently, the First World's conception of peace is a construct of middle-class, intellectual societies determined by the economic and political context within which those, who believe in it, reside[10]:

> Peace, as we have seen, is not an order natural to man; it is artificial, intricate and highly volatile. All kinds of preconditions are necessary, not the least a degree of cultural homogeneity (best expressed through a common language), to make possible the political cohesion that must underlie a freely accepted framework of law, and at least a minimal level of education through which that culture can be transmitted. Further, as states develop they require a highly qualified elite, capable not only of operating their complex legal, commercial and administrative systems, but of exercising considerable moral authority over the rest of society.[11]

Such conditions, first noticeable in the Anglo-American world of the early to mid-nineteenth century and then spreading at times to Europe and beyond, have required decades if not centuries to emerge. Nothing better suggests the gulf between those who currently inhabit the industrialized, global First World and those in the world beyond than the bizarre belief

---

[10] Perhaps the silliest notion to emerge in the last two decades from modern-day American political science is the idea that globalization has rendered the modern state obsolete and that it will therefore disappear. Indeed, the modern state will mutate, as it has been doing over the past three and a half centuries, but it will not disappear. A few simple examples from the real world of Somalia, Panama in December 1989, Los Angeles in the early 1990s, and Iraq after April 2003 underline what happens when the state is no longer around to provide internal and external security to its citizens. There is simply nothing to protect civilization, and globalization would simply disappear from the threats that abound; without states, the world would then descend into a nightmare Hobbesian universe governed by the most ruthless and powerful, while in the words of Thucydides, "the weak [would have to] accept what they have to accept." Such a world would contain none of the protections and framework that Michael Howard has suggested are required for peace. Quotation from Thucydides, *History of the Peloponnesian War*, p. 402.

[11] Michael Howard, *The Invention of Peace: Reflections on War and International Order* (New Haven, CT, 2000), pp. 104–5.

of American military and political policy makers in early 2003 that the emergence of a Western-style democracy and rule of law would quickly and inevitably follow the fall of Saddam Hussein's brutal and incompetent regime.[12] Some even went so far as to imagine they could mold that "instant democracy" with an American-style icon of free-market capitalism.[13]

But, then, ahistoricism lies at the heart of the modern world's *Weltanschauung*, especially that of Americans.[14] The comforts of modern life allow for a deep-seated belief that the past has little relevance for understanding the modern world, where history has ended. And even those who do recognize the value of history all too often assume that their own particular history provides the model for all situations, no matter what the political, cultural, geographic, or religious contexts within which they find themselves.[15]

The making of peace, both historically and in our era, however, has taken place in entirely different contextual frameworks, which seemingly makes comparisons difficult. Yet, the making of peace after the two great world wars of the twentieth century proved to involve the same complex mix of honor, expediency, and morality that has marked other efforts through the ages. In fact, understanding the difficulties involved in the making of peace requires that one have a general as well as a specific understanding of the actual conditions of the war that has occurred. Without the former, the latter is impossible.

For example, those who argue that the peacemakers at Versailles in 1919 should have displayed a kinder, gentler approach to the defeated Germans in order to make a more lasting peace miss entirely how the Germans had conducted the First World War against their enemies – with a level of brutality that would outrage modern twenty-first–century sensibilities – as well as how the war had ended.[16] In other words, the smooth, seemingly sensible arguments about how a "kinder, gentler" peace could have saved Europe from another world war are both irrelevant and nonsensical – removed

---

[12] For discussions about the planning for the making of peace in Iraq, see particularly Thomas Ricks, *Fiasco: The American Military Adventure in Iraq* (New York, 2006).

[13] For an excellent discussion of this phenomenon, see Rajiy Chandrasekaran, *Imperial Life in the Emerald City: Inside Iraq's Green Zone* (New York, 2006).

[14] Astonishingly, this is true even among a considerable number of those who call themselves conservatives. In particular, the "neo-cons," who inhabited the Department of Defense in 2003, could not recall major historical events which had occurred as recently as December 1989, when the destruction of the Panamanian government, military, and police forces occasioned massive looting and the general breakdown of civil society.

[15] Thus, the American belief in 1964 and 1965 among policy makers in Washington that a refusal to stand up to the Communists in Vietnam would be similar to the surrender of Czechoslovakia at the Munich Conference in late September 1938 with similar long-term results.

[16] For how the Germans waged the First World War, see particularly Isabel Hull, *Absolute Destruction: Military Culture and the Practices of War in Imperial Germany* (Ithaca, NY, 2006).

entirely from the context and realities of the time that so entangled the efforts of the peacemakers at Versailles.

The chapters in this volume do not attempt to present a clear, unambiguous road map toward the making of peace. Rather, they seek to delineate the general complexities and ambiguities that have confronted statesmen, nations, and polities in the making of peace through the ages. The making of peace, like the making of strategy, is a messy, complex, and uncertain process that suggests few, simple, clear directions for the future. At best, these chapters constitute a first draft to guide those charged with the making of peace in the future and who will confront the equally difficult task of maintaining the peace once achieved. They reflect the conviction that historians need to address this subject with as much care and detail and with the same enthusiasm that they have heretofore dedicated to the study of wars, military organizations, campaigns, battles, and military victories. Only when the historical record provides greater clarity can there be some hope of avoiding, or at least assuaging, the egregious errors of the past.

Some may criticize this volume and its chapters for failing to provide case studies that involve other cultures and civilizations in the making of peace. Our only reply is that we have spread our net as widely as limitations of time and resources would permit. Moreover, we also contend that wandering off into the experiences of other civilizations without seriously analyzing the difficulties the West has confronted in the making of peace is simply to cater to the intellectual prejudices of irrelevant academic fashion. It might be politically correct to have a chapter on how the Ottomans, or the Mayans, or the Chinese have made peace, but to what purpose, if we do not understand how the West has made peace – especially since it is our past that we need as a starting point for understanding the options open to us in the future? If we cannot understand ourselves, how can we possibly understand others?

THE HISTORICAL BACKGROUND: ANCIENT AND MEDIEVAL

It is well to remember where humanity has been and its attitudes toward war through the ages before attempting to understand the problems involved in the making of peace. History does suggest that there have been periods of peace in which war has been a distant rumble away from the centers of civilized life. The Romans certainly managed to create an empire where, for nearly three centuries, from 30 B.C. to 250 A.D., the *Pax Romana* provided the citizens of the Empire a period of extended peace, broken only rarely by civil war, barbarian invasion, or rebellions.

This period of peace stretched all the way from the deserts of Arabia and the Upper Nile to northern Britain and the Straits of Gibraltar. The great eighteenth-century historian of the Empire's decline, Edward Gibbon, eloquently described this period of prolonged peace in the following terms:

> In the second century of the Christian era, the empire of Rome comprehended the fairest part of the earth, and the most civilized portion of mankind. The frontiers of that extensive monarchy were guarded by ancient renown and disciplined valour. The gentle, but powerful, influence of laws and manners had gradually cemented the union of the provinces. Their peaceful inhabitants enjoyed and abused the advantage of wealth and luxury....

> If a man were called to fix the period in the history of the world during which the condition of the human race was most happy and prosperous, he would, without hesitation, name that which had elapsed from the death of Domitian to the accession of Commodus.[17]

Yet, the Romans paid a price for that peace: They created and lived under a system of tyranny, which, if in some periods it provided a modicum of good government under emperors like Trajan or Marcus Aurelius, in others it witnessed the murderous, monstrous rule of the insane or the criminally demented, like Tiberius or Caligula, so acidly chronicled by Tactitus.[18] Nevertheless, unlike the present era, the behavior of the worst tyrants touched the lives of only the senators and upper classes in Rome, while rarely disturbing the peace of the provinces or even of Rome's urban plebes.[19] As to the barbarian threat on the frontiers, which at least until the end of the second century largely consisted of small raids, approximately 150,000 legionaries in 30 legions, supported by 150,000 auxiliaries, sufficed to protect the vast empire with its approximately 60 million-plus inhabitants.

However, Rome – and China – appear as anomalies on history's landscape. In China's case, the extent of its empire, the size of its population, and the allure and strength of its culture served to mitigate internal strife while absorbing even the most ferocious of invaders. In the case of Rome, it took three centuries of ferocious wars, external and civil, to create the empire that at last brought peace to the Mediterranean world. In effect, Rome created peace by destroying all her immediate threats and then walling the Empire

---

[17] Edward Gibbon, *The History of the Decline and Fall of the Roman Empire* (New York, 1946), pp. 1, 61.

[18] The *Annals* and the *Histories* of Tacitus recount the crimes and follies of the emperors from Augustus through Nero and then the blowup in 69 A.D. with Nero's fall. For a brilliant dissection of the destruction of the last vestiges of the Roman Republic, the rise of tyranny, and the creation of the Empire, see Ronald Syme, *The Roman Revolution* (Oxford, 1939). In the early third century, Emperor Caracalla, one of the worst of a bad lot, is reputed to have considered slaughtering the entire population of Alexandria, only to be persuaded against such a decision by his advisers, simply because it was too great a task for the number of soldiers available.

[19] In Tacitus' eyes, Domitian was one of the worst Roman emperors; modern historians, looking at Domitian's reign from the point of view of the provinces and administration of the Empire, have developed a different and more favorable view of the emperor's reign.

off from the barbarian world. But when demographic, economic, and civil problems debilitated the Empire in the third century, the structure proved incapable of standing. Even then, the persistence of Latin-based languages, as well as the myth of the Empire, succeeded in eventually absorbing the barbarian invaders in Western Europe.[20]

In both cases of enduring peace, the fact that an overarching power possessed the resources, manpower, military forces, ruthlessness, and economic viability to *enforce* its concept of peace against all comers suggests that these two examples are anomalies, which cannot speak to the world of the twenty-first century. They certainly cannot speak to the present with its globalized world of European states, which lacked the will to intervene even against a murderous petty tyrant like Slobodan Milosevic, despite the fact that his actions were threatening to destabilize the entire Balkans, their immediate neighborhood.

In the interactive world of the twenty-first century, the problem is three-fold: How are those who have successfully embraced globalization going to maintain peace? When that fails, how will they limit the conflicts that occur? And, finally, how will they then make a more lasting, inherently more stable peace in war's aftermath? The first and the last of these three problems present the most difficult of challenges because they inevitably involve human emotions.

In the period that followed the fall of the Roman Empire, peace as the Romans – or the moderns – conceived of it simply ceased to exist. The *Pax Romana* collapsed in the third and fourth centuries, never to be restored. What followed the fall of the Roman Empire in the west was a series of ferocious barbarian invasions that lasted for more than six centuries, culminating with the Viking raids of the tenth and eleventh centuries. Moreover, from the seventh century on, the Europeans confronted constant pressure from Muslim invaders on the frontiers of the Balkans, Sicily, and particularly Spain. But the war against the outsiders represented only a portion of the wars in Europe. From its inception, the medieval world of Western Europe presented a scene of constant conflict. Internecine wars among kings and great nobles, among the great nobles themselves, and among what one can best describe as marauding knights and mercenaries fell on the backs of peasants and emerging towns.

Admittedly, all was not war, at least among monarchs. The Hundred Years' War between France and England did see truces between the major contestants, the kings of England and France and the Duke of Burgundy. After all, there were only three great battles: Crecy, Poitiers, and Agincourt. But the problem for the peasants and villagers of France was the fact that

---

[20] Rumania is the exception in the Balkans.

even then there was scarcely what we might regard as peace. Truces among the great had little impact on the local nobility, much less the unemployed soldiery. Bands of marauders and mercenaries kept the countryside in a constant state of turmoil, which at times was all too much for an enraged peasantry, which resorted to murderous rebellion against its lords and masters, who had not only refused to keep the peace but gloried in war against their neighbors.[21]

There were efforts to bring some order out of this Hobbesian world. In 1095, Pope Urban II preached a crusade against the Moslem infidels who held Christ's city, Jerusalem. His aim seems to have been twofold: obviously, to regain Jerusalem, but also to persuade a substantial portion of Europe's fractious noblemen to focus their constant state of war against Christianity's external enemies rather than their fellow Christians. But others, particularly within the church, saw peace as "resulting not from some millennial divine intervention that would persuade the lion to lie down with the lamb, but from the forethought of rational human beings who had taken matters into their own hands."[22] Out of that sustained effort that begins with St. Thomas Aquinas emerged eventually the doctrine of "just war" – a concept that concerned war between Christians and left the world outside Christianity beyond the pale. Unfortunately, such efforts largely foundered on the nature of Europe's politics and standards of behavior. Quite simply, at every level, Europe's rulers had no desire to give up wars of aggression against their neighbors.

When the monarchs of early modern Europe were finally able to bring their fractious, quarrelsome, and ferocious nobility to bay in the fifteenth and early sixteenth centuries, they replaced the conflicts of earlier ages with a greater willingness and ability – the latter being the crucial factor – to engage in wars against each other. The Italian city-states set the stage for inter-state conflict in the fifteenth century with a constant series of wars against each other, conflicts largely conducted by trained and highly paid mercenaries. The results were hardly impressive in terms of great battles. The mercenaries, who were in it for the money rather than the glory, earned Machiavelli's undying scorn by their efforts to limit both the damage and casualties involved in their campaigns. But at least their selfish motivations placed some constraints and limitations on the level of conflict and violence among the complex web of relations among the Italian city-states. However, those limitations were to last no longer than the time it took the major European powers to intervene in the affairs of the peninsula.

---

[21] The *Jackerei* is the term used to describe these outbreaks, *Jacque* being the contemptuous name for the French peasantry given by their masters. For a discussion of these rebellions, see Jean Froissart, *Chronicles*, trans. by Geoffrey Brereton (London, 1978).
[22] Howard, *The Invention of Peace*, p. 6.

Thus, at the end of the fifteenth century, such efforts to constrain war ended with the intervention of first the French and then the Spanish in the Italian wars. The Italian wars soon assumed the ferocity that marked conflicts outside the peninsula. Moreover, in the sixteenth and early seventeenth centuries, with the advent of the Reformation, religious quarrels further exacerbated the ferociousness as well as the pervasiveness of conflict throughout Europe. Nothing better illustrates the lack of peace and the consequences of constant war than the Thirty Years' War (1618–1648), which wrecked the Germanies from the Mark of Brandenburg-Prussia to Alsace. The sack of Magdeburg, in which the attacking Habsburg armies slaughtered the city's thirty thousand inhabitants, suggests how far the parameters of human behavior had sunk toward barbarity. There was no question of peace.

So disastrous were the wars of religion, especially the Thirty Years' War, that Europe was able to break loose from the dark incitement of religion to unlimited violence – at least until the appearance of religion in its modern garb of ideology in the first half of the twentieth century. With its removal of the religious factor from international conflict, the Treaty of Westphalia represented a significant break with the past thousand years of European history.[23] Moreover, not only did the treaty remove religion from the context of European war, it also established the state and its representatives as the arbiters of peace and war. The emergent modern state of the late seventeenth and eighteenth centuries may have had little interest in what its citizens thought, but it also had little interest in waging unlimited conflict against its neighbors, since the territories thus ravaged might well be under its control with the making of peace. Thus, even if they had no vote in the waging of war or the making of peace, most Europeans benefited because war remained limited in its goals and conduct and in the damage it inflicted on the landscape.[24]

For the most part, European monarchs waged war for relatively small territorial gains, such as Frederick the Great's seizure of the province of Silesia, an action which kicked off the War of Austrian Succession and indirectly contributed to the outbreak of the Seven Years' War. Moreover, the establishment of disciplined, organized military forces, subordinate to sovereign authority, provided the means to project military force without doing irreparable damage to the territory crossed. The downside was that the making of peace in the eighteenth century rarely, if ever, aimed at the creation of a lasting settlement and instead concentrated on preparation for

---

[23] For the complexities of the making of peace in the mid-seventeenth century, see Derek Croxton and Geoffrey Parker's chapter in this volume.

[24] It is worth noting that none of this applied in the Balkans in the contest between the Austrian and the Ottoman Empires, where religion remained very much on the table.

the next conflict by gaining the best strategic vantage points. At best, peace was a continuation of war by other means, a state of affairs that even so represented an improvement over what had existed and what was to come.

All changed radically with the wars of the French Revolution. Quite simply, the revolutionaries in Paris tossed the rule book of war and peace in the fire and radicalized the conduct of war. As Clausewitz points out:

> [B]ut in 1793 a force appeared and beggared all imagination. Suddenly war again became the business of the people – a people of thirty millions, all of whom considered themselves to be citizens.... The people became a participant in war; instead of governments and armies as heretofore, the full weight of the nation was thrown into the balance. The resources and efforts now available for use surpassed all conventional limits; nothing now impeded the vigor with which war could be waged, and consequently the opponents of France faced the utmost peril....

> War, untrammeled by any conventional restraints, had broken loose in all its elemental fury. This was due to the peoples' new share in the great affairs of state; and their participation in turn, resulted partly from the impact that the revolution had on the internal conditions of every state and partly from the danger that France posed to everyone.[25]

Driven by the popular nationalism of the French nation, the Republic completely overthrew the European balance of power. Its successor, the Napoleonic Empire, came close to establishing France's hegemony over the continent.

But the success of the French unleashed a savage response from the conquered. Ironically, it was in the areas farthest from the heart of Europe's enlightenment – Spain, Russia, the Tyrol – where resistance emerged in its most effective form. When it was over, an exhausted Europe, led by the victors, cobbled together a peace that managed to put the genie of nationalism, as well as war, back in the jar for the next three decades. Equally important to the maintenance of peace during the period was the fact that Europe's exhaustion after a quarter century of devastating conflict provided a major incentive for the peaceful settlement of international disputes, at least during the near term.

Whatever their motives, the peacemakers at Vienna enjoyed the major advantage over their successors in the twentieth century. From Westphalia to Vienna, the making of peace, like the making of war, was the business of kings, princes, generals, and their diplomats. In many ways, the making of peace resembled a cotillion among the great, in which popular opinion had neither say nor vote. Thus, the complexity of negotiations reflected the

---

[25] Carl von Clausewitz, *On War*, ed. and trans. by Michael Howard and Peter Paret (Princeton, NJ, 1975), pp. 591–3.

challenge of reconciling traditional territorial ambitions with the need for a stable and broadly legitimate European equilibrium. It certainly did not reflect public opinion outraged by its enemies. In all of this, none of the diplomats felt the slightest need to consult public opinion, which hardly existed in 1815, with the limited exception of France and Britain.[26] And so they did not. The result was that those who made the settlement were able to suppress the deep bitterness of those who had suffered under French depredations and rule in deciding how Europe would treat Napoleon and his successors.

The near century of peace from 1815 through 1914 resulted from two factors: The settlement at Vienna kept a modicum of peace for nearly half a century. Then, with nationalism's reemergence, beginning in 1848 with its revolutions and the late 1850s with the wars on the Italian peninsula but in its most virulent form in the Franco-Prussian War, accident as well as incompetence conspired to limit the damage, at least until 1914. In the Franco-Prussian conflict, the incompetence of Louis Napoleon's Second French Empire, as well as the French passion for political fragmentation, resulted in a decisive Prusso-German victory, one magnified by the brilliance of Bismarck's strategy. Thus, the implications of the reappearance of nationalism as a major driver in war and the making of peace remained hidden even to the most sophisticated analysts. The lid remained on until the catastrophe of 1914.

As Sir Michael Howard has pointed out in two significant works, it was during this period that present conceptions of "peace" as a condition wholly distinct from war emerged full-blown. The making of peace between the British and French on one side and the Russians on the other at the end of the Crimean War found an altered world. The telegraph now allowed reports from both the front and the negotiating table to reach Paris and London newspapers the next day.[27] However, it did not matter until the denouement of the Franco-Prussian War, when public opinion in Prusso-Germany and France played major roles, first in driving the two sides into conflict and then in making it exceedingly difficult for Bismarck and the Republic's negotiators to arrive at a settlement, even considering the decisive nature of Prussia and its German allies' battlefield victories.

---

[26] And even then the lack of speedy means of communications meant that the decisions of British negotiators in Vienna were invariably overtaken by events by the time they reached London.

[27] Interestingly, that factor exercised relatively little influence over the making of peace, but it certainly resulted in a massive public outcry in Britain over the inexcusable incompetence of the War Office in the clothing, feeding, and medical services provided British soldiers in the field.

If the 100 years of relative stability that ended in 1914 created the expectation that peace was the norm in human affairs, the catastrophe of the First World War should have disabused most of that notion. It did not. Unfortunately, after 1919, the prevailing opinion among many in the democracies, with the possible exception of France, was that the First World War had all been a tragic mistake, largely caused by miscalculation and error rather than deliberately set in motion by any one power.[28] Others in the Anglo-American community believed that the outbreak of the war was the inevitable consequence of evil, balance-of-power machinations by selfish, secretive, and largely unaccountable governments – ironically, the very features that had underwritten the success of the Vienna settlement. Such attitudes go far in explaining the fact that Britain and the United States so totally ignored the strategic and moral threat posed by the rise of Nazi Germany and its burgeoning military power in the 1930s.[29]

For their part, the ideologies of both Nazism and communism in the Soviet Union absolutely rejected the idea that peace, whether between races or classes, was the norm – the latter at least until the entire capitalist world had been overthrown, the former until the "biological revolution" had completely altered the world's racial balance. As General Erich Ludendorff was to argue after the First World War, peace was simply a continuation of war by other means, a complete reversal of Clausewitz's dictum. It was a dictum that Adolf Hitler's Third Reich would even manage to exceed.[30]

The *Wehrmacht*'s absolute defeat in the Second World War and the destruction and occupation of the Reich solved the first problem together with those posed by Imperial Japan and Fascist Italy. There could now be no quarrel on the part of the Germans, east or west, with the terms the victors imposed on them as there had been in 1919, when the victors had not even reached German territory when the war ended. The German problem, at least as far as the threat the Reich represented to its neighbors, had been

---

[28] The massive German campaign of disinformation certainly encouraged and abetted such opinions. See Holger H. Herwig, "Clio Deceived, Patriotic Self-Censorship in Germany after the Great War," *International Security*, Fall 1987, vol. 12, no. 2.

[29] In fact, the Bank of England played a major role in helping the Germans overcome their serious liquidity crisis in 1934 and 1935, support that prevented an economic crisis in the Third Reich that might well have brought German rearmament to a halt for a considerable period of time with huge implications for the future of European peace, as well as the ability of the Germans to wage war in 1939 with some prospect of success. Throughout the 1930s, the Nazi economy, considering Hitler's massive program of rearmament, was always in a tenuous situation. For a fuller discussion of German rearmament and these issues see Adam Tooze, *The Wages of Destruction: The Making and Breaking of the Nazi Economy* (New York, 2006), particularly pp. 15–16, 18.

[30] See MacGregor Knox, *Common Destiny: Dictatorship, Foreign Policy, and War in Fascist Italy and Nazi Germany* (Cambridge, 2000).

solved once and for all.[31] In contrast, the unresolved ideological conflict between Soviet communism and American capitalism–democracy should by all rights have led to the Third World War. But the existence of nuclear weapons as well as the belief by each side that the other's internal contradictions would eventually bring it down prevented the outbreak of another world war, which would have placed humanity's survival in doubt.

Of course, nuclear standoff did not mean the end of war or, for that matter, the concomitant problems raised by the need to make peace. In the case of the wars of colonialism – the Dutch East Indies, French Indo-China, Malaya, Cyprus, Kenya, Algeria, the second Vietnam war, and so on – the making of peace found solution by the defeat of the colonial power (or its replacement) and absolute victory by the insurgency. However, in conflicts such as the Arab-Israeli wars, the India-Pakistan conflicts, or perhaps even the Falkland Islands War of 1982, military operations have produced neither a protracted war nor an enduring peace.

The defeated in each case simply refused to accept the report cards of military operations, no matter how decisive they might have appeared to outside observers. In effect, the seeds of the next conflict found themselves firmly implanted in the soil of bitterness left after the "decisive" victory of the last conflict. And that looks to be the problem the United States confronts in the aftermath of its "decisive" victory in the three-week war of March–April 2003 against Saddam Hussein's Ba'athist regime.[32]

PROBLEMS WITH THE MAKING OF PEACE

What conclusions might one draw from the problems that peacemakers have confronted in the aftermath of conflicts or, for that matter, the mistakes that they have made in their efforts to find a satisfactory solution to those problems? The last section of this chapter attempts to sketch out some thoughts on why the making of peace has remained so flawed throughout history, so intractable, so ambiguous, and so uncertain.

As noted earlier, there have been sustained periods of peace. After all, Roman power did result in an unalloyed period of more than two and a half centuries of peace throughout the entire Mediterranean basin.[33] It did so by

---

[31] A fact that the swift agreement of Germany's neighbors to reunification with the collapse of the German Democratic Republic in 1989 underlined.

[32] For the misapprehensions with which U.S. policy makers embarked on the war against Saddam Hussein's regime, see, among others: Ricks, *Fiasco*; and Michael Gordon and Bernard Trainor, *Cobra II* (New York, 2006). For the disastrous results in terms of how matters were actually handled on the ground by the Coalition Provisional Authority, see Chandrasekaran, *Imperial Life in the Emerald City*.

[33] Although, admittedly, the Romans did conduct consistent small wars on the frontier and occasionally a civil war among themselves to determine who would rule the Empire.

the simple expedient of confronting Rome's opponents with either extermination, if they resisted, or absorption, if they chose instead to accommodate
to Roman demands and join the protection racket the Romans were so successful at running. Masada suggests the extent to which Rome was willing
to pursue its ends against the recalcitrant within the Empire. Against the
barbarians outside the Empire's frontiers, the Romans followed a policy of
the velvet glove covering the iron fist within, mixing diplomacy with political
manipulation of the tribes on the other side of the Rhine and the Danube
with extermination of tribes or political entities which became too dangerous
or truculent, such as the Dacians in the early second century A.D.[34]

Yet, as suggested earlier in this chapter, the *Pax Romana* represented an
anomaly in the turbulent path history has followed over its course. In most
of the historical landscape, if the contenders in war were willing to cease hostilities for a time, they nevertheless viewed peace merely as an interregnum
between wars, an opportunity to prepare for the next conflict. Thus, lasting
periods of peace were the last thing on the mind of those drawing up the
articles and agreements that ended military operations. Rather, peacemakers aimed at establishing conditions that would best position strategically
their polis or state for the inevitable and expected resumption of conflict.
Even then, compared to much of history, such attempts to control war and
its impact represented a substantial advance over what had occurred before
or what was to happen afterward. The world wars of the twentieth century
hardly represented an advance over what had occurred during the eighteenth
century, when the opposing sides at least were willing to limit the scale of
the conflicts on which they had embarked.

There were exceptions. The most obvious was the Congress of Vienna,
in which the contenders had suffered through nearly a quarter century of
constant, seemingly endless conflict, with battles and losses on a scale never
before seen in history. Something similar occurred in the making of peace at
Westphalia in the mid-seventeenth century and perhaps even in the aftermath
of the Second World War, at least as far as most Europeans were concerned.
The crucial point that led to a peace establishing a less ferocious international

---

[34] Making war was expensive, particularly if the war aimed at extermination, which was
something the Romans of the Empire understood. In the case of the Dacians, they attempted
diplomacy and politics before they embarked on war, and even then they attempted to make
peace with the Dacian king before embarking on the final effort of complete conquest. On
the other hand, in Britain, the Romans conducted a series of punitive campaigns against
the Scots and the Picts but never settled on complete conquest, most probably because the
economic gains failed to equal the costs of maintaining the territory as a Roman province.
The same might be said for the Roman approach to Germany after the massacre of Varus'
legions in 7 A.D. There, diplomacy and military force minimized the German danger, but
conquest just did not appear to be worth the financial cost. For a discussion of these
campaigns, see, among others, Adrian Goldsworthy, *In the Name of Rome: The Men Who
Won the Roman Empire* (London, 2003).

environment was the fact that both the perils and the damage that prolonged conflicts inflict on all had become clear to rulers and negotiators.

The vast differences in the context within which wars have ended make it extraordinarily difficult to develop a realistic theory that would improve either the conduct of war or the processes through which nations must negotiate some sort of a settlement that possesses some prospect of creating political stability, without which peace is simply not possible. To have any relevance, one must tie any theory of peace making closely to the harsh reality of historical examples. As Claudewitz suggests:

> [Theory] is an analytic investigation leading to a close *acquaintance* with the subject; applied to experience . . . it leads to thorough *familiarity* with it. The closer it comes to that goal, the more it proceeds from the objective form of a science to the subjective form of a skill, the more effective it will prove in areas where the nature of the case admits no arbiter but talent. . . . Theory then becomes a guide to anyone who wants to learn about war [or peace making] from books.[35]

That said, there are a number of issues raised by the past which may shed some light on how statesmen and political leaders – and military leaders, for that matter – might best think about the making of peace. To begin with, they must understand not only the nature of war but also the attributes and consequences of the conflict they are setting out to fight. In some cases, they will find themselves involved in war due to the actions of others, but even then it is essential that they think through the nature of the peace that will come afterward. Failing to consider present actions in terms of future risks holds that future hostage to ill-considered arguments of military or political "necessity," which subsequently may place intolerable burdens on those tasked with making peace in the wreckage left by war.

The first and certainly the most important factor in the making of peace lies in the nature of war itself. Second, and equally important, is the nature of the international environment; perhaps the human condition is a better way to describe it. Third, and heavily influenced by the nature of the war that has occurred, is the context within which statesmen and political leaders have to operate after a conflict has ended. One of the real dangers of history is the fact that it is easy for historians with their after-the-fact knowledge to "Monday-morning quarterback" decisions that occurred in conditions of uncertainty and ambiguity that are beyond their comprehension. Finally, there is the persistent problem of ahistoricism, which has encouraged far too many political and military leaders during the past three millennia to ignore the errors of their predecessors – no more so than at present, when

---

[35] Clausewitz, *On War*, p. 141.

history seems not even to get a nod from policy makers or senior leaders in the military and political worlds of Washington, DC.

THE NATURE OF WAR

In Book 1 of *On War*, Carl von Clausewitz laid out the most systematic and thoughtful examination of the fundamental nature of human conflict that has ever been written. In simple terms, *"[w]ar is thus an act of force to compel our enemy to do our will."*[36] Simple indeed, but the complexity lies in the fact that in war, the enemy is a thinking, breathing human with deeply held aspirations and thoughts of his own.[37] And, as a thinking, breathing human, the enemy, because of his aims, culture, history, and perceptions, often will act in a fashion which we do not expect. The result may be to lengthen, embitter, and expand the conflict beyond its intended bounds, no matter how carefully statesmen or soldiers have considered the implications of war.[38]

Thus, factors beyond pure military calculations become increasingly important, if not dominant, not only in the conduct of war but in the making of peace. It was for some years a dangerous trend within the American military to believe that one can fight wars in the clear world of high technology, precision, and computers when, in fact, civilian casualties, unforeseen incidents, and other incalculable results of military actions directly impact the political context within which the West has attempted to wage its wars since the Treaty of Westphalia.[39] War, *certainly within the framework of American policy,* is by nature a political act, and the violence of military operations by their *nature* will directly affect the political and strategic context, which in turn will determine the success or failure of the use of military force.

Inevitably, war involves the deepest of human emotions: anger, hatred, bitterness, fury, and a desire for revenge on the part of both those who wage it and those whom it impacts. Again, Clausewitz: "Consequently, it would be an obvious fallacy to imagine war between civilized people as resulting merely from a rational act on the part of their governments and to

---

[36] Clausewitz, *On War*, p. 75.
[37] As soldiers and marines in Iraq have taken to saying about the reaction of their Iraqi opponents to U.S. decisions and actions: "The enemy gets a vote."
[38] In this regard, Bismarck is a particularly good example because, while he was impressively successful in limiting the form and results of the wars against Denmark and Austria, the Franco-Prussian War proved to be an entirely different case.
[39] Of course, if the American military were real students of Clausewitz, this would not be the case, but heavily influenced not only by Baron d'Jomini but also by the Prusso-German military example, they have all too often attempted to separate war from politics, an exceedingly dangerous notion, as the German military managed to prove in its disastrous conduct of two world wars, particularly at the strategic level.

conceive of war as gradually ridding itself of passion, so that in the end one would never really need to use the physical impact of the fighting forces." Perhaps more than any other form of war, wars between civilized people have descended almost to the brink of what Clausewitz termed "total war."

The savageries of the last year of the Second World War, which extended from the final flickers of the holocaust; to the Soviet invasion of East Prussia, Pomerania, Silesia, and Brandenburg; and to the atomic bombings of Hiroshima and Nagasaki, suggest all too clearly the collapse of human values in the process of six years of brutal, murderous killing.[40] As the greatest of all historians, Thucydides, suggested at the end of the fifth century B.C. about the dark results of war – in this case the worst of all forms of conflict, civil war,

> [T]here were the savage and pitiless actions into which men were carried not so much for the sake of gain as because they were swept away into an internecine struggle by their ungovernable passions. Then, with the ordinary conventions of civilized life thrown into confusion, human nature, always ready to offend even where laws exist, showed itself proudly in its true colours, as something incapable of controlling passion, insubordinate to the idea of justice, the enemy to anything superior to itself; for if it had not been for the pernicious power of envy, men would not so have exalted vengeance above innocence and profit above justice. Indeed, it is true that in these acts of revenge on others men take it upon themselves to begin the process of repealing those general laws of humanity which are there to give a hope of salvation to all those who are in distress.[41]

How then is the statesman or political leader to make peace among nations, given the all-too-frequent collapse of civilized values during war and the wreckage left in its wake? The troublesome answer would appear to be that those directly involved in the struggle will find it almost impossible to separate themselves from the anger and bitterness that are the inevitable end by-product of war. Moreover, the democratization – perhaps *popularization* is a better word – of conflict since the American Civil and the Franco-Prussian Wars has only enlarged the impact of such emotions, heavily influencing both the conduct of war and the making of peace and significantly constraining the freedom of maneuver enjoyed by statesmen and diplomats alike. As the Prussian Chancellor, Otto von Bismarck, discovered to his considerable discomfort, his unleashing of German nationalism in 1870 to defeat the French came back to haunt him in his efforts to patch together a peace that would satisfy the many internal constituencies that would comprise the German Reich he was attempting to cobble together.

---

[40] For what the last months of the Second World War in Europe looked like, see Max Hastings, *Armageddon: The Battle for Germany, 1944–1945* (New York, 2005).
[41] Thucydides, *History of the Peloponnesian War*, pp. 244–5.

In fact, it would appear that the wreckage of bitterness left by wars lingers in many cases not for decades but sometimes for centuries, as the sad, dark events in the Balkans since the breakup of Yugoslavia have underlined. That bitterness is not just a matter of historical memory, although that plays its role, but also of myths, legends, and folktales that lie deep beneath the surface – yet form the core of the popular world and its cultural values. For statesmen or diplomats, attempting to put together what seems to them a reasonable peace, as did the United Nations' (UN's) negotiators in the Balkans, such folk memories are unseen and more often unnoticed. But they are there, nevertheless, and their insidious influence on any population will affect whatever "reasonable" settlement others may attempt to create. In the mind of many Serbs, the Battle of Kossovo in 1389, in which the Ottoman Turks crushed the main Serbian army, is as alive in their consciousness as if it had happened yesterday.

Thus, above all, statesmen and their military advisers must never forget that war is about killing, even in an age of technological marvels. As Clausewitz, drawing on the experiences of the nineteenth century, warned,

> Kind-hearted people might of course think there was some ingenious way to disarm or defeat an enemy without too much bloodshed, and might imagine this is the true goal of the art of war. Pleasant as it sounds, it is a fallacy that must be exposed: war is such a dangerous business that the mistakes which come from kindness are the very worst. . . . This is how the matter must be seen. It would be futile – even wrong – to try and shut one's eyes to what war is from sheer distress at its brutality.[42]

Unleashing that brutality – no matter how one might attempt to limit the "collateral damage" (that dreadful euphemism dreamt up by the American military) – in turn stokes the anger that makes war such a treacherous means of pursuing policy goals. Moreover, the casualties that one's own side has suffered in the conduct of military operations create their own legacy of anger and bitterness among one's own people. Such emotions help to explain why human passion is the least measurable and controllable variable among Clausewitz's trinity.

Perhaps the most salient warning that the nature of war suggests about the making of peace has to do with the aims with which the opposing sides wage the conflict. It was far too easy for those removed from the conflict to believe that their limited aims – themselves a reflection of their removal from the conflict – will allow them to achieve a peace of understanding with those against whom they are engaged in bitter, internecine conflict. That is rarely the case.

[42] Clausewitz, *On War*, pp. 75–6.

Moreover, just because one side has only limited aims and goals does not mean that the same is true of the opposing side. Nazi Germany possessed unlimited goals. There was and could be no compromise that could bring the murderous conflict to an end in Europe without the absolute destruction of Nazi Germany. And the means employed included the massive, destructive, and, in the end, murderous strategic-bombing campaign against Germany's economy *and* population.[43] The peacemakers in 1945 had no choice but to exterminate the political framework of the Third Reich. Luckily, they received considerable help from how the war had ended, with Germany wrecked from end to end and Allied military in occupation of the entire nation. Virtually no one in Germany at that time could argue, as so many had done in 1919, that the German military had not been defeated. Indeed, the entire nation had stayed the course to "the bitter end."

WAR'S HUMAN LEGACY

By its nature, war leaves to those who hope to sketch out a successful peace a dog's breakfast of hatreds, anger, bitterness, and, invariably, complexities, many of which are beyond the understanding of even the most brilliant statesmen. In his discussion of the origins of the First World War, Winston Churchill sketched out what he believed to be the greatest difficulties that had confronted Europe's leaders in the runup to war. His words are equally applicable to the difficulties which confront statesmen in the aftermath of conflict:

> One rises from the study of the causes of the Great War with a prevailing sense of the defective control of individuals upon world fortunes. It has been well said, "there is always more error than design in human affairs." The limited minds of even the ablest men, their disputed authority, the climate of opinion in which they dwell, their transient and partial contributions to the mighty problem, that problem itself so far beyond their compass, so vast in scale and detail, so changing in its aspect – all this must surely be considered [in any analysis of the outbreak of the war].[44]

For the peacemakers, the problem is doubly complex in that they must consider not only the present with its myriad demands, all resulting from the fury of the war just concluded, but a dim and uncertain future that will inevitably find itself influenced by their decisions as well as the *desiderata* of war. Rarely, if ever, do those charged with making the peace consult the past. In 1919, making an impossible task more difficult, the British commissioned one of their diplomat/historians to research the lessons of the past with a

---

[43] In this regard, see particularly Tooze, *Wages of Destruction*, chs. 17, 18, and 19.
[44] Winston S. Churchill, *The World Crisis* (Toronto, 1931), p. 6.

view to applying the results to the Versailles peace-making efforts. They then entirely ignored the study. On the other hand, the Americans, bathed in Wilson's heady visions of international nirvana, never bothered to consult the past at all.

One should also not forget that those involved in the processes of peace confront an insatiable set of demands on their time, of which they often possess too little, unlike their eventual critics, the historians, who possess infinite amounts of time to analyze what *should* have been done. Under the pressure of too little time, incomplete knowledge, and limited foresight, particularly about the future, politicians and diplomats must simultaneously seek to satisfy both the needs of the hour and the hopes of the future.

Yet, some historians persist in analyzing the efforts of statesmen as if their subjects had access to the historian's hindsight. For example, there are those who blandly criticize Bismarck for having created the conditions that made possible the First World War. Undoubtedly, there is a certain truth to such charges. But they miss the vast problems that the "Iron Chancellor" confronted in putting together the Peace of 1871, while at the same time creating a Germany which for more than a thousand years had been known as the "Germanies." They also grant Bismarck too little credit for keeping Europe at peace for the subsequent twenty years. Even then, war came only after another quarter century of peace, and only after Bismarck's successors had made a hash of his foreign policy and created the disastrous strategic framework of Germany against the other major European powers.[45]

THE CONTEXT OF PEACE MAKING

Clausewitz in *On War* makes a particularly sarcastic comment about those who embark on war: "No one starts a war – or rather, no one in his senses ought to do so – without first being clear in his mind what he intends to achieve by that war and how he intends to conduct it."[46] In fact, throughout history there has been a lack of clarity in the thinking of those who unleash war, particularly in terms of the larger strategic and political aims.

The Germans, for example, had no clear vision of the postwar world when they launched the Schlieffen Plan in 1914. Militarily defeating their opponents was the whole basis of their planning. They had prepared no coherent set of strategic goals defining what Europe would look like were they to win. Without clear strategic and political goals, the momentum of the war simply drove them down the road to megalomania, the Peace Treaty

---

[45] One might, of course, count Austria-Hungary as a major power, but given its record in the First World War, that is a doubtful claim.
[46] Clausewitz, *On War*, p. 579.

of Brest-Litovsk being a case in point. Their goals in the west were equally immoderate, which made the Allies at Versailles in 1919 even less willing to grant the Germans a peace of reconciliation.

In sum, the making of peace confronts statesmen with a world in which the first-order effects are still not clear, while second- and third-order effects are entirely opaque. We live in a nonlinear world, where seemingly unimportant decisions reached in the heated aftermath of one conflict can have a disastrous and totally unintended impact on the future course of events. Thus, the decision pushed by Lloyd George at Versailles to limit Germany to an all-professional military force of 100,000 soldiers – including 4,000 officers – instead of Clemenceau's proposal for a conscript army of 300,000 men would have the totally unintended effect of providing the Germans by 1939 with the best military machine of all the European powers.[47] Unintended effects, incalculable in thinking about the future, make the task of the peacemaker almost impossible. In effect, they ensure that no matter how clear-headed he or she might be, there are issues and decisions, the ultimate effects of which cannot be foreseen.

The larger the scale of conflict, the truer that tends to be. Thus, the human landscape of Eastern Europe in 1919, with its intractable historical legacies, set an impossible task for those seeking to resolve the more recent hostilities prompted by the war itself. Nothing better exemplified that than the difficulties posed by the new Czech Republic to Wilson's desire to base "the peace to end all wars" on solving the nationality problem of Eastern Europe. Virtually its entire borderlands, its mountainous strategic frontiers, were inhabited by Sudeten Germans, nearly all of whom preferred to join the new German state.

Thus, the dilemma was either to force the Sudeten Germans to remain in the Czech Republic, which would thwart one of Wilson's basic principles, that of national self-determination. The alternative was to create an indefensible Czech state by allowing the Sudeten districts to join the Reich. *Real politic* won out, but less than two decades later, Adolf Hitler was to throw that decision in the face of Chamberlain and Daladier.

In the end, one suspects that about the best one can expect from statesmen is a willingness to recognize and accept the intractability of the tasks they confront and the consequent incompleteness of any solution. The hope that negotiations and diplomatic decisions made in the aftermath of war can entirely resolve problems that were insoluble before conflict is, indeed, more often than not an idle dream.

---

[47] For a particularly thorough and imaginative examination of the impact of nonlinearity on human conflict – and, by inference, on other human endeavors – see Barry D. Watts, *Clausewitzian Friction and Future War* (Washington, DC, revised edition, 2004).

At best, when confronting the uncertainties of the future, one can patch together a peace that will last for some length of time; one can try to erect arrangements enabling its later amendment as circumstances change; and one can hope that those who follow will display more wisdom than those who unleashed the dogs of war. Even then, whatever peace emerges will remain conditional – dependent not only on the ever-changing context of international relations but also on the willingness and ability of those who inherit the peace once made to maintain it, even as memories of the prompting conflict dim. Nothing better underlines this reality than the dark and troubled decade of the 1930s, during which Hitler's dissolution of the Versailles settlement was less the result of the Reich's inherent economic and military power than of the general unwillingness of the Western Powers, in particular Britain, to enforce the strictures laid down by the peacemakers in 1919.[48]

THE PROBLEM OF MEMORY AND AHISTORICISM

In 432 B.C., the Spartan king Archidamus addressed the Spartan assembly with the clear warning that one should not embark on war without a clear understanding of the parameters within which one hoped realistically to fight it. In particular, he warned,

> Spartans, in the course of my life I have taken part in many wars, and I see among you people of the same age as I am. They and I have had experience, and so are not likely to share in what may be a great enthusiasm for war, nor to think that war is a good thing or a safe thing."[49]

Therein lies the problem of generational transition because the young Spartan warriors in the assembly had no knowledge of the horrors of hoplite warfare, of standing in the bloody, terrifying Spartan phalanx that had battered its way through Sparta's opponents for more than three centuries without defeat. But those successes never made the battles of hoplite phalanxes any less terrifying.[50] For the young Spartans, however, brought up on the myths of Spartan triumphs, not to mention the *Iliad*, war appeared enticing – even thrilling – with the opportunities it offered them to write

---

[48] In this regard, see, among others, Tooze, *The Wages of Destruction*; and Williamson Murray, *The Change in the European Balance of Power, 1938–1939: The Path to Ruin* (Princeton, NJ, 1984), ch. 1.
[49] Thucydides, *History of the Peloponnesian War*, p. 82.
[50] In this regard, see particularly Victor David Hanson, *The Western Way of War: Infantry Battle in Classical Greece* (Berkeley, CA, 2000).

their names in the book of Spartan heroes, such as Leonidas and the three hundred who had stood alone at Thermopylae.[51]

Yet, the knowledge of what war was like has always remained confined to those who have experienced its horrors firsthand.[52] Thus, while the peace-makers at the Congress of Vienna possessed a deep sense of the horrors that war had imposed on their world over the past quarter century, those memories gradually faded in the collective memory of Europeans, as new generations, who held no such memories of the cost of war, emerged to take the reigns of power. The Revolutions of 1848 were a signal that that transference of power was occurring, as were the conflicts that followed in their wake. Even the most virulent of those conflicts, however – the Seven Weeks War and the Franco-Prussian War – led to relatively short wars, in which decisive results – at least for the Germans – appeared to be the norm rather than the exception. By the early twentieth century, the reality of war had become entangled in a deep covering of myth – for the French the Napoleonic Wars, for the Germans the War of Liberation and the Franco-Prussian War – epitomized by the paintings of glorious cavalry charges and infantry squares.[53]

All that changed after 1914, but the price extracted by the first clash of arms was so high that none of the leaders of the major powers had the moral courage to call a halt.[54] Both sides continued to double the bets until the final crackup in 1918, when the Germans collapsed under the massive costs of conducting an attritional war against the rest of the world. But the nature of the war as well as its apparently indecisive conclusion then confronted the peacemakers with an impossible task.

If that generational change helps to explain the persistent willingness of statesmen and soldiers to embark on war without having thought through its darker possibilities, then the creation of myths about war may be equally

[51] And here, the Greek and Roman worlds of classical antiquity would never lose their reverence for Homer's *Iliad* until Christianity took over the cultural framework within which the Mediterranean world thought and acted.

[52] In this regard, the United States had a liberal secretary of state in the late 1990s who complained bitterly that the wonderful American military was there to be used, and its leaders should not so consistently argue against its use in contingency actions.

[53] The reality of Napoleonic War was another matter. See Clausewitz's description of war in *On War*, pp. 113–14; or John Keegan's discussion of the Battle of Waterloo in *The Face of Battle*. As the Duke of Wellington is reputed to have said, the only thing more depressing than a battlefield won was a battlefield lost. Goya's paintings and sketches of the partisan war in Spain brought reality to the horror of war in the Napoleonic age.

[54] Only the chief of the German general staff had the sense to recognize the path that lay ahead. In November 1914, General Erich von Falkenhyn went to the German chancellor, Theobold von Bethmann-Hollweg, and indicated that Germany could not win the war but should seek a compromise peace. Bethmann-Hollweg refused his advice and commented that Germany must fight to "the bitter end." Holger H. Herwig, *The First World War: Germany and Austria-Hungary, 1914–1918* (London, 1997), pp. 116–17.

important in distorting the possibilities of creating a lasting peace. Certainly, the Greek world of the polis found its deepest cultural roots in the *Iliad*, but the creation of myths that form the general impression of the war just past is clearly one of the most important factors in determining the stability of the peace that statesmen attempt to mold in war's aftermath.

Thus, the Germans created a series of deeply false myths in the immediate period after the ending of the First World War: that their army had remained unbeaten in the field in 1918, only to be stabbed in the back by revolutionary Communist and Jewish traitors in the homefront; that Wilson's "Fourteen Points" had tricked them into agreeing to an armistice and that military necessity had played no role in that decision; and that Germany was no more responsible for the outbreak of the war than any other power.[55]

A massive disinformation campaign organized and, in some respects, directed by the German government then persuaded not only the great majority of Germans of these "truths" but significant numbers of British and American leaders, policy makers, and intellectuals, not to mention academics, as well.[56] Similarly, in the post–Civil War period, the losers managed to create the myths about both the *ante bellum* South and the war itself that fundamentally distorted the understanding of the causes and course of the Civil War until the 1960s.[57] Even more disastrously, those myths helped to perpetuate the dark paths of race relationships in America for nearly a century.[58]

The disastrous impact of such myths on the work of the peacemakers hardly needs emphasis, but at least the myths of German and Southern innocence have largely disappeared from the pages of history books. Yet, as American and NATO peacemakers discovered in the Balkans, myths still exercise an impressive influence on how many human beings evaluate the world. Already, there are many in the Middle East who view the events of September 11, 2001, as a pernicious plot by the American government, undoubtedly aided and abetted by the international Jewish conspiracy, to take over the region's oil supplies.[59] Whatever the outcome of America's ill-considered venture in Iraq, myths are adding to the impossible task that any peacemaker will confront in attempting to bring some modicum of stability to the dismal state of affairs currently in train throughout the Mesopotamian Valley.

---

[55] For Germany's responsibility for the outbreak of the war, see Holger H. Herwig, "Germany," in *The Origins of the First World War*, ed. by Richard F. Hamilton and Holger H. Herwig (Cambridge, 2003).
[56] For this campaign, see Herwig, "Clio Deceived."
[57] The work of Bruce Catton was particularly important in rethinking the war's history.
[58] I am indebted to Professor James McPherson for this point.
[59] A claim that a Congressman from Minnesota has recently echoed, a comment that will undoubtedly add veracity to the myths that constantly surface in the Middle East.

Beyond myths and their pernicious impact lies the influence of the general ignorance of history. Nothing has displayed the dangers of an ignorance of the past more clearly than the postconflict stage in Iraq. Here, a set of deeply held beliefs by American policy makers, particularly in the Department of Defense, ignored not only the vast tableau of Middle Eastern history but even the recent past of American history as well. Barely fourteen years before operation "Iraqi Freedom" kicked off, the U.S. military launched an equally successful takedown of Manuel Noriega's corrupt regime in Panama. Within a matter of hours, American military forces had eliminated Panama's military and police forces and removed its government from power. The result: massive looting that wrecked the economy and the discovery that Panama's infrastructure had deteriorated far beyond American estimates. All of this occurred despite the fact that the United States had had extensive involvement in Panama over the previous century. Yet, virtually every experience of operation "Just Cause" appears to have disappeared from the collective memory of those in Washington at the onset of the invasion of Iraq in March 2003.

But the American crackup in Iraq after the brilliant initial conventional campaign is hardly atypical of the pattern of ahistoricism that has marked Western behavior during the past several centuries, particularly in the Anglo-American world. The great classicist, Bernard Knox, has perhaps best encapsulated the reasons lying behind the Western denial of historical experience as of relevancy to thinking about the future in an essay on the differences between the *Weltanschauung* of the modern world and that of the ancient:

> The early Greek imagination envisaged the past and the present as in front of us – we can see them. The future, invisible, is behind us. . . . Paradoxical though it may sound to the modern ear, this image of our journey through time may be truer to reality than the medieval and modern feeling that we face the future as we make our way forward into it.[60]

In the end, any successful attempt at peace making must bring to the table an understanding of the context, not only of the conflict just past but also of the larger cultural and historical framework within which it has taken place. And here, history must be a dominant player. That is because only a knowledge of the past can provide a sense of the causes, the cultural and political perceptions, and the influence of the past on the thinking of those who are directly involved. If, as Sun Tzu suggests, a knowledge of one's opponent is crucial to success in war, then a knowledge of the "other" in peace making is equally important. Unfortunately, the record of the past suggests that those who make peace as well as those who make war are

---

[60] Bernard Knox, *Backing into the Future: The Classical Tradition and Its Renewal* (New York, 1994), pp. 11–12.

equally likely to be ignorant of history and the differences that delineate the "other" – or "others," as the case may be. Without guideposts from the past to suggest paths to the future, then any road, no matter how irrelevant and inappropriate, will do. And such roads will inevitably lead to future conflicts.

CONCLUSION

The problem with history is that it offers no comfortable or easy answers. The past suggests that there are no "silver bullets" for complex problems, and of all the complex problems that human beings manage to construct, there is no doubt that war and its aftermath are the most difficult to solve. So, then, what is one to suggest? Perhaps above all, history suggests that war must always be a last resort because its aftermath will inevitably raise problems that may be and often are more daunting than those that the war was supposed to solve.

On the other hand, there are times when war can be the only alternative. Such was the case with the Second World War. Particularly with Nazi Germany, a true "rogue state," there was no alternative but a war to the end, a war of extermination. Perhaps of all the conflicts examined in this volume, that conflict proved the most open to a lasting settlement, at least among the nations of Western Europe and then, after the demise of the Cold War, Eastern Europe. Here, though, the mistakes of Versailles, as well as how the First World War had ended, provided statesmen and political leaders guideposts that were directly relevant to the making of peace. Yet, even then, postwar factors, such as the emergence of the Cold War, proved crucial in establishing the context within which a relatively stable peace could emerge, at least in Europe.

The great difficulties, which the First World – with its ignorance of history – will continue to confront in attempting to make a modicum of peace in places where the culture and political framework are entirely antithetical, have to do with its general inability to understand the complex underpinnings of its societies and how conditional its world really is. Thus, the idea that democratic ideals of restraint and individual responsibility for the whole is entirely irrelevant to societies closer to Bedouin tribes than the modern world.

Yet, that represents a reality the First World finds difficult to comprehend. The American experience in Iraq should be a salient warning to those who still may believe that a market economy based on Friedrich von Hayek or the democratic complexities evolved by the Founding Fathers in writing the U.S. Constitution can be implanted in societies where there is simply not even a basic rule of law and where the rule of violence is the order of the day. But, then, without even the most basic understanding of the complexities and ambiguities of their own society, it is not surprising that the Coalition Provisional Authority and its military support floundered so disastrously in the initial year of the Baghdad occupation.[61]

There are two crucial points that history suggests about the making of peace. The first is that war is, in every respect, an uncertain and unpredictable affair, which will inevitably present as many new problems as the ones that it may solve. Thus, the making of peace demands that both in the conduct of war and then thinking about its aftermath, *military* as well as political leaders must devote substantial efforts to preparing the landscape and thinking through the attendant problems involved in the aftermath of war.

The second is that history has consistently underlined that there are cases in which there is no solution, no appeasement, except absolute surrender, with some opponents. There will be no accommodation with the likes of Al Qaeda. Nor should those who have accepted the Western definition of peace ever believe that the remainder of the human race has willingly accepted that definition. At best, one may destroy them, but if that is not politically possible, then the creation of a context that limits their ability to inflict damage may be the only solution. In other words, in some cases in the making of peace, there may be no satisfactory way to fashion a lasting peace. That recognition is essential to the casting of realistic and sensible policies that attend to the world as it is rather than to what we hope it to be.

In the end, there are no easy solutions to the making of peace. As with all things of worth in life, that task demands hard, unremitting attention to detail, a real understanding of the context, including history and culture – in other words, the other – and a recognition of the limitations of military power. Sir Michael Howard has perhaps said it best in his discussion of the realities involved in the maintenance of peace:

> We have thus not yet escaped from the world of power politics and *raison d'état*. Nor does the increasing multiplicity of national actors in itself guarantee a more peaceful and better-ordered world. Kant was right when he said that a state of peace had to be 'established.' What perhaps even he did not discern was that this is a task which has to be tackled afresh every day of our lives; and that no formula, no organisation and no political or social revolution can ever free mankind from this inexorable duty.[62]

The chapters that follow this introduction examine how Western belligerents have addressed – or failed to address – the making of peace across a span of two and a half millennia and in contests reflecting a broad range of

---

[61] See, particularly, Chandrasekaran, *Imperial Life in the Emerald City*.
[62] Howard, *War and the Liberal Conscience*, p. 135.

prompting disputes. In some cases, peace making engaged only the contestants themselves; in others, a much larger audience intruded. Some efforts produced, at best, a momentary suspension of hostilities; others transformed the very context of international relations. All ultimately failed, if one defines success only as the permanent elimination of violence as a means of settling political disputes. Defined more modestly, however, as the control and moderation of such violence, some peace-making efforts were notably more successful than others. The chapters that follow attempt to elucidate why this was so.

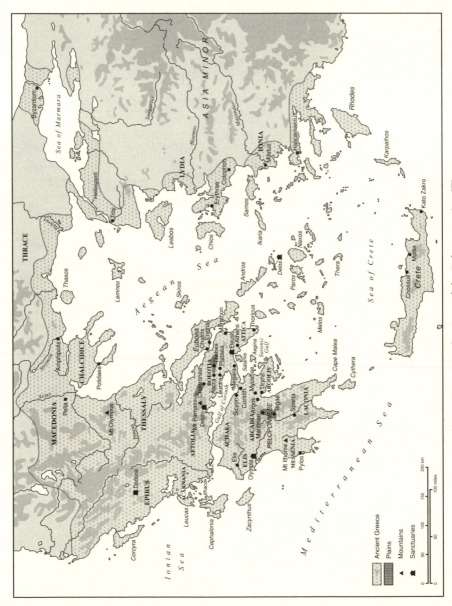

MAP 1. Greece in the time of the Peloponnesian War.

2

The Peace of Nicias

PAUL A. RAHE

For Donald Kagan

It is much easier to start a war than to end one. The former, a single, willful party can ordinarily accomplish with ease; to achieve the latter, it usually takes two. Often, it takes more parties than that. Such was the experience of those who found themselves engaged in what is conventionally called the Archidamian War – the first stage in what Thucydides termed "the great war" that took place "between the Athenians and the Peloponnesians" (Thuc. 1.1).[1]

The Archidamian War began in the spring of 431 B.C. It ended, if that is the proper word, ten years thereafter in the spring of 421 B.C., when ambassadors from Athens and Sparta met to swear an oath on behalf of their rival cities that for fifty years they would honor the terms of what came to be called the Peace of Nicias (5.17-20). The fact that the Athenians and the Spartans set a term to the agreement, that they regarded it as a long-term truce and never even imagined that it would be a lasting peace, should occasion on our part a brief digression. Peace making in antiquity was not the pious process that it pretends to be today.

With regard to war and peace, the ancient Greeks entertained few of the illusions that govern twenty-first–century rhetoric and shape policy making as well.[2] The ordinary Hellene would have nodded his approval of the

In citing the classical texts, I have used the standard abbreviations found in *The Oxford Classical Dictionary*, second edition, eds. N. G. L. Hammmond and H. H. Scullard (Oxford, 1970). I first formulated this argument more than thirty years ago in a seminar taught by Donald Kagan; and, though my argument was then and is now directed against his, I owe him a profound debt. I am also grateful to Oswyn Murray, who read this chapter in manuscript and made suggestions.

[1] This stage in the great war is covered in detail in Thuc. 2.1-5.16. The standard modern history is Donald Kagan, *The Archidamian War* (Ithaca, NY, 1974).

[2] For the foundations of the change in attitude that took place, see Thomas L. Pangle and Peter Ahrensdorft, *Justice Among Nations: On the Moral Basis of War and Peace* (Lawrence,

opinion attributed by Plato to Minos, the mythical lawgiver of Crete: "What most men call peace, he held to be only a name; in truth, for everyone, there exists by nature at all times an undeclared war among all the cities."[3] War was for the Greeks a constant presence, an ineluctable brute fact, that they simply took for granted. This presumption had profound cultural and political consequences.

When twenty-first–century students read in Plato's *Republic* that Polemarchus ("war-leader") defines justice as "doing good to friends and harm to enemies," they know not what to think. Rarely do they recognize that this pleasant and rather conventional young man is merely reasserting on the personal level the grim civic and martial ethic suggested by his name,[4] and even when they are told as much, it often fails to register. In classical Greece, outside the marginal sphere occupied by the philosophers, cosmopolitanism was virtually unknown, and patriotism went hand in hand with xenophobia. If "civil war is not to thunder in the city," Aeschylus' divine chorus warns the Athenians, the citizens "must return joy for joy in a spirit of common love – and they must hate with a single heart."[5]

It was with this ethos in mind that Greek cities, when they made a treaty of peace, ordinarily confined it to a limited span of years. They knew better than to think that it would last much more than a generation, and they usually recognized that even this was a pious hope. Never did they fight a "war to end all wars." Such a notion was simply beyond their ken. They owed their formation neither to the Jewish Bible nor to the Christian New Testament. For wisdom regarding this world and the next, they looked to Homer's *Iliad* and *Odyssey*. They had little inclination to beat their swords into ploughshares or to turn the other cheek and little expectation that even after death they would rest in anything one could intelligibly call peace.

KS, 1999); and Michael Eliot Howard, *The Invention of Peace: Reflections on War and International Order* (New Haven, CT, 2000).

[3] Pl. *Laws* 1.626a.

[4] Cf. Pl. *Resp.* 1.332a-d with Thuc. 2.41.4-5. This ethic was in origin a reflection of the aristocratic individualism so visible in Homer's *Iliad*. To be able to repay one's debts to friends and enemies alike rendered one a god among men: Theog. 337-40 (West). Cf. Hom. *Od.* 6.180-85; Archil. 23.14-15, 126 (West); Theog. 869-72, 1032-33, 1107-8 (West); Pittakos *Vorsokr.*[6] 10.3.e.8; Solon F13.5 (West); Pind. *Pyth.* 2.83-85, *Isth.* 4.52; Aesch. *Cho.* 120-23; Gorg. *Vorsokr.*[6] 82 B11a.18, 25; Eur. *Med.* 807-9; Ar. *Av.* 416-26; Dissoi Logoi *Vorsokr.*[6] 90.2.7; Lys. 6.7, 9.20; Xen. *Mem.* 2.3.14, 6.35, 4.5.10, *An.* 1.9.11, *Cyr.* 1.4.25, 8.7.7, 28, *Hiero* 1.34, 2.1-2, 6.12, 11.15; Pl. *Meno* 71e, *Cleitophon* 410a; Isoc. 1.26; and Arist. *Rh.* 1363a19-21, 33-34, 1399b36-37, with Xen. *Mem.* 4.8.11, Pl. *Cri.* 49b-c, and Matt. 5:43. Sophocles explores the logic of this understanding of human (and, by implication, civic) excellence in his *Ajax* and elsewhere: see Bernard Knox, "The *Ajax* of Sophocles," *Word and Action: Essays on the Ancient Theater* (Baltimore, 1979), pp. 125-60; and Mary Whitlock Blundell, *Helping Friends and Harming Enemies: A Study in Sophocles and Greek Ethics* (Cambridge, 1989).

[5] Aesch. *Eum.* 976-87.

BY LAND AND BY SEA

The Archidamian War was an especially difficult war to end. Athens was a sea power. As a consequence of "the Long Walls" that the Athenians built during the First Peloponnesian War to link the city proper with its seaport at Piraeus some miles away (1.107.1, 108.3; Plut. *Per.* 13.6-7), Athens had, well before 431 B.C., made of itself an artificial island, the city itself virtually impervious to invasion by land. Sparta was a land power; and, with the exception of Corinth, its allies were land powers as well. In 431 B.C., the Corinthian navy was no match for that of the Athenians; and, initially, at least, there was little inclination on Sparta's part to build up and deploy an armada sufficiently large and to train a host of oarsmen and commanders skilled enough so that the Peloponnesians could pose a credible threat to the masters of the sea.

By the same token, even if the Athenians had been inclined to send a large expeditionary force overland to the Peloponnesus to take on Sparta's league, they could not have done so. It was easy to fortify the territory of Megara and the Isthmus of Corinth; and though Athens could dispatch and land smaller amphibious forces virtually anywhere on the Peloponnesian shores, and though it did so during the war on a modest scale from time to time, it lacked the manpower needed if it was to take on the Spartan alliance.

Athens' so-called allies had long before become its subjects. After the Persian Wars, when they had voluntarily banded together with Athens in the so-called Delian League, the islanders of the Aegean and the various Greek cities on the shore of Asia Minor and Thrace had agreed to contribute ships to the common force, and what each owed had been specified soon thereafter. Over time, however, as the decades passed, most of the cities had opted to substitute a financial contribution for their quota of ships, and what had begun as an alliance gradually, imperceptibly, inexorably became an empire as the fear of Persia faded and a peace was negotiated, as the balance of power within the league shifted decisively in Athens' favor, as the more formidable of its allies became restive, and as Athens resolutely refused to relinquish hegemony in what had from the outset been intended to be a permanent league.

The very word *phóros*, which originally meant "contribution," came to mean "tribute." From such an alliance, from what the Athenians themselves in their decrees had carelessly come to call an empire (*archē*), one could easily extract the resources needed for the maintenance of a great Athenian navy, and, in 431 B.C., a handful of the larger cities were still willing and able to provide ships. But Athens' subject allies could not field a reliable hoplite army to fight in phalanx alongside the citizens of Athens – not, at any rate, one of any size, and certainly not one capable of facing the Spartans and their Peloponnesian allies in pitched battle. This they simply could not do.

Nor were the Athenians eager that their allies become formidable in such a fashion, for in their resentment of the Athenian yoke, by 431 B.C., Athens' subject allies were far more likely to turn such a force against their common hegemon than to deploy it against its Greek foes.[6]

In short, it is not easy to see how either of the two alliances which squared off in 431 B.C. could have brought the war to a decision and a fully successful conclusion. At the outset, neither had the wherewithal to put the other in sufficient jeopardy. Each was supreme in its own element. Each was more or less impervious to assault – as long as its alliance remained intact. There, in both cases, lay the Achilles heel, but in neither case was it easy to reach. To exploit the genuine tensions which did exist in each of the two alliances, the enemy power would have to field a credible force on the very element on which it was comparatively inexperienced and at a grave disadvantage. Nor is it any wonder that Thucydides' great war lasted twenty-seven long years. It is no wonder that, in the event, upsetting the not-so-delicate balance between the two powers required the intervention of a third: the Achaemenid Persians, whom the Athenians, the Spartans, and their allies in the Hellenic League had expelled from the Greek world so many decades earlier.

All of this suggests that there was a certain geopolitical logic to the vision of a dual hegemony in Hellas, propagated in the 470s and the 460s by the Athenian Cimon and successfully supported for a time by his like-minded friends in Lacedaemon. It is, in consequence, easy to see why an exceptionally well-informed and thoughtful modern scholar should argue that Pericles, the figure dominant in Athens after Cimon's death, eventually came to see the wisdom of the policy pursued by his onetime rival. It is no less easy to see why he should suggest that Pericles blundered in spring 431 B.C., when he failed to seize on a last-minute Spartan proposal that might have headed off the war.[7] In fact, on the face of it, both suggestions would seem to make excellent sense.

Whether either suggestion really makes sense is, however, an open question. Cimon's kinsman Thucydides entertained neither – he thought the war, in fact, inevitable – and this should give us pause, for he knew much more than we will ever know, and he was no fool. In any case, if we are to come to understand what it was that occasioned the Peace of Nicias, we will first have to consider why Athens and Sparta went to war in the first place, how each proposed to fight, how each expected to win, and why in the decade-long struggle that constituted the Archidamian War the expectations of both came to naught.

---

[6] See Russell Meiggs, *The Athenian Empire* (Oxford, 1975), p. 305.

[7] Note Thuc. 1.139.1-2, and see Donald Kagan, *The Outbreak of the Peloponnesian War* (Ithaca, NY, 1969), and *On the Origins of War and the Preservation of Peace* (New York, 1995), pp. 15–79.

THE SPARTAN DISPOSITION

The Spartans started the Archidamian War. Of that, there is no doubt. In 432 B.C., they voted for war and rallied their allies. At the end of Winter 431, in anticipation of the struggle to come, the Thebans – Sparta's principal allies outside the Peloponnesus – launched a surprise attack on Athens' longtime Boeotian ally Plataea,[8] and the Spartans then gathered an army and marched into Attica itself, fully expecting a fight (Thuc. 2.10.1-24.1). The Athenians could plausibly claim to be innocent. After all, they had been willing to submit the matter in dispute to arbitration, as required under the terms of the Thirty Years Peace, which both sides had solemnly sworn oaths to uphold in 446 B.C. (1.78.4, 85.2, 140.2, 141.1, 144.2, 145). Technically, the Thebans and their Spartan allies had broken the agreement; and, when things did not go well, the Lacedaemonians, who were notoriously superstitious, began to wonder whether in contravening their oaths, they had not, in fact, outraged the immortal gods (7.18.2-3).

This is not, however, the whole story. Nor can it be. The Spartans were notoriously slow to embark on war. They had nearly always been behindhand in the past. They arrved at Marathon too late to participate in the battle (Hdt. 6.105-7, 120; Pl. *Leg.* 698e; Isoc. *Paneg.* 87); at Salamis, it took a trick on Themistocles' part to get them to fight at all (Hdt. 8.40-97, esp. 49, 57-64, 68, 74-81). For all their prowess, they had always been reluctant warriors, and everyone knew it. On the eve of the war, Sparta's Corinthian allies tell the Lacedaemonians,

> The Athenians are innovators, keen in forming plans, and quick to accomplish in deed what they have contrived in thought. You Spartans are intent on saving what you now possess; you are always indecisive, and you leave even what is needed undone. They are daring beyond their strength, they are risk-takers against all judgment, and in the midst of terrors they remain of good hope – while you accomplish less than is in your power, mistrust your judgment in matters most firm, and think not how to release yourselves from the terrors you face. In addition, they are unhesitant where you are inclined to delay, and they are always out and about in the larger world while you stay at home. For they think to acquire something by being away while you think that by proceeding abroad you will harm what lies ready to hand. In victory over the enemy, they sally farthest forth; in defeat, they give the least ground. For their city's sake, they use their bodies as if they were not their own; their intelligence they dedicate to political action on her behalf. And if they fail to accomplish what they have resolved to do, they suppose themselves deprived of that which is their own – while what they have accomplished and have now acquired they

---

8 Consider Thuc. 2.2-6 and Hdt. 7.233 in light of 6.108, 111, 113, 7.132, 8.1, 66, 9.7, 28, 31; and see Kagan, *The Archidamian War*, pp. 43-8.

judge to be little in comparison with what they will do in the time to come. If they trip up in an endeavor, they are soon full of hope with regard to yet another goal. For they alone possess something at the moment at which they come to hope for it: so swiftly do they contrive to attempt what has been resolved. And on all these things they exert themselves in toil and danger through all the days of their lives, enjoying least of all what they already possess because they are ever intent on further acquisition. They look on a holiday as nothing but an opportunity to do what needs doing, and they regard peace and quiet free from political business as a greater misfortune than a laborious want of leisure. So that, if someone were to sum them up by saying that they are by nature capable neither of being at rest nor of allowing other human beings to be so, he would speak the truth (Thuc. 1.70).

Such was the common sense of the matter. The Athenians were enterprising. They had long been so, and the Spartans were cautious in the extreme.

For all of this, there was reason. Enterprise and daring had paid off for the Athenians. In 499 B.C., in a moment of enthusiasm, they had foolishly lent support to the Ionian revolt against Persian rule (Hdt. 5.28-38, 49-51, 54-55, 97-6.34); and, in 490 B.C., when a Persian expeditionary force arrived at Marathon to inflict on the Athenians the punishment they had so manifestly earned, Athens' hoplites, supported by Plataea alone, had with audacity charged, routed, and massacred the hitherto invincible Mede (6.94-119). Ten years later, when Xerxes, the Great King of Persia himself, marched into Greece with a sizable army and a great fleet drawn from a vast empire that stretched from Egypt in the west to the Indian subcontinent in the east, the Athenians had boldly evacuated their own territory and had taken to the sea. Their commander Themistocles had then tricked Xerxes into forcing a naval battle on the Hellenes in the bay dividing the island of Salamis from Attica, where his armada – superior in numbers and in skill – could not effectively maneuver, where the Greek triremes could immobilize his ships, and where the marines aboard those triremes could fight from shipboard almost as if on land (8.40-97). In the wake of this great victory, the members of the Hellenic League had agreed to carry the war across the Aegean to the Asia Minor shore (8.131-32, 9.102, 105-6) where, in 479 B.C., on the day the armies of the Hellenes defeated the Persians and their Theban allies at Plataea, the Greek naval forces and the hoplites they landed opposite the island of Samos at Mycale on the Anatolian shore inflicted on the Mede a no less impressive defeat (9.90-106). Then, when the Spartans had proved reluctant to make an ongoing commitment to defend the Greeks of Asia Minor and those who lived on the islands of the Aegean against Achaemenid Persia (9.106), the Athenians had enthusiastically stepped into the breach and offered their services (9.106, 114-21). In this fashion, in little more than a decade, a city of thirty thousand adult male citizens (5.97, 8.65),[9] a backwater just a short time before, had achieved naval hegemony in the eastern Mediterranean. Contemplation of the Athenian accomplishment in this brief span of time takes one's breath away.

If in 431 B.C. the Athenians had reason to be daring, the Spartans were no less right to be cautious. To begin with, they were few in number. In 480 B.C., if Herodotus is to be trusted, there had been 8,000 adult male Spartiates (7.234.2).[10] In time of war, they tended to dispatch two thirds of their soldiers on campaign (Thuc. 2.10, 3.15); and, at the time of the battle of Plataea, they reportedly sent out 5,000 Spartiate hoplites and a like number of hoplite soldiers from among the *períoikoi* – the free-subject population – of Laconia and Messenia; and this force they supplemented with a sizable body of nonhoplite auxiliaries drawn from among the helots – the servile population in Laconia and Messenia which tended Lacedaemon's farms (Hdt. 9.10-11). Herein lies the rub. The mere existence of these helots posed a grave danger to Sparta.

In 480 B.C., if Herodotus is reliable, Lacedaemon's servile population outnumbered its Spartan population by a ratio of seven to one or more (9.10.1, 29,1, 61.2). In the half century that followed, we have reason to believe that the population of Spartiates endowed with full political rights dwindled dramatically,[11] and we have no grounds for supposing that the same can be said for the helots. To make matters worse, the helots of Messenia constituted a people in bondage. They were not comparable to the slaves of Athens: They were not drawn from a considerable array of peoples speaking a variety of languages, worshipping divers gods, and possessing no ground for solidarity apart from their common condition. Until the late eighth century, the Messenians appear to have been an independent – if perhaps not fully defined – community.[12] Thereafter, they were a conquered people, reduced to servitude and forced to farm their ancestral land for a foreign occupier, and they knew it. They spoke a common language, a dialect of Dorian Greek; they worshipped the same gods; and they intermarried and reared families. They had grounds for mutual trust and, from time to time,

---

[9] The number provided by Herodotus is plausible: see A. H. M. Jones, *Athenian Democracy* (Oxford, 1957), pp. 8–10.

[10] This figure is consistent with the evidence provided in Plut. *Lyc.* 8 and Arist. *Pol.* 1270a36.

[11] This can be inferred from Thuc. 5.68 and Xen. *Hell.* 4.2.16. Note also 6.1.1, 4, 15, 17; *Ages.* 2.24; and Arist. *Pol.* 1270a36. Cf. Isoc. *Panath.* 255ff.

[12] Cf. Nino Luraghi, "Becoming Messenian," *Journal of Hellenic Studies* 122 (2002), pp. 45–69, who supposes the "absence of clear archaeological evidence" for "regional cohesiveness" a refutation of the literary evidence indicating that the Messenians as a people rallied and fought for their liberty, with Thuc. 1.10.2, who foresaw and warned against what one might dub "the archaeological fallacy."

as one would expect, they did revolt.[13] We hear of no more than three such occasions, but the Spartans were notoriously secretive about internal matters (Thuc. 5.68.2), and there may well have been other revolts.[14] The Messenian helots rose up in a dramatic fashion in the first half of the seventh century (Strabo 8.4.10). There is reason to believe that they did so once more on the eve of the battle of Marathon (Pl. *Leg.* 3.692d, 698d-e).[15] And they did so, to devastating effect, in 465 B.C. On this last occasion, the Spartans and their allies in the Hellenic League were able to drive the rebels from the cultivated land in the lowlands of Messenia, but they failed in their attempts to extricate them forcibly from the mountainous region near Mt. Ithome, where the terrain was unsuitable for the hoplite phalanx – and, in the end, they had to negotiate a humiliating evacuation of their formerly servile foe (Thuc. 1.101.1-103.3).

If the Spartans were a martial people, if they systematically indoctrinated their young in the city's traditions, if they encouraged a fierce xenophobia and taught their children loyalty, if they required young men to be physically fit and trained them in the martial arts, if they encouraged erotic attachments between men likely to fight in phalanx alongside one another, if the men of the city lived until an advanced age in barracks, ready to roll out of bed and fight at a moment's notice,[16] it was because they had to do so. They could not fully trust the *perioikoi*, who deeply resented their rule and the arrogance the Spartans displayed (Xen. *Hell.* 3.3.6).[17] And they confronted the fierce hatred of their subject population, which Aristotle (*Pol.* 1269b36-39)

---

[13] See Xen. *Hell.* 3.3.4-7; Pl. *Leg.* 6.776c-d, 777b-d; Arist. *Pol.* 1264a32-36, 1269a34-1269b12, 1272b16-22 (with 1330a25-28). To assess the impact on Spartan policy of the fear to which the helot danger gave rise, one should read Hdt. 7.235 (with Xen. *Hell.* 4.8.8; Diod. 14.84.5); Thuc. 4.3-5, 8-23, 26-41, 53-57, 5.35, 39.2-3, 44.3, 56.2-3, 115.2, 6.105.2, 7.18.3, 26.2, 86.3; Diod. 13.64.5-7 in light of Critias *Vorsokr.*⁶ 88 B37; Thuc. 4.80 (with 1.132.4, 4.6, 41.3, 55.1, 5.14.3, 23.3, 35.6-7); Xen. *Lac. Pol.* 12.4; Plut. *Lyc.* 28, *Sol.* 22.1-3. The fact that the Spartans found the means to contain the helot threat should not be taken as evidence that it was not serious: cf. Richard J. A. Talbert, "The Role of the Helots in the Class Struggle at Sparta," *Historia* 38 (1989), pp. 22–40.

[14] Cf. George L. Cawkwell, "Sparta and her Allies in the Sixth Century," *Classical Quarterly* n. s. 43:2 (1993), pp. 364-76 (at. 369), who is too quick to take an absence of evidence in this case as evidence of absence.

[15] In this connection, see W. P. Wallace, "Kleomenes, Marathon, the Helots, and Arkadia," *Journal of Hellenic Studies* 74 (1954), pp. 32–5, who makes a strong case for the view that the events described at Paus. 4.23.5-10 took place at this time and not in the seventh century. In this connection, see also E. S. G. Robinson, "Rhegion, Zankle-Messana and the Samians," *Journal of Hellenic Studies* 66 (1946), pp. 13–20; and *A Selection of Greek Historical Inscriptions to the End of the Fifth Century*, ed. by Russell Meiggs and David Lewis (Oxford, 1973) no. 22. Herodotus' silence concerning the revolt (6.120) is arguably a token of the effectiveness of Spartan attempts to maintain strict secrecy concerning matters of this sort.

[16] See Paul A. Rahe, *Republics Ancient and Modern: Classical Republicanism and the American Revolution* (Chapel Hill, NC, 1992), pp. 136–62.

[17] Note the manner in which the *perioikoi* comported themselves when the opportunity for rebellion presented itself: Thuc. 1.101.2; Xen. *Hell.* 6.5.25, 32, 7.2.2; *Ages.* 2.24; Plut. *Ages.* 32.12.

The Peace of Nicias

describes as a hostile force "continuously lying in wait for misfortune to strike," as it did, for example, in 465 B.C. when an earthquake leveled the five villages constituting Lacedaemon proper and killed an untold number of Spartan women and men.[18]

The same motive that made the Spartans warlike made them exceedingly reluctant to go to war and engage in battle. The Athenians were tolerably numerous. There is reason to suspect that their population may have grown in the wake of the Persian Wars, as the *phóros* contributed by those among their allies who chose not to contribute ships made it possible for poor Athenians to earn a living by serving in public office or rowing in the city's fleet.[19] The Athenians could suffer a setback and remain confident they could recover. After all, they had done so in the past. In 454 B.C., for example, in the midst of the First Peloponnesian War, when Athens first found itself engaged in a struggle against the Spartans and their Peloponnesian allies, the Athenians had lost approximately 250 ships and 50,000 citizen and allied rowers in a quixotic attempt to oust the Persians from Egypt. This blunder had cost the Athenians as much as one fifth of the city's adult male population, if not more.[20] But, in short order, they sent out another fleet and inflicted on the resurgent Persians off Cypriot Salamis a devastating defeat (Thuc. 1.112.1-4), and it was in the wake of this battle that both sides thought it prudent to negotiate a peace, leaving the Athenian Empire intact; the cities of the Hellespont, the Anatolian coast, and the Aegean free from Persian control; and Athens unchallenged at sea in the northeastern Mediterranean, the Hellespont, and the Black Sea (Diod. 12.4.5-6; Plut. *Cim.* 13.4-6, *Per.* 20.1-2).[21]

---

[18] Note Thuc. 1.128.1, 132.4; then compare Diod. 11.63-64 and Plut. *Cim.* 16.4-7, 17.3 with Paus. 3.11.8; see also Plut. *Lyc.* 28.12 along with Polyaen. 1.41.3; Ael. *VH* 6.7.

[19] For a survey of the evidence concerning the size of Athens' population at various points, see Barry Strauss, *Athens after the Peloponnesian War: Class, Faction, and Policy, 403–386 B.C.* (Ithaca, NY, 1986), pp. 70–86.

[20] After considering Moshe Amit, *Athens and the Sea: A Study in Athenian Sea-Power* (Brussels, 1965), pp. 30–49, cf. Thuc. 1.104, 109-10, and Isoc. 8.86 with Diod. 11.71.3-6, 74-75, 77.1-5; Ctesias *FGrH* 688 F14; and Justin 3.6.6-7; and see Jan M. Libourel, "The Athenian Disaster in Egypt," *American Journal of Philology* 92:4 (October 1971), pp. 605–15; and Meiggs, *The Athenian Empire*, pp. 92–151, 473–6. In this connection, see Hdt. 3.12.4, 160.2 (with 7.82, 121.3), 7.7. Even those who believe these figures to be inflated concede that something like one Athenian citizen in five died in the Egyptian campaign: see A. J. Holladay, "The Hellenic Disaster in Egypt," *Journal of Hellenic Studies* 109 (1989), pp. 176–82.

[21] I see no reason to doubt that there was a Peace of Callias: for the evidence, see Meiggs, *The Athenian Empire*, pp. 129–51 (with 487–95). There is reason to suppose that the Athenians were looking for such an agreement in the early years of Artaxerxes' reign (Hdt. 7.151), perhaps before Cimon's ostracism, more likely thereafter; and, although its achievement under Pericles is among the many developments that Thucydides does not mention in his potted history of the fifty years separating the great Peloponnesian War from the Persian Wars (1.89–118), he takes it for granted that his readers are aware of the event (3.10.3). In this connection, see also Ernst Badian, "The Peace of Callias," *Journal of Hellenic Studies* 107 (1987), pp. 1–39, which is reprinted in Badian, *From Plataea to Potidaea: Studies in*

The Spartans were not in a comparable position. Even more than the Israelis of our own time, they were highly sensitive to the loss of life. In Messenia and Laconia, they ruled by intimidation and, at the slightest provocation and sometimes without any overt provocation at all, they could be ruthless in the extreme.[22] Their hold on their subject population was, as is always the case, more psychological than real. This they knew and they recognized that there would be serious trouble, possibly fatal to their city, should they ever display weakness in any fashion. If they were reluctant to embark on war, if they generally avoided decision by battle, it was because a single, shattering defeat might seal their fate. In the conduct of foreign policy, they were generally as prudent and patient as they were formidable when they actually fought. Thucydides is right at least in this: When they went to war in 431 B.C., the Lacedaemonians did so because they were genuinely persuaded they had no other choice. The elaborate skein of alliances that they had formed in the sixth century to bolster their security was in jeopardy (Thuc. 1.86, 88, 118.2) and their future well-being was at stake. This, as Thucydides goes to some lengths to make clear,[23] they had good reason to believe.

THE SPARTAN ALLIANCE

The five villages in which the Spartans lived lay deep in the Eurotas Valley in a region called Laconia, which made up the southeastern fifth of the Peloponnesus. This region they controlled; and, as we have seen, by conquest, in the late eighth century, they came to control Messenia, the southwestern fifth of the Peloponnesus, as well. They profited from the fact that they were cut off from the outside world not only by a range of mountains that ran along the east coast of the Peloponnesus but by rough, mountainous terrain to the north of Laconia as well. In effect, the Spartan homeland was a fortress. In the absence of strife within Laconia itself, a modest number of men could make considerable trouble for an hostile army intent on entering that region through the passes to the north.

---

the *History and Historiography of the Pentecontaetia* (Baltimore, 1993), pp. 1–72, who believes that there was more than one such peace.

22   See, for example, Thuc. 4.80.

23   Cf. Ernst Badian, "Thucydides and the Outbreak of the Peloponnesian War: An Historian's Brief," in *Conflict, Antithesis, and the Ancient Historian*, ed. June W. Allison (Columbus, OH, 1990), pp. 46–91, which is reprinted in Badian, *From Plataea to Potidaea*, pp. 125–62, who argues in an essay as ingenious as it is perverse that Thucydides was a purveyor of "disinformation," no less dishonest than the reporters of the *Washington Post*, who aimed, "in his account of the origin and outbreak of the War, to show that it was started by Sparta in a spirit of ruthless *Realpolitik*," with Raphael Sealey, "The Causes of the Peloponnesian War," *Classical Philology* 70:2 (April 1975), pp. 89–109, who quite rightly recognizes that Thucydides held Pericles and Athens responsible for the outbreak of the war at this time.

Geography posed one problem for the citizens of Lacedaemon, as the Spartan polity was called, and it was quite serious, indeed. Mt. Ithome to the west also cut the Spartans off from Messenia. The only safe route by which they could march an army into that district ran north from Laconia through the mountain passes exiting into southernmost Arcadia, then west through that upland region, and south again from the high plains and the rolling hills of southern Arcadia into the great fertile plain of Messenia itself. In the long run, if they were to hold Messenia, the Spartans had to control this route. To do so without fear of interference, they needed the help or at least the connivance of Tegea, the most important of the Arcadian cities immediately to the north. This they had presumably learned during the great Messenian revolt in the seventh century – when, for a time, the Arcadians had come to the aid of the rebels.[24]

Initially, the Spartans sought to conquer Tegea outright; when this attempt foundered, they successfully sought to draw it into an alliance by force. This event, which appears to have taken place in the middle of the sixth century,[25] meant in turn that the Spartans came to have an interest in the wellbeing of the Tegeans and in the political stability of that *pólis*, which could support Sparta properly only if it was properly supported in turn. This then led by an inexorable process to Lacedaemon's involvement farther afield. Eventually, the Spartans found they could subdue and draw into alliance the better part of the Peloponnesus if they championed the interests of the propertied classes and overturned the populist tyrannies that had sprung up in the seventh and sixth centuries B.C. within many of the cities there and elsewhere.[26] In this fashion, step by step, the Spartans established their hegemony within the Peloponnesus as a whole,[27] and this made it highly likely that, if the helots of Messenia or even those of Laconia were ever to rise up in rebellion, they would face the combined forces of what modern scholars call the Peloponnesian League, and the same claim could be made with regard

---

24 The claim advanced by Pausanias (4.17.2-3) is confirmed by *POxy* 3316 = Tyrtaeus 23a (West)², lines 15 and 19. In the aftermath of this war, some Messenians reportedly found refuge and were even given citizenship in cities within Arcadia: Polyb. 4.33.35.

25 See Hdt. 1.65.1, 66-69 with Plut. *Mor.* 292b – on which, cf. Felix Jacoby, "Chrēstoùs Poieîn (Aristotle fr. 592R)," in *Abhandlungen zur Griechischen Geschichteschreibung*, ed. Herbert Bloch (Leiden, 1956), pp. 342-3, with Thomas Braun, "Chrēstoùs Poieîn," *Classical Quarterly* n. s. 44:1 (1994), pp. 40-5. See also D. M. Leahy, "The Spartan Defeat at Orchomenus," *Phoenix* 12:4 (Winter, 1958), pp. 141-65.

26 See Thuc. 1.18.1; Arist. *Pol.* 1307b19-23 with Hdt. 5.92a.1; Xen. *Hell.* 5.2.

27 See Hdt. 1.68.6; Thuc. 1.18.1; Plut. *Mor.* 859b-d; *FGrH* 105 F1; and Paus. 7.1.8 with D. M. Leahy, "Chilon and Aeschines: A Further Consideration of Rylands Greek Papyrus fr. 18," *Bulletin of the John Rylands Library* 38 (1955-56), pp. 406-35; and "The Bones of Tisamenus," *Historia* 4 (1955), pp. 26-38. In general, see George Leonard Huxley, *Early Sparta* (London, 1962), pp. 67-76. Although his treatment of Spartan–Tegean relations is unpersuasive, there is much of value in Cawkwell, "Sparta and her Allies in the Sixth Century," pp. 364-76.

to any power from outside the Peloponnesus which dared to go to war with Lacedaemon.

Some years after the conclusion of Athens' great struggle with Sparta, a Corinthian leader is said to have summed up Sparta's strategic position by comparing Lacedaemon to a mighty stream. "At their sources," he noted, "rivers are not great and they are easily forded, but the farther on they go, the greater they get – for other rivers empty into them and make the current stronger." So it is with the Spartans, he continued. "There, in the place where they emerge, they are alone; but as they continue and gather cities under their control, they become more numerous and harder to fight." The prudent general, he concluded, will seek battle with the Spartans in or near Lacedaemon, where they are few in number and relatively weak (Xen. *Hell.* 4.2.11-12).

On the part of Sparta's enemies, such a consummation was devoutly to be wished, but its accomplishment was, of course, easier said than done – for the Peloponnesian League was a considerable obstacle. As such, it was not, however, insuperable. In sustaining its hegemony within the Peloponnesus, Sparta encountered grave difficulties. In the course of constructing what perhaps should properly be called the Spartan alliance, Lacedaemon ousted Argos – which had also been allied with the Messenian rebels[28] – from its traditional position of leadership within the Peloponnesus. To add injury to insult, the Spartans then seized from Argos for their own use a swatch of fertile territory, called Cynuria, which was located near the coast to the northeast of Laconia, southwest of the Argolid (Hdt. 1.82). This meant that the Argives, comprising a sizable community, were a brooding presence within the Peloponnesus, ever intent on overturning the existing order and on regaining their lost territory and their prestige. Once in a generation, almost like clockwork, they tended to launch a war against Lacedaemon.[29]

---

[28] The recent discovery of a new fragment of Tyrtaeus (*POxy.* 3316 = F23a [West]²) confirms the contention of Pausanias (2.24.7, 3.2.2-3, 7.3-6, 4.5.1-3, 10.1, 6-7, 11.1-8, 14.1, 8, 15.7, 17.2, 7, 8.27.1) that Argos was already hostile to Sparta in the very early years of the archaic period. Note also Xen. *Hell.* 3.5.11, Strabo 8.4.10. Cf. Thomas Kelly, "The Traditional Enmity Between Sparta and Argos: The Birth and Development of a Myth," *American Historical Review* 75:4 (April 1970), pp. 971–1003.

[29] For the importance of Argive hostility, see Arist. *Pol.* 1269a39-1269b5. Note also Xen. *Hell.* 3.5.11, Strabo 8.4.10.The hatred between these two powers did not wane with the passage of time. For the battle of champions in about 546 B.C., see Hdt. 1.82 and Paus. 2.38.5. The battle of Sepeia occurred either shortly before 519 (see Paus. 3.4.1 with Hdt. 6.108.2, Thuc. 2.68.5, and Arnold W. Gomme, Antony Andrewes, and Kenneth J. Dover, *An Historical Commentary on Thucydides* [Oxford, 1945-80], vol. 2, p. 358) or – more likely – about 494 (Hdt. 6.76-83, 7.148). For subsequent relations, see Hdt. 7.148-53, 8.72-73, 9.12, 35.2; Thuc. 2.27.2, 4.56.2, 57.3, 5.14.4, 41, 69-83, 6.7.1-2, 95.1, 105, 7.26, 57.9, 8.25, 27.6, 86.8-9; Xen. *Hell.* 1.3.13, 2.2.7, 3.5.1, 11, 4.2.17-23, 3.15-17, 4.1-14, 19, 5.1-2, 7.2-7, 8.15, 5.1.34-36, 6.5.16-50, 7.1.29-33, 45, 2.1-10, 4.27-30, 5.5; Diod. 12.75.5-7, 77.2-3, 78.1-80.3, 14.82, 86, 92, 97.5, 15.23.4, 40.3-4, 62-65, 68, 70.3, 75.3, 84-85, 16.34.3, 39.

The second difficulty was twofold. To begin with, the cities within the Spartan alliance had their own particular interests, and they had territorial disputes with their neighbors, most of whom were also within the alliance. Their adherence to Lacedaemon limited their freedom of maneuver and, over time, this bred resentment – as, in alliances, it always does. Sometimes, their sense that they were being treated unjustly by their hegemon erupted into fury. At times, another development intensified this fury. The cities within the Spartan alliance tended to be oligarchies which excluded the great majority of citizens from political influence and control. Within nearly every city in Greece, there were tensions between rich and poor, and the Spartans had for understandable reasons sided with those like themselves: namely, the well-to-do. This guaranteed that a shift toward democracy within any of the allied cities would produce a government wary of, if not openly hostile to, Lacedaemon, a government beholden to poor men eager for the acquisition of adjacent land. It did not help that at some point, not long after the Persian Wars, Argos became a democracy,[30] sympathetic, at least in some measure – so we must presume – to democracies elsewhere. The Spartans had long been afraid that the Argives and Arcadians would form an alliance with the Messenians of the sort that had existed for a time in the seventh century, if not also in later times.[31] After the Persian Wars, the Spartans had all the more reason to be afraid.

In short, the Spartan alliance was fragile. Concerning events within the Peloponnesus, we are by no means well informed. We possess no ancient history written about Sparta or the region as a whole. We learn about incidents only in passing and generally by accident. Now and again, however, there is tantalizing evidence, suggesting that in the fifth century something was amiss within the Spartan alliance. On the eve of the battle of Marathon in 490 B.C., for example, we have good reason to believe that all of Arcadia was disaffected (Hdt. 6.74). Moreover, the Tegeans in particular appear to have been at odds with the Spartans shortly before the battle of Plataea (9.37-38), and they appear to have been so some years thereafter as well (6.72). The contingents from Mantineia and Elis, two of the principal cities within the Spartan alliance, showed up too late for the battle of Plataea in 479 B.C. For their tardiness, there can have been no excuse, as the Spartans knew all too well. The campaign was well planned; the Mantineians and the Eleans were forewarned; and it says a great deal about the fury of the Lacedaemonians that in the aftermath, the ruling order in both communities thought it prudent to banish the generals who had been in charge (9.77).[32]

---

[30] See Thuc. 5.28, 31.
[31] Consider Hdt. 5.49.8 and Arist. *Pol.* 1269b3-5, 1270a1-3 in light of *POxy* 3316 = Tyrtaeus 23a (West)².
[32] For the evidence and the details, see Antony Andrewes, "Sparta and Arcadia in the Early Fifth Century," *Phoenix* 6:1 (Spring 1952), pp. 1–5.

There is also scattered evidence indicating that at some point between the battle of Plataea in 479 B.C. and the helot revolt in 465 B.C., almost certainly in the early 460s, the Spartans had to fight two pitched battles – one at Tegea against the Tegeans and the Argives, another at Dipaea against all the Arcadians except the Mantineians.[33] Moreover, there is reason to wonder whether the Eleans may not have been involved as well.[34] Had this struggle coincided with the earthquake and helot revolt of 465 B.C., or had it followed hard on that cataclysm, especially if the Athenians had also taken advantage of Lacedaemon's moment of weakness and distress, the Spartans might well have found themselves driven from Messenia and reduced to the fastness of Laconia[35] – as, in fact, they were not much more than a century thereafter. Then, the Thebans defeated them in the Peloponnesus at Mantineia, liberated the helots of Messenia, built a capital for them on the slopes of Mt. Ithome, and established Megalopolis in southern Arcadia as an obstacle athwart the road leading from Laconia to Messenia.[36]

There was one additional difficulty, which emerged in the wake of the First Peloponnesian War, a struggle that took place between 461 and 451 B.C. and then flickered into existence for a brief moment five years thereafter. Sparta's most powerful Peloponnesian ally, the city within its alliance that was always the most independent, was Corinth – and, in the wake of this war, the Corinthians were left at their wit's end.

THE CORINTHIAN CONUNDRUM

Corinth occupied a position of great strategic significance on the isthmus at the entrance to the Peloponnesus that separated the Corinthian Gulf from the Saronic Gulf. Its central location athwart the trade routes and the fact that it possessed in the Acrocorinth an impregnable fortress gave it great influence. Prior to the Persian Wars, it was a great power in its own right, fielding the largest navy in Greece and maintaining exceptionally close relations with a commonwealth of independent colonies that it had scattered along the trade route to Italy in the west as well as in Thrace to the east.[37] In those years, on the rare occasions in which an over-ambitious Spartan king sought to extend

---

[33] See Hdt. 9.35, where the list of battles is clearly in chronological order. Note also Paus. 3.11.7, 8.8.6, 45.2; Isocr. *Arch.* 99.

[34] Consider Diod. 9.54 and Strabo 337 in conjunction with Paus. 5.9.5 and Thuc. 5.47.

[35] In this connection, see W. G. Forrest, "Themistocles and Argos," *Classical Quarterly* n. s. 10:2 (November 1960), pp. 221–41, whose reconstruction of events in this period I find not only ingenious but also plausible. Cf., however, J. L. O'Neill, "The Exile of Themistocles and Democracy in the Peloponnese," *Classical Quarterly* n. s. 31:2 (November 1981), pp. 335–46.

[36] See John Buckler, *The Theban Hegemony, 371–362 B.C.* (Cambridge, MA, 1980).

[37] For a thorough account, see J. B. Salmon, *Wealthy Corinth: A History of the City to 338 B.C.* (Oxford, 1984), pp. 1–252, 387–96.

Spartan hegemony beyond the Peloponnesus, Corinth was perfectly capable of inducing Sparta's allies to refuse cooperation. There was even a moment in the late sixth century B.C. when Athens itself owed its independence to truculence and obstinacy on the part of Lacedaemon's Corinthian ally (5.74-77, 90-93).[38]

In the aftermath of the Persian Wars, Athens quickly came to overshadow Corinth, and though there is reason to suspect that the assertiveness of the Athenians during the war made the Corinthians nervous from the outset (8.43-44, 59-63, 74-78, 94),[39] there is little indication of outright hostility on their part.[40] Corinth was, after all, a commercial power, far more interested in trade than it was in war. Moreover, for the most part, it looked to the west. Nearly all of its colonies lay beyond the aptly named Corinthian Gulf, along the coast of the Ionian Sea, or in Sicily; and, in this region, the Athenians played no special role. For Corinth, however, the First Peloponnesian War marked a great change.

This war began, as we have seen, in 461 B.C., some thirty years before the long and bitter struggle depicted by Thucydides. The desultory conflict that erupted between Sparta and Athens that year resulted from a long-festering territorial dispute between Corinth and its neighbor Megara, from Corinth's seizure of the district in dispute, and from the refusal of the Spartans to come to Megara's defense. In fury, the Megarians turned to Athens, which came to their aid, fortified the mountain passes leading to the Isthmus of Corinth, and built long walls to link the town of Megara to Nisaea, Megara's port on the Saronic Gulf (Thuc. 1.103.4).[41] When Corinth appealed to Sparta for help, the Spartans declared war but, in the struggle that followed, they proved feckless in the extreme. The hoplites of the Spartan alliance were unable to make their way through the mountain passes in the Megarid the Athenians had fortified; and, apart from Corinth and Aegina early in the war (1.105.1-2), the cities in that alliance made no known effort to confront Athens on the sea.

Moreover, in the interim, when the Spartans agreed to evacuate the rebellious Messenians occupying Mt. Ithome, the Athenians settled them at Naupactus near the mouth of the Corinthian Gulf, within sight of the narrowest point in that lengthy body of water (1.103.1-3). Although we do know that the Corinthian losses were considerable on both sea and land (1.105-106; Lys. 2.49-53), we are otherwise exceedingly ill informed concerning the conduct of this war. In particular, we are not expressly told whether the

---

[38] Prior to the Persian Wars, when the Aeginetans were a formidable naval power, the Corinthians were on excellent terms with the Athenians: Hdt. 6.89, 108.

[39] In this connection, note Thuc. 1.90.1.

[40] It is noteworthy that the Corinthians were willing to resort to Themistocles soon thereafter as an arbitrator: Plut. *Them.* 24.1, and Theophrastus ap. *P. Oxy.* 1012, F9.23-34.

[41] Note, in this connection, Plut. *Cim.* 17.2.

Athenians parked a fleet in Naupactus and conducted from there a blockade of Corinthian trade. We are not expressly told whether the Athenians used Pegae, Megara's port on the Corinthian Gulf, to similar effect; and nothing is said in the meager sources to suggest that a similar blockade was mounted from Salamis in the Saronic Gulf. But given that, almost from the outset, the Athenians used Naupactus and Salamis in such a fashion during the later war described in such fine detail by Thucydides (Thuc. 2.69.1, 93.4), it is reasonable to suppose that they did so earlier as well, and we do know that they kept a fleet in Pegae during the First Peloponnesian War (1.103.4, 107.3, 111.2). The Athenians were not lacking in strategic imagination and enterprise.[42]

Most of the ancient cities were farming communities, based on agriculture and little else.[43] Corinth was, as we have seen, an exception to the rule.[44] Within this *pólis*, there were some landholders, to be sure, and agriculture and animal husbandry were not unknown. But the territory of the city was quite small, and most of what its citizens consumed had to be imported from abroad. Its wealth – even in Homer's day, Corinth was famous for its wealth – rested almost entirely on trade. Unless merchants intent on transporting goods between the Black Sea and the Aegean, on the one hand, and the central and western Mediterranean, on the other, were prepared to risk everything by circumnavigating the Peloponnesus and rounding the notoriously dangerous Cape Malea, they had to unload their cargoes at Corinth and sell them on the spot or arrange for them to be carted across the isthmus to another ship – or, if their vessels were small, they had the option of paying to have them moved across the dragway linking the Saronic and Corinthian Gulfs. On all such trade, the Corinthians exacted a toll, and the merchants of Corinth were themselves in an ideal position to operate as middlemen, which they did. The Corinthians profited as well from providing for the needs of the sailors and merchants who passed through the town: The city was renowned not only for the work done by its artisans[45] but also for the quality and number of its prostitutes.

The long period of blockade – if, as seems likely, there was one – and the years of terrible hardship associated with it would help explain why in the late 430s the Corinthians should display such bitterness – against the Athenians, whose benefactors they once had been,[46] and against the

---

[42] Cf. Salmon, *Wealthy Corinth*, pp. 257–69, who fails even to consider this possibility.

[43] See Victor Davis Hanson, *The Other Greeks: The Family Farm and the Agrarian Roots of Western Civilization* (New York, 1995).

[44] For the details, see Salmon, *Wealthy Corinth*, pp. 101–85. There is also material of value in Donald W. Engels, *Roman Corinth: An Alternative Model for the Ancient City* (Chicago, 1990).

[45] The respect that the Corinthians accorded artisans was thought noteworthy: Hdt. 2.167.

[46] In this connection, note Hdt. 5.93, and see Thuc. 1.103.4.

Spartans, who had done next to nothing in their defense. The elaborate comparison made of these two peoples in the remarkable passage that I have quoted at length from Thucydides' history tells the tale, as does their reckless conduct on the eve of the Peloponnesian War.

There is reason to believe that in the period following the First Peloponnesian War, the Corinthians did everything in their power to improve their strategic position within the Corinthian Gulf and along the ancient trade route stretching from its mouth north past the island of Corcyra to Epidamnus in what is now Albania, then across the Ionian Gulf to the heel of Italy's boot and on to Sicily.[47] There were two obstacles to their success. Megara revolted against the Athenians in 446 B.C., slaughtered the Athenian garrison, and returned to the Spartan alliance; however, when the Thirty Years Peace was signed, Athens' allies the Messenian émigrés retained control of Naupactus. Moreover, to the north and west, another power of some considerable importance – Corinth's renegade colony Corcyra – maintained itself in splendid isolation, fielding the second largest fleet in Hellas, treating its metropolis with an infuriating disdain, and refusing to be party to any of the quarrels that affected the Greeks (1.13.2-4, 25.3-4, 38.1-3). If Corinth was once again to be secure, if it was not to be a pawn in the rivalry between Athens and Sparta, it would have to reassert itself, build up its fleet, and, by diplomacy or war, regain control of its lifeline to the west.

In 436 or early 435, a fateful opportunity presented itself. Civil strife, the bane of nearly all Greek cities, had erupted at Epidamnus, and the democratic party, which controlled the city, found itself besieged by the Epidamnian oligarchs and their allies among the Illyrians. For help, they had turned to their mother city Corcyra, a democracy. In keeping with their customary policy, the Corcyraeans, who had earned notoriety by failing to aid the Greeks against the Persians in 480 B.C. (Hdt. 7.168), spurned their colonists' appeal (Thuc. 1.24.3-7). In desperation, the Epidamnian democrats then sent an embassy to the oracle at Delphi, hoping that it would sanction an appeal on their part to Corinth, which, as it happens, was at this time an oligarchy. Centuries before, when relations with Corcyra had been everything they were supposed to be, in accordance with their custom, the Corinthians had appointed a founder (*oikistēs*) to lead colonists drawn from

---

47 See Salmon, *Wealthy Corinth*, pp. 270–80. One indicator is the status of Leucas. At some point not long after the Persian Wars, Corinth and Corcyra asked Themistocles to arbitrate a dispute they had with regard to their political rights vis-à-vis the island: see Plut. *Them.* 24.1, and Theophrastus ap. *P. Oxy.* 1012, F9.23-34. That he ruled in favor of Corcyra is indicated in the sources cited and is confirmed by the fact that he was subsequently regarded as a benefactor of that city: Thuc. 1.136.1. But, on the eve of the Peloponnesian War, when trouble breaks out between Corinth and Corcyra, Leucas is firmly allied with Corinth: 1.26.1, 27.2, 30.2-3, 46.1.

among the citizens of Corcyra to the place chosen for the establishment of Epidamnus on the Illyrian shore. This provided the Epidamnian democrats with the requisite excuse; the oracle, when asked, opined that their city was, in fact, a Corinthian colony; and the Corinthians leapt at the opportunity they were then offered (1.24.1-2, 25.1-3, 26.1).[48]

With little delay, they dispatched colonists drawn from among their citizens and those of their allies to join with the Epidamnian democrats in refounding the city, knowing full well that, in doing so, they might become embroiled with Corcyra, as they had been on occasion in the past (Hdt. 3.48, 54; Thuc. 1.13.2-4), for the Corcyraeans would certainly not welcome direct Corinthian intervention in their immediate neighborhood. In this regard, the fears of the Corinthians were fully realized, for the Corcyraeans responded by accepting an appeal for support from the exiled Epidamnian oligarchs and their Illyrian allies and by initiating a siege of the city by both land and sea (1.26). The Corinthians then began to equip a relief force and, to this end, they drew material support from nearly all of their Peloponnesian allies – apart, that is, from Sicyon, Sparta, and the landlocked Arcadian cities of Tegea and Mantineia (1.27). At this point, the Corcyraeans blinked. They sent an embassy to Sparta and Sicyon and, with the encouragement and support of these two cities, approached the Corinthians. At first, they demanded that the latter abandon Epidamnus as no concern of theirs (1.28.1) and then they suggested that, if this was unacceptable, the oracle at Delphi or one or more of the cities in the Peloponnesus as agreed upon by both parties arbitrate the dispute (1.28.2). In effect, in suggesting that powers allied with Corinth or an oracle that had already sanctioned Corinth's intervention at Epidamnus arbitrate, the Corcyraeans were offering to surrender if the Corinthians were willing to allow them to save face. In the process, they warned the Corinthians that, if they had to do so, they would seek help elsewhere (1.28.3). When the Corinthians replied that no such discussions could take place until and unless the Corcyraeans lifted the siege, the latter offered a series of alternatives: They would withdraw their forces if the Corinthians were willing to do the same; the struggle could continue while arbitration was under way; or there could be an armistice and arbitration (1.28.4-5).[49]

It is easy to see why the Spartans sent ambassadors to support the Corcyraeans. They recognized that, if the Corcyraeans were driven to seek help from the Athenians and succeeded in securing it, they might become embroiled in the dispute themselves. When the Corinthians refused to let the Corcyraeans gracefully back down, at least some of those in authority at Lacedaemon must have thought the situation dire.

---

[48] See Kagan, *The Outbreak of the Peloponnesian War*, pp. 205–21.
[49] See ibid., pp. 222–6.

The conduct of the Corinthians is explicable only in terms of bitterness and ire. The Corcyraeans had been a thorn in their side for more than two centuries (Hdt. 3.48-53, 7.168; Thuc. 1.13.2-4). This was certainly a part of the story. More important was the fact that, if the Corinthians annihilated the Corcyraean fleet and seized the island, especially if they managed to secure Epidamnus in the bargain, they would have in hand the resources necessary to confine or eliminate the Messenians at Naupactus and to reestablish their own hegemony in the Corinthian Gulf and the Ionian Sea along the trade route between Greece and Italy. It was a gamble, but – given what they had been through during the First Peloponnesian War – the risk was worth taking. Or so it must have seemed at the time.

Had the fleet dispatched by Corinth and its allies defeated the Corcyraeans at Leukimne in 435 B.C., they probably would have won the game. But they lost that battle. Epidamnus fell to the Corcyraeans and their allies (1.29-30); and when the Corinthians responded by mounting a supreme effort to build a great armada capable of reversing the decision at Leukimne (1.31.1), the Corcyraeans made good on their threat. They turned to Athens, and the Athenians were drawn in. The latter had no interest in the quarrel; they owed Corcyra nothing; and, when faced with the facts, they initially evidenced great reluctance. But they could not stand idly by while the city fielding the third largest fleet in Hellas conquered the city fielding its second largest fleet – not, at least, if they were given an opportunity to prevent this from happening. Corinth's bold venture threatened the naval balance of power and did so in a manner they could not tolerate. To such a possibility, the Athenians, who depended for their nourishment on grain imported by sea from the Crimea, could not be indifferent, and so they made a defensive alliance with the Corcyraeans and sent to Corcyra a flotilla (1.31.2-45.1).[50] Had the Corcyraeans proved victorious at Sybota in 433 B.C. without Athenian help, the diplomatic crisis looming on the horizon might have been averted. But it took Athenian intervention to save the Corcyraeans,[51] and this left the Corinthians not only frustrated but deeply enraged. At this point, they appealed to Lacedaemon, threatening ominously that, if the Spartans failed to come to their defense, they would do what the Corcyraeans had done. They would look elsewhere for help – and they would take other members of the Spartan alliance with them. So they said (1.71.4-7).

It is unclear what the Corinthians meant. There were, in fact, only two possibilities, and it is not plausible to suppose that either would have conferred on them the naval hegemony they had quite recently with such vigor

[50]   See ibid., pp. 226–42.
[51]   See ibid., pp. 243–50.

sought. In the Peloponnesus, there was Argos, the only power mentioned by the scholiast who glossed this passage; and, abroad, there was Athens. Argos lacked the wherewithal to aid Corinth in this fashion, and Athens was not about to sponsor the emergence of another great naval power. Either way, however, the Corinthians would have disburdened themselves of Sparta, and this was surely the point.

Corinth's suffering derived from its close relationship with Lacedaemon. When Athens accepted Megara into alliance in 461 B.C., it did not do so out of any particular solicitude for the welfare of the Megarians. Nor was it acting out of hostility to Corinth. Its aim was to guarantee its own security by bottling up the Spartans and their Peloponnesian allies within the Peloponnesus. Its larger purpose may have been to disrupt and dismantle the Spartan alliance. In any case, if Corinth abandoned Sparta for Argos or Athens, it would not regain thereby the standing it had once possessed, but it would gain this: No one with the ability to cause it trouble would have any particular interest in interfering with its trade.

Of course, the Corinthians were not especially eager to be confined to the status of a wealthy, commercial backwater. For this reason, they pressed the Spartans, and they pressed them hard. The Athenians made their task of persuasion considerably easier when, at some point not long after negotiating the alliance with Corcyra,[52] they passed a decree barring the Megarians from trading in the markets at Athens and in its empire and from entering the ports belonging to the cities in the Delian League (1.67.4; Plut. *Per.* 29.4-30.2). The so-called Megarian Decree was occasioned by a minor territorial dispute that pitted Megara against Athens and by the fact that the Megarians had begun giving refuge to slaves that had run away from Athens (Thuc. 1.139.2; Plut. *Per.* 30.1-2), but there was almost certainly another motive as well.[53] Of the members of the Spartan alliance nestled along the Saronic Gulf within the immediate vicinity of Athens, Epidaurus, Hermione, Troezen, and Megara had sent ships to join the Corinthian fleet that had fought at Leukimne (Thuc. 1.27.2). Only one of these cities opted to send ships to Sybota as well (1.46). It was against this city that Athens passed the Megarian Decree.[54]

---

[52] The date can be inferred from a comparison of the speech in which the Corinthians sought to dissuade the Athenians from making an alliance with Corcyra (Thuc. 1.36.4-43.4), in which there is no mention of the decree, and Thucydides' summary of the arguments presented at Sparta after the battle of Sybota by the Megarians (1.67.4), in which the decree is not only mentioned but stressed.

[53] See Kagan, *The Outbreak of the Peloponnesian War*, pp. 254–67.

[54] For an elaborate, ingenious, and ultimately unpersuasive piece of special pleading aimed at getting around the evidence strongly suggesting that in passing the Megarian Decree, the Athenians voted to adopt a policy tantamount to an empire-wide embargo on Megarian trade, cf. G. E. M. de Ste. Croix, *The Origins of the Peloponnesian War* (Ithaca, NY, 1972), pp. 225–89.

PERICLES' CALCULATED RISK

On the face of it, the conduct of Athens would appear to be consistent with the hypothesis that Pericles, who was firmly in control of the direction of policy, had come to see the wisdom of the grand strategy pursued in the late 470s and most of the 460s by his rival Cimon. When the Corcyraeans appeared before the assembly at Athens, the Athenians at first rejected their pleas. Only after sleeping on the matter, at a second assembly the next day, did they agree to make an alliance with Corcyra; and, apparently at Pericles' suggestion (Plut. *Per.* 29.1), they stipulated that it be a defensive alliance only (Thuc. 1.44.1). Moreover, when they sent a fleet to support the Corcyraeans, it was a tiny flotilla of ten ships only, commanded by the *próxenos* of the Spartans at Athens, a son of Cimon, who tellingly bore the name Lacedaemonius. His instructions were to enter the battle only if the Corcyraeans were on the verge of defeat (1.45; Plut. *Per.* 29), and it appears to have been only as an afterthought that the Athenians pressed Pericles to dispatch twenty additional ships to reinforce Lacedaemonius' ten (Thuc. 1.50.5; Plut. *Per.* 29.3).[55] All of this was clearly intended as a signal to Sparta that Athens had no desire for war. All of it was aimed at pinning responsibility for the battle to come, and the troubles that might follow, on Corinth alone.

In the aftermath of Sybota, the Athenians followed the same course. They could argue, and argue they did, that nothing that they had done involved a breach of the Thirty Years' Peace. That agreement specified that neutral powers, such as Corcyra, could be accepted into either alliance (Thuc. 1.35.1-2). Nowhere did it stipulate that one could not cut off all contact with a member of the opposing league (1.144.2).[56] In any case, they insisted, there was provision within the treaty for the peaceful settlement of disputes, which were supposed to be submitted to arbitration (1.78.4, 144.2). Everything that the Athenians said was clearly aimed at putting the onus on Lacedaemon.

It need not, however, have been Pericles' intention that the dual hegemony be sustained. Athenian conduct admits of another quite different interpretation, and this interpretation jibes far better with the passage of the Megarian Decree and with Pericles' adamant refusal – in the face of a suggestion on the part of Sparta's ambassadors that such a gesture would be sufficient for the avoidance of war – to even consider that measure's repeal (1.139.1-2, 140.2-5, 144.2, 145).[57] To make sense of this possibility, we must situate Pericles within a foreign-policy tradition.

---

[55] See Kagan, *The Outbreak of the Peloponnesian War*, pp. 222–50.
[56] I see no reason to join George Cawkwell, *Thucydides and the Peloponnesian War* (London, 1997), pp. 31–4, in supposing that Thucydides deliberately or inadvertently omitted to mention a clause within the Thirty Years Peace guaranteeing freedom of the seas and access to the Aegean ports.
[57] Cf. Kagan, *The Outbreak of the Peloponnesian War*, pp. 254–72, 278–81, 321–4, 347–9, 369–72.

The founder of this tradition was Themistocles. He it was who persuaded the Athenians, well in advance of Xerxes' great expedition, that they needed to build the great navy that he then deployed against the Mede at the battle of Salamis (Hdt. 7.143-44; Thuc. 1.14.3; [Arist.] *Ath. Pol.* 22.7; Plut. *Them.* 4). He it was who subsequently tricked the Persians into fighting in unfavorable circumstances in the bay about that island (Hdt. 8.40-97). He was also the man who advised his compatriots soon after the Persians were driven from Greece that, in the altered situation, the real danger to Athens came from Lacedaemon (Cic. *Off.* 3.11.49; Plut. *Them.* 20, *Arist.* 22.2-4); and on an embassy sent to Lacedaemon in the immediate wake of the Persian withdrawal, he capitalized on the extraordinary prestige that he had gained at Salamis (Hdt. 8.124) to put off the Spartans, who objected to anyone north of the isthmus rebuilding their walls, until the Athenians, working day and night, had managed to do just that (Thuc. 1.89.3-91.7).

Here is what Thucydides has to say about Themistocles on the occasion in which he remarks on the Athenian statesman's death:

> Themistocles was a man who in a fashion quite reliable displayed strength of nature, and in this regard he was outstanding and worthy of greater admiration than anyone else. By his own native intelligence (*oikeía xúnesis*), without the help of study before or after, he was at once the best judge (*krátistos gnómōn*) in matters, admitting of little deliberation, which require settlement on the spot, and the best predictor (*áristos eikastés*) of things to come across the broadest expanse. What he had in hand he could also explain; what lay beyond his experience he did not lack the capacity adequately to judge. In a future as yet obscure he could in a pre-eminent fashion foresee both better and worse. In short, by the power of his nature, when there was little time to take thought, this man surpassed all others in the faculty of improvising what the situation required (*krátistos ... autoschediázein tà déonta*) (1.138.3).[58]

Of no one else did Thucydides speak with comparable awe. Indeed, the only other individual he singled out for even remotely comparable praise was Pericles, of whom he wrote,

> As long as he presided over the city in time of peace, he led it in a measured manner (*metríōs*) and in safety; and in his time it was at its greatest. When the war broke out, in this also he appears to have foreknown the city's power. He lived on thereafter for two years and six months; and, when he died, his foreknowledge with regard to the war (*pronoía ... es tòn polémon*) became still more evident. For he told them that they would prevail if they remained at rest and looked after the fleet and if, during the war, they made no attempt to extend their dominion and refrained from placing the city at risk. What they did was the contrary in all regards, governing themselves and their allies, even in matters

---

[58] For at least some of the events that Thucydides has in mind, see Hdt. 7.143-44, 8.22, 56-64, 74-83, 108-10, 123-25; Thuc. 1.137.3-138.2.

seemingly extraneous to the war, with an eye to private ambitions and private profit in a manner quite harmful, pursuing policies whose success would be to the honor and advantage of private individuals, and whose failure brought harm to the city in the war. The cause was that Pericles – as a consequence of his standing, his understanding, and the fact that he was clearly impervious to bribes[59] – held (*kateîche*) the multitude under his control in the manner of a free man (*eleuthérōs*) – in short, he led them instead of being led by them; for, since he never came into the possession of power by improper means, he never had to go out of his way to please them in speech, but enjoyed so high an estimation that he could get away with contradicting them even to the point of angering them. Whenever he perceived that they were in an untimely manner emboldened to the point of insolence (*húbris*), by speaking, he reduced them to fear; on the other contrary, if they fell without reason (*alógōs*) victim to fear, he could restore in them again their confidence. What was, in name, a democracy was, in fact, rule by the first man. Those who came later were more on an equal plane with one another, and each desiring to be first, they sought to please the people and to them handed over public affairs. In consequence, as tends to happen in a great city also possessed of an empire, they blundered in many regards (2.65.5-11).

If we compare the two passages, we can infer from Thucydides' silences what we know from other sources: that Themistocles was not as "clearly impervious to bribes" as was Pericles,[60] that he never possessed the standing at Athens and the trust that Pericles eventually secured for himself, and that the foresight possessed by the latter was less a matter of "native intelligence" than something learned by experience. If Pericles told the Athenians "that they would prevail if they remained at rest and looked after the fleet and if, during the war, they made no attempt to extend their dominion and refrained from placing the city at risk," it was presumably because he had been Athens' leader in the midst of the First Peloponnesian War when the Athenians had dispatched 250 ships to Egypt on an ill-fated mission to help wrest the Nile Valley from Persian control and because he had learned something about the dangers associated with overreaching from having to cope with the fallout from that catastrophic campaign.

It is difficult to believe that Thucydides would have praised those two men in such a fashion had they held radically different opinions regarding the dangers faced by Athens and the foreign policy proper to it. They had, we know, a great deal in common. Themistocles appears to have been at odds with Pericles' father Xanthippus in the 480s, and he was almost certainly

---

59 Apparently, this fact did not prevent him from being charged with bribery toward the end of his life: see Pl. *Grg.* 516a1-2, Plut. *Per.* 32-35.

60 See, for example, Hdt. 8.4-5, 108-12 (with an eye to 74-75), along with Thuc. 1.137.3-138.2.

responsible for the man's ostracism in 484 B.C.[61] But when the great crisis came and Xerxes began making his way toward Hellas with a great army and fleet, Themistocles sponsored the recall from temporary exile of some of those whose ostracism he had himself procured, and he is known to have worked closely with both Xanthippus and Aristeides in 480 and 479 B.C.[62] Eight or nine years thereafter, Themistocles was himself ostracized in the course of a struggle with Cimon that turned on the question of the posture that Athens should adopt toward Sparta.[63] There is reason to think that the young Pericles may have been among Themistocles' supporters at the time. His future associate, Ephialtes, appears to have been allied with Themistocles in the 470s.[64] It was with Pericles' help that Ephialtes subsequently secured Cimon's ostracism in 461 B.C.,[65] and Pericles was almost certainly a proponent of allying with Argos (1.102.4), of settling the Messenians at Naupactus (1.103.1-3), of making an alliance with Megara (1.103.4), and of the war with Sparta that followed. Moreover, earlier in 472 B.C., shortly before Themistocles was ostracized, at a time in which the political dispute between Themistocles and Cimon was at its height, Pericles served as the *chorēgos* for the production at a public festival of a play by Aeschylus that had as its focus Persia's defeat at the battle of Salamis and that the Athenians could plausibly have interpreted as propaganda written on Themistocles' behalf.[66] That Pericles was Themistocles' disciple seems likely; that he was his successor is abundantly clear.

If this is so, it would make sense of Pericles' decision to abandon Cimon's ongoing war against Persia and to send Cimon's brother-in-law Callias to negotiate the peace he reached with the Great King in 449 B.C.[67] Once Persia was driven from the Aegean, Themistocles had believed, it ought not to be the primary focus of Athenian fears and concerns (Cic. *Off.* 3.11.49; Plut. *Them.* 20, *Arist.* 22.2-4). This presumption would also make sense of Pericles' conduct on the eve of the Archidamian War. When Themistocles was ostracized, Thucydides tells us, he withdrew from Athens to Argos, and

---

61 Note Hdt. 6.131.2 and [Arist.] *Ath. Pol.* 22.3-7; then, see A. E. Raubitschek, "The Ostracism of Xanthippus," *American Journal of Archaeology* 51:3 (July–September, 1947), pp. 257–62; and A. J. Podlecki, *The Life of Themistocles: A Critical Survey of the Literary and Archaeological Evidence* (Montreal, 1975), pp. 10–12.

62 Note [Arist.] *Ath. Pol.* 22.3-8, 28.2; Plut. *Them.* 3-21, and *Arist.* 1-25; then, consider Hdt. 6.136, 7.33, 8.79-82, 95, 131-33, 9.26-65, 90-106, 114-21; Thuc. 1.89-97, 5.18; and [Arist.] *Ath. Pol.* 23.3-5; and see Podlecki, *The Life of Themistocles*, pp. 14–34.

63 Note Plut. *Arist.* 25.7-26.3; see Thuc. 1.135.3; Plut. *Them.* 22-24, *Cim.* 5-8, 16; and consider Podlecki, *The Life of Themistocles*, pp. 34-7.

64 Consider [Arist.] *Ath. Pol.* 25.2-3 in light of R. G. Lewis, "Themistokles and Ephialtes," *Classical Quarterly* n. s. 47:2 (1997), pp. 358–62.

65 See [Arist.] *Ath. Pol.* 25.1-27.1, 28.2; Plut. *Cim.* 14.1-17.2, *Per.* 6.5-6, 9.3-4.

66 See Podlecki, *The Life of Themistocles*, pp. 36-7.

67 See Diod. 12.4.5-6 and Plut. *Cim.* 13, which should be read in light of Hdt. 7.151 and Thuc. 3.10.4.

from there he traveled within the Peloponnesus (Thuc. 1.135.3). We do not know precisely where he went and why, and we do not know what he said and did – but we can guess. In or shortly before 465 B.C., the Spartans sent an embassy to Athens to bring charges of Medism against Themistocles, shortly after they had caught Pausanias – the disaffected Spartan regent who had won the battle of Plataea – conspiring with the helots (1.128.1-138.2). All of this appears to have taken place not long after the Argives, Mantineians, and Tegeans had taken up arms against the Lacedaemonians.[68] We cannot be certain that Themistocles bore any responsibility for the difficulties that the Spartans encountered within the Peloponnesus in these years. Nor can we be fully confident that Themistocles was cooking up something with the disaffected regent Pausanias, as the Spartans charged. But no one closely familiar with the machinations he engaged in during the Persian Wars would find it surprising that he should do such a thing.[69] The man was a fox.

In any case, events in this period revealed the fragility of the Spartan alliance; they indicated the location of Lacedaemon's Achilles heel; and they raised the possibility that someone in the future might put together a coalition fatal to Sparta, involving the Athenians, the Argives, and various disaffected Spartan allies. This is surely what the Athenians were up to when, after ostracizing Cimon, they made an alliance with Argos and, soon thereafter, Megara, knowing full well that this encroachment on the Spartan alliance meant war with Lacedaemon; and it explains why they settled the Messenian exiles at Naupactus; why they made an alliance with Achaea on the Peloponnesian shore opposite that town; and why, in the course of the war, they pried Troezen loose from the Peloponnesian League (1.115.1). That, in the wake of the debacle in Egypt, Athens' leader Pericles had to reverse course, arrange for Cimon's recall (Plut. *Cim.* 17.4-6, *Per.* 10; Nepos *Cim.* 3.3), and support him in negotiating a five-year truce with Sparta (Thuc. 1.112.1; Diod. 11.86; Plut. *Cim.* 18.1, *Per.* 10.4); that, in 446 B.C., when the Megarians rebelled and massacred the city's Athenian garrison,

---

[68] The account given by Thucydides (1.136.1-138.2) of Themistocles' flight from Argos to Ephesus by way of Corcyra, the kingdom of the Molossians, Pydna, and Naxos does not make chronological sense, for he has Themistocles passing through Naxos at the time of the Athenian siege in 468 B.C., arriving at Ephesus, and writing a letter forthwith to Artaxerxes, the Great King of Persia, who did not attain the throne until three years later in 465/4 B.C. Naxos is almost certainly a scribal error that has crept into the text and should be replaced with Thasos, the island referred to in its stead in the parallel passage in the best surviving manuscript of Plutarch's *Life of Themistocles* (Plut. *Them.* 25.2). Thasos was not only under siege in 465 B.C. but also has the virtue of being on the route that a ship sailing from Pydna in Macedon to Ephesus is most likely to have taken.

[69] Note Mary White, "Some Agiad Dates: Pausanias and his Sons," *Journal of Hellenic Studies* 84 (1964), pp. 140–52; and see Forrest, "Themistocles and Argos," pp. 221–41; along with Podlecki, *The Life of Themistocles*, pp. 37–42.

when the Boeotians and the Chalcidians on the island of Euboea revolted, and the Spartans with their Peloponnesian allies marched into Attica, Pericles negotiated the Thirty Years Peace (Thuc. 1.114.1-115.1; Diod. 12.5-7; Plut. *Per.* 22-23)[70] – these developments tell us a great deal about the straits in which the Athenians then found themselves, but they say nothing that would prove a change in overall attitude on Pericles' part with regard to Lacedaemon. That Pericles had learned that it is unwise to fight a two-front war is perfectly clear. That he came to think of Athens as a saturated power is not.

In fact, if we are to judge his attitude from what he said to the Athenians in the three speeches that Thucydides records, he thought the opposite. He warned them to be cautious, to be sure, and he specifically warned them not to attempt to add to their empire *until the war with Sparta was won* (Thuc. 1.144.1). He had not forgotten the disaster in Egypt; no one in his generation could. But he evidently thought that an expansion of the empire might properly follow a victory over Sparta. This, in fact, he clearly implied. He told the Athenians that they were masters of the sea, and he held up before them an image of glory and grandeur. Pericles' Athens was, by his own admission, a tyrant *polis* – the unwanted mistress of a great empire (2.63.2), but this did not bother him at all. "We inspire wonder now," he observed, "and we shall in the future. We have need neither for the panegyrics of a Homer nor for the praises of anyone to whose conjecture of events the truth will do harm. For we have forced every sea and every land to give access to our daring; and we have in all places established everlasting memorials of evils [inflicted on enemies] and of good [done to friends]" (2.41.4). Moreover, in the last speech that he delivered to the Athenians before his death, Pericles encouraged them to dream of a universal dominion over the sea, extending well beyond the bounds of the empire they currently held (2.62); and, at that time, he exhorted them:

> Remember that this city has the greatest name among all mankind because she has never yielded to adversity, but has spent more lives in war and has endured severer hardships than any other city. She has held the greatest power known to men up to our time, and the memory of her power will be laid up forever for those who come after. Even if we now have to yield (since all things that grow also decay), the memory shall remain that, of all the Greeks, we held sway over the greatest number of Hellenes; that we stood against our foes, both when they were united and when each was alone, in the greatest wars; and that we inhabited a city wealthier and greater than all.... The splendor of the present is the glory of the future laid up as a memory for all time. Take possession

---

[70]   The terms can be pieced together from Thuc. 1.35.2, 40, 44.1, 45.3, 67.2, 4, 78.4, 140.2, 144.2, 145, 7.18; Diod. 12.7; Paus. 5.23.3.

of both, zealously choosing honor for the future and avoiding disgrace in the present (2.64.3-6).

Such is not the outlook that one would be inclined to encourage in the citizenry of what one regarded as a saturated power. It was in Pericles' heyday that Athens dispatched colonies to Thurii on the boot of Italy (Diod. 12.7, 11-12; Plut. *Mor.* 835c; Strabo 6.1.13),[71] to Brea on the Thermaic Gulf,[72] and to Amphipolis at a strategic crossroads in Thrace (Thuc. 4.102.1-3); he it was who led an Athenian armada to circumnavigate the Black Sea and display to citizen and foreigner alike the greatness of Athenian arms (Plut. *Per.* 20.1) – and all of this he did not before, but after, negotiating the Thirty Years' Peace.[73]

There was, moreover, good reason for Pericles and his countrymen to regard the Spartans with dislike and distrust. At the end of the 460s, the Athenians lost confidence in Cimon and in his policy and turned to Ephialtes and Pericles for two reasons. In 462 B.C., some three years after the great helot revolt of 465, the Spartans sent an embassy to ask for Athenian help. The Spartans had little experience with storming walled places and the Athenians had a great deal. The rebel helots had holed up on Mt. Ithome, and the Spartans had been unable to dislodge them from the fortifications they had cobbled together. Cimon persuaded the Athenians to send an expeditionary force to Messenia to aid the Lacedaemonians, but the latter, disturbed by grumbling on the part of some of the Athenians and fearful that they would side with the helots, soon sent it back in disgrace (Thuc. 1.102; Plut. *Cim.* 16.8-17.4; Diod. 11.63.2-3, 64.2-3). It was, moreover, that same year that the Athenians captured Thasos, which had revolted from their alliance in 465 B.C.

It was presumably its surrender that occasioned their learning that, shortly before the helot revolt, the authorities at Sparta had promised the prospective rebels Lacedaemonian aid (Thuc. 1.100.2-101.3). Cimon's ostracism, Athens' alliance with Argos, the settlement of the Messenians at Naupactus, and the Athenian decision to accept Megara into its alliance in 461/60 were the immediate consequence of this turn of events. Any wishful thinking that Pericles and his fellow Athenians may have engaged in after 446 B.C. and the commencement of the Thirty Years Peace was shattered six years later,

---

71 The evidence leaves something to be desired and admits of a number of quite different interpretations: see H. T. Wade-Gery, "Thucydides, the Son of Melesias: A Study of Perikleian Policy," *Journal of Hellenic Studies* 52:2 (1932), pp. 205–27, reprinted in Wade-Gery, *Essays in Greek History* (Oxford, 1958), pp. 239–70; Victor Ehrenberg, "The Foundation of Thurii," *American Journal of Philology* 69:2 (1948), pp. 149–70; and Kagan, *The Outbreak of the Peloponnesian War*, pp. 154–69.
72 Note *A Selection of Greek Historical Inscriptions to the End of the Fifth Century* no. 44; and see Kagan, *The Outbreak of the Peloponnesian War*, pp. 182–6.
73 In this connection, see Cawkwell, *Thucydides and the Peloponnesian War*, pp. 22–5.

at the time that Samos and Byzantium revolted from the Delian League (1.115-17), when the Spartans called a meeting of the Peloponnesian League and tried to persuade Corinth and their other allies that they should send a fleet to aid Athens' rebellious allies.[74]

The evidence suggests a certain consistency on the part of the Spartans. They were timid and hesitant, but they were also profoundly uncomfortable with the reality of Athenian power; and when the Athenians were in distress, they could be expected to make at least a halting attempt to take advantage.[75] Thucydides reports that, when the Corcyraeans came to Athens seeking help, they argued that conflict with Sparta was nigh (1.33.3) and described the Athenians as "anxiously scanning the horizon that you may be in readiness for the outbreak of the war that is all but upon you" (1.36.1). He indicates soon thereafter that, in depicting his compatriots, the Corcyraeans were right: The Athenians regarded "the coming of the Peloponnesian War" as "merely a question of time" (1.44.2). That they should have thought otherwise would have been decidedly odd. As Pericles stated it in spring 431 B.C., on the eve of the war, "It was clear *before* that Sparta was conspiring against us; it is even clearer now" (1.140.2, emphasis added).[76]

In judging Athens' conduct on the eve of the Archidamian War, we have to be open to the likelihood that, like Thucydides himself, Pericles regarded war with Sparta as inevitable in the long run, that he did not believe that peaceful coexistence could be more than a temporary expedient, and that he hoped, therefore, to be able to fight the upcoming war at a time when the terms on which it would be fought would be highly favorable to a decisive victory on Athens' part. In short, we have to be open to the possibility that Pericles' ultimate aim was Sparta's demise, that his immediate aim was the dismemberment of the Peloponnesian League, and that in the mid to late 430s, the means he adopted for achieving these aims were indirect and quite circumspect.

Everything that Pericles did in those years was aimed at strengthening Athens while depriving the Spartans of any genuinely plausible justification for going to war. This much is clear. But, by the same token, everything he did

---

[74] Given that the league did not meet except when summoned by Sparta, this can be inferred from Thuc. 1.40.5-41.2. Moreover, given the semipublic nature of these gatherings, it is highly likely that the Athenians heard about it quite soon thereafter. The reference to this event made by the Corinthians certainly presupposes that their listeners are already fully familiar with what took place. Cf. Kagan, *The Outbreak of the Peloponnesian War*, pp. 170-9, and *On the Origins of War and the Preservation of Peace*, p. 77, n. 20, with A. H. M. Jones, "Two Synods of the Delian and Peloponnesian Leagues," *Proceedings of the Cambridge Philological Society*, 182 (1952-53), pp. 43-6, and Ste. Croix, *The Origins of the Peloponnesian War*, pp. 200-205.

[75] See C. A. Powell, "Athens' Difficulty, Sparta's Opportunity: Causation and the Peloponnesian War," *L'Antiquité Classique* 49 (1980), pp. 87-114.

[76] See also Plut. *Per.* 8.7

appears to have been calculated also with an eye to enraging the Corinthians. For both purposes, the alliance with Corcyra and Athens' conduct at Sybota could not have been more finely calibrated. Technically, neither the alliance nor Athens' fulfillment of its terms was a breach of the Thirty Years Peace (1.35.1-2). Moreover, one could plausibly argue, as the Corcyraeans did argue (1.32-36), that the Athenians had no alternative. The Corinthians were certainly behaving recklessly. But, given their bitter experience in the First Peloponnesian War, on their recklessness and fury in these circumstances one could bank – especially if, at the same time, one skillfully raised the Megarian question. This was a sore subject for both Corinth and Sparta. Athens' occupation of Megara in the period stretching from 461 to 446 B.C. had been a disaster for Corinth and a humiliation for Lacedaemon. Pericles had brilliantly designed the Megarian Decree. Technically, it was not a breach of the Thirty Years Peace. But it put the Megarians, who depended for their welfare to a considerable degree on trade to the east, in a terrible bind. It heightened the anxiety of the Corinthians by reinforcing their sense that they were beleaguered, and it caused them to fear that, if the Spartans stood idly by while the Megarians faced deprivation and possibly starvation as well (Ar. *Ach.* 495-556, 729-64, *Pax* 246-49, 605-14), the Megarians themselves would once again leave the Spartan alliance and join the Athenians. It is difficult to believe that Pericles had no notion of what he was doing when he induced the Athenian assembly to pass the Megarian Decree; and, even if at that time he had not a clue, he surely recognized its significance when the Spartan ambassadors told the Athenians that they might avoid war if they repealed the decree (Thuc. 1.139.1-2).

In the end, if this account is correct, Pericles got exactly what he wanted: a war that Sparta lacked the resources to win, a war for which Sparta was technically at fault, a war which the Spartans would later regret and for which that superstitious people would blame themselves when they found themselves in duress – in short, a war that would end in a peace, humiliating for Sparta, that would virtually guarantee the disintegration of the Spartan alliance. For when the war was over and nothing had been done to satisfy Corinth, that power was bound to bolt as, in fact, it had threatened to do; and where the Corinthians went, as they had predicted and everyone understood, others would follow. The key to understanding what Pericles had in mind is that he had a grand strategy,[77] and that the Spartans had none.[78]

---

[77] That Pericles' strategy was offensive is but rarely appreciated: For an exception to the rule, see H. T. Wade-Gery, "Thucydides," in *The Oxford Classical Dictionary*, pp. 1067-70 (at 1069). Cf. Kagan, *The Archidamian War*, pp. 24-123.

[78] See P. A. Brunt, "Spartan Policy and Strategy in the Archidamian War," *Phoenix* 19:4 (Winter, 1965), pp. 255-80; and Kagan, *The Archidamian War*, pp. 18-24. Cf., however, Thomas Kelly, "Thucydides and Spartan Strategy in the Archidamian War," *American*

GRAND STRATEGY

Of course, the Spartans were initially unaware they lacked a strategy. Archidamus, the well-informed Agiad king of Lacedaemon, had warned them that it would not be possible to defeat Athens without securing a mastery over the sea, and he had spelled out in some detail the preparations requisite for the attempt (1.80-84). Nevertheless, the Lacedaemonians persisted in supposing that they need only march into Attica and polish off the Athenians in a pitched battle or that the latter would give way after a year or two when they saw their land repeatedly ravaged (4.85.2, 5.14.3, 7.28.3).[79] In the event, in spring 431 B.C., when they actually did march into the territory of Athens, the Athenians under Pericles' direction withdrew behind the Long Walls and waited for the Peloponnesians to cease ravaging the countryside and leave. There was considerable grumbling on the part of the Athenians, but Pericles persuaded them to exercise self-restraint. Even before the Peloponnesians had withdrawn, he dispatched a fleet of 100 ships to circumnavigate the Peloponnesus, reconnoiter with a squadron of 50 Corcyraean ships, and make landings here and there on the coast for the purpose of ravaging the territory of the Lacedaemonians and their allies (2.10-23, 25). In the summer, the Athenians turned to the Aeginetans, who had laid complaints against Athens before the Spartans and the other Peloponnesians (1.67.2), expelled them from their island, and settled Athenians in their place (2.27). And, toward autumn, under Pericles' command, the Athenians invaded the Megarid with their entire levy, ravaging the territory in as thorough a fashion as they could. This, as a matter of settled policy (Plut. *Per.* 30.3), they did in one fashion or another twice every year thereafter until, in 424 B.C., they managed to capture Nisaea, the Megarian port on the Saronic Gulf (Thuc. 2.31, 4.66-69).[80]

In this fashion, the war continued from year to year – with the Peloponnesians invading Attica in the spring and the Athenians deploying their cavalry to harass the invaders when the latter dispersed for the purpose of ravaging the land (2.22.2),[81] with the Athenians sending out a fleet to ravage the coastline of the Peloponnesus and probe its defenses in the summer,

---

    Historical Review 87:1 (February 1982), pp. 25–54; and Cawkwell, *Thucydides and the Peloponnesian War*, pp. 40–3.

[79] There were those at Athens who presumed that Sparta would win: see Thuc. 6.11.5.

[80] See Kagan, *The Archidamian War*, pp. 48–69.

[81] Note Thuc. 7.27.3-5; *Hell. Oxy.* 16.5 (Bartoletti). The Athenian cavalry was apparently a force to be reckoned with: Some Athenians were even persuaded that in the absence of the Boeotian cavalry, which presumably served to protect the Peloponnesian infantry when it was dispersed, the Peloponnesians would not have dared to invade Attica (Thuc. 4.95.2). Note, in this connection, Diod. 13.72.2-9. See Josiah Ober, "Thucydides, Pericles, and the Strategy of Defense," in *The Craft of the Ancient Historian: Essays in Honor of Chester G. Starr*, ed. by John W. Eadie and Josiah Ober (Lanham, MD, 1985), pp. 171–89; and

and with the Athenians ravaging the Megarid before the Peloponnesians came and after they had returned home. At or soon after the outset of the war, the Athenians mounted from Salamis a blockade of Megara's port on the Saronic Gulf (2.93.4), and they no doubt did the same with regard to Corinth; and in the second year, they sent twenty ships to Naupactus to interfere with the western trade of the Corinthians and the other Peloponnesians (2.69.1). On two occasions, when the Corinthians and their allies sent a much larger force in an attempt to wipe out the fleet at Naupactus, the Athenian general Phormio and his sailors showed them just how much skill and experience mattered in battles at sea (2.83-92).[82]

Some events of significance did take place in the first few years, but these were few. Pericles and the Athenians came close to taking Epidaurus in the second year of the war (2.56.3-4; Plut. *Per.* 35.3). And, that winter, the city of Potidaea in Thrace, a colony of Corinth and a subject ally of Athens, which had revolted in 433 B.C. at the instigation of the Corinthians and with a secret promise of support from the authorities at Sparta (Thuc. 1.56-66), surrendered on terms (2.70). Otherwise, the war continued in a desultory and predictable fashion – with neither side being able to land a decisive blow. This was, in fact, what Pericles had expected; and, if the hypothesis presented here is correct, he expected also that as the Athenians repeatedly hammered Megara, put severe economic pressure on both Megara and Corinth, and ravaged the Peloponnesian shore – seizing whatever opportunities might present themselves – they would wear down the Spartans and their allies.[83] Then, when the Spartans offered peace, by imposing humiliating terms, they might be able to create conditions favorable to picking apart the Spartan alliance in the fashion in which Themistocles seems to have picked it apart in the early 460s.

This was a strategy that might have worked with reasonable alacrity had Athens not been struck by the plague.[84] We do not know how many Athenians the disease killed; and though we have a detailed account of the symptoms, no one really knows their cause. The one pertinent piece of evidence suggests that somewhere between one in four and one in three Athenians died from the disease.[85] In its immediate demographic impact, it was at least as important as and probably more significant than the losses that Athens suffered during the Egyptian expedition in 454 B.C. The Athenian response

I. G. Spence, "Perikles and the Defence of Attika during the Peloponnesian War," *Journal of Hellenic Studies* 90 (1990), pp. 91–109.

[82] See Kagan, *The Archidamian War*, pp. 107–17.

[83] See H. D. Westlake, "Seaborne Raids in Periclean Strategy," *Classical Quarterly* 39:3/4 (July, 1945), pp. 75–84.

[84] For a discussion of the consequences, see Kagan, *The Archidamian War*, pp. 78–100, 117–19.

[85] Cf. Thuc. 3.87.3 with 2.13.6-8.

to their predicament was as predictable as it was foolish: After enduring two Spartan invasions and the plague, they briefly sidelined Pericles and sued for peace (2.59.1-2). But, of course, they did this to no avail – for their display of weakness served only to encourage those in Sparta intent on depriving Athens of her empire altogether, and no one in Athens could contemplate abandoning the city's mastery over the sea. Even worse for the Athenians, however, was the fact that in the end, after they had fined and re-elected Pericles a general (2.65.2-4), the plague killed the mastermind himself (2.65.6), leaving Athens adrift without a coherent strategy or even a strategist and what is worse: with no one in charge, able to guide, rather than follow, the vagaries of public opinion (2.65.7-12).

None of this was of much use to the Peloponnesians. Eventually, to be sure, the Spartans invested Plataea (2.71-78); and, after a prolonged siege (3.20-24), the Plataeans surrendered on terms and were executed after a show trial (3.52-68).[86] In 428 B.C., the Mytilenians on the island of Lesbos rebelled (3.2-6), and the Spartans and their allies sent a fleet out into the Aegean in support of their efforts (3.8-15.1, 25). But the Peloponnesians were anything but zealous (3.15.2-16.4), and the Lacedaemonian commander was too dilatory, timid, and xenophobic to be of any help to the Mytilenians or to any of Athens' other subject allies (3.16.3, 26.1, 29-33, 69.1): So, the Athenians were soon able to crush the rebellion (3.18, 27-28).[87]

In the aftermath, the Peloponnesians made various unsuccessful attempts to take advantage of factional struggles, which they had fomented on Corcyra for the purpose of gaining control of the island (1.54.2-55.1, 3.69.2-85.3, 4.2.3, 8.2-3, 46-48); and with the help of the Leucadians and the Aetolians, they made a stab at gaining leverage in the region to the north and west of Naupactus, with an eye to seizing that city from the landward side (3.7, 94-98, 100-102, 105-14). For their part, the Athenians, intent on preventing the Syracusans and the other allies of the Peloponnesians in Italy and Sicily from building ships and sending them help, dispatched a fleet of twenty ships to support their own allies in the war that broke out in that region.[88]

Eventually, in 425 B.C., the Athenians decided to send forty additional ships to reinforce the twenty already in Sicily (3.115, 4.2.2-3), and they instructed the generals in charge to pause en route around the Peloponnesus to help the former general Demosthenes effect an ambitious and ingenious scheme that he had in mind. This Demosthenes had in the recent past demonstrated a measure of tactical brilliance in the conduct of campaigns to the

---

[86] See Kagan, *The Archidamian War*, pp. 102–5, 154, 171–4.
[87] See ibid., pp. 132–53.
[88] Consider Thuc. 3.86, 88, 90, 103, in light of 2.7.2. See Kagan, *The Archidamian War*, pp. 175–86.

north and west of Naupactus, and he had developed especially good relations with the Messenian émigrés who resided in that settlement (3.94-98, 100-102, 105-14).[89] It may have been from them that he had learned of the impressive natural harbor that lies along the coast of Messenia at Pylos, and his aim was to build a fort on a headland there and to post a handful of triremes and a garrison of Messenians who might make incursions into the heartland of Messenia and threaten the Spartans where it mattered most. This he did – while the Spartans elsewhere in Messenia and in Laconia dithered, celebrating a religious festival.

On Agis, the son and successor of King Archidamus, however, the news of Demosthenes' gambit had an electric effect. He was at the time in Attica, where he had arrived with the Peloponnesians earlier than usual, at a time when the grain was still green and not suitable for harvesting, and the army there – accustomed, as it was, to living off the land – was in some distress. The moment he learned of the Athenian presence in Messenia, Agis ordered the withdrawal of the Peloponnesian army from Attica. According to Thucydides, the Agiad king thought that "the matter touched" the citizens of Lacedaemon "intimately," as, indeed, it did. Soon thereafter, the Spartans in the region and the *períoikoi* from nearby marched to Pylos; the Lacedaemonian contingent that had been in Attica followed at a more leisurely pace; and, in time, the Peloponnesians were summoned to Pylos (4.2.4-6.2, 8.1-2).

The details of the struggle that then ensued need not detain us.[90] Suffice it to say that with support from the fleet intended for Sicily, Demosthenes managed to deploy forces sufficient not only to fend off the Peloponnesian assault but also to isolate a substantial contingent of Lacedaemonians posted on the island of Sphacteria in the middle of the bay (4.8.2-14.5). Many of those on the island were Spartiates. The prospect that the Athenians might capture or kill so many full citizens was more than the Spartans could bear, and so those in authority at Lacedaemon negotiated with the Athenian generals present at Pylos an armistice on terms highly favorable to the latter, involving the surrender of sixty Peloponnesian triremes; and to Athens they immediately dispatched an embassy, offering not only peace but an alliance (4.15-20).

It is unclear how Pericles, had he been alive, would have responded to the Spartan offer. If, of course, as some suppose, he had become persuaded that Cimon's policy of dual hegemony was viable, he would no doubt have regarded the offer as the basis for a lasting peace, and he would have accepted it forthwith.[91] But if, on the contrary, as I have argued, he remained convinced throughout that Themistocles had been right all

---

[89] See Kagan, *The Archidamian War*, pp. 187–93, 201–17.
[90] For an overview, see ibid., pp. 218–59.
[91] For a valuable discussion of the available options, see ibid., pp. 330–49.

along, or if the Spartan decision to go to war in 431 B.C. had restored his faith in the strategic analysis of that great mastermind, as it might well have, he would have confronted a real dilemma. In foreign affairs, to a considerable degree, power rests on illusion. Prestige is what soldiers call a force-multiplier. Quite often, it enables one to work one's will without deploying one's forces at all. By the same token, a dramatic loss of prestige can trigger the collapse of one's position. For the Spartans to make peace on such an occasion would have shattered the confidence of their allies. They had gained immensely in prestige when they had sacrificed the three hundred with Leonidas at Thermopylae (Hdt. 7.201-33). To have made peace over a like number of Spartiates trapped on Sphacteria would have cost them dearly.[92] So Pericles might have thought.

He might also have thought otherwise. The simple fact that they had sought peace he might have thought a sufficient blow to their prestige. There was, moreover, another consideration. In 451 B.C., when, in the wake of the Egyptian debacle, Athens negotiated a five-year truce with the Lacedaemonians, the Argives had signed with the latter a thirty years' peace. That the Argives were still eager for the recovery of Cynuria Pericles would have known, that they were inclined to honor their oaths he would have known as well, and he would not have been oblivious to the passage of years. He might have calculated that the Athenians had some time to kill, that in the short run they had more to gain from pressing their cause, and that Sparta's strategic situation was, in the interim, likely to worsen.

If his compatriots captured the Spartiates on Sphacteria and imprisoned them in Athens; if they staged raids from Pylos on the lowlands of Messenia; if they captured the island of Cythera just off the Peloponnesian coast, within easy reach of the one area of Laconian coastline not protected by mountains, and used it as a base from which to raid the Spartan heartland;[93] if they intensified the pressure on Megara and Corinth, which were certainly by this time in exceedingly difficult straits; if they seized Troezen, Hermione, Halieis, Epidaurus, or territory nearby lying on the overland route to Argos, as Pericles had already once tried to do (Thuc. 2.56.3-4; Plut. Per. 35.3), then, when the Argives felt free to launch a war, the Athenians would be in a better position to join them in exploiting the genuine tensions that existed within the Spartan alliance between Corinth, Mantineia, Elis, and Tegea, on the one hand, and Lacedaemon, on the other. Such appears to have been the thinking of Cleon, who initiated discussions with the Argives at about this time or soon thereafter (Ar. Eq. 465-67), and Pericles might well have entertained similar thoughts.

In the event, of course, Pericles was long dead, and Athens found itself divided along factional lines. In 425 B.C., Nicias, the son of Niceratus,

---

[92] See Cawkwell, *Thucydides and the Peloponnesian War*, pp. 64–6.
[93] Note Hdt. 7.235.

favored the policy once championed by Cimon, and Cleon, the son of Cleaenetus, opposed him at every turn. When the Spartan embassy arrived, the latter persuaded his compatriots to demand as a condition of peace the surrender of the men on Sphacteria and their arms and the restoration to Athens of the Megarian ports Nisaea and Pegae, of Troezen and Achaea, and of all the other places that they had given up in 446 B.C.; and when the Spartans were reluctant to discuss in public betraying their allies and suggested that commissioners be appointed to work out an arrangement in private, Cleon denounced them, and the Spartan ambassadors gave up hope (Thuc. 4.21-22).

In the aftermath, the Athenians killed some of the Lacedaemonians on Sphacteria and captured the others, threatening to execute the 120 Spartiates among their captives if the Spartans invaded Attica (4.23, 26.1-41.1). Then, as the Spartans quailed, they seized Cythera and staged raids, more or less at will, on Messenia, Laconia, and Cynuria (4.41.2-4, 53-57).[94] The Megarid they invaded twice a year, as before (2.31, 4.66-69; Plut. *Per.* 30.3); on the Corinthiad, they staged a raid in force (Thuc. 4.42.1-45.1); and they built a fort and left a garrison at Methana on an isthmus lying between Epidaurus and Troezen from which they could easily raid the territory of Troezen, Halieis, and Epidaurus (4.45.2). This had an effect. In 424/3, we learn from an inscription, Halieis made an alliance with Athens.[95]

The pressure put on Megara eventually had an effect as well.[96] At some point prior to the summer of 424 B.C., there had been a popular revolution at Megara; the oligarchs expelled by the popular party had seized Pegae; and from there they had conducted raids on the civic territory, which compounded the suffering caused by the semiannual Athenian invasions. In 424 B.C., the leaders of the revolution came under pressure from their own supporters to re-admit the exiles; and, in the expectation that this would prepare the way for their own demise, the former entered into negotiations with the Athenians to betray the city (4.66).

The plot was only partly successful, however. The Athenians managed to seize the long walls extending from Megara to Nisaea, and they soon secured the surrender of the Peloponnesian garrison at Nisaea itself (4.67-69). But, at Megara, the conspiracy was thwarted (4.68.5-6). Moreover, Brasidas – the one genuinely enterprising Spartan officer – happened to be in the immediate vicinity with a small force intended for deployment against the Athenians in the Chalcidice. He summoned the Boeotians and, with their support, he confronted the Athenians outside the walls of Megara. Upon reflection, the Athenians then backed off; the forces of the

---

[94] See Kagan, *The Archidamian War*, pp. 260–4.
[95] See *IG* I² 87. The First Peloponnesian War opened with an Athenian landing at Halieis: cf. Thuc. 1.105.1.
[96] See Kagan, *The Archidamian War*, pp. 270–8.

Peloponnesian League were admitted into the city and the oligarchs in exile at Pegae returned and installed a narrow oligarchy in the city (4.70-74). Had the Athenians succeeded in this particular endeavor, the Peloponnesians would have been unable to renew their annual invasions of Attica, and the Boeotians, cut off from the Spartans and their other allies, might have been forced to make a separate peace.

The seizure of Nisaea marked the high tide of Athenian fortunes. In the winter of 424 B.C., the Athenians made an attempt to establish a fort in the territory of Tanagra, hoping to conduct raids from there and to stir up a democratic revolution in Boeotia.[97] While en route home, they encountered the Boeotian army and suffered serious losses at the battle of Delium, and the Boeotians soon thereafter managed to seize the fort (4.76-77, 89.1-101.2). In the meantime, Brasidas had made his way through Boeotia and Thessaly on to Thrace, accompanied by a force of 1,700 hoplites, including 700 helots who had been freed for this purpose, and he had managed to persuade the citizens of Acanthus and Stagirus to revolt (4.78-89). In the winter, he managed to strike a powerful blow against the Athenians by taking Amphipolis – the Athenian colony, rich in timber, that Pericles had established at a strategic crossing on the river Strymon (4.102.1-3) – and he made an abortive attack on Eion, three miles downriver on the Thracian coast (4.102.1-107.2). This enabled him to deploy his forces east of the Strymon and to sound out the subject allies of the Athenians throughout Thrace (4.108.1), which he subsequently did (4.109.2-116.3).[98] That same winter, the Megarians managed to wrest from the Athenians and raze the long walls linking their city with Nisaea (4.109.1).

These setbacks caused the Athenians to rethink. Since the capture of the Spartiates on Sphacteria, the Lacedaemonians had repeatedly sued for peace (4.41.3-4), and in spring 423 B.C., the two sides agreed to an armistice (4.117-19), which occasioned a battle in the Peloponnesus between Tegea and Mantineia (4.134) but did not, in fact, stop the warfare in Thrace (4.120-133, 135). The following summer, when the truce expired, Cleon headed for Thrace with 1,200 hoplites and 300 cavalrymen, recovered one of the cities in the Chalcidice taken by Brasidas the previous year, and moved on to Eion in the hope of recovering Amphipolis. There, not far from the city he hoped to regain, both Cleon and Brasidas lost their lives in battle (5.1-3, 6-11).[99]

By removing from the scene the two most determined proponents of war (5.16.1), this last event occasioned what we now call the Peace of Nicias.[100]

[97] See ibid., pp. 278–87.
[98] See ibid., pp. 287–304.
[99] See B. Mitchell, "Kleon's Amphipolitan Strategy," *Historia* 40 (1991), pp. 170–92. In this connection, see also Kagan, *The Archidamian War*, pp. 305–33.
[100] See Kagan, *The Archidamian War*, pp. 333–49.

The war had exhausted both sides. The Athenians, who had not yet fully recovered from the plague and who had suffered one great blow at Delium and another at Amphipolis, feared that there might be further revolts within their empire. The Spartans were beleaguered. They longed to recover the men captured at Sphacteria; they suffered from the raids launched from Pylos and Cythera; they stood by helpless while their helots deserted to the enemy; and they greatly feared a helot revolt. To make matters worse, the thirty years' peace that they had made with Argos was about to expire; the Argives refused to renew it unless Cynuria was returned to them; and the Lacedaemonians feared, not without reason as it turned out, that some of their allies within the Peloponnesus intended to go over to the Argives (5.14.1-15.1).

THE PEACE OF NICIAS

Given their mutual exhaustion, it is entirely understandable that both the Spartans and the Athenians should want peace. Moreover, in the Spartan case, it was crucial for their security that the war be brought to an end. As long as the Athenians were actively conducting a war from Pylos and Cythera, there was reason to be fearful of a helot uprising, it was absolutely essential they be on guard at home, and this meant that the Argives would have a free hand within the Peloponnesus, where, the Spartans knew, they might wreak havoc. The Mantineians were restive, as were the Eleans. There might be trouble at Tegea. The entire position of the Lacedaemonians within the Peloponnesus was in greater danger than it had ever been in the recent past.

It is less obvious that at this point peace was in the Athenian interest. Of course, if they could sustain Cimon's vision of a dual hegemony in practice, they could regard the moment of mutual exhaustion as providing a genuine opportunity for a lasting settlement. If, however, it was not at all likely that this vision could be realized, the Athenians would have to look on peace as a truce and judge it accordingly.

In conducting the war, the Athenians had at one crucial moment blundered badly. It was essential that they defend Corcyra and Naupactus. The attacks on Megara and Corinth made perfect sense, as did the seizure of Cythera, the establishment of the forts at Pylos and Methana, and the raids they mounted against the Lacedaemonians and their allies within the Peloponnesus from those places. After all, the Athenians' only chance for decisive victory depended on the disintegration of the Spartan alliance *within* the Peloponnesus. The invasion of Boeotia had been foolish, however. Athens was short of manpower and, for the purpose of erecting the fort at Delium, the Athenians had exposed their entire hoplite army to no real purpose. Even had they managed to conquer Boeotia, it would not at this point have given them any appreciable strategic advantage with regard to Sparta.[101] They had done so during the First Peloponnesian War to no avail; and, when the Boeotians revolted in 446 B.C., Pericles, recognizing that there was little to be gained from their reconquest and danger in the attempt, had argued against bothering (Plut. *Per.* 18). The Boeotians, moreover, were formidable, as they had demonstrated on that occasion at the battle of Coronea (Thuc. 1.113; Diod. 12.6; Plut. *Per.* 18.2-3). Nor were there good grounds for Athens' involvement in Sicily. No great damage was done as a consequence of their presence there, but there were risks involved, and Athens' commitment in the central Mediterranean did reduce the forces available for guarding their empire. That the Athenians should have allowed Brasidas and his men to make their way unhindered to Thrace, that there should have been no garrison established in a city as important as Amphipolis was[102] – this suggests on the part of the Athenians an unjustifiable mood of complacency.

There was only one genuinely powerful argument to be made in favor of Athens' negotiating a truce at this time. Sparta's withdrawal from the war might well force the Corinthians to bolt from the Spartan alliance. They had threatened to do so on the eve of the war; Sparta had once again proved feckless in their defense; and a peace between Athens and Sparta would place them in a difficult position: Either they would have to endure humiliation and accept as a given that, should war return, they would be the ones to suffer, or they would have to make good on their threat, leave the alliance, and seek help from the Argives or the Athenians. If they did the latter, as they would most likely do, an opportunity was likely to present itself, for other cities, such as Mantineia and Elis, were likely to follow suit. And, once they were committed, the Athenians could reverse course, make an alliance with Argos and the hoplite powers that had abandoned the Peloponnesian League, and force the Spartans to fight a decisive battle on unfavorable terms.

One could also argue that, by making a truce, the Athenians would lose more than they gained. Their ability to mount raids on Laconia from Cythera and on Messenia from Pylos really did put the Spartans at risk; and if Argos could be drawn into an alliance, as was surely the case, the likelihood that the Argives could lure the Mantineians and the Eleans into revolt was very high. Under the circumstances, it would arguably no longer matter whether

---

[101]　Cf. Cawkwell, *Thucydides and the Peloponnesian War*, pp. 50–1. Had the Athenians not held captive the Spartans from Sphacteria, and had they not been in a position to execute them should the Peloponnesians invade Attica (Thuc. 4.23, 26.1-41.1), the claim that the latter would not dare to do so without the support of the Boeotian cavalry (4.95.2) would have been a weightier assertion than it, in fact, was.

[102]　There is no mention of a garrison in Thucydides' narrative of the city's seizure by Brasidas: 4.102-6.

Corinth left the Peloponnesian League or stayed within it. Either way, a great opportunity was about to present itself.

In the end, as they pertained to Athens, such arguments were moot. After the death of Cleon, Nicias was preeminent, and his stature was at the crucial moment sufficient for the Athenians to follow his lead. In sum, they agreed to the peace and, in the aftermath, even made an alliance with the Spartans, hoping that it would bolster what would be a lasting peace; and they harbored no intention of ruthlessly exploiting the opportunities that it might produce. To the Spartans, they returned the prisoners captured at Sphacteria; and when the Spartans proved to be unable to return to them Amphipolis in Thrace and Panactum, a fort on the border of Boeotia, they became suspicious and retained Pylos and Cythera while suspending for a time the raids that they had mounted against Messenia and Laconia and removing the Messenians from the fort at Pylos. Moreover, when Corinth refused to join in the peace, left the Peloponnesian League, made an alliance with Argos, and induced Mantineia and Elis to abandon Sparta for Argos, Athens as a city, in its frustration with Sparta, flirted with the idea of supporting the coalition emerging within the Peloponnesus and even made a defensive alliance with its members. But, as the character of this treaty suggests, they were halfhearted. When the Argives, the Mantineians, and the Eleans drew the Spartans into fighting a pitched battle in the plain between Mantineia and Tegea, the only Athenians present were 1,000 volunteers and 300 cavalrymen who accompanied Pericles' onetime ward and Nicias' outspoken opponent Alcibiades (Thuc. 5.16.1-83.3).[103] Had there been 6,000 Athenians at the battle of Mantineia, the outcome would almost certainly have decided the contest between Athens and Sparta once and for all.

When, under the leadership of Nicias, the Athenians once again embraced Cimon's vision of a Greece governed by a dual hegemony, they threw away every advantage that they had gained in ten long years of war. In the process, they gave the Spartans the breather they needed to consolidate control once again within the Peloponnesus and then rededicate themselves to the dismemberment of the Athenian empire and the subjugation of Athens – which, of course, once the Athenians formally broke the peace (6.105.2, 7.18.2-4), is precisely what they did.[104]

---

[103] For a far more thorough examination of events in this period than is needed here, see Donald Kagan, *The Peace of Nicias and the Sicilian Expedition* (Ithaca, NY, 1981), pp. 17–137.

[104] Note Thuc. 6.11.5, and for the details, see Donald Kagan, *The Peace of Niclas and the Sicilian Expedition*, pp. 138–372, and *The Fall of the Athenian Empire* (Ithaca, NY, 1987).

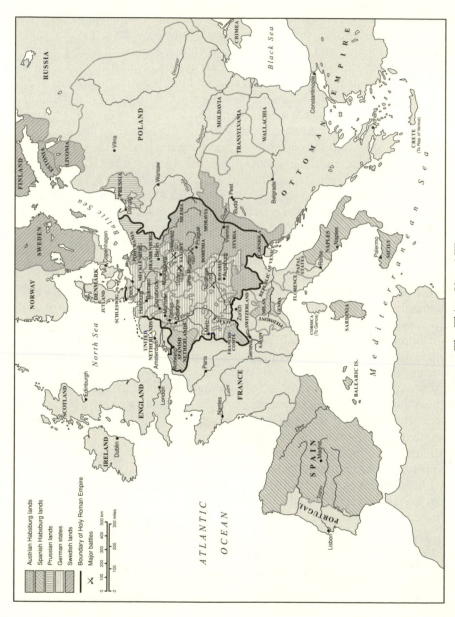

MAP 2. The Thirty Years' War.

Austrian Habsburg lands
Spanish Habsburg lands
Prussian lands
German states
Swedish lands
Boundary of Holy Roman Empire
X Major battles

3

"A swift and sure peace": the Congress of Westphalia 1643–1648

DEREK CROXTON AND GEOFFREY PARKER

The Congress of Westphalia began just like medieval peace conferences. First of all, it was initiated by the pope, Urban VIII (1623–1644), who saw it as his responsibility to end the shedding of Christian blood. Since 1634, he had repeatedly urged France, Spain, and the Holy Roman Empire to resolve their differences in a conference mediated by a papal nuncio. Like his predecessors, Pope Urban also feared that the Thirty Years' War (1618–1648) would allow the Ottoman Turks to seize Christian territory. In fact, the Ottomans did invade the Venetian-held island of Crete in 1645 and, thus, initiated a war that lasted twenty-four years and delivered the island to Ottoman control until 1898. Both before and during the Congress of Westphalia, the idea of uniting the Christian powers and launching a new crusade against the Ottomans ran just beneath the surface. France was well aware of the Ottoman threat. For many years, the Capuchin Father Joseph, the guiding force behind France's chief minister, Cardinal Richelieu, saw a crusade against Islam as the ultimate goal of French foreign policy. Only later did he and his master change their minds: France alternately sought to provoke an Ottoman attack in the Balkans in order to force the Habsburgs to concede French terms, and offered the Habsburgs military assistance against the Ottomans in order to make their demands seem more palatable.[1]

---

[1] Derek Croxton, *Peacemaking in Early Modern Europe: Cardinal Mazarin and the Congress of Westphalia, 1643–1648* (Selinsgrove, NJ, 1999), pp. 192, 198. The changing views of Father Joseph exemplified France's changing policy: In 1617, he founded the Order of the Christian Militia to spearhead an anti-Turkish crusade and spent the next eight years composing "La Turciade," a Latin epic of almost four thousand verses designed to mobilize international support for that crusade. In 1625, just as he presented his finished poem to Pope Urban VIII, he became convinced that the Habsburgs presented the greater challenge and argued that the pope should send Capuchin missionaries to the Ottoman empire instead of crusaders. After 1634, he argued that France should send money to Istanbul to encourage the sultan to attack both the Spanish and Austrian Habsburgs. See Benoist Pierre, "Le

Of course, this medieval paradigm for peace did not last.[2] To begin with, the Ottoman Empire was a menace, but it no longer threatened to overrun Europe as it had done in the previous two centuries. Moreover, *Christendom* – the term statesmen still typically used to describe the states in what we call Europe – was no longer uniformly Catholic. Two Protestant participants in the war, Sweden and the Dutch Republic, did not recognize the pope's authority, while the papacy refused any contact that would provide even a hint of legitimacy to those Protestant governments. Likewise, a number of German principalities, which, although not sovereign powers, nevertheless played a military and diplomatic role in the civil war in the Empire, were also Protestant, and the papacy would not mediate any peace with these states. The original plan for an all-Catholic Congress, to meet in the Catholic city of Cologne, therefore gave way to a bi-confessional congress meeting in two nearby yet different towns. The popes and their representatives not only refused to meet with Protestant ambassadors in any official capacity but declined to negotiate in the same place where the Protestant envoys had assembled: the Protestant city of Osnabrück. Instead, the papal envoys and those of other Catholic powers converged on the Catholic city of Münster, 30 miles away. The two parallel series of negotiations, collectively known as the Congress of Westphalia, eventually involved 176 plenipotentiaries, representing 194 European rulers (almost 150 of them German). It formed, by far, the largest – as well as the longest lived – peace conference held to that date.

France played the key role in getting the Protestants to the conference table because although a Catholic power, its strategy in the war depended for success on Protestant alliances. It could have sanctioned some arrangement in which the Catholics would negotiate under papal mediation, while Protestants would carry on their negotiations with Catholic powers separately; but this would have made it too easy to separate France from its allies, particularly Sweden – a prime aim of Habsburg policy. The Habsburgs – Spanish and Austrian – fighting together would have overmatched an isolated France, so the French insisted on the conduct of Catholic and Protestant negotiations with as much coordination as possible. Although France's representatives resided in Münster and Sweden's in Osnabrück, they met frequently to coordinate policy, and they made a point of presenting their peace proposals at the same time and in as similar terms as possible.

The papacy still participated in the negotiations as mediator, but its refusal to deal directly with any Protestant state, whether on foreign policy issues or

Père Joseph, l'Empire ottoman et la Méditerranée au début du 17e siècle," *Cahiers de la Méditerranée* 71 (2005), pp. 187–202.

[2]   See, e.g., Carl Conrad Eckhardt, *The Papacy and World Affairs as Reflected in the Secularization of Politics* (1937).

on the settlement of the Empire's own political affairs, rendered it powerless to prevent the Catholics from making major concessions to their Protestant enemies in return for a settlement. Pope Innocent X (1644–1655) found these so obnoxious that in November 1648 he issued a bull, *Zelo domus Dei*, formally condemning the Peace of Westphalia just concluded, and he steadfastly refused to recognize its legitimacy thereafter. Whereas the negotiations had begun under the auspices of the papacy, they ended with a peace the papacy refused to accept.[3]

This was an important break, practical as well as symbolic, with the diplomatic world of medieval Europe. Admittedly, the papacy's disconnect with European diplomacy had been evident since the beginning of the Reformation, and the problems involved in arranging papal mediation at the Congress of Westphalia are a perfect example of its consequences. For more than a century, the papacy had managed to sidestep the issue of Protestant legitimacy: It would not negotiate with Protestants but it would compromise to the extent of carrying on negotiations in which it knew Protestants to be intimately involved. The papacy had silently tolerated the 1555 Peace of Augsburg, which granted German Protestant rulers and their subjects freedom of worship. The papal approach appeared based on a belief that it was better to accept the inevitable and pretend it did not exist than to oppose an accomplished fact openly. Westphalia was different: By declaring the peace treaties of 1648 null and void, the papacy set itself squarely against established international law and thereby virtually sacrificed its ability to assume the same mediating role in future conflicts.

In effect, the papacy sacrificed this role late in 1646, when the papal mediator Fabio Chigi leaked a draft protest to key Catholic representatives and threatened to make it public if they made concessions he did not accept. Inevitably, his threat became generally known, making the Protestants all the more insistent on gaining further security for any concessions, out of fear that Catholics would appeal to the papal bull as an excuse to disregard all oaths, however solemn, that they had made in signing and ratifying the treaties.

The parties openly addressed the question of whether Catholics were morally obliged to keep promises they made to non-Christians or to Protestants during the negotiations. Some Catholics argued they could not legitimately surrender rights to Protestants, and any such concessions would be *ipso facto* null and void. Although other Catholics disagreed and felt they had to keep promises even with heretics, the existence of a party of Catholics

---

[3] Martin Heckel, "Zelo domus Dei? Fragen zum Protest des Heiligen Stuhls gegen den Westfälischen Frieden," in *HUMANIORA Medizin – Recht – Geschichte Festschrift für Adolf Laufs zum 70. Geburtstag*, ed. Bernd-Rüdiger Kern, Elmar Wadle, Klaus-Peter Schroeder, und Christian Katzenmeier (Berlin, 2006), ch. 5.

prepared to disregard their oaths was in itself a source of insecurity to Protestants. Many Protestants argued that the unreliability of Catholic promises made even greater concessions and more solid security for their execution necessary. Gradually, the Catholics themselves saw that they must exclude and declare of no effect any papal declarations nullifying the treaties. This was the origin of a specific "anti-protest" clause in the Peace of Westphalia, which declared in advance that any denunciation of the treaties would be invalid. (The source of possible denunciations was not specified, and several smaller estates of the Empire also protested the treaty; but everyone had the papacy in mind.) The papal condemnation of the Peace of Westphalia thus not only marked the papacy's self-declared separation from international law but also the declaration on the part of the signatories that the papacy's opinions carried no weight. Europe had come a long way from the time of Innocent III (1198–1216), when the pope's interpretation of international law partially determined how politicians behaved.

Innocent X's celebrated denunciation of the Peace of Westphalia offers a curious contrast with the lesser known denunciation of the Treaty of Münster, signed by Spain and the Dutch Republic earlier in the same year to end a war that had raged for decades. Again, the mediator and nuncio, Fabio Chigi, was the driving force behind the denunciation, but he was not so naïve as to expect Spain to continue the war until it won ultimate victory – or went down to total defeat – for the sake of re-Catholicizing the rebellious provinces. However, he did object to the failure to secure a promise of religious freedom for Catholics in the Meierij of 's-Hertogenbosch, a territory comprising some two hundred villages conquered by the Dutch in 1629 and still staunchly Catholics. The Spanish ambassador, the Count of Peñaranda, did his best to wrest a concession from the Dutch on this issue, holding up the negotiations for several months but, in the end, he proved unwilling to sacrifice a lasting settlement for the Meierij and ultimately gave in. Chigi felt compelled to issue a protest against the resulting treaty, but he did so in a fashion different from the later Peace of Westphalia. This time, he drew up the protest in secret and had it signed and notarized in the privacy of his own chambers, with only enough witnesses to allow him to claim that it was a public (and, therefore, official) act but with all witnesses sworn to absolute secrecy. He evidently feared the consequences of his declaration on Dutch treatment of the Catholics in the Meierij, so he made sure the announcement received no more publicity than absolutely required for the sake of his conscience.[4] The failure of the papacy to meet either the needs of the

---

[4] Jan Joseph Poelhekke, *De Vrede van Munster* ('S-Gravenhage, 1948), pp. 502–8. Tadhg ó hAnnracháin, *Catholic Reformation in Ireland: The Mission of Rinuccini 1645–1649* (Oxford, 2002), pp. 111–15 and 253–4, notes that Innocent X's nuncio in Ireland, Gian Battista Rinnuccini, followed a similar policy, repudiating treaties made by Catholics that made concessions to Protestants which he deemed unacceptable.

Congress of Westphalia or its own goals constituted a public marker of the transition of European diplomacy from the medieval to the modern era. But the Congress of Westphalia marked a departure from previous negotiations in another way and, although the effects of this shift remained less visible in 1648, they proved no less important.

Traditionally, those who wrote on international relations in Europe viewed the existence of multiple, competing powers as undesirable. Their ideal was a single, unified empire ruled by a Christian monarch, who maintained peace and justice in all of Christendom. This hearkens back to the golden ages of Augustus, the five good Roman emperors, and the later Roman Empire under the Christian rulers after Constantine – and also to the revived empire under Charlemagne, the last time Western Christendom had been more or less united. The subsequent fragmentation of Europe into different states was accepted as a fact but hardly ever celebrated. Instead, hope continued that Christendom could again be united and the wars caused by divided sovereignty brought to an end. Dante Alighieri's tract *De Monarchia* (*On Monarchy*), written in about 1317, expressed the ideal most memorably. Although it remained unachieved (no ruler was willing to subordinate his own authority to another regardless of the theoretical benefits to peace), it lived on as a goal, reflected in the fact that states stood in a hierarchical relationship with monarchies at the top, republics at the bottom, and the Emperor at the pinnacle – at least, where matters of diplomatic precedence were in question.

At the beginning of the seventeenth century, a new concept of the international system began to take hold, which, although still operating within the traditional framework of Christendom, began to endorse multipolarity not only as real but also desirable. One can see this in the imaginative plans to bring peace to Europe conceived by Emeric Crucé in *The New Cyneas* and by the Duke of Sully in his *Grand Design*, both published during the Thirty Years' War.[5] The interesting thing about these peace plans is that they start from the basis of a multistate system: Sully visualized a Europe consisting of fifteen roughly equal states, under the direction of a Council of Europe that would resolve differences and maintain a common army. Unlike Dante, who believed that union under a single state is necessary to create peace, Crucé and Sully considered a multilateral international system both desirable and a feasible framework for peace.

Although such utopian schemes were far removed from the practice of statecraft, they share some of the same assumptions and biases as the

---

[5] Elizabeth V. Suleyman, *The Vision of World Peace in Seventeenth- and Eighteenth-Century France* (New York, 1941); Sir John A. R. Marriott, *Commonwealth or Anarchy? A Survey of Projects of Peace from the Sixteenth to the Twentieth Century* (London, 1937); Crucé's *Le Nouveau Cynée* first appeared in 1623; Maximilien de Béthune, Duke of Sully, supervised the first printing of his "Mémoires des sages et royales Oeconomies d'Estat" in 1638.

policies actually pursued by the leading statesmen in the war, especially Cardinal Richelieu in France and Chancellor Axel Oxenstierna in Sweden. They turned on its head the traditional view that a single monarch for all of Christendom was desirable, raising the threat of "universal monarchy" to incite support for their kingdoms, who alone, they alleged, could guarantee the continuing liberty of individual European states.[6] Rather than focusing on specific rights that needed redressing, Richelieu and Oxenstierna wanted to establish the preconditions for lasting peace in a multilateral framework. Their watchwords were *liberty* and *balance*, their fear was universal monarchy, and their goal was security.

The extent to which these policies departed from prior practice becomes evident, if one considers the reasons typically used until the seventeenth century to justify a declaration of war. They normally fell into three broad categories[7]:

- First, wars against non-Christians typically required no further explanation. European states routinely fought against Native Americans, South Asians, and Muslims (just as they had in the Middle Ages against domestic heretics, such as the Cathars, and against Baltic and Slavic heathens) without feeling any need to explain why. Admittedly, Christian states could and did sign treaties with non-Christians, but they were usually born of exhaustion and proved of limited duration.

- Second, a noble, city, or province might rebel against its sovereign. Justification for rebellion followed traditional Christian teaching and the specific laws of the state in question. It was not primarily a matter for international law, although other states might intervene in support of the rebels.

- Third, states initiated wars to enforce their hereditary claims to provinces or kingdoms. England and France had a long history of conflicts over feudal rights: wars over Aquitaine in the twelfth century, wars over Normandy in the thirteenth century, and the Hundred Years' War over the succession to the French throne in the fourteenth and fifteenth centuries. Spain had fought wars over the inheritance of Portugal, and

---

[6] On the concept of "monarchia universalis," see Franz Bosbach, *Monarchia universalis: Ein politischer Leitbegriff der frühen Neuzeit* (Göttingen, 1988), and ibid., "Die Habsburger und die Entstehung des Dreißigjährigen Krieges: Die *"Monarchia Universalis,"* in *Krieg und Politik 1618–1648: Europäische Probleme und Perspektiven,"* ed. by Konrad Repgen (Munich, 1988), pp. 151–68.

[7] See the discussion in Sharon Korman, *The Right of Conquest: The Acquisition of Territory by Force in International Law and Practice* (Oxford, 1996). She does not consider the case of rebellions, in which, indeed, the concept of "conquest" might seem to play no part. However, it was an important concern in the later stages of the Eighty Years' War between Spain and the Dutch Republic because, although the Dutch were functionally an independent state by that time, their conquests still fell under the justification of their original revolt.

had fought France over the rights to the Kingdom of Naples and the Duchy of Milan. Moreover, Emperor Charles V (1519–1558) spent much of his reign trying to recapture the Duchy of Burgundy, ruled by his ancestors until seized by France in 1477. In most of those cases, questions over the application of inheritance laws and the relative rights of feudal lord against fief holder left room for dispute over the legitimate claim. This is not to say that states did not fight for political reasons as well, but they rarely fought without some semblance of a dynastic claim. The papacy had a legitimate role in this system as arbiter of these claims.

In this chapter, we are chiefly concerned with the third case – that of disputes between Christian states over feudal rights where the remedy was obvious: transfer of ownership to the victorious party. The Thirty Years' War marked a departure from this system because few powers justified their acts of war with references to inheritance or legal rights. Consider Spain's intervention in Mantua in 1627–1631, for example. On his deathbed in 1627, the last native Duke of Mantua recognized Charles of Gonzaga-Nevers, a Frenchman, as his heir. Spain feared that if Nevers took over, France would gain a power base from which to threaten the adjacent Duchy of Lombardy, which formed the nerve center of the Spanish monarchy: the link between Spain and Spanish Italy on the one hand, and its possessions in the Netherlands and the lands of the Austrian Habsburgs on the other. Nevertheless, the legal situation was clear enough and, left to make the decision, King Philip IV's favorite and chief minister, the Count-Duke of Olivares, would probably have allowed Nevers to take possession without serious dispute. However, when the old Duke of Mantua died, the governor of Spanish Milan immediately intervened without waiting for royal permission and began to occupy the disputed territories. Olivares judged it best to support him once the war was already under way. Here was a war whose only justification was the prevention of a threat to the Spanish Empire. Looking back, many observers clearly saw the folly of the war. Pope Urban VIII commented in 1632,

Everyone knows that, before that war, the Habsburgs, the French and all other Catholic princes were in accord, and that public tranquility and the progress of the Catholic religion proceeded most favorably in Germany, in France and everywhere else. But the war in Italy then introduced the Devil's cunning and the seeds of jealousy and unrest.

A decade later, Philip IV still felt uneasy about it: "I have heard it said that the wars in Italy over Casale in Monferrat could have been avoided. Although I have always followed the advice of my ministers in such serious matters, if I have made a mistake in some way and given Our Lord cause for displeasure, it was in this."[8] But by then it was too late.

This trend continued with Sweden's attack against the Empire and France's declaration of war against Spain in the 1630s. For most of the 1620s, Sweden fought a traditional dynastic war against Poland: King Sigismund III of Poland had also briefly ruled Sweden during the 1590s, and his life's ambition was to regain the Swedish throne. Gustavus Adolphus invaded Poland to preempt this threat and convince Sigismund to abandon his claims to Sweden. He only gave up this attempt because of what he regarded as the growing threat posed by Emperor Ferdinand II to Sweden's position in the Baltic. Admittedly, part of his reason was dynastic – the Emperor had supported his brother-in-law Sigismund by dispatching "whole armies into Prussia against His Majesty and the kingdom of Sweden" – but in his manifesto (issued in five languages), Gustavus highlighted other Imperial acts which posed no immediate threat to Sweden, such as laying siege to the town of Stralsund in Pomerania. He had begun a preemptive war essentially to prevent one of his neighbors from becoming too powerful. What kind of peace settlement could fulfill such war aims? Certainly, Sweden had no legitimate demand to any German territory.[9]

France's declaration of war against Spain had a similar foundation. The immediate cause for the war was Spain's capture and imprisonment of the Elector of Trier, a French protégé. Richelieu could use this to portray France as intervening in defense of the Empire or at least in defense of one of the Empire's members, but his justification went beyond this one illegitimate act by Spain. Instead, Richelieu argued that Spain was a threat to other states *in general*, and that France was acting to defend the liberty of all Europeans against Spain's hegemonic aspirations. As in the case of Sweden, this brings up a difficult question: What sort of peace settlement would satisfy France, if it entered the war to counter the *threat* that Spain posed? Apart from the capture of the Elector of Trier, there was no specific act that France demanded be reversed – and the Elector was released in 1645, before the

---

8 Quentín Aldea Vaquero, *España, el Papado y el Imperio durante la guerra de los treinta años*, II (Comillas, 1958), 32, Urban's instructions to his nuncios going to Spain, 1 May 1632; Carlos Seco Serrano, *Cartas de Sor María de Jesús de Ágreda y Felipe IV*, I (Madrid, 1958: Biblioteca de Autores Españoles, CVIII), 28, Philip IV to Sor María, 20 July 1645, holograph. In 1630, the papal secretary of state could already see that the war of Mantua would prove "fatal" to the Catholic cause around the world: see Konrad Repgen, *Die römische Kurie und die Westfälische Friede*, I (Tübingen, 1962), p. 202, n. 64, Barberini to Nuncio Paliotto, 19 January 1630.

9 An English version of Gustavus's *Kriegsmanifest* is printed in G. Symcox, ed., *War, Diplomacy and Imperialism, 1618–1763* (London, 1974), pp. 102–13. Only at the end did the manifesto mention, with some reticence, the oppression of German liberties as a motive for invasion. It included not a word about saving "the Protestant cause."

negotiations got under way, yet France was clearly not satisfied with this result.[10]

France and Sweden's general strategic goals at Westphalia were, therefore, not so much rectification of specific wrongs as the prevention of future injustice on the part of the Habsburgs.[11] Their peace negotiations were, therefore, unusually forward-looking: Unlike, say, the war over the Duchy of Mantua, the powers could not resolve the Thirty Years' War by the transfer of one or even several tracts of land. The only way the "two crowns" (as contemporaries called France and Sweden) could succeed in their war aims was by making Christendom safe from Habsburg ambition, and this could only be judged after time had passed. This put France and Sweden in the unusual position of crafting demands that put more emphasis on the future than on the present, more emphasis on *securing* the peace than on actually *creating* the peace. Their language, which repeatedly emphasized the security of the peace over the justice of specific territorial acquisitions, reflected this reality. Certainly, previous diplomats had made an effort to make their peace treaties permanent, but it was never as important to them as it was to the two crowns at the Congress of Westphalia.

The principle of balance guided both states, but they imparted quite different meanings to that term. For Sweden, *balance* meant balance of power in its most basic sense. One of the principal Swedish negotiators at Westphalia, Johan Adler Salvius, complained to his government in September 1646,

> People are beginning to see the power of Sweden as dangerous to the "balance of power" [*Gleichgewicht*]. Their first rule of politics is that the security of all depends on maintaining an equilibrium between each individual state. When one begins to become more powerful and formidable, the others throw themselves onto the scale by means of alliances and federations in order to offset it and maintain a balance.[12]

Other statesmen, including Richelieu, would probably not have accepted at face value this remarkably prescient statement, which anticipated the value placed on the balance of power during the eighteenth century. The Cardinal viewed Christendom in more traditional, hierarchical terms, in

---

[10] On Richelieu's justification for war against Spain, see Hermann Weber, "'Une Bonne Paix:' Richelieu's Foreign Policy and the Peace of Christendom," in *Richelieu and His Age*, ed. by Joseph Bergin and Laurence Brockliss (Oxford, 1992), pp. 45–69; and, "Une paix sûre et prompte: Die Friedenspolitik Richelieus," in *Zwischenstaatliche Friedenswahrung in Mittelalter und Früher Neuzeit*, ed. Heinz Duchhardt (Cologne, 1991), pp. 111–29.

[11] In which Sweden was more concerned with the Austrian Habsburgs, and France with the Spanish.

[12] C. T. Odhner, *Die Politik Schwedens im Westfälischen Friedenscongress und die Gründung der schwedischen Herrschaft in Deutschland* (Gotha, 1877), p. 163: Johan Adler Salvius to Swedish council, 7 September 1646.

which some states naturally played a more preponderant role than others. For him, attaining a "just balance" meant each state occupying its true position in the hierarchy and all states respecting international legal norms and the rights of other sovereign powers. The means to achieve a lasting peace was, therefore, to establish a more just distribution of power – one that would leave France, to be sure, as the most powerful kingdom but not so powerful as to pose a threat to the liberty or security of others. Naturally, as the leading state, France would use its power to promote a Christian solution to international conflict and not abuse its position (as Spain allegedly had) to aggrandize itself at the expense of others.[13]

If balance were the goal, how best could one restore it? Obviously, the overmighty state that had disrupted the balance – in this case, the Habsburgs – must be weakened. In the same way that the Allies sought to cripple Germany by stripping away much of its territory at the Treaty of Versailles, France and Sweden determined to take enough territory away from Spain and Austria to prevent the Habsburgs from ever launching another aggressive war with any hope of success. But neither Richelieu nor Sweden's chief minister, Axel Oxenstierna, was confident that this measure alone would provide sufficient security, and they adopted different means of supplementing military security based on their particular circumstances.

Richelieu's chief concern was Spain, which he utterly distrusted. His instructions for France's representatives to the Congress of Westphalia noted that "experience has taught us that the Spanish keep their treaties only so long as is useful for them, and so long as they do not have any occasion to break them with advantage."[14] For Richelieu, therefore, the security of the peace became a specifically international problem. France alone could never have sufficient strength to guarantee that Spain would remain peaceful; only many states acting together could create the necessary balance. Thus, Richelieu conceived the idea of international leagues to enforce the treaties. The idea was not unprecedented – it had been tried, for example, at the Peace of Lodi (1454), which tried to end a vicious cycle of wars between the leading Italian states – but the Congress of Westphalia applied the concept of an international peace organization to all of Europe. Richelieu had become so focused on securing a peace that would prevent Spanish aggression that his

---

[13] Hermann Weber, "Chrétienté et équilibre européen dans la politique du Cardinal de Richelieu," *XVIIe siècle* 42 (1990), pp. 7–16. Richelieu's concept of "balance" more closely corresponds to the term *equilibrium* used at the Congress of Vienna and during the nineteenth century; for a detailed analysis of the distinction between "balance of power" and "equilibrium," see Paul Schroeder, "The Nineteenth Century System: Balance of Power or Political Equilibrium?," *Review of International Studies* 15 (1989), pp. 135–53; and Paul Schroeder, "Did the Vienna Settlement Rest on a Balance of Power?," *The American Historical Review* 97, no. 3 (1989), pp. 707–15.

[14] *Acta Pacis Westphalicae* Series I, 1:71. Initial instructions for the plenipotentiaries, 30 September 1643, incorporating Richelieu's instructions drafted the previous year.

original goals took little account of territorial acquisition. In the empire, his early demands included only official recognition of France's right to the so-called Three Bishoprics of Metz, Toul, and Verdun: three imperial enclaves in the Duchy of Lorraine occupied by the French in 1552 during a war against Charles V and administered by them ever since. The Empire had never formally ceded them, and so Richelieu only demanded formal recognition of a conquest that had already taken place long ago. Regarding Spain, the Cardinal sought to confirm the terms agreed to in previous treaties signed at Monzón (1626) and Cherasco (1631) and of acquiring some strategic fortresses in the Spanish Netherlands. It is true that he had signed a treaty with the Dutch Republic that foresaw the eventual conquest and partition of the entire Spanish Netherlands, but this decision rested on the insistence of the military and political leader of the Dutch Republic, Frederick Henry of Nassau, and went contrary to Richelieu's known intentions.[15]

In contrast to France, Sweden put little hope in international leagues. This partly resulted from the fact that Sweden's international situation was quite different from that of France. France was at war with both branches of the Habsburgs and could count on numerous allies, both in the Empire and in Italy; Sweden was at war only with the Austrian Habsburgs and publicly insisted that it had no quarrel with Spain. Moreover, Sweden's other neighbors and rivals – Denmark, Poland, and Russia – were not at Westphalia and thus were not present to endorse the settlement reached there. It is not surprising, then, that Sweden's approach to the peace emphasized the situation in the Empire to the exclusion of all else.

Axel Oxenstierna, who headed the Swedish regency government after the death of Gustavus in 1632, pinned his hopes for a secure peace on constitutional changes within the Holy Roman Empire that would make aggressive war impossible, much as Article Nine of the Japanese constitution after the Second World War forbids the maintenance of an army or declarations of war. This was a viable strategy because the empire's government was highly decentralized. It was normal for foreign powers to deal directly with individual imperial rulers – the dukes, counts, electors, and others whose territories constituted the empire – and, therefore, it was possible to make out how the empire would be governed an issue in the negotiations. This was far more difficult with regard to the Spanish monarchy, whose constituent parts – although fiercely independent – were not accustomed to having a voice in royal policy, especially foreign policy. Despite his generally realist approach to international affairs, Oxenstierna regarded changing the Imperial constitution as essential for a lasting peace. Even prior to the Congress of Westphalia, he quoted with approval a phrase of Gustavus: "While an

---

[15] Hermann Weber, "Vom verdeckten zum offenen Krieg: Richelieus Kriegsgründe und Kriegsziele 1634/35," in *Krieg und Politik* (op. cit.), 203–18.

Elector can sit safe as Elector in his land, and a Duke is Duke and has his liberties, then we are safe."[16]

The insistence of Sweden and, to a lesser extent, of France on imposing the concept of balance to the internal situation of the empire – a foreign country – was novel: There must be a balance between the estates and the emperor, or between Protestants and Catholics, in order for the empire to be safe from Habsburg absolutism. Oxenstierna seems to have deliberately aimed at "atomizing" Germany in order to create a permanent balance and never seems to have held scruples that his approach to international security rested squarely on the right to intervene in the internal affairs of the Holy Roman Empire. The Habsburgs did everything they could to thwart this intervention but, ultimately, they lost. Therefore, it is a fundamental mistake to see the Peace of Westphalia as the origin of the concept of sovereignty in international relations, however one may define it. The settlement rested on precisely the opposite of sovereignty.[17]

PACIFYING THE EMPIRE

One can divide the attempts by France and Sweden to deny the empire the means to wage aggressive war into three categories: restrictions on the election of Habsburgs as emperors, legal provisions to limit the institutional power of the Emperor, and friendship with German states. France, which feared the Austrian Habsburgs chiefly because of their close alliance with Spain, sought remedies specifically against the House of Habsburg: Their demands were the most radical and the least successful. They proposed two main alternatives to allowing the Habsburgs to monopolize the Imperial office. First, they proposed that two consecutive emperors could not come from the same family; rather like the debate around "term limits" in the United States, it was argued that this would prevent an ostensibly free election from turning into a perpetual office. French ministers seemed genuinely surprised when their German allies emphatically rejected this proposal on the grounds that it would obstruct the right of the seven electors to choose an emperor of their own choice, as guaranteed by the constitution of the empire. They also proposed that no emperor-designate could be elected while the existing emperor still lived. This practice, known as election *vivente imperatore*, limited the period of uncertainty that could follow the death of an emperor, as occurred after the death of Emperor Matthias in 1619, which

---

[16] Quoted by Michael Roberts in *The Thirty Years' War*, ed. Geoffrey Parker (2nd ed., London, 1996), p. 140. See also Sven Lundkvist, "Die schwedischen Kriegs- und Friedensziele 1632–1648," in *Krieg und Politik, 1618–1648: europäische Probleme und Perspektiven*, ed. by Konrad Repgen (Munich, 1988), p. 224.

[17] Sigmund Goetze, *Die Politik der schwedischen Reichskanzlers Axel Oxenstierna gegenüber Kaiser und Reich* (Kiel, 1971) makes a convincing case for "atomization" as Sweden's goal.

created an imperial interregnum for eight months. This proposal, too, gained little support among the Germans and was dropped.

The French also contemplated changing the composition of the Electoral College since the status quo favored the election of Habsburg emperors. The prewar balance of four Catholic and three Protestant electors had been challenged when the Bohemians deposed the Habsburg King-elect Ferdinand and instead chose Frederick, the Elector Palatine, in 1619. This gave Frederick two votes and the Protestants a majority of four to three. But they never got a chance to use this advantage because the imperial election of 1619 took place a few days before Frederick had accepted the throne of Bohemia; so, at the imperial conclave, Ferdinand voted for himself and was crowned. The following year, Ferdinand's troops reconquered Bohemia and, in 1623, he transferred Frederick's Palatinate electorate to Duke Maximilian of Bavaria, which gave the Catholics an advantage of five to two. Since no one at Westphalia suggested taking Bohemia from the Habsburgs again, the existence of a Catholic majority was not in question, only its extent. In the end, Bavaria kept its electorate, but an eighth was created for Frederick's son and his heirs, leaving the Catholics with a majority of five to three – more than enough to keep the imperial title in the Habsburg family until the Empire's dissolution in 1806.[18]

Although France and its Swedish ally failed in their particular attacks on the Habsburg family, they were more successful in the advancement of general constitutional provisions against the imperial office and in favor of the one thousand or so semi-autonomous states that comprised the empire. This served France's security interests nearly as well because French statesmen unanimously believed that the Habsburgs were betraying Germany for the sake of their own family ties and that if only the Germans as a whole could decide on foreign policy on the basis of their own interests, they would be more amicably inclined toward France. It happened that many Germans agreed with the French assessment of Habsburg policies, so they tended to favor proposals that gave more power to the estates. The first and most important issue was the so-called *ius belli et pacis*, the right of war and peace – that is, the right to declare war and make peace treaties. It was a fundamental demand of the two crowns that this right be vested not in the emperor but rather in the Imperial Diet: the assembly of the electors (who formed one chamber), the princes (with about 150 members in a second chamber), and about 50 towns (meeting in a third chamber). The final treaties made this explicit. It is interesting that the French based their view on the same foundation as what is now known as the "democratic peace theory," which posits that democracies will be less likely to go to war than

---

[18] With the exception of the contested tenure of Charles VII in 1740–1745.

dictatorships. Equally interesting is that the U.S. Constitution mirrors the arrangement created at Westphalia, with the right of war and peace vested solely in the Congress and not in the president.

While the transfer (some would say reestablishment) of the right to wage war to the Imperial Diet was an important victory, France and Sweden also considered it inevitable that Emperor Ferdinand would attempt to regain his lost power at any opportunity. Therefore, they sought to strengthen the constituent parts of the Imperial Diet materially so as to allow them to resist future Habsburg aggression. They accomplished this by establishing two other rights: the *ius armorum*, or "right to arms," and the *ius foederum*, or "right to alliances." The right to arms referred to the prerogative of each ruler to raise his or her own military forces. The existence of independent militias in the German states had been a cause of concern for centuries, and the establishment of two military alliances, the Catholic League and the Protestant Union, in 1608–1609 is generally seen as one of the causes of the Thirty Years' War. Ferdinand II had managed to overturn this right in 1635 by the Peace of Prague, whose signatories (led by the Protestant Electors of Brandenburg and Saxony) acknowledged the emperor as the sole military authority. In practice, of the three Imperial armies that operated independently after the Peace of Prague, known as *Reichsarmadas*, two were under the control of princes (i.e., Maximilian of Bavaria and John George of Saxony): The troops swore an oath to the emperor but they were recruited, paid, and commanded by the local ruler. Predictably, then, their loyalty was primarily with the electors rather than the emperor. When Ferdinand III attempted to use his authority to bring the Bavarian-controlled army back under his authority after Maximilian signed a separate truce with France and Sweden in 1647, all but a few officers remained with Maximilian. The evident impotence of the new imperial military system created by the Peace of Prague should not mislead us about its importance: Symbolic changes can have long-term consequences if the circumstances are right. The legal reestablishment of the right of German rulers to raise their own military forces in the Peace of Westphalia was a decisive step in weakening imperial power.

Along with the right to arm themselves against the emperor, France and Sweden also insisted that German territorial rulers should possess the right to contract alliances with foreign states. This was another sensitive matter because the ability of German princes to attract foreign support (English, Dutch, Danish, and Swedish) after they had been themselves militarily defeated had played a major part in keeping the war going. Except for the few rulers who had actually allied with France or Sweden – chiefly, Hessen-Kassel, Trier, Baden-Durlach, and Magdeburg – Germans were generally skeptical of the *ius foederum*, feeling that it had contributed to the long war and destruction that Germany had faced. Ferdinand III insisted that no ruler could make an alliance against the Empire or the emperor himself.

He won this qualification, but the inclusion of the right to alliances in the treaty was more important than the limitation placed on it – a limitation that could not be enforced. The *ius foederum* was important to France and Sweden not only because it vindicated their alliances with German estates retroactively, which they had used to justify going to war in the first place, but also because it could serve as a prospective justification for further intervention in Imperial politics, either to protect German liberties (the official justification) or to advance their own interests.

Once they had thus strengthened the power of territorial rulers, the two crowns had done much to secure their main goal of securing themselves against future Habsburg aggression. But one other point required attention: While the Habsburgs might no longer be in a position to wage an aggressive war, the Empire as a whole, acting through the Diet, might still do so. Therefore, both France and Sweden sought to strengthen their ties with individual German rulers to prevent them from ever wanting to launch a war against them. Both harped on their role as "defenders of German liberties" against a usurping emperor as evidence that they were friendly and that Germany needed them as allies. Their efforts achieved far less success than either had hoped, however, because the damage inflicted by the war made it difficult for any German ruler to see foreign intervention as benign, especially since both France and Sweden demanded Imperial territory for themselves which could serve as a bridgehead from which to start a new conflict.

Both France and Sweden, therefore, regarded the Germans as ungrateful for the assistance they had received in the past but, beyond general support for German liberties, France and Sweden tried to win allies for the future in different ways. France had gotten into the war to restore the imprisoned Elector of Trier but, beyond that, it could do little to identify a specific interest group it had aided. French policy, therefore, oscillated between various options. It certainly wanted to oppose the Habsburgs, but its chief allies in this struggle had been Protestant; and although France had a long history of supporting German Protestants, there was only so far it could go. The civil war against French Protestants (i.e., Huguenots) and their political suppression in 1629 made German Protestants skeptical of French motives. French officials were correspondingly dubious of allowing Protestantism to gain too strong a footing on the international scene: Thus, in 1644, their plenipotentiaries objected to a proposed alliance between the Calvinists rulers of Brandenburg and Hessen-Kassel because they saw "Huguenottism" in it.[19]

Many Frenchmen went further and opposed any support for Protestants. This group, known as the "dévots," had opposed the war against Spain and Austria and would have preferred an alliance with the Habsburgs to

---

[19] *Acta Pacis Westphalicae*, Series II B 1:602, d'Avaux and Servien to Brienne, 5 November 1644.

extirpate Protestantism in Germany, the Netherlands, and England. Although the dévots lacked the strength to take control of policy, even during Louis XIV's minority, nevertheless the head of the regency government, Cardinal Jules Mazarin, could not afford to inflame domestic Catholic opinion against him. Moreover, he had to justify every action to Anne of Austria, the Queen Regent who, although she trusted him totally, was still a devout Catholic (as well as the sister of Philip IV of Spain and sister-in-law of Emperor Ferdinand III).

If France could not ally too closely with German Protestants, allying with German Catholics proved equally problematic. Cardinal Richelieu had tried to build up a third party in the Empire behind Maximilian of Bavaria, one that would be Catholic but anti-Imperialist. He repeatedly ran into two difficulties. First, both he and his successor, Mazarin, underestimated the loyalty of Maximilian and other German Catholics to the Emperor, not out of religious reasons but rather because they still recognized him as their feudal overlord (even if, in practice, they preferred to keep him as far removed from their affairs as possible). Maximilian might withdraw his support from the Habsburg war effort, but he refused to fight against the Emperor under any circumstances. Second, France depended on the alliance with Sweden to achieve its military goals, and Sweden had no interest in building up a strong Catholic party, even if opposed the Emperor. In 1631 and again in 1647, treaties between France and Bavaria failed because Bavaria remained fundamentally loyal to the Emperor: On both occasions, Sweden, France's principal ally, attacked.

Sweden's position toward the territorial rulers of Germany was altogether different. As a Lutheran state, Sweden could and did promote Protestantism for religious as well as political reasons. Gustavus's invasion of the Empire in 1630 was primarily motivated by political consideration but, once in the war, Swedish propaganda stressed the need to uphold the "Protestant cause." Gustavus had aimed to establish a separate, semi-independent Protestant bloc within the Empire, a *Corpus Evangelicorum* that could defend itself against Catholic aggression – and, naturally, allied with its great protector, Sweden. These grandiose schemes disappeared with the king's death in 1632, but the idea of using their religious support for Lutherans and Calvinists to bind Protestants more closely to the Swedish crown continued to play an important part in Swedish policy. This led to some difficult moments during the negotiations at the Congress of Westphalia, where France was at pains to show that it was fighting a political war, not a religious one, whereas Sweden posed as a Protestant hero and tried to advance Protestant interests wherever possible.[20]

---

[20] Sweden generally supported Calvinists as well as Lutherans, though naturally Lutherans more strongly.

Sweden had another tie to Germany that France lacked: Many religious and political exiles from the Habsburg lands served in the Swedish army. By insisting on a general amnesty, Sweden simultaneously hoped to secure the goodwill of those exiles and to keep its own army loyal.[21] Its pressure on the Habsburgs to allow freedom of religious practice in Bohemia, Silesia, and Austria tended toward the same aim: The return of the exiles to the homes they had abandoned a generation before would not only strengthen pro-Swedish opinion in the Empire but also in the Austrian patrimonial lands themselves. In the words of the chief Imperial ambassador, Count Maximilian von Trauttmansdorff, to concede would be like planting so many rebels in the Emperor's own lands.[22] The Habsburgs, therefore, refused to concede this point.

POMERANIA

Despite their religious affiliation, Sweden put only limited faith in the support of the German estates, which they regarded as fickle allies. "This German war," Axel Oxenstierna exploded in 1634, "I don't know what it is, only that we pour out blood here for the sake of reputation, and have naught but ingratitude to expect." A few months later, he repeated: "We must let this German business be left to the Germans, who will be the only people to get any good out of it (if there is any), and therefore not spend any more men or money here, but rather try by all means to wriggle out of it."[23] Sweden's eventual success in securing the "German liberties" in the Peace of Westphalia did little to increase "gratitude." Henceforth, the Protestants would have little need for Sweden. This helps to explain the tenacity with which Sweden insisted on acquiring German territory, especially the Baltic duchy of Pomerania. Swedish statesmen viewed diplomacy in surprisingly defensive terms. Chancellor Oxenstierna once wrote that "Pomerania and the Baltic Coast are like an outwork of the Swedish crown; our security against the Emperor depends on them." Even Ambassador Salvius, who was more concerned with courting international opinion, saw Sweden as a fortress, "whose walls are its cliffs, whose ditch is the Baltic, and whose counterscarp is Pomerania."[24] Partly, this view echoed Gustavus's reasons for entering the war in the first place. Given Sweden's long coastline, he had argued, it was impossible to defend the country on its own shores; only by

---

21 The army had its own list of demands and, for a time, maintained its own representative in the Congress.

22 Fritz Dickmann, *Der Westfälische Frieden*, 7th ed. (Münster, 1998), p. 471.

23 Oxenstierna to his commanding general, Johan Baner, 28 October 1634, and to the regency council, 7 January 1635, both quoted by Michael Roberts in Parker, *Thirty Years' War*, p. 140.

24 Odhner, *Die Politik Schwedens*, p. 5.

occupying the potential launch pad for foreign invasion could Sweden really be safe.[25] By the time he invaded Pomerania, he and his predecessors had already secured Livonia and some of the key ports in Polish Prussia. Acquisition of Pomerania gave Sweden almost complete control of the Baltic littoral, with the notable exception of Denmark.

Pomerania was significantly different from Sweden's other Baltic acquisitions, however. Livonia had become a disputed land since the extinction of the order of Livonian Knights in the sixteenth century, and Sweden's conquests from Sigismund III formed part of the disputed succession to the Swedish throne (see page 78). By contrast, Sweden had no claim, legal or historical, to Pomerania. Bogislaw XIV, the last native duke, had tried to keep Sweden from invading and when that failed, he had tried to remain neutral. Only after the invasion was complete, leaving him little choice, did he sign a defensive alliance with Gustavus. Since Bogislaw had no heirs, Sweden might have been able to claim Pomerania on his death, had not Brandenburg and Pomerania sealed a treaty long before that if one dynasty died out, the other would automatically inherit. Sweden included in its treaty with Bogislaw a clause insisting that Bogislaw's successor must agree to continue the alliance with Sweden and must give Sweden recompense for the cost of the war: Gustavus himself, after occupying the duchy, had announced, "Now my army is in your city, by the law of war you belong to me!"[26] From the moment negotiations about ending the war began, Sweden laid claim to Pomerania and made this demand consistently – rarely referring to the treaty with Bogislaw for justification, instead relying on its right to an indemnity for their war costs.

The Swedish claim did not impress the Pomeranian estates. They regarded the inheritance treaty with Brandenburg as definitive and their oaths to uphold it as sacred – despite the fact that they were Lutherans and the Brandenburg elector had turned Calvinist. Even though Sweden went out of its way to administer the duchy as justly and mildly as possible and seems to have created a good impression, the Pomeranians regarded the Swedish claim as simply unjustified. Even Stralsund, which Sweden had saved from an Imperial siege in 1628, opposed it. This was also the general view in the Empire: Hardly any ruler favored Sweden's claim to Pomerania because it went contrary to law.[27]

It is easy to understand why Sweden wanted Pomerania so much: Any other territorial gains it made in the Empire would be highly insecure without

---

[25] How he reached this conclusion after Denmark had waged two wars against Sweden in the previous century with considerable naval superiority and yet had not accomplished much of anything via naval invasions is not clear.

[26] Dickmann, *Der Westfälische Frieden*, p. 216.

[27] Other territorial exchanges took place in northern Germany in the 1640s but all involved ecclesiastical land, where there was no heritable right.

a defensible foothold on the coast. And claims were made – although Sweden never claimed a right of occupation. When it came to the ports of Mecklenburg, which Sweden also wanted, it demanded only the right to garrison. Admittedly, this came close to control, but legally it was still limited and did not offend legitimacy as openly. Oxenstierna, aware that Brandenburg would need compensation for its title to Pomerania, proposed at an early stage the transfer of some secularized bishoprics, as well as part of Habsburg Silesia. Sweden might have browbeaten Elector George William, Gustavus's brother-in-law, into acceptance, but he died in 1640; his son, Frederick William (1640–1688) resolved to push his claims to Pomerania with the utmost forcefulness. It is a tribute to the importance that Sweden attached to Brandenburg's consent as an element of its security that it worked for so long to find a solution acceptable to a prince without an army and without possession of the land under dispute.[28] Even the imperial ambassador Trauttmansdorff, joined by other German rulers, urged Brandenburg to make concessions in order to end the war. It was only this threat of being bypassed – thereby losing any claim to compensation – that Frederick William finally accepted the compromise of partitioning the duchy so that Sweden got the western half and Brandenburg got the rest (as well as the secularized bishoprics).

ALSACE, NAVARRE, AND LORRAINE

France's demand for Alsace was even more problematic than Sweden's demand for Pomerania. Although France and the Austrian Habsburgs had several points of contention, they had gone to war with each other unwillingly. When France declared war against Spain in 1635, Emperor Ferdinand II had not obliged Spain by declaring war against France. Neither had France obliged its ally, Sweden, by declaring open war against the Emperor. Only when imperial troops invaded France in 1636 did the two powers declare war. At the Congress of Westphalia, France justified its participation in the war as an intervention in defense of German liberties against unjustified Habsburg absolutism. (This is contrasted with French absolutism, which the French claimed was established legally.) The fact that it had entered the war against Spain in support of the Elector of Trier seemed to justify this claim and to show that both Houses of Habsburg were colluding to exercise their arbitrary dominion over the Empire and Europe as a whole – the "universal monarchy" that France purported to defend against.

The French demand for the occupied parts of Alsace at least had the advantage of being directed against the Habsburgs, their enemies, and not

---

[28] On the importance Sweden gave to its occupation of Pomerania, see Lundkvist, "Die schwedischen Kriegs- und Friedenziele, 1632–1648," p. 229.

(like Sweden's demand for Pomerania) against an ally. The fact that the debate subsequently extended beyond the range of Habsburg possessions was partly the fault of the Habsburgs themselves, who proposed the surrender of Alsace in vague legal terms which seemed to offer France more territory than the House of Austria actually controlled. The French might be forgiven for initially misunderstanding the legal situation, but even when they were informed by a German legal expert of the limited extent of Habsburg lordship, they continued to insist on the full amount of the Habsburg offer, even where it extended unambiguously into territory not controlled by the Habsburgs.

In principle, there was no contradiction in France's demand of non-Habsburg territory: It all belonged to the Empire, and it might be considered pedantic to debate the exact Imperial administration of territory that was to be separated from the Empire anyway, as though one were to dispute whether territory annexed from the United States after a defeat by Canada should come from Montana or North Dakota. But the French justification for the war and for the right to annex territory depended heavily on whose territory, exactly, they were getting. They had claimed that they were not at war with the Empire but rather only with the House of Habsburg; it would be hypocritical, therefore, to demand territory that did not belong to the Habsburgs. Moreover, France justified its claim partly on the basis of the "law of war." This, if valid, would vindicate French acquisition of territory conquered from the Habsburgs, but it was much less convincing when applied to towns not under Habsburg jurisdiction. France had occupied many of these towns from 1632 to 1634, before its formal entry into the war, to protect them from Sweden or from the Emperor.[29]

Some of the towns had no garrison at all prior to accepting French protection, in which case the French negotiated with town officials; where towns were already garrisoned, the French negotiated with the commanding general to arrange an exchange of the existing garrison for a French one. In almost every case, the French had promised that the garrison would only continue during the war, and they would return the town when peace was made. The town of Colmar, one of the largest and most important, actually had a treaty with France guaranteeing its rights, and the parties had renewed the treaty in 1644 (to ensure its validity after the death of Louis XIII). This did not, however, stop France from demanding and taking Colmar in the Peace of Westphalia.

French demands were all the more problematic because not only the Alsatians themselves but also the estates of the Empire opposed them.

---

[29] Wolfgang Hans Stein, *Protection Royale: Eine Untersuchung zu den Protektionverhältnissen im Elsaß zur Zeit Richelieus, 1622–1643* (Münster, 1978).

Despite repeated attempts by the estates, France refused to accept any further specification or clarification of the exact rights being transferred to France. This is ironic because France itself had been at the forefront in insisting that the German estates had the final right to make peace treaties, not the Emperor. Yet, in this case, France chose to ignore the estates and accept the Emperor's ambiguous concession. The ambiguity of the transfer clauses would seem to make for an insecure conquest, but it was only insecure as far as they extended beyond Habsburg territory. French ambassador Abel Servien explicitly endorsed this ambiguity as an opportunity for future French encroachment, obviously in disregard of the actual terms of the treaty.

France's demands against Spain, although not actually finalized in 1648, are also illuminating. France's only prior claim against Spanish-controlled territory was in Navarre, part of which had been controlled by Spain for more than 100 years. (The other part became attached to the French crown in 1589.) Nevertheless, Navarre played only a diversionary part in France's demands at the Congress of Westphalia. Instead, Cardinal Mazarin insisted on making a treaty *à la hollandaise* – that is, with each side keeping every-thing that it occupied (what is conventionally known as *uti possidetis*).[30] In fact, in French demands at the start of 1646, he explicitly reserved not only all currently occupied lands but even included those that would fall to France in the ensuing campaign – even if an agreement should be reached before the campaign started. Obviously, this sort of negotiation owed noth-ing to prior legal claim, but that does not mean that it was entirely without thought for the future. Cardinal Mazarin, like his predecessor Richelieu, believed that Spain would never make a treaty except under duress and that it would attempt to recoup its losses at the first opportunity. Unlike Richelieu, however, Mazarin had no confidence in international leagues as a means of security. The only way to a secure peace, in his view, was to demand as much as possible because only by weakening Spain sufficiently would France's conquests be safe. This was reflected in French territorial demands, which expanded with each new conquest and with each Spanish concession. When Spain conceded the port of Rosas in Catalonia, France increased its demands to include Cadaques, between Rosas and Roussil-lon. When the French occupied Piombino and Porto Longone in Italy, they added those to their demands. Perhaps most egregiously, when it came time to clarify the extent of French conquests in Artois, they changed the nature of their demands entirely: Previously, they had demanded the rights over only those towns that they had conquered, leaving the title of Count of

---

[30] *Acta Pacis Westphalicae*, Series I, 1:69, 93–94. Initial instructions for the plenipotentiaries, 30 September 1643.

Artois to the King of Spain; now, by contrast, they wanted Louis XIV to become the Count of Artois, with Spain to retain only those specific towns it possessed. This changed both the territorial extent of French demands and the nature of French rights, opening up new arenas for legal combat and jurisdictional disputes. Ironically, French Ambassador Longueville characterized one of the last Spanish offers as "not a treaty of peace, but a seeding of new troubles and a source of contestation and debates."[31] In fact, while France wanted to have its core demands transferred as unambiguously as possible, it was always ready to accept ambiguity if it offered the possibility for future expansion.

Despite France's continually rising territorial demands, however, the treaty with Spain did not falter chiefly because of this point. The main source of difficulty was the Duke of Lorraine, Charles IV. Charles was a difficult character beyond doubt. He had obtained the duchy by questionable means, and he had used his position not only to wage war against France but also stir up trouble among the French royalty. Lorraine's position was awkward: The duke owed fealty to the Empire for some of his lands, to France for others, and held others in sovereignty. The close relation of the royal houses of France and Lorraine meant that it touched a sensitive spot in French governance. To make matters worse, Charles had repeatedly been defeated and signed treaties with France, only to break them again at the first opportunity. With each treaty, Richelieu had pushed the penalty for violation higher, until the Treaty of Paris of 1641, in which the duke agreed that he would forfeit his duchy in case of default. Nevertheless, he was hardly free before he again took up arms against France.

Defending Lorraine was no longer an issue: France had already occupied it for some years. But Charles IV maintained an army in the service of Spain and he continued to be a prickly problem for the French monarchy. Cardinal Mazarin seems to have been undecided about how to deal with him, but the two main French ambassadors, d'Avaux and Servien, both had strong (and contrasting) opinions. Servien insisted that Lorraine should not enter negotiations with foreign powers at all. France might consider some concessions to the duke, but only if he threw himself on the mercy of the court; he had forfeited any legal right to his duchy and France should not allow other states to interfere with that. D'Avaux's view on Lorraine, as with his opinion of the acquisitions from Spain, emphasized consent over conquest. D'Avaux was no friend of Lorraine, but he asked Mazarin whether it would not be better to acquire whatever territory they could with the consent and guarantee of everyone rather than leaving a smoldering

---

[31] Anuschka Tischer, *Französische Diplomatie und Diplomaten auf dem Westfälischen Friedenskongress: Außenpolitik unter Richelieu und Mazarin* (Münster, 1999), p. 392.

ember on the border; in the latter case, France might end up with "neither peace, nor Lorraine."[32]

OUTCOME

What was the result? The diplomats in Münster and Osnabrück signed a schedule of 128 clauses on 24 October 1648 that ended the Thirty Years' War and, since the Congress had the status of an Imperial Diet, its provisions went into immediate effect.[33] Protestant refugees returned to the cities and territories from which they had been banned (provided Protestant worship had existed there in 1624); those who had lost lands and property for supporting France or Sweden (although not those condemned for rebellion) received them back; and the Elector Palatine resumed his seat in the Diet. Before long, the diplomats were packing their bags and preparing to leave – albeit not before securing payment of their own salaries for the previous years, a charge of more than three million thalers. The diplomats' bill was dwarfed, however, by the cost of disbanding the 200,000 or so troops still under arms, who continued to draw pay until the day of their demobilization. The Swedish army alone earned almost a million thalers a month, on top of a settlement of five million thalers for their arrears since 1630. The taxpayers of the empire shared responsibility for payment of both bills – for the diplomats and for the troops – and only in June 1650 did the last troops begin a phased withdrawal, on prearranged days, from the areas they occupied.[34]

And what had the victors gained? France and Sweden had entered the war because they wanted security from the Habsburgs and they fought on until they attained that goal. France, indeed, fought on for another eleven years after Westphalia before making peace with Spain, and even then the terms it obtained were significantly less than those it could have gotten in 1648 (notably by Spain's reconquest of Catalonia). In addition, its territorial gains

---

[32] Ibid., p. 369. In 1659, Mazarin got peace but had to return most of Lorraine: see Daniel Séré, "La paix des Pyrénées ou la paix du roi: le rôle méconnu de Philippe IV dans la restauration de la paix entre l'Espagne et la France," *Revue d'histoire diplomatique*, (2005/2), pp. 243–61.

[33] For the text of the treaties, in the original Latin as well as several translations (including English for the Treaty of Münster but not the Treaty of Osnabrück), see *Acta Pacis Westphalicae: Supplementa electronica*, 1, "Die Westfälischen Friedensverträge vom 24 Oktober 1648. Texte und Übersetzungen." http://www.pax-westphalica.de/ipmipo/ (accessed March 22, 2007).

[34] On the costs of making peace, see Franx Bosbach, *Die Kosten des Westfälischen Friedenkongresses: Eine strukturgeschichtliche Untersuchung* (Münster, 1984). On the demobilization, see Antje Oschmann, *Der Nürnberger Exekutionstag 1649–1650: Das Ende des Dreißigjährigen Krieges in Deutschland* (Münster, 1991).

from Spain led to increasing unease within the Dutch Republic, long France's closest ally. For a power that had put such emphasis on alliances during the Thirty Years' War, France seemed strangely unconscious of the multilateral nature of international politics in the latter part of the seventeenth century. Its focus – one might almost say obsession – on bringing down Spanish power made it blind to the fact that other states might perceive its own growing strength as a threat and might respond with force of their own. Perhaps it reflected a French diplomatic mindset still rooted in the Middle Ages, focusing only on the possibility of "universal monarchy" – which it did not seek – at the expense of other forms of hegemony. The notion that other states would see a need to balance against France never seems to have occurred to French statesmen, steeped as they were in Richelieu's idea of France as the maintainer of European liberty, never the aggressor against it.

French policy in the Holy Roman Empire was analogous. Their leaders in the 1640s had a naïve belief that the Germans feared imperial aggression more than anything else and would, therefore, welcome France's intervention in the war on their behalf. Some even convinced themselves that the Germans would happily give France compensation in imperial territory since it would allow France the means to intervene in the Empire should the Habsburgs attempt once more to impose absolutism. At the same time, like Oxenstierna, these same French statesmen resented what they saw as the ungratefulness of the Germans for the liberation that French heroism and dedication had achieved for them. Evidently, the French were confusing their views of how things should be with how they actually were.

This attitude emerged most clearly in French reassurances to Alsatians about the possibility of their incorporation into France. The Alsatians (especially the representative of Colmar, Balthasar Schneider) argued strenuously that the Emperor did not have the authority to transfer them into French control because they were "immediate estates" with no direct feudal overlord. The French plenipotentiaries dismissed this complaint by saying that it was not their concern if Ferdinand III had offered them more than he could legally deliver – which is roughly equivalent to accepting a person's automobile as a gift when you know that it really belongs to someone else. The arguments advanced by Abel Servien in favor of the ambiguous terms for the transfer of Alsace to French control offer another example of French concern to acquire territory, whatever the legal situation. Servien recognized that the terms were unclear and that disputes were likely to derive from them, but he favored them anyway because they would give France an opportunity to extend its control at a later point – something it was not in a position to do at the time of the Congress of Westphalia. Servien's predictions came true in the 1680s, as Louis XIV's policy of "réunions" indeed led to the absorption of the remainder of Alsace, including Strasbourg – an Imperial Free City never subject to Habsburg control. As in the 1640s when the treaty terms were drafted, Louis XIV seemed unable to understand that this policy of expansion, covered with only a transparent gauze of legal justification, would excite resentment and reaction on the part of the empire. His conquest of Alsace stood, but only after he had fought the Nine Years' War in defense of it.[35]

Sweden's gains also depended on military strength to achieve its territorial goals. Although Pomerania had never come under Habsburg control, it became the target of Frederick William's lifelong ambition. Admittedly, it is difficult to see what acquisitions Sweden could have made on the Baltic coast of Pomerania without earning Frederick William's opposition, and no one could have anticipated that the elector would prove such a stubborn, long-lived, and effective opponent. Nevertheless, Sweden's failure to attempt any kind of reconciliation that would give Brandenburg an interest in maintaining Swedish presence in the Empire limited that for which they could hope. Instead of Pomerania being a "counterscarp" for the defense of Sweden, it proved to be an expensive outpost that drew Sweden into numerous wars in the next half century which it otherwise could have avoided. Once it renounced the disputed areas of Pomerania in 1720, Sweden's subsequent diplomatic relations with the Empire were almost entirely peaceful – contrary to their earlier fears of invasion from that quarter.

The efforts of France and Sweden to render the Austrian Habsburgs incapable of future aggression largely succeeded; certainly, Axel Oxenstierna was happy to report to the Swedish council that "now we have security that Germany will not become an absolute monarchy."[36] However, this success was limited on two major counts. First, neither France nor Sweden seemed to anticipate that the Empire as a whole could be brought to declare war on them if they showed themselves sufficiently contemptuous of international law, as occurred in 1689. Second, by paralyzing imperial institutions to such an extent, the two crowns had, in fact, destabilized the Empire and enhanced the possibility of military conflict among the estates. The possibility was not immediately realized because external threats, first by the Ottoman Empire and then by France, kept most of the empire at peace until 1740. However, the rise of Prussia, thanks in part to its gains at Westphalia and its growing rivalry with Austria, became one of the most important causes of war in Europe, and the significance of their struggle drew other countries into the conflict. The War of the Austrian Succession (1740–1748) demonstrated not only this limitation of the Peace of Westphalia but also the logical outcome of the two crowns' policy of annexation without prior legal claim. Frederick the Great's seizure of Silesia in 1740 on only the thinnest of pretexts and the

[35] Derek McKay and Hamish M. Scott, *The Rise of the Great Powers 1648–1815* (New York, 1983).
[36] Lundkvist, "Die schwedischen Kriegs- und Friedenziele, 1632–1648," p. 240.

notorious partitions of Poland later in the century are further elaborations of the same idea.

It is interesting to contrast the aggressive approach to territorial expansion adopted by France and Sweden with the other chief French negotiator at the Peace Congress, the Count d'Avaux. D'Avaux argued that consent, rather than simply military power, would be the key to a successful treaty: France's goal was not really its own expansion but rather the prevention of Spanish aggression. The important thing, he argued, was that the peace be secure, which could only occur if everyone got something and, therefore, had an interest in guaranteeing it. Cardinal Mazarin repeatedly overruled D'Avaux.[37] Although it is idle to speculate on the consequences had d'Avaux's views prevailed in the negotiations, it is worth noting that other approaches were available and might have been adopted under different circumstances.

Was the Peace of Westphalia, then, an unmitigated disaster? Some people have thought so. German indignation at the loss of parts of Alsace and Lorraine cooled in the ensuing century but became an issue again under the Second and Third Reichs. A 1940 exhibition in Münster called Westphalia "France's greatest triumph – Germany's deepest shame."[38] Two years before, an English historian came to a similarly pessimistic conclusion, though for entirely different reasons: "The war solved no problem," wrote C. V. Wedgwood. "Its effects, both immediate and indirect, were either negative or disastrous."[39] More recently, several works have appeared criticizing Westphalia for unleashing an era of international anarchy and, hence, conflict; they speak of moving "beyond Westphalia" or of "exorcising the ghost of Westphalia."[40]

But it would be misleading to focus only on the negative aspects of the peace since it certainly had positive results as well. Above all, the fact that all states involved in the conflict – and even some which were not involved – participated in the negotiations created a new paradigm for peace making. Obviously, there are many limitations and qualifications on the universality of the negotiations. Some states that were intimately concerned with their outcome, such as Denmark, did not participate. Other states that were legally

---

[37] Tischer, *Französische Diplomatie und Diplomaten auf den Westfälischen Frieden* Kongress, p. 345.

[38] Stadtmuseum Münster, *Dreissigjähriger Krieg, Münster Und Der Westfälische Frieden: 1648–1998* (Münster, 1998), pp. 214–15. The project was started in January and was originally to be a traveling exhibit. However, by the time it was completed in the fall, France had been defeated and Germany no longer needed such negative propaganda. The exhibition, therefore, never opened to the public; only a small group of officers saw it.

[39] C. Veronica Wedgwood, *The Thirty Years' War* (London, 1938), p. 526.

[40] Gene Martin Lyons and Michael Mastanduno, *Beyond Westphalia?: State Sovereignty and International Intervention* (Baltimore, 1995); Charles W. Kegley, *Exorcising the Ghost of Westphalia: Building World Order in the New Millennium* (Upper Saddle River, NJ, 2002).

recognized as sovereign entities by some of the participants, and which functioned as sovereign entities, did not participate because their sovereignty was disputed; Lorraine and Portugal fall into this category. The Congress was not entirely unified and resulted in two separate bilateral treaties; moreover, it did not result in peace between all participants since France and Spain remained at war, whereas other states (e.g., Spain and the United Provinces) signed a treaty that was in no way linked with the other treaties that are conventionally known as the Peace of Westphalia. Furthermore, Richelieu's original plan, which would have linked all signatories into two leagues to guarantee the execution and long-term effect of the treaties, was never carried out.

These are serious limitations, but they do not detract from the fundamental point that the conference was deliberately assembled with the intention of including as many interested parties as possible. Despite France and Sweden's lack of interest in consensus on the matter of their own territorial satisfaction, they were aware of the value of having their conquests secured by treaties signed by other powers, even those not directly involved in the transfer. In their more enlightened moments, they also saw that ending all European wars and creating an international peace endorsed by all states would create a powerful source of legitimacy for their conquests in adding prescription to positive law. Ultimately, Mazarin decided that conquests were more important than legitimacy and rejected a treaty with Spain for another eleven years. But, the concept of an international peace conference lived on. Henceforth, European states usually resolved international conflicts by international negotiations: Nijmegen (1668), Rijswijck (1697), and Utrecht (1713) were all, in some sense, consequences of the Congress of Westphalia. Although crude balance of power politics, often with little respect for international law, dominated during the *ancien régime*, the congress system was arguably a necessary precursor of the Concert of Europe that successfully maintained peace after 1815.

In removing religious issues from diplomacy, the Peace of Westphalia also made a positive contribution to international peace. It was not that the treaties explicitly or implicitly barred religion as a motivating factor in foreign policy: No treaty could do that. Nor did statesmen suddenly become more secular in the 1640s. To the contrary, religious feeling remained so intense that upon the resolution of one religious article, which created a new framework for the coexistence of Catholics and Protestants in the empire, delegates at the Congress were moved to the point of tears.[41] It was this resolution of the German religious problem that made it possible for diplomacy to become more secular and not the other way around. The period from

---

[41] Dickmann, *Der Westfälischen Frieden*, p. 460.

1517 to 1648 is often called an "age of religious wars" with good reason; but, it is a mistake to think that states normally went to war with the intent of converting their neighbors. Instead, the religious divide led to civil wars as people fought over the dominant religion in their state: France, the Low Countries, and the empire were all afflicted with civil wars fought primarily over religion. And where there was a civil war, there was an opportunity for foreign states to intervene, so civil wars often sowed the seeds of foreign wars.[42] France and the Netherlands had largely resolved their religious wars before 1648, and the Peace of Westphalia endowed the empire with a stable constitution that supported religious pluralism. With no more states torn apart by religious civil wars, foreign states no longer had the opportunity to intervene in (or be drawn into) wars fought primarily for religious reasons. Europe's period of religious wars was over.

Together with the beginning of Congress diplomacy, this made the Peace of Westphalia the foundation of the European international system. The year 1748 saw widespread celebration of its centenary and, as late as 1761, the incurable romantic, Jean-Jacques Rousseau, believed that the European state system of his day rested on a

> ... solid foundation, namely the German Empire, which from its position at the heart of Europe keeps all powers in check and thereby maintains the security of others even more, perhaps, than its own. The Empire wins universal respect for its size and for the number and virtues of its people; its constitution, which takes from conquerors the means and the will to conquer, is of benefit to all and makes it a perilous reef to the invader. Despite its imperfections, this Imperial constitution will, while it lasts, maintain the balance in Europe; no prince need fear lest another dethrone him. The peace of Westphalia may well remain the foundation of our political system for ever.[43]

Although Rousseau was wrong, the fact that the Peace of Westphalia came to be seen as a sort of "fundamental law" of European diplomacy demonstrates the great weight that it carried long after the issues at stake

[42] The United States faces a similar problem in Iraq. Although its invasion in 2003 to overthrow Saddam Hussein had no religious basis, the mutual hatred of Shi'ites and Sunnis made the goal of creating a stable Iraqi government far more difficult, and the proliferation of nuclear-weapon technology made the instability of Iraq a security issue for all states. Although no seventeenth-century state possessed "Weapons of Mass Destruction," instability in a neighboring state has always caused concern because of the danger that violence would spill over the border.

[43] J.-J. Rousseau, 'Extrait du projet de paix perpétuelle de Monsieur l'Abbé de St Pierre' (1761), in Oeuvres complètes de Jean-Jacques Rousseau, III (Paris, 1964). See other similar claims by later statesmen in Parker, Thirty Years' War, p. 193. On the centennial celebrations in Germany, see Konrad Repgen, "Der Westfälische Friede: Ereignis, Fest und Erinnerung," Nordrhein-Westfälische Akademie der Wissenschaften. Vorträge G. 358), p. 1. The bicentennial and tercentennial years, 1848 and 1948, saw no celebrations since Germany had other concerns.

in the Thirty Years' War had ceased to influence international relations.[44] The unprecedented duration of the war and the unparalleled sacrifices of the participants had, by the 1640s, created great pressure to "get it right": that is perhaps why the participants in peace conferences held earlier in the war – such as the Peace of Prague in 1635 – remained unwilling to make the compromises and concessions necessary for a lasting settlement. They had not yet suffered enough. But the Peace of Prague also failed to end the war for another reason: It consisted of individual agreements between Emperor Ferdinand II and some of his enemies and no bilateral treaty, nor even a series of bilateral treaties that settled the particular affairs of two states, could resolve the conflicts that wracked Europe in the 1630s and 1640s. Only an international congress between equally war-weary combatants could have produced a long-lasting peace; not even condemnation by the spiritual leader of half of Europe could change that outcome.

[44] See Heinhard Steiger, "Der Westfälische Friede – Grundgesetz für Europa?," in *Der Westfälische Friede: Diplomatie – politische Zäsur – kulturelles Umfeld-Rezeptionsgeschichte*, ed. Heinz Duchhardt (Munich, 1998).

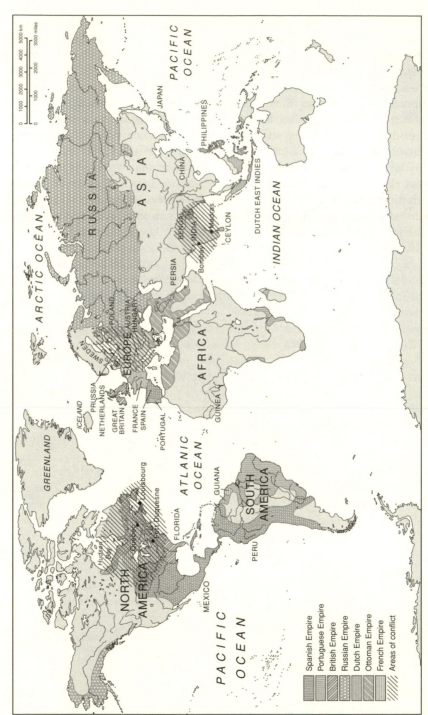

MAP 3. The Seven Years' War.

Spanish Empire
Portuguese Empire
British Empire
Russian Empire
Dutch Empire
Ottoman Empire
French Empire
Areas of conflict

4

The Peace of Paris, 1763

FRED ANDERSON

Contemporaries regarded the Peace of Paris, which concluded the Seven Years' War in 1763, as a diplomatic event of the first importance, if only because it transferred vastly more territory between European empires than had any previous treaty. Modern historians, by contrast, have accorded it little attention. Although every general account of the Seven Years' War, of course, mentions the treaty, few accord it more than cursory attention. Indeed, since 1950, the Peace of Paris has been the subject of a single monograph and only a handful of scholarly articles. The Peace of Westphalia, by contrast, has occasioned at least a dozen scholarly books and editions since the mid-twentieth century; the Congress of Vienna has been the subject of at least ten; and the Treaty of Versailles, somewhere between forty and fifty. Mere slothfulness among eighteenth-century scholars cannot explain so great a disparity. Rather, it reflects the prevailing view among diplomatic historians that the Peace of Paris simply had less enduring significance than those other great treaties, which, after all, appear to have constructed, restored, and undermined the modern European state system.

This chapter argues, however, that there is still something to be learned from the Peace of Paris. When seen in the context of the war it ended and the events that followed, it reveals much about the assumptions of peacemakers in the mid-eighteenth century, the effects of the Seven Years' War as a transforming event, and ironic interrelationships between peace making in the century's greatest imperial war and the wars of the revolutionary age that followed.

THE PAST AS FUTURE

Undistinguished as it may seem in comparison to the other great treaties of European history, the Peace of Paris can lay claim to one indisputable distinction: It inspired the first futurist novel in English, *The Reign of George VI, 1900–1925,* an anonymous political satire published in 1763. For our purposes, the significance of this volume arises less from its limited merits as a work of fiction than from its author's attempt to explore the long-run implications of "our late treaty of peace" – that is, the actual Peace of Paris in 1763, which the author argued "was not *altogether* so advantageous as ministerial writers would have us think it; and that the moderation which we showed on that occasion, was *rather* a little ill-timed."[1] What the author forecast was a century and a half of future history, in which a resurgent France would dominate European politics and cause endless problems for an increasingly beleaguered, politically corrupt, debt-ridden Britain.

In the author's imagined history, Britain's international position and power declined through the nineteenth century while France succeeded in conquering Holland, Spain absorbed Portugal and bankrolled French ambitions with American silver, and Russia – having conquered Lithuania, Denmark, Norway, and Sweden – built a navy more powerful than Britain's. By 1900, all that stood in the way of Franco-Russian dominion over Europe was a fragile entente between Britain and Prussia. Yet, even that alliance had found itself rendered problematic by Kaiser Frederick IX's dynastic union with the Austrian Habsburgs, a marriage that brought him the crown of the Holy Roman Empire but made a sorry schnitzel of the once "generous bravery, and political reputation," the Hohenzollerns.[2]

When the young George VI ascended the throne in 1900, Russia pounced on the sadly diminished Britain with a powerful fleet and an invading army. The new monarch, however, quickly proved himself to be the embodiment of the Patriot King, leading his forces with the skill of Frederick the Great and dealing with Parliament in ways that would have done credit to William Pitt. George sent the Russians reeling back from their invasion of Britain in 1901 and, when the French intervened, he crossed the Channel with a small army and recapitulated Henry V's campaigns in northern France. With Paris exposed to British attack, the French and Russians sued for peace at Beauvais in early 1902. The young king agreed to a remarkably generous

---

[1] *The Reign of George VI, 1900–1925* (London, 1763), p. xv. The book was republished as C. Oman, ed., *The Reign of George VI, 1900–1925: A Forecast Written in the Year 1763* (London, 1899); that volume was in turn reprinted with a new foreword by I. F. Clark in 1972 (London, 1972). Charles William Chadwick Oman (later Chichele Professor of Modern History at Oxford University and a Knight of the British Empire), was a noted historian of the Napoleonic Wars, and his preface and explanatory notes are still well worth reading. He also made numerous editorial changes, however, including omissions, rearrangements of sentence order, repunctuation, and other silent variations from the original. Hence, all page references to the text are to the digitized version of the 1763 edition available in *Eighteenth Century Collections Online* at http://galenet.galegroup.com/servlet/ECCO (Document Number CW109487203).
[2] Ibid., p. 20.

set of conditions, evacuating France in return for a £2 million reparations payment, which covered the costs of the war and enabled him to begin addressing his main domestic concern: Britain's staggering national debt.

Taming the debt was the new king's first step toward an illustrious reign and a cultural flowering that culminated in 1907 when he founded Stanley, a kind of English Versailles in Rutlandshire, far from the crowds and miasmas and filth of London. The lenient Treaty of Beauvais, however, allowed the French to resume their intrigues on the continent, and in fall 1917, they attacked the Prusso-Austrian Empire. George rushed to his ally's aid, determined to teach the incorrigible king of France a lesson. In less than a year, he had France on the ropes militarily, but the Spanish offered financial support and covert aid early in 1919 and in October declared war. Shortly thereafter, the Russians joined the grand alliance against Britain and a fundamentally useless Prussia.

Things looked grim for Britain but, instead of making peace, as a defeatist faction in Parliament headed by the Duke of Bedford urged, George mobilized the resources of the British Empire so effectively that soon "new ships were building... even in the immense colonies of America; four ships of forty guns each, were on the stocks at Quebeck; ten at Boston, and five at Philadelphia." The king's determination emboldened his friends in the Commons to overcome Bedford's bid to end to the war. Granting the crown a vast sum ("thirteen millions, every shilling of which was raised by taxes within the year, to the surprise of all Europe"), they enabled George to continue the fight without increasing the national debt.[3]

Britain's hero now transformed a European war into a worldwide struggle. Subsidizing several small states – the Swiss cantons, Bavaria, and the kingdom of Sicily – to attack France, he personally liberated the Netherlands (December 1919–January 1920) and launched a series of distant campaigns. In spring 1920, a Royal Navy task force invaded the Baltic and destroyed Russia's fleet at Stockholm and St. Petersburg. Losing not a moment, the navy then sailed for the Iberian coasts, trapping the Spanish fleet at Cadiz, while sending a modest squadron ("ten sail of the line, and eight frigates") with three thousand redcoats to New Orleans. There they joined some fifteen thousand colonial troops and marched overland into Mexico.[4] Turning then to Havana, the squadron "without any assistance reduced it," bringing Cuba "once more... under the dominion of Great-Britain, and with it a prodigious sugar trade."[5] Meanwhile, New Spain's defenses proved so paltry that Mexico City "surrendered on the first summons" to the invading Anglo-American army. The rest of New Spain fell in a matter of

---

[3]   Ibid., pp. 116–17.
[4]   Ibid., p. 144.
[5]   Ibid., p. 153.

three months, "together with the isthmus, across from La Vera Cruz to Acapulco."[6]

While the British lion roared in the halls of Montezuma, the East India Company launched an expedition from Batavia (Java having come under the Company's control at some earlier unspecified point) against the Philippines. Fifteen sail of ships and ten thousand Company troops surprised Manila and seized it "after an attack of two hours." By autumn 1920, then, Britain had made itself the master of the Pacific and all its riches. "The accession of trade was immense, which these distant conquests concurred to command; a vast and open trade which was carried on, almost immediately, from Acapulco to Manilla."[7]

As redcoats and tars repeated their great-great-grandfathers' victories of 1762 in the East and West Indies, on the continent, George VI won battle after battle, seizing Paris and capturing both the French king and dauphin, then dictating peace at Paris in fall 1920. The terms of the treaty could scarcely have differed more from those of the 1763 Peace of Paris:

> 1. That the King of Spain shall cede all the conquests of the English in the East and West-Indies to Great-Britain, as an indemnification for the expences of the war. 2. That the King of Spain shall acknowledge the King of Great Britain, King of France. 3. That the King of Great-Britain shall relinquish his conquests in Catalonia, in consideration of the King of Spain's ceding the island of Sardinia to Philip of France, which he shall enjoy for ever, with the title of King.[8]

Spain promptly acquiesced, and a British squadron "wafted" the king, the dauphin, and miscellaneous diehard nobles to Sardinia where the Bourbon dynasty met the shabby end that was, in fact, a lot better than it deserved. "The peace was no sooner signed, than it was proclaimed at London and Paris, and his Majesty was crowned King of France, at Rheims, the 16th of November, 1920, before an immense concourse of British and French nobility, &c."[9]

What followed, however, mattered far more than the treaty. George, rightly wary of a resurgent alliance against him, refused "to disarm himself . . . – a conduct which has often been fatal to conquerors"[10] and secured Parliamentary grants sufficient to maintain the navy at its present size, while instituting strict economy in all other government spending. The occupation troops in France were paid for from French revenues, while he reduced the army establishments of England and Ireland to prewar levels. George's

[6]   Ibid., p. 154.
[7]   Ibid., p. 155.
[8]   Ibid., pp. 157–8.
[9]   Ibid., p. 159.
[10] Ibid., p. 160.

well-known commitment to the domestic economy gave the Commons the courage to set public finance on the firmest of footings. British commerce, fattening on the riches of Mexico, Cuba, and the Philippines, increased customs revenues to the point that great expenditures could be made on public works.

The "truly magnificent" city that had grown up around the royal palace at Stanley attained new heights of splendor as "the metropolis of the three, or rather four, kingdoms." Contentment flourished in Britain's colonies as well, particularly in North America, where George was "Sovereign of a tract of much greater extent than all Europe."[11] America's Britons, eleven million strong and "in possession of, perhaps the finest country in the world,... had never made the least attempt to shake off the authority of Great-Britain: indeed, the multiplicity of governments which prevailed over the whole country – the various constitutions of them, rendered the execution of such a scheme absolutely impossible."[12] Now the colonists' numbers increased "so surprising fast" that American consumption became the engine that "most extended and forwarded... British manufactures" within the empire as a whole.[13]

George VI returned to occupied France in 1922 "to conquer" the "disaffection [of the French] by his clemency and [by] the mildness of his government." This he did, first of all, by "raising many French regiments" to provide employment for deserving gentlemen and to prevent insurrection; and then (equally important) by establishing freedom of the press. The latter was crucial because journalists and pamphleteers immediately published a torrent of works that "ridiculed and subverted the Roman Catholic religion" and, hence, "opened the eyes of the more sensible, and even awakened some of the ignorant, to a sense of the absurdities of popery." To have prohibited Catholicism outright would have summoned furies of resistance but, by means of free inquiry and expression, George cleansed even that wellspring of spiritual corruption, encouraging enlightened religious opinions to flourish, within both the Roman Church and the competing sects that sprang up everywhere around it.[14]

The king crowned these popular measures with an edict that "introduced the laws of England into France, with no changes, but such as respected religion, and his own authority: he even gave up every prerogative which he did not possess in England, except the raising of money." The French greeted the rule of law "with particular exultation; as [it] came from the hand of their conqueror; happy for France that it was conquered by such

---

11 Ibid., p. 180.
12 Ibid., p. 181.
13 Ibid., pp. 181, 180.
14 Ibid., pp. 184, 186–7.

a Patriot King!"[15] *Habeas corpus*, trial by jury, and judges "with salaries fixed for life . . . [who] had no inducement to favour either side" in any trial, instantly won the loyalty and gratitude of every ordinary Frenchman.

Only the aristocrats grumbled. But in the end, George mollified even the *noblesse* when he established magnificent palaces where the frivolous could flounce and prance at court, provided the ambitious with opportunities for employment in the military and the state, and captured the devotion of the sophisticated by patronizing the arts and letters "with a liberality unknown in France, and greatly to his honour."[16] In the end, then, this "philosophical king" won the hearts and minds of the French by delivering them from the tyranny under which they had so long labored. George VI conquered France to free the French, allowing them to fulfill their potential to become a freedom-loving race that might be compared – almost – to the English.

THINKING OF PEACE

This curious political fable repays our attention for many reasons beyond providing an early example of the fantasy that a well-conducted war of conquest can transform an enemy nation into one capable of enjoying the blessings of freedom and of displaying a decent gratitude to its conqueror. Above all, *The Reign of George VI* affords an unparalleled view of the way the people whom William Pitt called "the nation" – the newspaper- and pamphlet-reading, politically conscious, but unenfranchised "middling" Englishmen who admired him so extravagantly – thought about war and peace in the immediate aftermath of the Seven Years' War. It is clear that the author was one of Pitt's devotees because he modeled the policies and strategies of George VI in the great war of 1919–1920 on those Pitt had pursued from 1757 through 1761.

Even more telling, however, was the name he assigned to the leading villain of English politics in the early twentieth century: the Duke of Bedford. In the novel, Bedford is the immensely rich head of the largest "interest" in Parliament, a great man suspected of being in the pay of the Russians and perhaps even the French. He pursued peace in late 1919 with traitorous zeal, hoping to prevent Britain from seizing the greatest prizes of all in the contest with France and Spain. In the real world of 1763, of course, John Russell, the fourth Duke of Bedford, was a Francophile diplomat and politician whom Pitt's followers regarded with unsurpassable loathing. Bedford had begun to criticize Pitt's war policies in 1759, just as they were yielding the victories that made the Great Commoner a hero to virtually everyone but the Prince of Wales, who abhorred the war. When the prince ascended the throne in 1760 as George III, he rewarded the duke with a place in the cabinet; two years

<hr/>

[15]   Ibid., p. 188.
[16]   Ibid., p. 191.

later, he named Bedford his minister plenipotentiary and dispatched him to Paris. There, of course, Bedford negotiated the treaty that Pitt denounced as a shameful surrender of British interests at the moment of victory.

There are other clues to the author's sympathies, too: The author named the greatest military heroes of *The Reign of George VI* for Pitt's political allies, the Duke of Devonshire and the Duke of Grafton; the name he chose for George's imperial capital, Stanley, recalled Hans Stanley, the head of the first British peace delegation to France (June–September 1761). This last echo gained special significance because Stanley's peace mission ended when he remained loyal to Pitt's instructions and refused to budge on what was, for the French, the impossible demand that they surrender fishing rights off Newfoundland.

Even more important, however, were the ways in which the plot and structure of the book made clear that the author shared Pitt's convictions that the Peace of Paris had squandered Britain's greatest victory and that it would lead to future wars. In the author's imagined history, Britain prospered commercially after 1763, but it was a deceptive, enervating prosperity, for as the nation steeped in effeminizing luxury, it stagnated as a military power. Throughout the nineteenth century, France and its allies repeatedly drew Britain into wars that served only to hobble it by relentlessly increasing the national debt. By 1897, the nation had slipped so far that it lost a naval arms race with Russia. By 1900, the Royal Navy had grown so feeble that it could not even protect the home islands from a Russian invasion.

The lessons of all these woes could hardly have been clearer to the author. France had lost the Seven Years' War but, because the roots of its power had not been destroyed, nothing could prevent it from resuming its quest for universal monarchy. Seduced by peace, absorbed in commerce, and forgetful of virtue, Britons would inevitably succumb to political factionalism and decline. North American colonists, useful insofar as they consume British manufactures, would prove no real source of strength: They might be prosperous and safe (the colonies of Spain, their only plausible enemy, were militarily incapable of posing a threat) but were too distant, too indolent, and too unconcerned in Britain's affairs to be of use unless the crown took direct action to mobilize them for war.

Only when George VI finally seized the initiative in a war with France could Britain reverse a century and a half of slow decline – by precisely the same measures Pitt had used in the Seven Years' War. George VI, like Pitt, found himself threatened by a Bedfordite peace party but, in the end, overcame the challenge where Pitt could not and pressed on to the conclusion that (the author implies) Pitt *would* have achieved had he had a king and fellow ministers worthy of him: the extinguishment of French power in Europe. As far as the author is concerned, then, there could be no lasting peace as long as France survived. Or, more properly, there can be no peace as long as the Bourbon monarchy survived, for it is not the French people but rather their rulers who posed the problem. If only one could free the French from the shackles of absolutist tyranny, something unprecedented might just be possible: an indefinite cessation of war in Europe, the ultimate happy ending.

Fanciful as this might seem, and not forgetting that it was being proposed in a novel intended to skewer the Duke of Bedford and his treaty, this vision anticipates the dream of permanent peace that so captivated Thomas Paine, William Wordsworth, William Godwin, and other British radicals three decades later. Even in the teeth of the Terror, they found it possible to believe that the removal of the tyrannical Bourbon regime (and the aristocratic and ecclesiastical infrastructures that shored it up) would redeem the French, who could then develop as a free and virtuous people, capable of living in peace with the rest of the world. The anonymous writer of 1763 and the radicals of the 1790s, in other words, agreed that peace might flower among nations once the political ground had been cleared by violence. They saw peace not merely as an interval between one war and its inevitable successor but rather as a condition that had the potential to become permanent.

THE MAKING OF THE TREATY OF PARIS

Such an understanding of peace had little meaning for the Duke of Bedford or for Étienne-François de Stainville, duc de Choiseul, or Don Jerome, marquis de Grimaldi, the architects of the real Peace of Paris. They were, after all, diplomats who shared a hard-headed expectation that states which agreed to lay down their arms would not cease to pursue their competitive interests but would certainly prepare for the next war. Yet, even this supremely realistic trio evidently believed that the treaty they wrote might produce something more enduring than the temporary cessation of hostilities typical of eighteenth-century treaties. While there can be no doubt that they assumed war would eventually return to Europe, it also appears they believed they could delay the evil day by attending with care to the peace arrangements they made for North America. Indeed, from what we can deduce from their negotiations, they thought the Treaty of Paris would make peace a permanent feature of American life.

Bedford, Choiseul, and Grimaldi negotiated the Peace of Paris within a diplomatic framework buttressed by political and cultural assumptions sufficiently different from those of the present that it may be worthwhile to sketch them briefly before turning to the treaty itself.[17] For more than a century,

---

[17] For a splendid overview of these matters, see Michael Howard, *The Invention of Peace: Reflections on War and International Order* (New Haven, CT, 2000); the following discussion follows Howard's second chapter, "Priests and Princes: 800–1789," pp. 7–31.

European rulers had generally agreed that each state was solely responsible for maintaining domestic order within its own frontiers and defending itself from external threats. To achieve those ends, they had claimed, on behalf of the state, a monopoly on the means of violence.

Inasmuch as sovereigns acknowledged no power superior to themselves (except, of course, God, who helpfully sanctioned royal authority through whichever version of His church the monarch had pledged himself to defend but who otherwise refrained from intervening in day-to-day concerns of state), interstate relations typically proceeded in a bare-knuckled way. Kings decided when to make war on their fellow kings, and they alone decided when it was time for the bloodletting to stop. That this fundamentally anarchic approach did not lead to uninterrupted carnage had more to do with the expense of maintaining armed forces and the infrastructure of defense than with any sense that there might be something intrinsically undesirable about military conflict. Wars were simply what kings did, and warfare furnished one of the more reliable ways that monarchs had to control and reward the great aristocratic families upon whose consent their rule depended.

Making peace, in such a context, posed complex problems. To do so required sovereigns to reverse the course they had announced in formal declarations of war and begin to cooperate with their sworn enemies in finding some way to lay down arms without also sacrificing honor. In theory, such matters were solely up to the rulers. But, in reality, kings could only make peace with the acquiescence of their aristocratic supporters and that inevitably involved intricate, exquisite calculation. To make peace too soon, or on terms that did not sufficiently recognize the honor and interests of the nobility who led the state's military forces, could appear as analogous to that supremely dishonorable battlefield event: the premature surrender of a fortress. Since wars seldom produced decisive military results, it was the fear of dishonor and the risk of losing the support of their most important noble constituents that discouraged kings from making peace until military operations had exhausted their treasuries and they could borrow no more money for the continuation of war.

Fortunately for early-modern monarchs and their long-suffering subjects, European aristocracies produced not only military officers but diplomats to whom kings could turn when they could no longer afford war. Kings delegated what amounted to power of attorney to the ambassadors whom they sent to negotiate terms with the similarly empowered representatives of their enemies. These "ministers plenipotentiary," in turn, drafted treaties – contracts between their masters – that stipulated the terms on which wars might end. Only sovereigns could put those proposed treaties into effect by ordering them to be officially proclaimed. In practice, this allowed a monarch an interval in which he could consult with the significant members of his court, whose consent to the terms was as necessary as the agreement of his enemy.

As usual, the matter was somewhat more complicated in Britain, where the constitution in theory vested sovereignty in "King, Lords, and Commons in Parliament assembled." There, custom decreed that the House of Lords and the House of Commons debate the preliminaries of the treaty. Most important, the House of Commons alone could appropriate the funds needed to implement the preliminaries. Yet, even in Britain, the general pattern held: The crown managed foreign relations, delegated authority in settling peace terms to plenipotentiary ambassadors, and consulted with its major constituencies before confirming the preliminary articles as what was called a "definitive treaty of peace."

The negotiations that the Duke of Bedford, the duc de Choiseul, and the marquis de Grimaldi brought to completion at Paris between 14 September and 3 November 1762, therefore, reflected a thoroughly ritualized process.[18] They were well aware of the immense power they exercised on behalf of their masters, its contingent quality, and the potential pitfalls that lay in drafting terms of peace. Enormous consequences could arise from agreeing to seemingly innocent phrases and provisions that concealed unanticipated mischief. In negotiations such as these, involving not two but three parties, the additional danger lurked that two had secretly agreed to terms outside the knowledge of the third. The latter was a thoroughly justified suspicion at Paris in 1762.

In 1761, France had negotiated a secret treaty with Spain to bring it into the war as an ally without informing Spain that it was simultaneously, secretly negotiating potential terms of peace with Britain. As late as mid-August 1762, when the French and British delegates were preparing for their meeting in Paris after having worked out a full set of preliminary understandings through third parties, Choiseul was still selectively suppressing information about the terms in his correspondence with the Spanish

---

[18]   Zenab Esmat Rashed, *The Peace of Paris 1763* (Liverpool, 1951) is still the standard narrative account of these final negotiations, setting them in the context of previous peace overtures dating back to the Hague conversations of late 1759–early 1760, the Bussy–Stanley negotiations of mid-1761, and the protracted Anglo-French correspondence preliminary to the dispatch of Bedford to Paris; her account of the Bedford-Choiseul-Grimaldi talks is at pp. 169–87. See also Lawrence Henry Gipson, *The British Empire before the American Revolution*, vol. 8, *The Great War for the Empire: The Culmination* (New York, 1970), pp. 283–313; Walter L. Dorn, *Competition for Empire, 1440–1763* (New York, 1963), pp. 378–84; Julian S. Corbett, *England in the Seven Years' War*, vol. 2, *1759–1763* (London, 1907), pp. 327–65; Ronald Hyam, "Imperial Interests and the Peace of Paris (1763)," *Reappraisals in British Imperial History*, ed. by Ronald Hyam and Ged Martin (London, 1975), pp. 21–43; Max Savelle, *The Diplomatic History of the Canadian Boundary, 1748–1763* (New Haven, CT, 1940), pp. 103–46; Max Savelle with the assistance of Margaret Anne Fisher, *The Origins of American Diplomacy: The International History of Angloamerica, 1492–1763* (New York, 1967), pp. 467–510.

foreign ministry, with the intention of depriving Grimaldi of a decisive role in the negotiations.[19] Of such duplicitous actions, diplomats negotiated eighteenth-century treaties, and no one understood it better than they; not even those whose interests were being betrayed expected that it would be otherwise.

Above all, each diplomat's goal in peace negotiations was to define the postwar balance of power in the most advantageous terms possible for his nation. All eyes, therefore, remained fixed on Europe and on a future in which one could assume that nations would behave more or less as they had in the past. For the Duke of Bedford, it was absolutely clear that the French would seek to rebuild their power in the aftermath of defeat. The great question before him – in a sense, the only significant question – was how best to keep Britain secure against that inevitable revival and how to make a peace that would not invite another, potentially ruinous, war as a result. In May and July of 1761, he had explained his views on those matters in letters to the Duke of Newcastle and the Earl of Bute. To both, he observed that the worst thing Britain could do was to press its advantages relentlessly, and seek to remain as dominant in the peace as it had become during the last two years of the war. Such power, he told Newcastle, "would be as dangerous for us to grasp at as it was for Louis XIV when he aspired to be the arbiter of Europe, and might be likely to produce a grand alliance against us."[20] Therefore, he argued, "at the same time we are fair to ourselves, let us be just to others, and not think to impose such terms on France, as we are sure she cannot long acquiesce under and which, when she has taken breath she will take the first opportunity of breaking."[21]

This diplomatic application of the Golden Rule, Bedford told Bute, had a crucial maritime corollary: "endeavouring to drive France entirely out of any naval power is fighting against nature, and can tend to no one good to this country; but, on the contrary, must excite all the naval powers of Europe to enter into a confederacy against us." In practical terms, this meant that France should not be denied access to the Newfoundland cod-fishing grounds or the facilities to dry the catch for shipment back to France and other European markets. Pitt, who was still in power when Bedford wrote, above all opposed allowing France future access to the fisheries.

19 Fred Anderson, *Crucible of War: The Seven Years' War and the Fate of Empire in British North America, 1754–1766* (New York, 2000), pp. 484, 503–5; Rashed, *Peace of Paris*, pp. 133–65; Savelle, *The Origins of American Diplomacy*, pp. 503–4.
20 Bedford to Newcastle, 9 May 1761, British Library, Additional Manuscripts (Newcastle Papers) 32922, quoted in Corbett, *England in the Seven Years' War*, vol. 2, p. 172.
21 Ibid. (BL, Add. MS 32922, fol. 452), quoted in Martyn J. Powell, "Russell, John, Fourth Duke of Bedford (1710–1771)," *Oxford Dictionary of National Biography*, Oxford University Press, September 2004; online ed., October 2005 [http://www.oxforddnb.com/view/article/24320].

His stubbornness on this point doomed the Stanley–Bussy negotiations, which were just getting under way when Bedford delivered his views to Bute.

Before the war, the Newfoundland fisheries had supported a trade worth roughly £500,000 annually for France, but strategic rather than economic reasons led Pitt to determine to keep French fishermen away from the Grand Banks. The shipwrights who built fishing vessels could also build men-of-war, while the tens of thousands of mariners who made each year's fishing voyages could become the manpower backbone of a new navy. Pitt's nightmare of a resurrected French fleet, however, bothered Bedford not at all. Quite the opposite: It was the thought of a Britannia truly intent on ruling the waves that could wake him in a cold sweat. A British "monopoly of all naval power," he told Bute, "would be at least as dangerous to the liberties of Europe as that of Louis XIV was, which drew almost all Europe upon his back."[22]

As Bedford's letters suggest, the Sun King cast a long shadow over every judgment he made about the conduct of diplomacy. Above all, he believed, an England that had thwarted Louis's attempts to impose a Catholic universal monarchy on Europe by the patient building and rebuilding of coalitions against him should never allow itself to be seduced by the temptations of dominion. The temptation was particularly acute, and thus most to be feared, now that hegemony over not just Europe but the Atlantic world itself seemed to lie within Britain's grasp. Hence, Pitt's vehement insistence, in late summer of 1761, that Britain step up the war effort and even declare a preemptive war on Spain appalled Bedford; he boycotted the Cabinet in protest, beginning in August. Soon thereafter, the other ministers' support for Pitt waned until, finally, on 5 October with but a single supporter (his brother-in-law) remaining, he resigned his office as Secretary of State for the Southern Department. When the Duke of Newcastle assembled a new cabinet in November, he offered the office of Lord Privy Seal to Bedford, who accepted it with greater determination than ever to seek peace and restore something like a viable, stable balance of power in postwar Europe. Bedford could only have regarded the King's decision to appoint him as minister plenipotentiary in September 1762 as the most powerful of all endorsements for his position and for his view that magnanimity to an enemy so soundly defeated as France was the surest route to lasting peace in Europe.

Conservative, Francophile, historically conscious, Europe-minded, and aristocratic, the Duke of Bedford would have seemed ideally suited to the diplomatic role to which he was assigned. In his own mind, he certainly was: Once in Paris, he resisted and deeply resented as an infringement on

---

[22] Bedford to Bute, 9 July 1761, quoted in Corbett, *England in the Seven Years' War*, vol. 2, p. 172.

his plenary powers every attempt to advise him on the conditions of peace. Of all the politicians in Britain, therefore, Bedford may have been one of the least able to understand the significance of the interest that his countrymen were also taking in the terms on which peace should be made. Yet, that interest would have been manifest to anyone taking even a casual look at the pamphlets on sale in London booksellers' shops between the end of 1759 and late 1763, when at least sixty-five titles were published on the question of whether Britain in making peace would be best advised to retain Canada or the island of Guadeloupe.[23]

All of these pamphlets, of course, were politically inspired, emanating from the presses of either court or country interests in the aftermath of the great British victories in America and the West Indies. Those triumphs seemed to portend a vast expansion of the British Empire as a result of the war; but what was the character of that empire to be? The writers who advocated returning Canada and keeping Guadeloupe (or, in a more general case, all of the French sugar islands taken by British forces between 1759 and 1762: Guadeloupe, Marie-Galante, Dominica, Martinique, St. Lucia, St. Vincent, Grenada, and the Grenadines) conceived of Britain's Empire in more or less conventional mercantilist terms, with the colonies serving as a source of raw materials and tropical products, such as sugar and molasses, that Britain could not produce.

To those who thought of the Empire in this way, Canada would be the source of furs and forest products of trifling value but potentially great expense to the metropolis because Britain would have to defend and police it. What was worse, some of them argued, was that the North American colonies, having no enemy to threaten their frontiers, might decide that there was no longer any point in clinging to Britain and would therefore break away as independent states. It was possible, these skeptics argued, to be so dazzled by the grandeur of territorial possession as to forget that the immense colonies of the Spanish Empire had, in fact, overextended Spain and left it dangerously vulnerable in the late war.

The writers who argued for retaining Canada (and, later, Louisiana) saw matters in exactly the opposite way. The American colonies' great value to Britain lay not in their produce but rather in their people, who provided

---

23 On the Canada–Guadeloupe controversy, see William L. Grant, "Canada versus Guadeloupe, an Episode of the Seven Years' War," *The American Historical Review* 17 (1912), 4, pp. 735–43; Clarence Walworth Alvord, *The Mississippi Valley in British Politics: A Study of the Trade, Land Speculation, and Experiments in Imperialism Culminating in the American Revolution*, vol. 1 (Cleveland, Ohio, 1917), pp. 45–75; Jack M. Sosin, *Whitehall and the Wilderness: The Middle West in British Colonial Policy, 1760–1775* (Lincoln, 1961), pp. 8–10; and Paul W. Mapp, "British Culture and the Changing Character of the Mid-Eighteenth-Century British Empire," in *Cultures in Conflict: The Seven Years' War in North America*, ed. by Warren Hofstra (Lanham, MD, 2007), pp. 23–59 passim, esp. pp. 44–50.

a large and fast-growing market for British manufactures. It followed that the Empire would benefit from annexing territory into which colonial populations could continue to expand, to the seemingly unlimited benefit to the manufacturing economy of the metropolis. Given the immense extent of available land in Canada and Louisiana, colonists there would engage in agriculture for many generations to come. Widespread ownership of land would keep wages so prohibitively high that there was no reason to imagine that the Americans would ever develop a manufacturing sector to compete with Britain's. Nor was there any reason to imagine that the colonies would ever learn to cooperate well enough to break away from British rule. Apart from their common tie to the metropolis, the North American provinces had always been deeply divided among themselves; it was inconceivable that they could ever unite unless Britain itself began to oppress them politically, and that could never happen.

Moreover, these writers argued, to remove the French Empire from the interior of North America would ensure that France would never again incite Indians to attack the colonial frontiers. The more of North America the British possessed, the more secure their hold on it would be and the less likely that Britain would ever find itself drawn into a future war with France, as it had been in 1754–1755, over colonial affairs. Benjamin Franklin was eloquent on all of those points in his anonymous pamphlet, "The Interest of Great Britain Considered, With Regard to her Colonies and the Acquisitions of Canada and Guadeloupe" (1760). In the absence of the French threat, he wrote, the Indians had no alternative to "depending absolutely upon us for what are now necessities of life to them, guns, powder, hatchets, knives, and cloathing; and having no other *Europeans* near, that can further supply them, or instigate them against us; there is no doubt of their being always dispos'd, if we treat them with common justice, to live in perpetual peace with us."[24] As a consequence, "the [British] force now employ'd in that part of the world [America], may be spar'd for other service here [in Britain] or elsewhere." The colonists who had gained military experience in the war were more capable than ever of defending themselves; thus, "both the offensive and defensive strength of the *British* empire on the whole will be greatly increased" by the annexation of Canada and Louisiana.[25]

The point here is not that the pamphlets published in the course of this controversy had any bearing on British foreign policy, for it is almost certain that the officials responsible for formulating it did so without any significant

---

[24] [Benjamin Franklin,] "The Interest of Great Britain Considered, With Regard to Her Colonies And the Acquisitions of Canada and Guadeloupe" (London, 1760; reprinted Boston, 1760), p. 16. Digitized version available in *Eighteenth Century Collections Online*, at http://galenet.galegroup.com/servlet/ECCO (Document Number CW3304184656).
[25] Ibid., p. 17.

reference to them.[26] Rather, it is to suggest that the consumers of British political pamphlets – the same kinds of people who bought and read *The Reign of George VI*, which is best understood as a fictional extension of the Canada–Guadeloupe debate – were profoundly interested in the future of the empire. Their interest translated, inevitably, into concern for the nature of the peace settlement, and not only because it would have an impact on the imperial economy. They were also concerned, just as Bedford and his fellow politicians were, with minimizing the chances of future wars and particularly with securing British interests as thoroughly as possible against renewed threats from France.

The pamphlets suggest, however, that the authors worried less than Bedford and his fellow diplomatists about stabilizing the postwar balance of power and dreamed instead of eliminating, permanently if possible, the threat that France posed to their nation. Less than a decade earlier, an obscure clash of arms on the eastern fringe of the Ohio Valley had plunged the colonies of Britain and France into a war that expanded until it had drawn all of Europe into the maelstrom. If Benjamin Franklin and other writers like him were to be believed, the best way to avoid the repetition of such a vast calamity would be to annex as much American land as possible at the peace, encourage Anglo-American colonists to be fruitful and multiply, and do everything possible to spur their migration beyond the Appalachian Mountains. The farther west these American Britons carried the Union Jack, the more secure Britain itself would inevitably be.

As much as Franklin hoped that his arguments would influence the men who determined British policy at the peace, however, the Earl of Bute was almost certainly *not* thinking of them on 1 May 1762 when he informed Bedford that "the Mississippi should be the boundary between" the British and French Empires in North America.[27] The future security of Britain and its empire was much on his mind as he wrote those words. Yet, he reasoned about it from wholly different premises than the expansionist pamphleteers. Those assumptions informed the secret correspondence he had been carrying on with Choiseul through third parties since the previous October, immediately after Pitt's resignation; in a matter of a few more weeks, they would produce an agreement on preliminary terms, permitting Britain and France to appoint plenipotentiaries for face-to-face negotiations.[28]

The draft terms, still a profound secret, included the concessions that Pitt found outrageous and dishonorable when they finally became public in

---

[26] Although Alvord, *The Mississippi Valley in British Politics*, 1, pp. 35–37 and passim, suggested that the pamphlets did indeed help create policy, Sosin, in *Whitehall and the Wilderness*, pp. 9–10, convincingly argues that they did not.

[27] Bute to Bedford, 1 May 1762, quoted in Mapp, "British Culture and the Changing Character of the Mid-Eighteenth-Century British Empire," p. 47.

[28] Corbett, *England in the Seven Years' War*, vol. 2, pp. 285–7, 327–37.

the terms of peace – an agreement to allow the French to continue fishing off Newfoundland and to cede them two small islands in the Gulf of St. Lawrence, where they could erect drying stages and repair their ships; a promise to return the sugar islands of Martinique, Guadeloupe, and St. Lucia; and a *de facto* undertaking to abandon the alliance with Frederick of Prussia. Yet, there was also one provision that Pitt, later, heartily endorsed: France's cession of Canada and Louisiana east of the Mississippi. Why did Bute, concerned primarily with creating a viable postwar balance of power, insist that France should cede the eastern half of Louisiana as a condition of peace?

In part, it was sheer practicality, for his informants had made it clear that while Louis XV and Choiseul would never give in on the question of Newfoundland fishing rights, they would happily cede both Canada and at least the eastern half of Louisiana, territories that had never been anything but a drain on the French treasury. Bute, like his royal master, longed for peace, and he was prepared to give the French a powerful say in its terms in order to gain it quickly. Yet, he and the king also wanted that peace to be as durable as possible and saw the cession of Canada and Louisiana as critical to gaining it – not for reasons that had anything to do with the kind of expansionism Franklin envisioned but rather for reasons most fully expressed in July in a memorandum written by the Earl of Egremont, Secretary of State for the Southern Department. Writing as the minister formally responsible for diplomatic relations with France, Egremont commented at length on the intention of Article Five of Britain's draft peace conditions:

> What we have proposed in this article was not to draw any advantage from the extension of our territory into a country a great part of which is waste, and which we shall probably never clear nor people. It was to reëstablish peace on solid and lasting foundations and to forestall all disputes respecting the boundaries of the two nations on the American Continent.... [I]t is absolutely only to this end that we ask that the two banks of the Mississippi serve as boundaries to the two nations, and that each content itself with its own side of the river in order that they may have nothing to adjust in the future, we flatter ourselves that we shall encounter no difficulty on an article calculated as much for the welfare of France as for our own.[29]

This view, later imbedded in the king's instructions to Bedford of 4 September, required the duke to establish a boundary between French and

---

[29] "Observations on the Different Articles of the Memoir Containing the Conditions of Peace Proposed by Great Britain," 10 July 1762, in Theodore C. Pease, ed., *Anglo-French Boundary Disputes in the West, 1749–1763* (Springfield, IL, 1936), pp. 452–53; also partially quoted in Mapp, "British Culture and the Changing Character of the Mid-Eighteenth-Century British Empire," p. 47.

British territories down the center of the Mississippi, as embodied in what by then had become the sixth article of the proposed treaty:

> And whereas the great object We propose by the Limits above described, besides the Acquisition of an extended Territory, is the establishing [of] a certain, fixed Boundary between our Dominions in North America, and Those of the Most Christian King, which may ascertain beyond all possibility of doubt, the respective property of the Two Crowns in that part of the World, and which may, by that means, remove forever the source of those unhappy Disputes, which always arise from an equivocal and unsettled Frontier, and from which the Miseries and Calamities of the present war have sprung: Our Will and Pleasure is, that you do exert your utmost Attention with regard to this Article, which is to be treated in such clear and explicit Terms, as shall render it incapable of any Misconstruction. . . . [30]

Britain's goal, then, as understood by Bedford, Bute, Egremont, and the king, was to ensure that no future European war would arise, as the Seven Years' War had, from an American boundary dispute. That the proposed Mississippi boundary was 500 miles west of the westernmost British settlements added another layer of security, but the acquisition of so much territory was not itself an element of decisive importance. The addition to the British Empire of an area approximately the size of Western Europe was, in effect, an incidental result of the fact that the Mississippi River was too big to miss, and it divided North America more or less in two, along a north–south axis.

Given the anarchic quality of international relations of the eighteenth century, it is hardly surprising that an unambiguous border between empires would appeal to diplomats concerned with stabilizing the European state system. Spain's willingness to accept the western half of Louisiana when France secretly offered it, late in the Paris negotiations, demonstrates the same thinking in another context.[31] The British conquest of Havana made it imperative that Spain offer some "equivalent" to Britain in order to regain the city; Choiseul proposed to transfer the western half of Louisiana – the immense expanse of territory between the Mississippi and the Continental Divide – to induce Spain to hand over Florida to the British crown. The impulse behind Spain's rapid acceptance, however, had nothing to do

---

[30] "Bedford's Instructions, September 4, 1762 [S P France, 253]," ibid., pp. 505–6.

[31] Louis XV wrote to Charles III on 9 October 1762 to offer him Louisiana west of the Mississippi, together with New Orleans. Just two weeks later, the Spanish Foreign Minister, Don Ricardo Wall, directed Grimaldi to sign the peace preliminaries and accept Louisiana. France secretly transferred the territory to Spain by the Treaty of Fontainebleau on 3 November 1762, the same day that the plenipotentiaries agreed to the preliminaries of the Peace of Paris. Rashed, *Peace of Paris*, pp. 181–93; Arthur S. Aiton, "The Diplomacy of the Louisiana Cession," *American Historical Review*, 36 (1931) 4, pp. 717–18.

with a desire to expand New Spain northward to what is now Alberta. For two hundred years, Florida had been an expensive headache for the Spanish crown. Populated by a few thousand colonists and missionaries, a great many more troublesome Indians, and a steadily growing population of maroons from Georgia and South Carolina, the colony had been a lightning rod in Anglo-Spanish relations for most of the eighteenth century. Spain had no conceivable use for western Louisiana but every reason to establish a clear line of demarcation between the Spanish and British territories. Above all, an unmistakable border on the Mississippi River would prevent Britain and its mad-dog American colonists from manufacturing an incident in the pinewood wasteland of the Georgia–Florida frontier as an excuse for launching an expedition into Mexico and seizing its silver mines or perhaps staging a repeat performance of the Havana expedition.

In a world where security was all but impossible to come by, then, removing the potential causes of future wars could furnish a far more powerful motive for expansion than the desire to add lands to an imperial domain. That, at least, represented the logic behind Spain's speedy acceptance of the Treaty of Fontainebleau on 3 November 1762; that was the logic that drove Bedford's pen as he signed his name to the preliminaries of the Peace of Paris that same day.[32] It even made a kind of sense to William Pitt who, in a great speech to the House of Commons on 9 December, denounced every aspect of the preliminaries of peace *except* the acquisition of Canada and eastern Louisiana. Although he maintained that the treaty contained "the seeds of a future war," that was because it returned too many valuable territories to France and gave the French the means to rebuild their navy, not because he foresaw anything untoward emerging from the conditions of peace in North America.[33] Similarly, the powerful objections to the treaty that the Earl of Hardwick raised in the House of Lords centered on the erosion of British influence in Europe: "By this desertion of the King of Prussia," he observed, "we are left without any system or connection at all on the continent" and, hence, vulnerable to a France that would surely begin to build an anti-British coalition after the war.[34]

Most speakers, however, portrayed the Peace far more positively and particularly with respect to its likely impact on North America. The Earl of Shelburne, for example, argued that Britain had gone to war in the first place "for the security of our colonies" and had wholly succeeded in achieving

---

[32] Mapp, "British Culture and the Changing Character of the Mid-Eighteenth-Century British Empire," p. 50.

[33] *The Parliamentary History of England from the Earliest Period to the Year 1803*, ed. by William Cobbett (London, 1806–1820), 15: 1270; also quoted in Rashed, *Peace of Paris*, p. 191.

[34] Hardwick speech in the House of Lords, quoted in Gipson, *The British Empire before the American* Revolution, vol. 8, p. 308.

its military purposes. The treaty, he pointed out, would seal that triumph diplomatically, leaving the colonists "freed from the molestation of enemies and the emulation of rivals, unlimited in their possessions, and safe in their persons." The Peace assured the Americans' future and, in so doing, promised to create a postwar empire of "real grandeur."[35]

Bute in the House of Lords and his manager in the House of Commons, Henry Fox, spared neither effort nor expense in securing support for the resolution "to express to his Majesty their Approbation of the Advantageous Terms upon which His Majesty hath concluded Preliminary Articles of Peace." But even the most prodigal buying of votes could not have produced the lopsided result that followed the debates on 9 December, when the Commons voted 319 to 64 in favor of the resolution and the Lords passed it by acclamation.[36] Such an outcome suggests that only the most hardened devotees of William Pitt disagreed with the ministry's reasoning. Thereafter, no substantive issue remained that could prevent the formal proclamation of the Definitive Treaty of Peace at Paris on 10 February 1763.

THE UNINTENDED EFFECTS OF PEACE MAKING

The men who signed the Peace of Paris took pains to assure the conditions of a lasting peace in North America, and it would seem clear from the outcome of the debates in Parliament that in Britain even the most skeptical of the political elite agreed that the negotiators had succeeded at least in that respect, if not in others. Yet, three months after the signing, an Ottawa war chief, Pontiac, attacked Fort Detroit and sparked the greatest pan-Indian rebellion in North American history. Within weeks, only three interior forts remained under British control. Imperial authority remained effectively extinguished west of the Appalachians until British officials negotiated peace treaties that gave way on every significant Indian demand.

Peace had barely been restored to the West in 1765 when colonial settlements from New Hampshire to St. Kitts erupted in protests against a mild stamp tax, nullifying the law by violence. Parliament had no choice but to repeal the offensive act while passing another to assert sovereignty over the colonies, a compromise solution that left British ministers determined to demonstrate their authority over the colonists at the first opportunity. Their efforts to do so provoked increasingly determined resistance until civil war broke out in Massachusetts in April 1775. Fifteen months later, thirteen mainland colonies, calling themselves the United States of America, renounced their allegiance to the crown of Great Britain and declared themselves independent republics. Almost exactly fifteen years to the day after

35 Shelburne speech in the House of Lords, quoted ibid.
36 Resolution, ibid., p. 309; Anderson, *Crucible of War*, p. 505.

the proclamation of the Peace, on 6 February 1778, France concluded the treaty of alliance with the United States that, in 1783, served up the fine cold dish that sated Versailles' hunger for revenge. It would have been impossible to imagine two decades of developments less in keeping with the results that Bedford, Bute, and George III anticipated from the Peace of Paris. What went wrong?

Notwithstanding Lawrence Henry Gipson's famous argument that the absence of the French Empire from North America inexorably moved the colonists to seek independence because they no longer needed the British army and navy to protect them from the "Gallic peril," there was nothing inevitable about events in the two decades after the Peace of Paris.[37] Yet, it is also clear that the character and effects of the Seven Years' War in America, conditions that Bedford and the others understood poorly (if at all) when they wrote the treaty of peace, had enormous impact on those postwar events. We can best begin to understand those connections by recognizing how incredibly surprising it all was to contemporaries, all of whom assumed that after 1763, North America would no longer destabilize international relations. Even the author of *The Reign of George VI*, who loathed everything connected to Bedford and his treaty, described nineteenth- and twentieth-century wars between France and England as emerging entirely from European causes. His predicted history of British North America consisted of 150 years of uninterrupted peace, prosperity, and population growth.

The principal focus of contemporary British observers, in other words, remained fixed on metropolitan actors. Whether peace would endure, in their minds, depended on what future moves George III's fellow sovereigns would make in European international politics. What they did not fully understand was that the Seven Years' War had been a war like no other in their experience, with lasting effects that extended well beyond Europe. The constituencies which had interests at stake in the peace, therefore, were far more varied and numerous than those whom Bedford and the other

---

[37] That the North American colonists would move quickly for independence once the French threat to their borders had been removed had been predicted by several of the pamphleteers who advocated retaining Guadeloupe and returning Canada to France at the peace; see Grant, "Canada *versus* Guadeloupe," esp. pp. 740–1. Lawrence Henry Gipson picked up these prophecies and gave them substantial credit in "The American Revolution as an Aftermath of the Great War for the Empire, 1754–63," *Political Science Quarterly*, 65 (1950), 1: pp. 86–104; *The Coming of the Revolution, 1763–1775* (New York, 1954), pp. x–xii; and *The British Empire before the American Revolution*, vol. 13, *The Triumphant Empire* (New York, 1974), pp. 171–215. John Murrin thoroughly demolished this argument in "The French and Indian War, the American Revolution, and the Counterfactual Hypothesis: Reflections on Lawrence Henry Gipson and John Shy," *Reviews in American History*, 1 (1976), 3: pp. 307–18. See also Jack P. Greene, "The Seven Years' War and the American Revolution: The Causal Relationship Reconsidered," *Journal of Imperial and Commonwealth History*, 8 (1980), 2: pp. 85–105.

diplomats believed they were representing. The reactions of two of those unconsulted groups, American Indians and colonists in British North America, would prove the most dramatic of all. The ways they understood the world – both as remembered from the prewar era and as the war had remade it – were indeed far more crucial in determining the course of events in the 1760s and beyond than anyone whose gaze was fixed on the chessboard of European diplomacy could imagine.[38]

In fairness to the Duke of Bedford – and the Earl of Bute, George III, and virtually everyone else in British political life – there was no realistic way one might have expected them to regard the opinions of Indians and colonists as relevant to the Peace. The parties concerned in all treaty negotiations were, by definition, sovereigns and their direct representatives. The natives and provincials of eastern North America were merely subjects of the crown, whose interests the king would preserve and protect and who had in return the obligation to render him allegiance and obedience. But that conventional perception, in the radically altered world that emerged from the Seven Years' War, formed the heart of the problem.

The Indians felt the changes first and most acutely and reacted the most strongly. To a degree that no British commander except perhaps General John Forbes fully grasped, and which no imperial official understood better than the Northern Commissioner of Indian Affairs, Sir William Johnson, native people were essential to Britain's victory in America. Every stage of the war had reflected the decisive importance of native military power and diplomacy. The origins of the conflict lay in Iroquois miscalculations concerning the Ohio Valley and its peoples, supposed clients who, in fact, were eager to steer their own course in relations with European traders and empires. In 1754, it had been the combination of Iroquois cupidity and a longing for independence on the part of the Delawares and other Indians living in the upper valley that had allowed agents of the French and British empires to confront each other over control of the Forks of the Ohio, the strategic key to the trans-Appalachian West. The fortunes of war in North

---

[38] There were, of course, imperial impacts that extended far beyond North American groups, as well, including an expanded British stake in the West African slave trade and a vast new role in India, especially Bengal, where the war triggered the transformation of the commercial *imperium* of the East India Company into the fully developed British Raj of the nineteenth century. These topics are well beyond the scope of the present chapter, but can be explored in a series of excellent essays in Wm. Roger Louis, gen. ed., *The Oxford History of the British Empire*, vol. 2, *The Eighteenth Century*, ed. P. J. Marshall (Oxford, 1998); David Richardson, "The British Empire and the Atlantic Slave Trade, 1660–1807," pp. 440–64; Philip D. Morgan, "The Black Experience in the British Empire, 1610–1810," pp. 465–86; P. J. Marshall, "The British in Asia: Trade to Dominion, 1700–1765," pp. 487–507; Rajat Kanta Ray, "Indian Society and the Establishment of British Supremacy, 1765–1818," pp. 508–29; and H. V. Bowen, "British India, 1765–1813: The Metropolitan Context," pp. 530–51.

America ebbed and flowed thereafter according to the engagement and withdrawal of Indian allies whose leaders acted on calculations of advantage with a skill that would have done credit to the subtlest minds in Europe's foreign ministries.

The decision of Delaware, Shawnee, and Mingo Seneca warriors to ally themselves with the French in 1755 made a sanguinary wasteland of the Anglo-American frontier for the next three years, as raids that they conducted in company with other French-allied Indians from the upper Great Lakes basin and the Illinois country created refugee crises from New York to North Carolina. Teedyuscung, the leader of a band of Delawares living east of the Alleghenies, acted as a diplomatic intermediary in making approaches to the Delawares on the Ohio in 1756 and 1757, which in turn led to their decision to make a separate peace at the Treaty of Easton in the autumn of 1758. When the Ohio Delawares withdrew from the French alliance, the Shawnees and other Indians of the region followed suit, enabling Anglo-American forces under General Forbes to seize the Forks at the end of the year and restore peace to the Virginia–Pennsylvania frontier. Promises made by representatives of the crown at the Treaty of Easton – that following the war a well-regulated trade would be conducted west of the Appalachians and that white settlement would be prohibited in the region – would do much to structure events and to poison relationships within the empire during the coming years.

It was largely in the hope of regaining control over the Delawares and other Ohio Indians that the Iroquois League shifted its stance from neutrality to alliance with the British in 1759 – tipping the balance on the New York frontier enough to allow an Anglo-American expedition to take Fort Niagara, seize control of the Great Lakes, and cut off Canada from its interior Indian allies. Iroquois diplomats who preceded Jeffery Amherst's invading army down the St. Lawrence the following year persuaded the last Indian allies of New France to make peace and, indeed, to guide the approaching army through the Rapids of Richelieu, where a well-coordinated attack might well have destroyed the expedition. Stripped of the warriors without whom they could not resist the invading redcoats and provincial troops, French forces surrendered at Montréal in September 1760, without firing a shot.

Although great immediate advantages in trade and diplomatic gifts accrued to the Indians who abandoned their previous alliances with France and to those like the Iroquois who shifted from neutrality to active cooperation with the Anglo-Americans, the surrender of New France deprived native groups of the ability to play the British Empire off against the French – and, hence, of the means to preserve their autonomy. The Indians came to understand the tenuousness of their new position not long after the conquest of Canada, when Jeffery Amherst (over the strenuous objections of

Sir William Johnson) suspended the giving of diplomatic gifts, ended the trade in rum, restricted access to ammunition, and stopped the subsidies that had previously kept the prices of Indian trade goods low. Amherst did so in part out of necessity – the War Office had cut his budget without ceasing to make demands on him and his forces to support Britain's campaigns in the Caribbean – and in part because he intended to reform and civilize Indians by making them more industrious, particularly by arresting alcohol's destructive effects on their communities.

The Indians who understood themselves as having entered into an alliance with the British based on mutual respect could understand these measures only as treachery. Amherst was treating them as if they, not the French, had been conquered. Moreover, he was doing nothing to fulfill the promises made at the Treaty of Easton with respect to controlling white settlement in the interior. Between 1760 and early 1763, thousands of frontiersmen, whom long years of frontier warfare had made inveterate Indian haters, moved into the trans-Appalachian West. They came over roads that the army had constructed during the war and settled near forts the army still manned, growing crops to feed the garrisons. The army came to depend on them to such a degree that when white settlers killed Indians, military officials did little or nothing to find and punish the murderers.

Moderate native leaders, especially those from nations formerly allied with France, expected that the European peace treaties would restore Canada and Louisiana to French control, tried hard to control warriors who yearned to strike back at the invaders, and bided their time. But when news of the Peace of Paris arrived, they could no longer restrain the young men who followed Pontiac's example and attacked the interior posts to instruct the British in the proper behavior of ally to ally. By driving British troops from their forts and launching raids that embroiled the recently repopulated frontier in a new refugee crisis, the Indians compelled the British to rescind the offensive policies. Notwithstanding these spectacular successes, however, as early as 1764, it was unmistakably clear to native leaders that their ability to carry on a war was strictly limited. Without a competitor empire at hand to arm and supply them, they simply could not sustain resistance once they ran out of gunpowder, lead, and spare parts to repair their muskets. The Seven Years' War, which the Indians had understood as many local conflicts waged in parallel to the Anglo-French confrontation, had changed the face of North American politics and diplomacy forever. In ways that no native leader could have anticipated, its effects would reverberate through the next century, depriving Indians of the diplomatic and military power they had previously exercised to defend their ways of life and to shape their destiny on the continent.

In many ways, the reactions of the Anglo-American colonists to the new world order, announced by the Peace of Paris, paralleled those of the native peoples. Initially, their response to the great victories of 1759 and 1760 had been almost literally ecstatic. The Boston preacher, Jonathan Mayhew, was one of many divines who perceived nothing less than the dawn of the millennium in the defeat of France and the expulsion of the minions of Antichrist from North America. In a remarkable sermon preached at Boston following the Battle of Québec, he predicted a future in which the French would be completely subdued, while the Indians, freed from delusions of popery and heathenism, would become Protestants and adopt civilized ways. It was a vision of peace in which British North America would "by the continued blessing of heaven, in another century or two, become a mighty empire (I do not mean an independent one) in numbers little inferior to the greatest in Europe and in felicity to none."[39]

Mayhew was preaching to the converted, for New England had mobilized for war more fully than any other region in the British colonies. Modern estimates suggest that at least 40 percent, and perhaps as many as 60 percent, of Bay Colony and Connecticut men in the prime military age range of eighteen to twenty-nine served in provincial armies during one or more campaigns.[40] Although participation rates across the colonies as a whole were less extraordinary, they raised, on average, more than sixteen thousand men for provincial service annually in the critical years 1758–1760. The overwhelming majority were volunteers, attracted by wages that approximated those of civilian laborers and bounties that could double or even triple their total compensation. For these men, military service was a means of gaining money to help them advance to householdership and the economic independence that they called "competency."

The future they looked forward to was one in which no French and Indian enemy would threaten British frontiers, and they would be able to live in a real-world version of the millennial peace and prosperity that the Reverend Dr. Mayhew prophesied in the fall of 1759. Nor were provincial soldiers the only colonists who took part in the war or who anticipated a glowing future in the aftermath of victory: A number at least equal to the provincial troops raised, in every year of the war, served either in the British army as regulars enlisted for the duration; as crewmen on privateers; or as contractors, bateaumen, wagoners, artificers, sutlers, and other kinds

---

[39] "Two Discourses Delivered October 25th, 1759" (Boston, 1759), p. 60. [Digitized version, American Antiquarian Society and NewsBank, Inc., 2002; Early American Imprints, 1st series, no. 8417. Permanent URL http://docs.newsbank.com/openurl?ctx_ver=z39.88-2004&rft_id=info:sid/iw.newsbank.com:EVAN&rft_val_format=info:ofi/fmt:kev:mtx:ctx&rft_dat=0F301509468E2578&svc_dat=Evans:eaidoc&req_dat=0D0CB57A6677F68A].

[40] Anderson, *Crucible of War*, 288; also see Fred Anderson, *A People's Army: Massachusetts Soldiers and Society in the Seven Years' War* (Chapel Hill, NC, 1984), pp. 58–62; Fred Anderson, "A People's Army: Provincial Military Service in Massachusetts during the Seven Years' War," *William and Mary Quarterly*, 3d Ser., 40 (1983), 4: pp. 499–527; Harold Selesky, *War and Society in Colonial Connecticut* (New Haven, CT, 1990), pp. 166–70.

of camp followers employed by the armies. Taken together, it would seem that in the *anni mirabiles* of 1758–1760, the total number of British subjects under arms and active in war-related roles in America roughly equaled the entire *habitant* population of New France. The conflict in British America had been, to an extent perhaps unparalleled in the eighteenth century, a people's war.

Britain and the colonies could sustain such extraordinary levels of participation only because late in 1757 William Pitt had induced parliament to subsidize the colonial war effort by reimbursing colonial governments for a proportion – on average, approximately 40 percent – of their annual military expenditures. This policy reassured colonial legislators who had previously worried that the war might bankrupt their provinces, stimulated an economic boom in North America, and fostered a tremendous surge of patriotism among America's Britons. Canada's conquest did nothing to diminish their enthusiasm. Notwithstanding the return of safety to the frontiers and the elimination of virtually all direct enemy threat after 1760, more than nine thousand colonists enlisted as provincial soldiers in both 1761 and 1762 – numbers that suggest the Anglo-Americans had become enthusiastic participants in creating what they thought of as the most glorious empire since Rome.

Even before the Seven Years' War, the colonists' conception of their place in the British Empire had centered on the notion, best articulated by Benjamin Franklin, that the empire was in fact a trans-Atlantic partnership: a community of Britons who shared a common identity, heritage, language, interests, and rights, irrespective of on which side of the ocean they lived. This was not a view favored by British imperial administrators like the Earl of Halifax, an associate of the Duke of Bedford who had long been associated with a program of reform aimed at bringing coherence and efficiency to the Empire. The measures Halifax favored included restraining colonial settlement in the interior to diminish tensions between white settlers and natives. This was the rationale behind the prohibition of colonial settlements beyond the Appalachian crest in the Proclamation of 1763. Halifax also favored the imposition of mild colonial taxes to pay the salaries of administrative officials, such as governors and judges, whom the assemblies of their provinces had previously paid. Such financial support would immunize them to pressures from below and allow them to represent the sovereign king-in-Parliament with vigor and effectiveness.

These measures, which assumed the colonists were anything *but* the legal and constitutional equals of subjects who lived in England, seemed especially urgent in 1763, for two reasons. First, Pitt's win-the-war policies had granted the colonists exactly the sort of autonomy that encouraged them to imagine the empire was, in fact, a voluntary union of British patriots – notions that now seemed especially pernicious and in desperate need of correction.

Second, Pitt's strategies had nearly doubled the national debt, which was estimated at war's end to be £146 million sterling. In the first years of peace, interest payments alone consumed nearly half of the government's annual revenues, and the remainder barely covered the fixed costs of administration. The reformers agreed that Britain had no choice but to make the colonies bear their fair share of the expense of administering and defending the now vastly extended dominions of the crown in America. Nor, they agreed, was there any question that the king-in-Parliament, as the locus of sovereign power in the Empire, had the authority to impose the measures necessary to make the administration of the colonies honest, efficient, and fiscally sound.

This, then, was the context for the revenue measures that George Grenville pursued with fatal efficiency once he became prime minister after the resignation of the Earl of Bute in April 1763, with the Earl of Halifax, in office as Secretary of State for the South, to advise him on matters of imperial reorganization and reform. The Proclamation of 1763 and the revenue and reform measures that followed close behind all responded to the demands of the moment and reflected Grenville's and Halifax's senses of what the main lessons of the Seven Years' War had been. But they reflected those lessons as understood at the highest echelons of government, in Westminster and Whitehall, with no reference to the very different perspectives of the Americans who would feel their impact.

When Grenville, Halifax, and other metropolitan politicians asserted their hierarchical conception of empire as the new norm in the postwar period, colonists were shocked to find that the reforms being proposed were ones that seemingly recognized no limits on the exercise of sovereign power. The colonists, not surprisingly, phrased their protests in the republican language of British political opposition; lacking any other way to define constitutional limits to the exercise of metropolitan power, they virtually had to do so. What *was* surprising – or, at least, what astonished the metropolitan authorities – was the intensity and, indeed, the violence of the colonists' responses. One can best understand the emotional tenor of the Stamp Act protests and the later Townshend Acts and Tea Act boycotts as reflecting feelings of betrayal rooted in the recent experience of war and victory. The generation of men, who had shared the experience of war most directly, had, by the ordinary operation of the male life cycle, become householders and community leaders by the mid-1770s. What happened, they now wondered, to the patriotic union that had won the war? Why were lands they had helped win for the Empire suddenly reserved for the exclusive use of the Indians and the French? Why should they have to pay taxes to which they had not consented, when they had never refused to tax themselves for the empire's defense in the late war? Why did the ministry suddenly seem bent on treating them as if they were Britain's conquered instead of her fellow conquerors?

During the twelve years between the end of the war and the outbreak of fighting at Lexington and Concord, the colonists clarified their beliefs and articulated them in language sufficiently inclusive to build a broad base of support for opposition to the authority of a Parliament they blamed for deceiving the king and subverting their rights. In time, these same political principles would become the basis for a new political order, a republic, but those revolutionary implications remained latent until civil war had torn the Empire apart. What took place between 1763 and 1775 was a prolonged, increasingly acrimonious debate over what the Empire meant: a dispute over who belonged to it and on what terms of membership, a disagreement about whether it was to function according to voluntarist or coercive principles. Those debates grew so bitter *not* because the colonists wanted independence and certainly not because they had formed an American cultural identity but rather because they could think of themselves as nothing but British. It took more than a year of civil war to persuade the colonists that they were anything except the loyal, if aggrieved and inexplicably abused, subjects of the king.

CONCLUSION

Thus, a diplomatic attempt to restore the European balance of power by taking North America off the table of European imperial competition set in train events that would make North America the stage on which France exacted revenge from Britain for its humiliation in 1763. Britain had emerged from the Seven Years' War as the closest thing the eighteenth-century world had to a superpower and, despite Bedford's best efforts at Paris to reassure the nations of Europe that his sovereign wished only to establish a viable post-war international order, they sufficiently feared this emergent hegemon to align themselves against it. Conscientious British administrators undertook badly needed imperial reforms only to mystify and alienate the American colonists, uniting them against the authority of the metropolis. Then, when Britain finally applied its overwhelming military and naval power to cut the knot of colonial resistance by forcing the colonists to submit, it turned a resistance movement into a revolution. Force, and force alone, was the argument that finally convinced North America's Britons that shadowy metropolitan conspirators intended to enslave them and that the only way to preserve the rights they cherished was to take up arms and, ultimately, to secede from the British Empire.

The irony here is worth pondering. An epochal military victory and a seemingly definitive peace treaty, almost overnight, rained disaster after disaster on the victorious power. In general, it would seem clear that winning a great victory can create equally great dangers for the victor, if only because a decisive outcome in war can foster the illusion that military power is less limited and contingent than, in fact, it is. In this specific case, Bedford, Bute, and the others who created the postwar settlement confronted the further handicap of being able to see the war only as having affected relations among states, not as having profoundly altered the state of relations among groups *within* the empire. One should not necessarily fault them for this, for they had no analytical vocabulary available to characterize the inhabitants of the empire as anything but subjects of the sovereign power. Because they understood the sovereignty of king-in-Parliament as the unarguable, ultimate power of the state to take property and life in defense of public order, they could not recognize as valid, or even arguable, the constitutional principles that the colonists were struggling to articulate in defense of their political rights. Most damaging of all to their ability to deal with the crisis of empire that confronted them, however, was the powerful memory of a war in which Britain had reduced not one but two rival empires to submission: a memory that fatally inhibited their ability to grasp the limits of military power as applied *within* the empire.

Thus, *The Reign of George VI* makes it possible for us to measure the range of alternative approaches to peace and its preservation, as thoughtful Englishmen could understand them at the end of the Seven Years' War. Bedford, Bute, and the king accepted that the continuing risk France posed could be managed. France should continue to participate as before in European politics, provided that it could no longer make mischief in America. The author of the novel, in contrast, believed only unconditional surrender could remove the perennial threat that France posed for Britain. Nothing short of destroying the Bourbon monarchy and liberating the French nation could root out the kind of evil it represented. Neither the diplomatists nor the author could see war within the British Empire emerging from the peace because neither understood the Seven Years' War as having in any significant way altered conditions in the New World or as having affected the relationship among the metropolis, its colonies, and the native people of North America.

But, the Seven Years' War had, in fact, changed everything. The fantastic, unforeseeable developments that followed in its train – in North America, a revolution that created an imperial republic, which in seven decades' time extended its sway across the continent; in Britain, a new empire based on the successful application, in an Asiatic context, of the same principles that had torn the old Atlantic empire asunder; in France, a revolution that would generate both the empire of Napoleon and an ideological legacy that would reverberate through Europe and the world for another two centuries – could surely not have been arrested if the men who negotiated the Peace of Paris had written a different treaty from the one they did. But *that* they wrote the one they did, assuming that nothing fundamental had changed as a result of the war and that prudent adjustments to the existing system would therefore be sufficient to recover and sustain the peace, catalyzed the changes that followed, accelerating them toward the revolutions that would forever sweep away the world that Bedford, Choiseul, and Grimaldi had assumed was theirs to preserve.

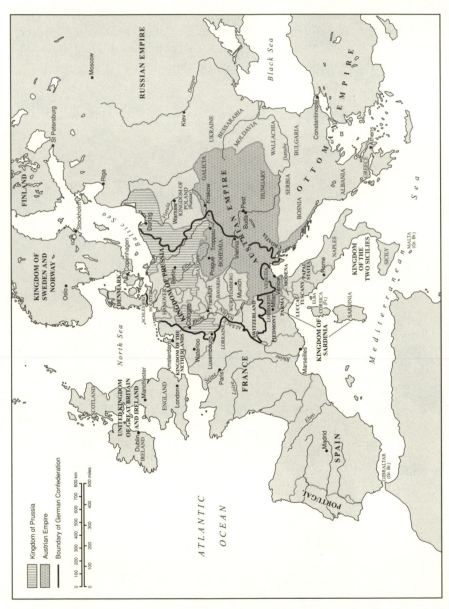

MAP 4. The settlement of 1815.

Kingdom of Prussia

Austrian Empire

Boundary of German Confederation

5

In search of military repose: the Congress of Vienna and the making of peace

RICHARD HART SINNREICH

> Whether or no one adopts the determinist view of history, whether or no one believes that events are influenced by individuals or individuals by events, it must be recognized that the combinations of circumstances are governed as much by invisible as by visible factors, as much by the unapparent as by the apparent.[1]

In September 1814, with Napoleon exiled to Elba and a Bourbon king installed once more on the throne of France, rulers and diplomats from virtually every European state and principality assembled in Vienna, capital of a diminished but still formidable Habsburg Empire, summoned by the victorious Allies to help settle political and territorial issues resulting from a quarter century of revolutionary and military upheaval.

This chapter offers only the barest sketch of the Congress of Vienna and the events that framed it. What took place in 1813–1815 among Napoleon's former allies and enemies – often one and the same – reflected a bewildering tangle of issues, interests, and personalities defying brief description. Nevertheless, the chapter's purpose is not to narrate that convoluted history in detail.[2] Rather, it seeks through an examination of the Congress and what followed to address a question with more contemporary relevance: How did those who gathered in Vienna from September 1814 through June 1815 manage despite daunting obstacles to negotiate, still more actually implement, a settlement that effectively prevented great power conflict in Europe for nearly forty years and contained it for another sixty years thereafter?

---

[1] Harold Nicolson, *The Congress of Vienna* (New York, 1946), p. viii.
[2] Tim Chapman, *The Congress of Vienna: Origins, Processes, and Results* (London, 1998) is agreeably short and readable. A more comprehensive but much lengthier history is Paul W. Schroeder's *The Transformation of European Politics 1763–1848* (Oxford, 1994). I have relied heavily on both.

"When the fate of empires is at stake," wrote Henry Kissinger in his doctoral dissertation, "the convictions of their statesmen are the medium for survival."[3] The settlement reached in Vienna reflected the convictions as well as the diplomatic skills of some extraordinary statesmen. They were men of their time, however, and in part because of that, their achievement has suffered a checkered reputation among both their successors and diplomatic historians.

Even its detractors acknowledge that the Congress's Final Act of June 1815, ratified again after Waterloo by the Second Treaty of Paris, produced the most enduring European peace since the emergence of the modern nation-state system more than 150 years earlier.[4] Only four significant European conflicts marred the remainder of the century. All were limited in objective, scale, and duration. None threatened the national survival or sovereignty of the major powers involved. Nevertheless, the agreements through which Vienna's principal actors achieved that condition of relative military quiescence were roundly attacked by late nineteenth-century historians as reactionary and shortsighted, contrary to the emerging liberal "spirit of the age" and thus doomed to eventual repudiation and renewed great power conflict.[5]

This chapter acknowledges both Vienna's prolonged success and its eventual failure. But it argues that neither was a product solely of the convictions and talents of the statesmen who labored there, however prescient or shortsighted they may have been. Success and failure also reflected an underlying conflict dynamic that independent of political beliefs and diplomatic deftness, intrinsically affects belligerents' ability to control war's outbreak, conduct, and results. That the great powers that were Vienna's principal beneficiaries failed in the end to modulate that dynamic successfully is not surprising. Their modern successors have done little better, with a good deal less excuse.

WAR AND ITS ENVIRONMENT

If wars between civilized nations are far less cruel and destructive than wars between savages, the reason lies in the social conditions of the states themselves and in their relationships to one another. These are the forces that give rise to war; the same forces circumscribe and moderate it.[6]

---

[3] Henry Kissinger, *A World Restored* (Boston, 1973), p. 8.
[4] Generally dated by scholars to the 1648 Peace of Westphalia ending the Thirty Years' War.
[5] Twentieth-century historians have been more generous, unsurprisingly given the convulsions of their own era.
[6] Carl von Clausewitz, *On War*, ed. and trans. by Michael Howard and Peter Paret (Princeton, NJ, 1976), p. 76.

War, Clausewitz informs us, comprises a "remarkable trinity" oscillating continuously among the competing pressures of unfettered violence, the unpredictable but decipherable fortunes of war, and the deliberate aims of state policy. The first of these pressures, he argues, arises from individual and collective human passions, while the second reflects and furnishes scope for the creativity and energy of armies and their commanders. The last, however, derives – or should – from reasoned political goals, which, he asserts, "are the business of government alone."[7]

In its clarity and simplicity, Clausewitz's trinity is easily the most compelling model of war ever conceived.[8] Among other contributions, it helps explain why war's outbreak and termination so often fail to conform to rationalist theories of human behavior,[9] and why neither generalship nor statesmanship invariably dictates its outcome. Above all, his analogy of war to an object suspended amid three magnetic poles suggests that any change in the relative influence of human passions, military behavior, and reasoned policy perforce will profoundly affect both the conduct of war and the making of peace.

In fact, history suggests that variations in those influences, and especially between the first and last, tend to produce two alternating and wholly different strategic environments, which Kissinger and others have denoted "legitimate" and "revolutionary." "A legitimate order," Kissinger argued, "does not make conflicts impossible, but it limits their scope. Wars may occur, but they will be fought in the name of the existing structure and the peace which follows will be justified as a better expression of the 'legitimate,' general consensus." In a revolutionary environment, in contrast, "it is not the adjustment of differences within a given system which will be at issue, but the system itself. Adjustments are possible, but [only] as tactical maneuvers to consolidate positions for the inevitable showdown, or as tools to undermine the morale of the antagonist."[10]

Beginning with the Treaties of Westphalia in 1648, Europe has seen three such shifts from a revolutionary to a legitimate environment and from total to limited conflict. In all three cases, the motive force was a war or series of wars so long and exhausting that it produced a tacit agreement by the

---

[7] Ibid., p. 89.
[8] Which has not prevented critics like Sir John Keegan from attacking *On War* as an anachronism. See Christopher Bassford, "John Keegan and the Grand Tradition of Trashing Clausewitz." *War in History*, November 1994, pp. 319–36. Perhaps its most eloquent defender is Colin Gray. See "Clausewitz, History, and the Future Strategic World," in *The Past as Prologue*, ed. by Williamson Murray and Richard Hart Sinnreich (Cambridge, 2006), pp. 117–18.
[9] For an alternative explanation, see Graham Allison, *The Essence of Decision* (Boston, 1971).
[10] Kissinger, *A World Restored*, p. 2.

survivors to discipline their territorial and/or ideological ambitions in return for military repose. And in all three cases, the result was not a peace wholly free of conflict but rather an informal commitment to forms of military competition that while limiting contestants' strategic returns, also bounded their strategic risks.

The settlement of 1815 signaled precisely such a shift, just as Westphalia had done 166 years earlier and Lake Success would do 131 years later. Of the three, however, Vienna was probably the most successful. As one appraisal states, "[j]udged primarily not on how well it met the demands of rulers, élites, and the general populace, but on how well it faced and met the permanent, structural problems of international politics.... [no] other general peace settlement in European history... comes anywhere close to [its] record."[11]

In part, that was because in Vienna, to an extent we scarcely can imagine today, the settlement producing the shift was largely "the business of government alone." The plenipotentiaries who assembled in Vienna in 1814 were almost entirely unfettered by public opinion, reflecting both limited information mechanisms and the character of the governments they represented.[12] Alone, Britain's Robert Viscount Castlereagh labored at some risk of political disavowal, and that threat ultimately materialized only after Vienna.

Not so for their successors. In the century after Waterloo, war aims increasingly ceased to be wholly controllable even by autocratic rulers. As political power diffused, as ideology began to supplant *raisons d'état*, and as dependence on mass armies and the growing industrialization of military power held the conduct of war increasingly hostage to popular as well as élite support, so too the aims to which war was directed. Meanwhile, exploding communications progressively eroded the insulation of national publics from the fortunes of war and of military commanders and statesmen from the resulting domestic pressures.

Partly in consequence but even more because, during a century of relative peace, both nations and their rulers tended to forget the afflictions that had prompted it when Europe's great powers marched to war once again in August 1914, their political and military leaders' confidence in their ability to control its intensity, costs, and duration proved fatally mistaken and so also, in the end, their ability to dictate its results.

That, unfortunately, was by no means the last such episode. On the contrary, since 1945, making peace successfully has proved increasingly difficult,

---

[11]   Schroeder, *The Transformation of European Politics, 1763–1848*, p. 577.
[12]   Sir Charles Webster, *The Congress of Vienna* (New York, 1963), pp. 22–6. Webster's actually is the earlier (1919) of two excellent histories of the Congress by former British scholar–diplomats (Nicolson's, cited earlier, is the second). Significantly, each was written in the wake of a world war.

at least if one defines "successful" to include "enduring." If, as one writer recently has argued, "war termination may be more vital in its implications for the international system than how wars begin,"[13] it would be difficult to imagine a more compelling reason to revisit one of history's most enduring settlements.

BACKGROUND TO THE CONGRESS

> If we wish to learn from history, we must realize that what happened once can happen again; and anyone with judgment in these matters will agree that the chain of great events that followed the march on Moscow was no mere succession of accidents.... It was a vast success; and it cost the Russians a price in blood and perils that for any other country would have been higher still, and which most could not have paid at all.[14]

The French Revolution and its military aftermath radically altered the map of Europe. By the beginning of 1812, with Napoleon at the apex of his power, France dominated the European continent from the North Sea to the Mediterranean and from the Atlantic to the Russian frontier. In Western Europe, only Sweden in the north and the Iberian Peninsula in the south continued to resist French domination, the former ruled by a former Bonapartist general, the latter a ferocious battleground between occupying French armies and Spanish insurgents sustained by British troops, arms, and money.[15] In Eastern Europe, the French had dismembered Frederick the Great's Prussia, dissolved the once-powerful Holy Roman Empire, and militarily emasculated its Austrian inheritor. To all intents and purposes, Eastern Europe south of the Baltic, north of the Ottoman Empire, and west of Russia had become a French dependency.

Then, on June 24, 1812, angered by Czar Alexander I's growing obstinacy and his refusal to conform to the decrees of the Continental System,[16] Napoleon crossed the River Nieman into Russia with an army of more than half a million men. Discounting Russian political and military stamina, like the rest of Europe, he confidently anticipated Alexander's rapid capitulation.

Instead, before the year ended, fewer than twenty-five thousand tattered survivors of the *Grande Armée* escaped Russian territory only hours ahead of their vengeful pursuers. The magnitude of the French disaster and its

---

13 Audrey Kurth Cronin, "How al–Qaida Ends," *International Security*, Summer 2006, p. 8.
14 Clausewitz, *On War*, p. 616.
15 Napoleon called the war his "Spanish ulcer" with good reason. French costs in men and money from 1808 to 1814 were staggering. For a comprehensive treatment, see David Gates, *The Spanish Ulcer* (New York, 1986).
16 An economic embargo intended to weaken Britain by depriving her merchants of European markets and products.

revelation of Napoleon's vulnerability shook chancelleries across Europe. Setting aside earlier defeats at his hands and their own habitual enmity, Austria and Prussia joined with Russia, Sweden, and Britain in the last of a long series of anti-French coalitions and, after another year of fighting culminating in the Battle of Leipzig on October 18, 1813, finally forced Napoleon back on French soil.

Five months later, shrugging off the emperor's brilliant but futile last-ditch maneuvers, Allied armies entered Paris.[17] At the Palace of Fontainebleau on the morning of April 13, 1814, threatened from north and south, bereft of resources, deserted by his generals, and having unsuccessfully attempted suicide, a bitter but resigned Bonaparte scrawled his signature on a treaty abdicating the throne of France and renouncing any further dominion "over the French Empire and the Kingdom of Italy, as over any other country."[18]

By any standard, the Treaty of Fontainebleau was astonishingly lenient with the upstart Corsican who had terrorized aristocratic Europe for the better part of two decades.[19] It allowed Napoleon and Marie-Louise to retain their imperial ranks and titles. It granted Elba to him and the Duchy of Parma to her in perpetuity, together with a lifetime pension from the French government of 2 million francs a year. Finally, it permitted Napoleon to take a modest guard of French soldiers with him to Elba and retain the ship transporting them. The treaty made equally generous provision for his extended family.[20]

But, while (presumably) disposing of Bonaparte, Fontainebleau left unresolved the question of who would rule France in his wake and under what constitutional provisions. Beyond this troublesome question, moreover, far more serious issues divided the victorious Allies, from the governance of the Low Countries and of Germany's numerous states and principalities; to the future of thrice-partitioned Poland, now occupied by Russian armies; to the sovereignty of the Piedmont and the Italian city-states; to the disposition of France's overseas colonies, many seized during the war by Britain. Resolution of these and other territorial and political issues was made no easier by their varying importance to the several Allies and by the existence of prior commitments between and among those Allies to which not all of them and none of the other states affected were party.[21]

---

[17] Even Wellington praised Bonaparte's final operations as "excellent, quite excellent." Nicolson, *The Congress of Vienna,* p. 83.

[18] Ibid., p. 95.

[19] The terms were negotiated almost unilaterally by Alexander. His Allies were by no means as comfortable as he was with the selection of Elba as Napoleon's retirement home, Metternich in particular warning that leaving Bonaparte so close to France invited another war within two years. Susan Mary Alsop, *The Congress Dances* (New York, 1984), p. 66.

[20] Including an annual stipend of a million francs to his former Empress Josephine.

[21] Notably the treaties of Kalisch (February 1813, Russia and Prussia), Reichenbach (June 1813, Russia, Prussia, and Austria), Teplitz (September 1813, Russia, Prussia, and Austria),

For Russia, after France's defeat the most powerful nation on the continent, honor and interest required some intrinsic acknowledgment of her enlarged stature, as well as reparation for the damages inflicted by Napoleon's brief but costly invasion. In addition, Alexander professed himself committed to resurrecting a Polish kingdom, which the powers had erased from the map by successive partitions among Prussia, Austria, and Russia herself. Historians differ concerning how much this reflected a genuine if romantic liberalism and how much a more cynical acquisitiveness. The answer probably was some of both. "[T]he tension between liberalism and autocracy [was] deeply rooted in Alexander's personality – his wish, to paraphrase Czartoryski, that the whole world should be free to do what he wanted."[22]

For Prussia, humiliated by military defeat at Jena–Auerstadt in 1806, reduced by the Treaty of Tilsit less than a year later to four impoverished provinces and wracked by domestic unrest, the desire for revenge and territorial aggrandizement compounded the urgent need to refurbish King Frederick William's domestic reputation, tarnished by his repeated submission to Napoleon's impositions and insults.[23] Alexander's Polish ambitions, underwritten by Russia's military occupation of formerly Prussian Poland, offered little hope of the latter's return to its previous master. Prussia, accordingly, sought territorial compensation in Germany, specifically in Saxony and the northern Rhineland.

That ambition, however, put Prussia at loggerheads with Austria, equally fearful of Prussian expansion southward and Russian expansion westward, and which, while happy to see Napoleon's back, shared none of Prussia's visceral hatred of the French.[24] Above all, for Habsburg Austria with its polyglot nationalities, no settlement would be acceptable that encouraged nationalism and self-determination. Instead, for Austria's Francis I and his equally conservative foreign minister, Prince Clemens von Metternich, any durable settlement would require restoring as far as possible the political and territorial *status quo ante bellum*.

In turn, that objective initially put Austria at odds with Britain, Napoleon's most remorseless enemy and the principal financial if not military author of his defeat. Apart from ridding France of Bonaparte and

and Chaumont (March 1814, Russia, Prussia, Austria, and Great Britain). In all but the last, the future of Poland was a central issue.

22   Schroeder, *The Transformation of European Politics*, p. 504.
23   "[F]ear underlay Prussia's policy and ambitions in general, a consciousness that its power base was fragile and its great-power status marginal. More than once, Frederick remarked that Prussia's crest should feature a monkey rather than an eagle, for it could only ape the great powers." Ibid., p. 24.
24   As Webster noted concerning Prince Hardenberg, "Like all Prussians, he expressed always, and without abatement, an undying hatred of France, which no victories or conquests could assuage." Webster, *The Congress of Vienna*, p. 25.

depriving it of possession of the Low Countries and their Channel ports,[25] British concerns focused almost exclusively on retention of its maritime supremacy, preventing external domination of the Iberian Peninsula and Sweden at the gateways to the Mediterranean and Baltic, respectively, and satisfying domestic pressures to abolish the African slave trade. Beyond that, the acute preference of its politicians and public alike to avoid permanent continental military entanglements heavily counterbalanced Britain's interest in Europe's internal security arrangements. As one historian noted, "Behind the moderate and sensible Castlereagh stood a Cabinet, a Prince Regent, a Parliament, and a public whose war aims were to defeat France and strip it of its conquests, overthrow Napoleon, perhaps through a revolution within France, restore the Bourbons and a so-called balance of power, and then leave Europe to its devices."[26]

Finally, no settlement was likely to endure without the cooperation of France herself, a reality that all the Allies apart from Austria initially had difficulty accepting, and to which Prussia especially never was wholly reconciled. Even reduced to her "ancient" territorial limits, France was too large, too populous, and too strategically positioned to ignore. In foreign minister Charles Maurice de Talleyrand, moreover, France enjoyed the services of a negotiator easily the equal of any Allied diplomat in skill, subtlety, and determination. One way or another, France's interests, chiefly that it neither be humiliated politically nor denied representation in determining Europe's future, would have to be accommodated.

All of these conflicting interests and pressures were in play long before Napoleon abdicated, and only the well-founded belief that he would instantly exploit any perceived breach in Allied unity prevented the rupturing of the coalition before hostilities ended. In February 1814, in fact, they nearly did, when the czar, determined to seize Paris in revenge for Bonaparte's occupation of Moscow, threatened to disregard his allies' objections and install Sweden's Crown Prince Bernadotte on the throne of France with or without their concurrence or the acquiescence of the French people.

The effect was to throw Britain and Austria together for the first time as partners in restraining Russia. Metternich's threat to withdraw Austrian forces from the combined armies and Castlereagh's promise of continued British subsidies finally convinced the czar to compromise; and, at Chaumont on March 9, deferring the question of France's eventual governance, the four powers committed themselves not to make a separate peace until France had

---

25 The port of Antwerp was the chief concern, regarding which Castlereagh warned his colleague Aberdeen that "The destruction of that arsenal is essential to our safety. To leave it in the hands of France is little short of imposing on Great Britain the charge of a perpetual war establishment." Ibid., p. 32.

26 Schroeder, *The Transformation of European Politics*, p. 486.

been reduced to her ancient geographic limits and – what would become equally important in the long run – to collaborate in keeping her inside those limits thereafter.[27] Even so, as one historian notes, "The four great powers that signed the Treaty of Chaumont were reluctant allies, made to co-operate only in extreme need. They came together not to help each other but simply to defeat France after twenty years of largely unsuccessful wars in which the individual pursuit of separate aims had failed."[28]

After Fontainebleau, however, with Napoleon eliminated from the equation, Prussia's Prince Hardenberg proposed a settlement that threatened to unravel that fragile mutual commitment. In effect, with minor changes, he demanded implementation of 1813's secret Kalisch Accord between Prussia and Russia, giving the latter a free hand in Poland in return for Prussia's acquisition of most of northern and central Germany, including Saxony[29] and Westphalia. The Austrians would find themselves compensated for the loss of the Austrian Netherlands and its former Polish provinces by accessions in Italy and the Tyrol, while the remaining German principalities, in particular Bavaria, Hanover, and Württemberg, would be required to federate in some fashion.

Hardenberg's proposal represented an unapologetic return to the previous century's pattern of territorial forfeits and indemnities, a pattern that "regularly helped make eighteenth-century alliances, whether defensive or offensive, into power-political instruments designed for ... expansion and acquisitions as well as mutual security."[30] Like earlier such settlements that, grounded in no legitimizing principle, invariably sooner or later were repudiated producing a new round of hostilities, Hardenberg's scheme threatened to sacrifice any prospect of durable peace to Prussia's desire for revenge on France and its ambition to replace Austria as Germany's dominant power.

Meanwhile, neither Austria nor Britain had been party to Kalisch.[31] To both states, for different reasons, its provisions were strategically unacceptable. To Britain, Hardenberg's proposal was objectionable, above all, for what it failed to address, particularly deterrence of renewed French aggression and Britain's maritime concerns. For Austria, the expansion of

---

[27] Other clauses included restoring the Bourbons to Spain and enlarging Holland, but those cited were key.

[28] Chapman, *The Congress of Vienna*, p. 31. Castlereagh considered Chaumont with some justice to be his particular achievement. As Schroeder points out, however, Napoleon himself deserved much of the credit. Schroeder, *The Transformation of European Politics*, pp. 500–504.

[29] Whose prince loyally but unwisely had refused to abandon Napoleon until made prisoner by the Allies.

[30] Schroeder, *The Transformation of European Politics*, p. 7.

[31] Instead, in the treaties of Reichenbach joining Austria to the coalition and of Chaumont formalizing the Quadruple Alliance, Poland's future intentionally had been left ambiguous, its disposition to be determined "amicably" among the Allies.

Prussia southward and of Russian power westward both threatened its strategic position. Even more dangerous, from Metternich's perspective if not his generals', was Alexander's quixotic ambition, encouraged by reformist advisers like Poland's Adam Czartoryski and Prussia's Karl vom Stein, to reunify Poland as a constitutional monarchy, injecting the seductive poison of national self-determination into Central Europe. For his part, the czar was not to be satisfied only with the Duchy of Warsaw; where the rest of his resurrected Kingdom of Poland would come from was only too apparent.

Unable in Paris to resolve these differences, and with France becoming restive under Talleyrand's caretaker administration (and he himself seeking a freer diplomatic hand), the Allies decided to postpone resolution of the broader European issues in favor of settling the immediate problem of who would rule France. With Prussia and Britain firmly opposed to any sort of Bonapartist succession, and at Talleyrand's urging, the Allies finally agreed to restore France's Bourbon monarchy in the person of Louis XVIII, subject to a charter not unlike that adopted by the French prior to the regicide of his unhappy elder brother.[32]

Ratified on May 30, 1814, the first Treaty of Paris, like that of Fontainebleau, was extraordinarily magnanimous. Though it stripped France of her Napoleonic conquests and compelled her to surrender several colonies, the treaty actually added modestly to her pre-revolutionary territory.[33] It imposed no monetary indemnity and even allowed the Louvre to retain artworks looted during Bonaparte's campaigns. Finally, apart from confirming the independence of the Netherlands and restoring the King of Sardinia to the Piedmont, the treaty deferred resolution of major territorial issues associated with erecting Castlereagh's "real and permanent balance of power" to a subsequent Europe-wide congress, to be held in Vienna that fall. "This," Harold Nicholson suggests, "was a diplomatic formula for stating that the Polish question had been shelved and that when eventually it came up for discussion France would not be permitted to intervene."[34]

Ironically, it ended by having precisely the opposite result. By settling France's territorial limits and thus assuring her ejection from the Low Countries, the treaty instantly diminished the continental Allies' diplomatic leverage against Britain. Meanwhile, by inviting to Vienna delegates from "all the powers engaged on either side of the late war," it implied discussions

---

[32]   Which Louis XVIII promptly rejected as an intrusion on his royal prerogatives but much of which he eventually grudgingly accepted.

[33]   Principally by boundary adjustments and by a decision not to return French papal territories to Rome.

[34]   Nicolson, *The Congress of Vienna*, p. 100.

far broader than just the reconciliation and ratification of the Allies' own prior agreements. It thus almost automatically promised to reopen territorial questions which Russia and especially Prussia had considered settled and that they strongly desired to keep closed. Finally, as Talleyrand had foreseen, with France no longer a belligerent, the powers could not reasonably exclude her from discussions concerning overall European arrangements. Moreover, allowed no territorial claims of her own, France's apparent disinterest would only lend her voice weight.

The czar's undiplomatic behavior during the interval between the signing of the Treaty of Paris and the assembly of plenipotentiaries in Vienna only compounded his and Prussia's strategic shortsightedness in allowing the postponement of contested issues such as Poland and Saxony. Before leaving Paris, annoyed by Louis XVIII's careless public attribution of his royal restoration to British efforts and what Alexander with some justification considered cavalier treatment during a visit to Compèigne to welcome Louis back to France, the Czar infuriated the new king by paying public court to Marie–Louise, Josephine, and other prominent Bonapartes. Then, during his subsequent visit to London, even while being lionized by the British public, he and his entourage managed repeatedly to offend both the Prince Regent and the Liverpool government.[35]

Why he behaved that way, no one was quite sure. "So far as his motives were political and not personal," wrote Sir Charles Webster, "he seems to have thought that he could best win support for his Polish schemes by an alliance with the leaders of the Opposition, while the unpopularity of the Prince Regent and some of his ministers may have given him the idea that the Tories would not remain long in power. If these were his motives, never was a greater political mistake committed."[36] Indeed, whatever his motives, the result was to drive Britain even closer to Austria and, thus, also – ironically but inevitably – closer to France.

THE CONGRESS

When the Powers, by Article XXXII of the Treaty of Paris, agreed that the settlement of European affairs should be regulated at a Congress, they struck the imagination of all Europe. The peoples did not know of the first secret article by which the Allied powers intended to keep affairs in their own hands . . . they looked on the Congress as a constituent body of Europe which should settle on

---

[35] Liverpool was so incensed by the Czar's sister's insolent behavior at one state dinner – to which she invited herself – that he reportedly admonished the wife of the Russian ambassador, "When folks don't know how to behave, they would do better to stay home." Ibid., p. 116.

[36] Webster, *The Congress of Vienna*, p. 67.

lofty principles of justice and equity the great problems resulting from twenty years of war.[37]

In September 1814, Vienna, then a city of around 200,000 souls, found itself invaded not by an army but instead by a horde of foreign dignitaries and their retinues.[38] Virtually every European principality sent delegates, together with nearly as many uninvited groups ranging from a deputation of German Jews to a petitioner for the dispossessed Knights of Malta. History records that the Hofburg alone played host to "an Emperor, an Empress, four Kings, one Queen, two Hereditary Princes, three Grand Duchesses, and three Princes of the Blood,"[39] while 200-odd lesser princes and their entourages, to say nothing of mere diplomats and their families, had to make do with more modest accommodations. An army might have been easier to manage and certainly would have been cheaper. The care and feeding of this self-important multitude presented a major financial and logistical burden. As Nicolson notes, "The affluence of so many otiose visitors to Vienna created serious problems of housing, maintenance, and expense."[40] The Congress's not altogether unjustified reputation as a prolonged bacchanalia for Europe's nobility financed by Vienna's hapless burghers in no small part reflected these problems.

More immediately important, however, the superabundance of delegations created an organizational problem for which the convening Allied powers were wholly unprepared. "[T]he invitation had been given and accepted by all the States of Europe; and the great powers were committed to admit them in some way to their councils. . . . [But they arrived] only to find no principle which should govern their procedure and no machinery by which they could be made into a coherent body."[41] As Talleyrand commented mordantly on arrival in a report to Louis XVIII, "Not even the English, whom I thought more methodical than the others, have done any preparatory work on this subject."[42]

Assembling in Vienna by prior agreement two weeks before the Congress's scheduled convocation on October 1, the Allied ministers found themselves frantically playing procedural catch-up. By a secret article of the Treaty

---

[37] Ibid., p. 73.

[38] No formal census was taken, but some estimate that the city's population temporarily increased by as much as half. Also, *The Congress Dances*, pp. 90–1. See also Hilde Spiel, ed., *The Congress of Vienna: An Eyewitness Account*, trans. by Richard H. Weber (London, 1968), p. xv.

[39] Nicolson, *The Congress of Vienna*, p. 160.

[40] Ibid., p. 133. Costs to the Austrian civil list for entertainment alone were estimated at the time to be between 30 million and 40 million florins (roughly $10 million to 12 million in today's dollars). To help cover them, a 50 percent trade tax was imposed on both the Viennese and their visitors. Spiel, *The Congress of Vienna*, p. xiv.

[41] Webster, *The Congress of Vienna*, p. 74.

[42] Nicolson, *The Congress of Vienna*, p. 137.

of Paris, reaffirmed in a later protocol drafted by Prussia specifically to preclude French influence on the negotiations, they had agreed to retain control of major territorial questions among themselves. The problem they now faced was how to impose that readily contestable resolve on a collection of delegations much larger and potentially more unruly than any of them had anticipated.

Their initial solution was to declare themselves and, at Castlereagh's insistence, France and Spain, "great powers" in relation to the smaller states and adopt a procedure by which decisions agreed to by the Allies would first be shared with the French and Spanish delegates, then presented by all six to the full Congress for formal ratification. In addition, a committee of the principal German states – Prussia, Austria, Bavaria, Hanover, and Württemberg – would be constituted to design some form of German federation.

All of this, of course, presumed Spanish and especially French acquiescence; neither was forthcoming. On the contrary, informed of the proposed procedure at a lengthy and contentious meeting with the Allied ministers on September 30, Talleyrand and Spain's Don Pedro Labrador both balked.[43] The Allies had pledged to convene the entire Congress on October 1, Talleyrand reminded them pointedly, and added with impeccable logic that peace having mooted the Quadruple Alliance, the only credible authority apart from the Congress itself, upon which a smaller directing council might conceivably have rested, was the Treaty of Paris – to which, he pointed out, Portugal and Sweden also were signatories.

Unprepared for so direct a challenge to the legitimacy of the Congress even before it convened, the Allies had little choice but to postpone its commencement.[44] There followed a prolonged and, for the Allies, intensely frustrating diplomatic ballet in which Talleyrand, appointing himself guardian of the interests of the smaller states, repeatedly demanded that the Congress convene in its entirety.

This, above all, the Allies were determined to avoid. As Webster notes, "Hardenburg was clearly on unshakeable ground when he said that no plan could be considered which would give the minor princelings the right to interfere in the general arrangements of Europe."[45] In self-defense, the Allies chose instead to begin including Talleyrand in their deliberations, upon which he promptly abandoned his guardianship pretensions.

Annoying though the Allies certainly found it, Talleyrand's successful opportunism merely underlined their acute sensitivity to a challenge, even

---

[43] Metternich's assistant Von Gentz recorded in his diary that "Talleyrand protested against the procedure we have adopted and soundly rated us for two hours. It was a scene I shall never forget." Alsop, *The Congress Dances*, p. 120.

[44] As it turned out, effectively indefinitely. It convened officially on June 9, 1815, only to ratify the Final Act.

[45] Webster, *The Congress of Vienna*, p. 87.

by a defeated former enemy, to the perceived legitimacy of the settlement process, and their profound reluctance to risk a similar challenge to its outcome. "[T]he doctrine of legitimacy was often restricted, twisted, manipulated, and shunted aside at Vienna, not least by Talleyrand himself. But in its real meaning – the rule of law, not the divine right of kings – it was widely believed, followed, and practiced at Vienna."[46]

Meanwhile, business had somehow to be transacted and was. Although, as one historian has noted, "[i]t seems inconceivable that after such a violently contentious meeting, the statesmen involved should have continued their daily round of festivities as though nothing had happened," she notes perceptively that in 1814 "there were no eager reporters on the scene to track down the story of Talleyrand's disruption of the plans of the Big Four, there were no press conferences, no television cameras."[47]

Instead, negotiations took place privately and informally in the drawing rooms and dining rooms – and, occasionally, the boudoirs – of the various delegations and at the nonstop balls, hunts, concerts, sleigh rides, and other entertainments devised by the beleaguered Austrians in a desperate effort to occupy the time and energies of several thousand largely unemployed dignitaries and their families. Throughout, diplomatic notes, memoranda, and rumors flew back and forth like confetti.

Eventually, the Congress established formal committees to address Germany, Tuscany, Genoa and Sardinia, the Duchy of Bouillion, the slave trade, and international rivers, along with a committee on diplomatic precedence, a statistical committee to establish agreed population numbers, and a drafting committee. All were organized *ad hoc*. "[T]he organisation for the transaction of business grew out of the necessities of the situation; and machinery was set up which derived its authority from no consistent principle."[48]

For the most divisive questions, however – the dispositions of Poland and Saxony – there would be no committees. The Allies alone could settle those issues, or so they believed, and until they had, not much else in the way of territorial adjustments would occur. Like the proverbial house of cards, "On the question of Poland depended the fate of Saxony; and on the disposal of Saxony depended all the other arrangements in Germany, so that the frontier of almost every German State was likely to be affected."[49]

At the heart of the Polish–Saxon problem was the question of whether, in the face of Prussian–Austrian rivalry, the smaller German principalities' self-importance, Alexander's ambitions, and Britain's indifference, some stable equilibrium could be erected in Central Europe and, if so, in what form.

---

[46] Schroeder, *The Transformation of European Politics*, p. 530.
[47] Alsop, *The Congress Dances*, p. 122.
[48] Webster, *The Congress of Vienna*, pp. 90–1.
[49] Ibid., p. 75.

Such an arrangement was unlikely to survive a resurrected Poland, in the true independence of which, notwithstanding Alexander's romantic dreams, none of the other Allies believed for a moment. Poland had been partitioned in the first place thanks in no small part to the persistent unruliness of its nobility. Reformers like Czartoryski and nationalists like Kosciusko notwithstanding, no evidence promised that a restored Poland would be any better behaved. In 1814, a reunified Poland could survive only as the appendage of a stronger power, and that power could only be Russia.

Instead, for Metternich especially, insulation simultaneously from threats north, east, and west could be assured only by some form of concert among the German states. In the end, real unification awaited Bismarck. However, to avoid what he perceived as the greater threat of a reconstituted Poland, Metternich was willing to subordinate his own and his generals' distrust of Prussia.[50] Accordingly, on October 22, 1814, he informed Hardenberg that Austria would agree to Prussia's digestion of Saxony (but not Westphalia) in return for support against Russia's ambitions in Poland. The offer encouraged Castlereagh to believe that, together, his allies might convince Alexander to reconsider.

That hope vanished almost immediately. Belabored by a furious Alexander, Prussia's King Frederick William repudiated Hardenberg and ordered him to break off private discussions with Castlereagh and Metternich. Meanwhile, back in London, alerted by Alexander's agents, Britain's Whig opposition loudly attacked Castlereagh for exceeding his instructions and the government for seeking to rob the "good old King of Saxony" of his throne. During parliamentary debate on November 8, opposition leader Samuel Whitbread thundered that "the annexation of Saxony by Prussia would be as unprincipled a partition as the world ever saw"[51] and warned that opposing Alexander's beneficent desire to reestablish Poland's independence was not only morally unconscionable but also risked transforming Russia from an ally into an enemy, inviting another war.

The uproar produced the only directive instructions Castlereagh received during the entire Congress. On November 27, in a note drafted for the cabinet, Lord Henry Bathurst, Secretary of State for War, warned him that "It is unnecessary for me to point out to you the impossibility of His Royal Highness consenting to involve this country in hostilities at this time for any objects which have hitherto been under discussion at Vienna."[52]

---

[50] As Schroeder points out, "Austria could tolerate a major expansion of Russian power, but not a Polish Kingdom; it would breed Polish nationalism and revolution and make Poland ungovernable for Russia, Austria, and Prussia alike." Schroeder, *The Transformation of European Politics*, pp. 525–6. Worse, such a disease threatened to spread.

[51] Nicolson, *The Congress of Vienna*, p. 183. A disingenuous exaggeration given the competition for that honor, starting with Poland.

[52] Webster, *The Congress of Vienna*, p. 107.

It also was pointless. Undeterred, in less than a month Castlereagh would propose to do just that. The central problem for both Britain and Austria was Alexander, who, to the intense frustration of the other Allies and his own ministers alike, insisted on acting as his own negotiator. In Susan Mary Alsop's description, "[h]e appeared to trust no one, least of all his own foreign minister. The other ministers would obtain Nesselrode's agreement on a point at issue at their daily conference, only to have the Czar reverse the decision that very evening."[53] Polite efforts by Castlereagh to persuade Alexander that self-restraint in the matter of Poland offered the only hope of restoring a stable European equilibrium predictably went nowhere. Nor, having grounded his argument in the balance of power, could he easily rebut the Czar's shrewd counterargument that, with France diminished as a continental power, Russia now alone balanced Britain's undisputed maritime supremacy.

Meanwhile, the social festivities continued nonstop, prompting the Prince de Ligne's classic diplomatic putdown, "*Le congrès danse, mais il ne marche pas.*"[54] Disconsolately advising London of his failure to sway Alexander, Castlereagh instead sought some way to bring Austria and Prussia to terms. It was a quixotic effort unless both were willing to modify their claims: Prussia by accepting less of Saxony and the Rhineland than Prussian generals demanded, Austria by conceding Prussia more of both than Austrian generals were willing to countenance. By the beginning of December, discussions on both Poland and Saxony were deadlocked and tempers were rising. On December 5, Castlereagh warned Liverpool that renewed war was entirely possible, this time among the former allies, and that should it erupt, Britain almost certainly would be unable to remain aloof.

The situation was made to order for Talleyrand, who, rightly judging Prussia a greater future threat to France than Russia, also recognized that in opposing Prussia's annexation of Saxony on the argument that its king's legitimate sovereignty must be preserved, he would at the same time establish grounds for ousting the detested Murat from Naples.[55] He therefore convinced Louis XVIII to order a partial mobilization. At the same time, to woo Castlereagh, he formally endorsed Britain's commitment to abolish the African slave trade.

Finally, temporarily reassuming his mantle as protector of the smaller German states, he threatened to convince them to denounce Prussia collectively

---

[53] Alsop, *The Congress Dances*, p. 138. Russia's nominal head of delegation, Count Karl Vasilyevich Nesselrode, became foreign minister in 1822.

[54] "The congress dances, but it doesn't work."

[55] Joachim Murat, Napoleon's brother-in-law and former cavalry commander, was named by him King of Naples in 1808. After Leipzig, he deserted Napoleon on Austria's assurance that he could keep his throne. Louis XVIII naturally opposed leaving formerly Bourbon Naples in the hands of a Bonapartist turncoat.

as an aggressor. That posture was not entirely contrived. Writing to King Louis in October, Talleyrand had complained more presciently than he knew, "To the Germanomanics" – Stein and the Prussian reformers – "German unity is the battlecry, the doctrine and religion they defend with the utmost fanaticism. Who can calculate the results if a mass like the German, amalgamated into a single whole, should turn aggressive? Who can tell where such a movement would stop?"[56]

For his part, having failed to secure Prussian support against Russia, Metternich, with the diplomatic agility[57] for which he was notorious, reversed field and instead urged the Czar to apply pressure to Prussia. By this time, alarmed by the British and French ministers' growing hostility and his own advisers' doubts about the wisdom of encouraging Polish nationalism, while suppressing any similar hint of self-determination in Russia, Alexander himself had begun to have second thoughts. The crisis came in late December. Sensing Alexander's eroding support, Hardenberg stunned his colleagues by threatening to annex occupied Saxony unilaterally and treat any objection as a declaration of war. In response, on January 3, ignoring Bathurst's instructions and emboldened by Britain's timely conclusion of peace with the United States,[58] Castlereagh joined Metternich and Talleyrand in a "secret" agreement committing France and Austria each to furnish 150,000 troops and Britain the equivalent in funds or mercenaries in the event of war. For a British statesman, it was an extraordinary gamble, fully justifying Schroeder's judgment that "The difference [Castlereagh] made to British policy was as important as the difference it made that, in May 1940, Winston Churchill rather than Lord Halifax succeeded Neville Chamberlain."[59]

It was Castlereagh's great good fortune that his courageous but probably impracticable commitment never had to be put to the test. Instead, leaked almost immediately, the January 3 agreement proved too much for Alexander, who, no more eager for another war than anyone else, persuaded Prussia to yield.[60] By January 5, Castlereagh could reassure Liverpool that the crisis

---

[56] Spiel, *The Congress of Vienna*, p. 32.

[57] Or unscrupulousness, according to one's view.

[58] The Treaty of Ghent ending the War of 1812 was signed on December 24, 1814.

[59] Schroeder, *The Transformation of European Politics*, p. 458. As Talleyrand reported to Louis on January 4, "Peace with America, the arrogance of Russia and Prussia, all this has changed Castlereagh's mind...." Spiel, *The Congress of Vienna*, p. 38.

[60] To his diary, Austria's Archduke Johann confided, "Austria, England, and France must stand firm... no one will dare to start an unpopular war, exhausted as their lands are." Spiel, *The Congress of Vienna*, p. 23. Indeed, according to Webster, "[T]here can be no doubt that, if war had broken out, all Europe would have joined in opposing Prussia, the behavior of her soldiers having made her detested in every quarter." Webster, *The Congress of Vienna*, p. 134. Whether "all Europe" would have included Britain is not nearly as certain.

was over; and, on February 8, the Allies concluded an agreement surrendering nearly half of Saxony to Prussia but far less than half its population and
neither of its two principal cities. Resolving Poland took longer, but eventually the Allies reached a settlement that essentially reinstituted partition.
Most of the Duchy of Warsaw became the Kingdom of Poland, effectively
a Russian protectorate.[61] The rest of Poland – apart from Poznan, returned
to Prussia, and Crakow, declared a free city under joint Prussian, Russian,
and Austrian supervision – was turned back over to a relieved Austria.

The Polish–Saxon problem scarcely had been settled when the Congress
confronted still another crisis. On February 26, 1815, Napoleon escaped
from Elba. The news reached Vienna on the morning of March 7. Within
hours, the ministers of all four Allied powers were meeting, but several days
elapsed before Bonaparte's destination and intentions were clear.[62] Then, the
Allies wasted no more time. On March 13, together with the other Treaty of
Paris signatories, they issued a declaration reading, in part, "By abrogating
the contract that designated the island of Elba as his residence, Bonaparte
has destroyed the one and only legal title to his existence. . . . Therefore, the
powers declare that Napoleon Bonaparte has removed himself beyond the
pale of decent social intercourse and, as enemy and disrupter of world peace,
has bound himself over to the public courts of law."[63] In other words, they
declared Napoleon an international outlaw.

The "Hundred Days" prompted some nervous moments, especially among
the smaller states. The real threat presented by Napoleon's return, however,
was not that he might prevail – barring Britain's or Russia's withdrawal
from the struggle, his eventual defeat was almost certain – but rather that it
would resurrect the challenges so painfully overcome in Paris and Vienna,
particularly Alexander's ambition and France's rehabilitation. By averting
any excuse for Russian armies to re-invade Germany, Wellington's decisive
victory at Waterloo deflected the former. In declining to impose a significantly more punitive peace in place of the earlier generous one, the Allies'
forbearance after Waterloo preserved the latter.

Even so, the French could not wholly evade accountability for the eagerness with which they had welcomed back their exiled war dog, nor reparation for the lives and treasure that rekenneling him had cost. In the Second Treaty of Paris, signed on November 20, 1815, France was made to

---

[61] Alexander would be its first and only monarch. As Metternich had foreseen, "Congress
Poland" survived only fifteen years before annexation by Russia in the wake of two successive internal rebellions.
[62] Metternich later claimed to have been in no doubt: "He proceeds by the most direct route
to Paris." Spiel, *The Congress of Vienna*, p. 43.
[63] Ibid., p. 48.

surrender additional territories and fortresses to her neighbors,[64] submit to a five-year occupation of her northern provinces, expend something over a million francs in government and private indemnities, and return to their original owners the artworks she had earlier been allowed to retain. Still, none of these impositions was unreasonably harsh. As one historian notes, "The Second Treaty of Paris, 20 November 1815, did not substantially alter the territorial settlement despite Prussia (predictably) and the Netherlands calling for vengeance."[65] France paid off the indemnity in three years and the Allies' occupation ended forthwith.

Other results of the Hundred Days and the treaty ending them proved to be more enduring. Bonaparte was immured on St. Helena, where he ended his days. Murat, having unwisely abandoned his new allies, was defeated by Austria at the Battle of Tolentino and Naples was restored to the Bourbons in the person of Sicily's Ferdinand III.[66] The principal territorial and political agreements hammered out in Vienna were ratified, among them establishment of a Kingdom of the Netherlands comprising Holland and Austrian Belgium, Denmark's cession of Norway to Sweden, and replacement of the Holy Roman Empire's three-hundred-odd German states with a loose confederation of thirty-nine under Austrian supervision.

Finally, in ratifying the Congress, Paris also ratified significant changes in the conduct of diplomacy. It reduced, if it did not altogether end, the wars of dynastic succession that had plagued the two preceding centuries. It solved long-standing disputes regarding diplomatic precedence and promoted cooperative solution of cross-border issues such as regulation of waterways. Above all, it established the principle that states, not just their rulers, henceforth would be bound by the treaties their governments contracted.[67]

THE FALLOUT

No international settlement can be expected of itself to promote a better, more just society, or judged primarily on how well it does so.... To expect it to do so is not only to ignore the necessary, inescapable priority of the pursuit of order over justice in international affairs, but to demand of an international order

---

[64]　Notably to Sardinia and Switzerland, the latter granted independence and neutrality under great power guarantees.

[65]　Chapman, *The Congress of Vienna*, p. 54.

[66]　Thereafter, Ferdinand IV, King of the "Two Sicilies." Concerning Italy, "As Castlereagh told Bentinck [who had incautiously promoted Genoese independence], an insurrectionary policy was fine so long as the goal was to weaken Napoleon. But now Italy had to settle down, Austria and Sardinia–Piedmont were the powers with which Britain had to work, and liberal experiments would have to wait." Schroeder, *The Transformation of European Politics*, p. 511.

[67]　Ibid., pp. 578–9.

what it cannot deliver and what would ruin it for its other central purposes if it tried.[68]

The Europe that emerged from Vienna and Paris was not the millennial Europe that its architects later were criticized for failing to create but neither was it the Europe of 1789. Dynastic rulers, it is true, were in some cases – by no means all – restored to the thrones from which Napoleon had ejected them, but in no case, including France, did they replace anything approaching a democracy or even a tolerably liberal oligarchy. Indeed, most of Napoleon's former conquests, especially Holland, Spain, and Italy, were wholly delighted to be rid of the arrogant and incompetent rulers he had imposed on them.

In short, if the settlement "almost entirely subordinated considerations of nationality to the idea of the balance of power and strategical necessities; yet, if this was so, a great advance on previous conditions had been made, even in respect to national interests in the case of Poland."[69] Most important, the Europe created in 1814–1815 was one in which all states, but especially the great powers, accepted that there were limits on sovereign freedom of action. How far they would observe these, for how long, and at what sacrifice in national interests, no one in 1815 could be certain.[70] But the fact that the powers were willing to accept a principle of limits at all was at least as world-changing an event as the revolution that prompted it. As Stein's biographer, G. H. Pertz, wrote in 1856, "The merit of the Congress of Vienna is that . . . it replaced the vanquished Napoleonic tyranny with the return to a confederacy of coequal sovereign states. . . . And if the latter was later warped and stunted, it is not the Congress that should be blamed, but lesser men that followed and a deterioration in the times."[71]

There remained the question of how that principle would be enforced. Two different answers were offered to that question, one by Castlereagh, the other by Alexander and Metternich. The former recognized that not all political change was baneful; the latter increasingly identified stability with stasis. In that irreconcilable difference and Britain's discomfort with its implications germinated the Vienna settlement's ultimate collapse.

On April 3, 1815, in reaction to Napoleon's return to France, the Allies had renewed the Quadruple Alliance originally established in March 1814 by the Treaty of Chaumont. On November 20, 1815, concurrent with the Second Treaty of Paris, they reaffirmed it. In addition, they committed themselves to meet periodically with a view to preserving the peace. That

---

[68] Ibid., pp. 576–7.
[69] Webster, *The Congress of Vienna*, p. 139.
[70] Indeed, as Webster points out, "there were few optimists among the statesmen; and scarcely one expected that the peace of Europe would long remain undisturbed." Ibid., p. 164.
[71] Quoted in Spiel, *The Congress of Vienna*, p. 9.

commitment, Castlereagh's particular achievement, was unprecedented, the precursor of such twentieth-century deterrent alliances as North Atlantic Treaty Organization (NATO) and the Warsaw Pact.[72]

Alexander, however, dreamed of more than just a deterrent alliance. At his urging, on September 26, Russia, Prussia, and Austria joined in what became known as The Holy Alliance, declaring their monarchs' "fixed resolution, both in the administration of their respective States, and in their political relations with every other Government, to take for their sole guide the precepts ... of Justice, Christian Charity and Peace, which, far from being applicable only to private concerns, must have an immediate influence on the councils of Princes, and guide all their steps, as being the only means of consolidating human institutions and remedying their imperfections."[73]

The alleged instigator, if not the actual author of this peculiar document, was a Baroness von Krüdener, a Russian religious mystic whom Alexander had met during the Hundred Days and who briefly became his personal adviser.[74] As a practical agreement, it was worthless, specifying neither actionable obligations nor the conditions in which they would take effect; and, although eventually nearly every European ruler signed it,[75] most shared Castlereagh's appraisal of the agreement as a "piece of sublime mysticism and nonsense."[76] Whatever its authorship and utility, however, its subliminal effect was to raise questions about just what was meant by the phrase, "preserve the peace."

For the Quadruple Alliance, preserving the peace meant implementing the Second Treaty of Paris and the Vienna settlement, specifically by ensuring that France abided by the former and was deterred from interfering with the latter. Agreement on that definition began to erode, however, at the very first post–Vienna Congress, held late in 1818 at Aix-La-Chapelle.[77] Although convened for the precise purpose Castlereagh had intended – to review implementation of the Treaty of Paris and the Vienna settlement – in the interval, as Gentz pointed out to Metternich, relations among the great powers had mutated. Prussia had begun moving toward Austria and away from Russia, the latter was becoming aligned more closely with France, and Britain was beginning to distance herself from all four.

---

[72] With the important qualifier, of course, that, unlike its twentieth-century successors, the Quadruple Alliance established no supranational institutional structures for consultation and decision making.

[73] http://www.1911encyclopedia.org/The_Holy_Alliance.

[74] Webster, *The Congress of Vienna*, p. 164. She eventually was replaced by Metternich of all people, whence his informal and by no means unjustified title, "prime minister of Europe."

[75] Apart from the sultan, for obvious reasons, the Pope, suspicious of its Russian (Orthodox) sponsorship, and Britain's Prince Regent, who, wisely pleading constitutional obstacles, offered only his private endorsement. Chapman, *The Congress of Vienna*, p. 61.

[76] Webster, *The Congress of Vienna*, p. 163.

[77] Today's Aachen, Germany.

Aix-La-Chapelle accelerated that transformation. France having paid her indemnity, the Allies agreed to end her occupation early. Then, at the Czar's insistence, reflecting Russia's concern over Austria's rapprochement with Prussia, they agreed to admit her to what thus became a Quintuple rather than Quadruple Alliance.

In the process, however, the Alliance's deterrent rationale inevitably became diluted, much as NATO's later would become on the collapse of the Soviet Union. And, as it would in NATO, pressure thereupon arose to expand the meaning of "preserve the peace." In 1818, it took the specific form of a proposal by Alexander to convert the Holy Alliance into an *Alliance Solidaire*, in which all the great powers would agree to support each other militarily not just to deter or defeat external aggression but also to prevent or suppress internal upheaval.[78] Just such a threat already was manifesting itself in Germany, Italy, and Latin America.

Britain's reaction was unequivocal. In a "Memorandum on the Treaties of 1814 and 1815" submitted to the congress in October 1818, the foreign office pointed out that both treaties had as their sole purpose "The restoration and conservation of Europe against the power of France," and argued that any alliance "by which each State shall be bound to support the state of succession, government, and possession within all other States from violence and attack, upon condition of receiving for itself a similar guarantee, must be understood as morally implying the previous establishment of such a system of general government as may secure and enforce upon all kings and nations an internal system of peace and justice" – in other words, universal government.

Absent such a(n unlikely) development, the memo added, "nothing would be more immoral or more prejudicial to the character of government generally than the idea that their force was collectively to be prostituted to the support of established power without any consideration of the extent to which it was abused.... [Instead] States must be left to rely for their [internal] security upon the justice and wisdom of their respective systems."[79]

With that declaration, Britain divorced herself politely but unmistakably from her allies' growing preoccupation with the challenges of nationalism and self-determination. In the event, the focus of subsequent congresses at Troppau in 1820, Laibach in 1821, and Verona in 1822, was indeed internal upheaval: in Iberia, the Piedmont, and the Balkans, respectively. At each

---

[78] Anticipating the Brezshnev Doctrine and, some might argue, NATO's recent "stabilization" efforts. Interestingly, in October 2006, Reuters reported U.S. intentions at a forthcoming NATO summit meeting to transform the alliance into "a global security organization" intended to help "instill democratic principles." The philosophical kinship with Alexander's *Alliance Solidaire* is hard to avoid.

[79] Webster, *The Congress of Vienna*, p. 189 *passim*. The memorandum is worth reading in its entirety, for style as well as substance.

successive conference, British participation became increasingly *pro forma* and, with Castlereagh's death in August 1822 and his replacement as foreign minister by long-time rival George Canning, it effectively ceased altogether.[80]

The upheavals in question were almost uniformly unsuccessful[81]; not so twenty-five years later. In 1848, Europe erupted. Beginning in Paris in February, revolution spread rapidly to Germany, Italy, and Hungary. In France, the Bourbon monarchy fell for good, its successor Second Republic surviving only briefly before being replaced by a Second Empire with another Napoleon at its head. In Germany, revolution began in Berlin and spread rapidly until finally suppressed by the Prussian Army. In Italy and Hungary, only Russian military assistance enabled Austria to defeat concurrent separatist movements.

The revolutions of 1848 produced the first cracks in the post-Vienna system. Their subsequent exploitation by the Piedmont's Count Camillo di Cavour and Prussia's Otto von Bismarck widened those fissures beyond repair, albeit almost certainly unintentionally. Both believed that by launching limited military operations to secure limited political gains, they could thereafter control the fallout. Both were wrong. As in 1792, once unleashed, nationalism proved much more difficult to discipline than to exploit.

Thus, Cavour's ejection of Austria from Lombardy in 1859 was achieved only with the help of Garibaldi's insurgents and the French Army. The one led to Italian unification, the other to France's recovery of Nice and Savoy, breaching the *cordon sanitaire* erected by Vienna; similarly with Prussia, which demonstrated the success of Scharnhorst's military reforms with its lightning defeats of Austria in 1866 and France in 1870. Achievement at last of the true German unification that Vienna was unable to produce was intentional; not so the instability in Austria, revanchism in France, and paranoia in Russia produced by those defeats, each of which contributed its own tinder to the conflagration of August 1914.

As revolution began eroding the Concert of Europe from within, the Crimean War of 1854–1856 began unraveling it from without. Originating in long-standing Russian designs on the European territories of a dying Ottoman Empire, its immediate trigger was the collapse of the Bourbon monarchy in France and the accession to power of Napoleon III. Seeking to broaden his Roman Catholic support, Bonaparte's nephew bullied the

---

[80] Nicolson, *The Congress of Vienna*, pp. 271–3. It is far from clear, however, that Castlereagh would have been any more successful than his successor in keeping Britain committed to continental involvement in conditions so increasingly at odds with British political predilections.

[81] The exception was Belgium's divorce from the Netherlands in 1830, producing an internal linguistic and cultural split that persists to this day.

Ottoman sultan into granting France in 1852 formal supervision of Christian sites in the Holy Land. The concession infuriated Orthodox Russia, in which it earlier had been vested and, after months of unproductive diplomacy, Czar Nicholas I marched his armies into Moldavia and Wallachia on the pretext of the Porte's repudiation of those earlier treaties.

The initial fighting heavily favored Russia, and when representations by the other great powers failed to convince the Czar to accept an armistice, Britain and France declared war. The land battles were fought entirely in the Crimea[82]; and, apart from prompting an epic poem, making Florence Nightingale a legend, and convincing the British Army to abandon commission by purchase, they had little permanent result, Russia already having withdrawn her troops from Ottoman territory before the first Allied soldier landed.

What did have enduring consequences, however, was Austria's refusal to support Russia despite the latter's earlier support of Austria in Hungary, a failure that – as Austria's regent Prince Felix Schwarzenberg earlier had forecast would happen – "amazed the world" with Austria's ingratitude. From that moment, she was increasingly isolated. Hence, when a decade later she found herself at war with Prussia, it should have come as no surprise that Russia stood aside while Prussia made mincemeat of Austrian armies in only seven weeks.

Four years later, it was France's turn, Napoleon III having inherited neither his uncle's military brilliance nor his army, and the Vienna settlement was dead. Compelled by its allies in 1814 and again in 1815 to grant France a generous peace, Prussia in 1870 chose to ignore Bismarck's warnings and inflict on its long-hated and envied enemy the humiliations that its generals earlier had been denied. Thus, ironically, a European settlement conceived in the defeat of one Napoleon finally was interred by the defeat of another.

CONCLUSION

Although every war is fought in the name of peace, there is a tendency to define peace as the absence of war and to confuse it with military victory. [But] the logic of war is power, and power has no inherent limit. The logic of peace is proportion, and proportion implies limitation.[83]

Historians writing about the Vienna settlement and its aftermath generally have offered three alternative explanations for both its prolonged success in deterring European conflict and its eventual catastrophic collapse. The

---

[82] Minor naval skirmishing took place along the Baltic Sea, White Sea, and Russian Pacific coasts.
[83] Kissinger, *A World Restored*, p. 138.

first, popular among late-nineteenth-century progressives, held that Vienna succeeded only by ruthlessly suppressing nationalism and self-determination and failed when these no longer could be contained.[84]

More recent chroniclers have argued, however, that relatively few ordinary people at the turn of the eighteenth century embraced what we would recognize today as nationalism or self-determination. "Nationalism had no champions except a few radicals and later nineteenth-century historians. The diplomat who was most interested in nationalism was Metternich, and he wanted it suppressed."[85] Instead, loyalties still tended to inhere in ruler, faith, and locality. Indeed, as Napoleon discovered in Spain to his sorrow – and as others have rediscovered since – local rule, however despotic, incompetent, or corrupt, often trumps more detached rule, however enlightened.[86] Finally, the fact that the upheavals of 1830–1848 were resolved without instigating military conflict among the major powers is the best evidence that the Vienna settlement was anything but a rigid obstacle to political change.[87]

The other two explanations are separately more convincing but also more directly competitive. The one attributes Vienna's success to the establishment of a stable balance of power that diminished the temptation of any European state to seek territorial aggrandizement at the expense of others and its failure to the ultimate erosion of that balance, propelled by the selfishness and shortsightedness of the continental powers and accelerated by Britain's unwise withdrawal from continental engagement.[88]

The other, far from holding the balance of power a contributor to peace, instead holds it directly responsible for the beggar-my-neighbor eighteenth-century behavior that permitted a Napoleon to flourish in the first place. In this view, it was precisely the indiscipline of relations among states seeking thoughtlessly to enhance their own relative strategic and economic advantage that repeatedly rendered all of them militarily and diplomatically vulnerable. Speaking for that view, Schroeder, among others, contends that "Seeking a durable peace through a balance of power was futile. The size,

---

[84] "The spectacle of a dozen statesmen transferring 'souls' by the 100,000 from one sovereign to another has inspired many mordant pens; and in light of the history of the nineteenth century the validity of these criticisms cannot be disputed." Webster, *The Congress of Vienna*, p. 164.

[85] Chapman, *The Congress of Vienna*, p. 56.

[86] Bonaparte's effort to impose an extraordinarily liberal constitution on an unyieldingly feudal Spain was a resounding failure. See John Lawrence Tone, *The Fatal Knot: The Guerrilla War in Navarre and the Defeat of Napoleon in Spain* (Chapel Hill, NC, 1994), p. 51.

[87] Schroeder, *The Transformation of European Politics*, p. 799.

[88] "To a generation...which had seen the dominance of a single Power, it is not strange that the principle of the Balance of Power should have appealed with great force." Webster, *The Congress of Vienna*, p. 165.

structure, power, and geographical position of the various European states virtually guaranteed that the free play of competitive forces among them would not result in a general stability, independence, and balance, but in destruction for some, mutilation for others, dependence for still others, and hegemony, if not outright empire, for one or two."[89]

Instead, in his view, the durability of the Vienna settlement was attributable largely to the grudging emergence among Europe's great powers of a sense of international *system*, a recognition of the inescapable interdependence among states and agreement on rules of behavior acknowledging it, limiting the resort to force to ends and means consciously self-disciplined to avoid undermining the system overall. When, after 1870, that agreement on the rules of the game vanished, a relapse to the unrestricted use of force became inevitable.

There is truth in both explanations, just as there is in Kissinger's attribution of Vienna's success to "the convictions of [its] statesmen." That a belief in the need to achieve a stable equilibrium among sovereign states influenced those statesmen, especially Castlereagh and Metternich, cannot be doubted. Both wrote of it, and their actions even more than their words confirmed it. Likewise, it is undeniable that those statesmen's and their rulers' behavior before, during, and after Vienna reflected unprecedented sensitivity to the need for legitimacy and the behavior required to claim it.

But the reality also was both simpler and more complicated than these explanations. It was simpler in the sense that, by 1815, all the combatants, not just France, were materially and psychologically exhausted. Even Britain, the least damaged, had expended over £700 million and not a few lives, and the British too yearned for peace. That powerful desire for military repose fortified both those, like Metternich and Castlereagh, who sought stability in equilibrium and those, like Talleyrand and Alexander, convinced that stability required adherence even under compulsion to some legitimizing principle. Only Prussia emerged from Vienna unconvinced in either respect and, thus, it is unsurprising that Prussia ultimately would drive the final nail in Vienna's coffin.

The reality was more complicated because none of these explanations, least of all belief in the disciplining effect of community, gives enough weight to the erosion of memory over time. Pondering this problem, Talleyrand wrote, "The general equilibrium of Europe cannot be composed of simple elements.... [It] can only last so long as certain large States are animated by a spirit of moderation and justice which will preserve that equilibrium."[90] Such a spirit of moderation and justice, however, becomes more difficult to sustain as generational change occurs, the memories of the horrors of

---

[89]   Schroeder, *The Congress of Vienna*, p. 10.
[90]   Charles Maurice de Talleyrand, quoted in Chapman, *The Congress of Vienna*, p. 19.

total war fade, and foreign policy once more becomes the handmaiden of domestic politics conducted by leaders ignorant of or impervious to history.

As Kissinger perceptively warned, "[W]hile powers may appear to outsiders as factors in a security arrangement, they appear domestically as expressions of a historical existence. No power will submit to a settlement, however well-balanced and however 'secure,' which seems totally to deny its vision of itself."[91] After 1848, those visions began to change among all of Vienna's principal players and, by 1870, they had largely ceased to be compatible. The cataclysm of 1914, in that sense, merely ratified the collective loss of memory.

That loss of memory was only compounded by the concurrent transformation of the political process about which Clausewitz had warned. Explaining the shift toward total war at the turn of the eighteenth century, he noted that the change reflected "the new political conditions which the French Revolution created both in France and in Europe as a whole, conditions that set in motion new means and new forces . . . the transformation of the art of war [thus] resulted from the transformation of politics."[92]

Still more was that true after 1848, as royal absolutism increasingly gave way to popular limitations on monarchical power and as the increasing need for and evolving mechanisms of social mobilization progressively eroded the political monopoly of élites. Prussian Field Marshal Leopold von der Goltz's *The Nation in Arms* found its French counterpart in the French left's belief "in the principle of the 'nation in arms' as the only safeguard of the Republic."[93] And, as the aims, methods, and outcomes of war increasingly ceased to be "the business of government alone" and instead became that of the people, Clausewitz's "object suspended between three magnets" began to swing more powerfully toward untrammeled violence, just as he had predicted it would.

The Vienna settlement was a unique historical event reflecting a set of unrepeatable circumstances in a strategic environment profoundly unlike our own. Drawing lessons from it concerning peace making today, therefore, is inherently dangerous. But the conditions that made the Vienna settlement possible and those ultimately responsible for demolishing it still may have something useful to tell us at a time when achieving a durable peace seems especially remote.

One of those was the Allies' success in convincing the French of both the desirability of peace and the impossibility of achieving it while Napoleon ruled. In April 1814, French armies were far from shattered. Several still occupied territories from which dislodging them would have been difficult

---

[91] Kissinger, *A World Restored*, p. 146.
[92] Clausewitz, *On War*, p. 610.
[93] Barbara W. Tuchman, *The Guns of August* (New York, 1962), p. 35.

and costly. But that it eventually could have been done was not in doubt. A year later, of course, there was no question at all: At Waterloo, the French Army ceased to exist as an effective fighting force, and Napoleon himself likely escaped execution only by throwing himself on the mercy of the British.[94] In effect, the Allies made peace desirable by making France's defeat inevitable.

To induce French acceptance of that inevitability required a total effort on the part of the Allies. In that sense only, there was nothing "limited" about the final coalition or its prosecution of the war. From the Treaty of Chaumont through Napoleon's final defeat a year later, the Allies applied virtually every asset they could muster. Nothing less would have sufficed against as dangerous and resourceful an enemy as Napoleon Bonaparte. The Allied victory of 1814–1815 thus was decisive in the only meaningful sense of that word: It resulted in France's submission to the political will of the victors.

Because the French accepted defeat as inevitable, however, the generous terms extended by the Allies, not only to Bonaparte himself but also to France as a whole, appeared not as the prudential act of a coalition still uncertain of its success but rather as acknowledgment of the reality that a stable Europe required an actively cooperative France, and that as quickly as could safely be managed. Even the harsher terms imposed in 1815 failed to alter that fact. France was occupied but only to a limited extent and for a limited time and, above all, for a reason whose legitimacy even the occupied could not easily dispute. Similarly, while Louis XVIII may not have been the ideal monarch, he was acceptable to most Frenchmen, who understood (as, for that matter, he himself eventually did, however grudgingly) that in its political and social essentials, the Revolution of 1789 had become irreversible. While altering France's governance, in short, the Allies wisely eschewed any effort to reshape French society.

Because France remained a political player even after November 1815, first Britain and Austria, then Britain and Russia, had an interlocutor and make-weight in debates with Prussia, which, more than any other power, threatened first to prevent, then to upset, the equilibrium so devoutly sought by the others. The resulting relationships did not depend on a perfect identity of interests or even values; they did depend on mutual awareness that the alternatives to cooperation and compromise were immeasurably worse.

In turn, that awareness reflected the immediate memory of two decades of constant danger, devastation, and death. Few of the states and principalities represented in Vienna and of the major powers only Britain had not felt the Corsican's boot; even the British had endured their moment of peril, as they

---

[94] Had he been taken by the Prussians instead, he almost certainly would have been shot. Nicolson, *The Congress of Vienna*, p. 231.

would again in 1940. All were tired. All wanted peace and quiet. And all were wise enough to recognize that only self-discipline, above all on the part of the most powerful, could produce it.

When in the fullness of time that self-discipline finally vanished under the pressures of militant nationalism, societal boredom, the disappearance of historical memory, and political and military arrogance, so also did the peace of Europe and the world. If there is a lesson for today's soldiers and statesmen in the Congress of Vienna and its aftermath, there, above all, is where it most probably resides.

6

War and peace in the post–Civil War South

JAMES M. MCPHERSON

In his formal acceptance of the Republican presidential nomination in 1868, General Ulysses S. Grant concluded with four words that struck a deep chord with voters: "Let us have peace."[1] Historians have described the conflict in Vietnam as America's longest war. But, arguably, the nineteenth-century decades of sectional strife punctuated by a four-year conflict Americans call the Civil War truly represents the nation's longest war. It was certainly its most intense and violent war. In a country with less than one sixth of the population it contained a century later, the number of American soldier deaths in the Civil War was almost eleven times greater than those in Vietnam. And to this total of 625,000 Civil War dead, one must add hundreds more in the Kansas wars of the 1850s that anticipated the war of 1861–1865 and the thousands of deaths in Reconstruction battles that illustrated a sort of Clausewitzian corollary that politics were the continuation of war by similar means.

Grant's plea for peace in 1868 resonated with such meaning because the country had not known real peace since the outbreak of war with Mexico in 1846. During congressional debates over the issue of slavery in the territories acquired from Mexico, fistfights broke out on the floor of the House, Senator Jefferson Davis of Mississippi challenged an Illinois congressman to a duel, Senator Henry Foote (also of Mississippi) drew a loaded revolver on the Senate floor, and Congressman Alexander Stephens of Georgia declared that to resist "the dictation of the Northern hordes of Goths and Vandals"

---

[1] John Y. Simon, et al., eds., *Papers of Ulysses S. Grant*, 29 vols. to date (Carbondale, IL, 1967–), vol. 18, p. 264.

the slave states must make "the necessary preparations of men and money, arms and munitions, etc., to meet the emergency."[2]

The initial crisis subsided with the Compromise of 1850 but flared up again after passage of the Kansas–Nebraska Act in 1854. At least two hundred men lost their lives in fighting between proslavery and antislavery forces in Kansas. Congressman Preston Brooks of South Carolina clubbed Senator Charles Sumner of Massachusetts almost to death with a heavy cane on the floor of the Senate in 1856. Two years later, a congressional debate over the question of admitting Kansas as a slave state under its fraudulent Lecompton constitution provoked a shoving and pummeling fight between Northern and Southern congressmen in the House. "There were some fifty middle-aged and elderly gentlemen pitching into each other like so many Tipperary savages," wrote a journalist with some amusement, "most of them incapable, from want of wind and muscle, of doing each other any serious harm." But one representative commented that "if any weapons had been on hand it would probably have been a bloody one."[3]

After John Brown's raid on Harper's Ferry in 1859, which stirred fear, outrage, and retaliation in the South, men began coming armed to the floor of Congress. One of them observed, with a degree of hyperbole, that "the only persons who do not have a revolver and knife are those who have two revolvers." A Southerner reported that a good many slave-state congressmen expected – even wanted – a shoot-out on the floor of the House: They "are willing to fight the question out, and settle it right there." The governor of South Carolina wrote to one of his state's representatives: "If... you upon consultation decide to make an issue of force in Washington, write or telegraph me, and I will have a regiment in or near Washington in the shortest possible time."[4]

The war of 1861–1865 transferred these conflicts from the political arena to the battlefield. Appomattox and the subsequent surrenders of other Confederate armies ended that battlefield war. But it did not end the cultural and ideological struggle in which the military conflict found itself embedded. The Civil War was actually two wars. One of them ended in 1865. But real peace was impossible until the other ended as well. Some contemporaries recognized this truth. Two months after Appomattox, the Boston lawyer and author (*Two Years Before the Mast*), Richard Henry Dana, the federal district attorney for Massachusetts, gave a widely publicized speech in which

[2] Quoted in Don E. Fehrenbacher, *The South and Three Sectional Crises* (Baton Rouge, LA, 1980), p. 40.
[3] *New York Weekly Tribune*, February 13, 1859; the representative is quoted in James A. Rawley, *Pace and Politics: "Bleeding Kansas" and the Coming of the Civil War* (Philadelphia, 1969), pp. 239–40.
[4] Quotations from Allan Nevins, *The Emergence of Lincoln*, vol. 2, *Prologue to Civil War 1859–1861* (New York, 1950), pp. 121–2.

he declared that "a war is over when its purpose is secured. It is a fatal mistake to hold that this war is over, because the fighting has ceased. This war is not over," and until the North had secured "the fruits of victory," it must continue to hold the South in the "grasp of war."[5]

These phrases, "fruits of victory" and "grasp of war," became part of the public discourse during the year immediately after the end of fighting between the armies. What did they mean? At a minimum, they meant that the victorious North had the power and responsibility to impose terms on which the South would be reincorporated into the Union. Suffering from the shock of defeat, many ex-Confederates were despondent and listless, without the will to resist any terms of reconstruction the North saw fit to impose. "They expect nothing," wrote a Northern journalist, "were prepared for the worst; would have been thankful for anything. . . . They asked no terms, made no conditions." Even South Carolinians admitted that "the conqueror has the right to make the terms, and we must submit."[6]

The problem was that the conquerors could not agree on what those terms should be. The assassination of Lincoln had removed a firm hand from the helm. At first, his successor, Andrew Johnson, seemed to favor draconian terms. Having fought the secessionists on the ground in Tennessee, the new president thundered that "*treason* is a crime. . . . Traitors must be punished and impoverished. Their great plantations must be seized and divided into farms, and sold to honest, industrious men."[7] This rhetoric seemed to place Johnson at the extreme end of a spectrum of Northern opinion with Thaddeus Stevens and other radical Republicans who wanted to overthrow the power of the old Southern ruling class, confiscate their land, and distribute it among freed slaves and Unionist whites. It also meant disenfranchising leading ex-Confederates and enfranchising freed slaves. The planter class had brought on secession and war, they believed. The United States would never achieve genuine peace until the planters were shorn of their wealth and replaced by a democratized biracial yeoman class that would constitute the backbone of the New South.

However, at heart, Johnson was a Democrat and a white supremacist, whom the Republicans had placed on the ticket in 1864 to broaden their appeal to War Democrats and border-state Unionists. Johnson's nomination turned out to have given the Republicans a short-term advantage in helping to win the election – and the war – but at the cost of disastrous long-term consequences in winning the peace. Not long after declaring that traitors

[5] *Boston Commonwealth*, June 24, 1865.
[6] Whitelaw Reid, *After the War: A Tour of the Southern States 1865–1866* (Cincinnati, OH, 1866), p. 296; Sidney Andrews, *The South since the War* (Boston, 1866), p. 68.
[7] Quoted in Hans L. Trefousse, *Andrew Johnson: A Biography* (New York, 1989), p. 197; and Brooks D. Simpson, *The Reconstruction Presidents* (Lawrence, KS, 1998), p. 68.

must be punished and impoverished, Johnson began a migration toward the conservative and even Democratic end of the spectrum. From there, he and like-minded Democrats saw Reconstruction as a minimalist process that would establish a mechanism whereby former Confederate states could return to the Union with little or no change except for the abolition of slavery. For the proponents of such a policy, the fruits of victory included simply the restoration of the old Union and a grudging admission that slavery had gone with the wind. They could best achieve a real and permanent peace, they believed, by the maximum conciliation of former enemies consistent with the actual outcome of the war.

Between these alternatives of Reconstruction as either revolution or minimum change were the imprecise and shifting ideas held by the majority of the Republican Party. For them, the fruits of victory included an irrevocable repudiation of secession, ratification of the Thirteenth Amendment abolishing slavery, some kind of Federal guarantee for the civil rights of former slaves – if not their immediate enfranchisement as voters – security and power for Southern white Unionists, and at least temporary political disqualification of leading ex-Confederates. When Andrew Johnson moved toward the conservative end of the spectrum in the period 1865–1866, the moderate Republicans moved in countervailing fashion closer to the radical position. This situation produced a growing polarization between the president and Congress, which in turn led to Johnson's impeachment in 1868 and his escape from conviction by a single vote in the Senate.

In the spring and summer of 1865, Johnson issued proclamations of amnesty and reconstruction that offered full pardons and restoration of property – except slaves – to most ex-Confederates who were willing to take an oath of allegiance. The president exempted several classes of high-ranking Confederate civil and military officers and wealthy Southerners who could nevertheless apply for individual pardons. Johnson pardoned them in large numbers – more that thirteen thousand. Once pardoned, these Southern whites – along with those who had never supported the Confederacy – could proceed to adopt new state constitutions and elect new governors, legislatures, congressmen, and senators.

Freed slaves remained excluded from this process. In fact, several of the new Southern governments enacted "Black Codes" that codified explicit second-class citizenship for freedmen. Johnson's restoration of property to amnestied and pardoned ex-Confederates also drove tens of thousands of freedmen off land they had farmed for themselves that year. Moreover, the president vetoed a Freedmen's Bureau bill that would have given the Bureau authority to place freedmen on abandoned land in the former Confederacy.

Under the new state governments, voters elected hundreds of ex-Confederate officials to state offices, along with no fewer than nine Confederate congressmen, seven Confederate state officials, four generals, four colonels, and Confederate Vice President Alexander H. Stephens to the United States Congress. To angry Republicans, and Northern people in general, it appeared that the rebels, unable to capture Washington in war, were about to do so in peace. They were determined not to let this happen. In December 1865, the *Chicago Tribune* expressed a growing sentiment in the North. Its editorial focused in particular on the Mississippi Black Code but, by implication, addressed the growing defiance of Southern whites in general: "We tell the white men of Mississippi," thundered *The Tribune*'s writers, "that the men of the North will convert the state of Mississippi into a frog pond before they will allow such laws to disgrace one foot of the soil in which the bones of our soldiers sleep and over which the flag of freedom waves."[8]

For the next two years, a bitter struggle in Washington made a mockery of the hopes for peace that had blossomed at Appomattox. With their three-quarters majority in Congress, Republicans refused to admit the representatives and senators elected by the Southern states. Congress passed a civil rights bill and a Freedmen's Bureau bill over Johnson's vetoes and adopted the Fourteenth Amendment to the Constitution, which Johnson counseled Southern state legislatures to reject. In the mid-term elections of 1866, Northern voters resoundingly repudiated a conservative coalition, which Johnson's supporters had cobbled together. The Republicans maintained their three-quarters majority in both houses of Congress. They proceeded to enact a series of laws over Johnson's vetoes that mandated new state constitutions in the South providing for universal manhood suffrage and for temporary disfranchisement and political disqualification of many ex-Confederates. New Republican-controlled state governments came into existence in 1868 and 1869, which created the first public school systems in the South and enacted other progressive social legislation. They also ratified the Fourteenth and Fifteenth Amendments to the Constitution that banned racial discrimination in civil and voting rights.

President Johnson tried to hinder every step of this process by executive obstruction, which is why the House impeached him and the Senate almost convicted him. The most pernicious effect of Johnson's obstructionism was its encouragement of growing white resistance throughout the South. By fall 1865, the immediate postwar passivity of Southerners was metamorphosing into defiance. After all, the president of the United States appeared to be on their side. In September 1865, a leading Alabama politician scoffed at Republican insistence on guarantees of Southern white loyalty and good behavior. "It is you, proud and exultant Radical, who should give guarantees, guarantees that you will not again... deny any portion of the people

---

[8] *Chicago Tribune*, December 1, 1865.

their rights." Two months later, Wade Hampton, one of the South's richest antebellum planters and Confederate cavalry commander, commented that "it is our duty to support the President of the United States so long as he manifests a disposition to support all our rights as a sovereign State."[9]

This sounded like 1860 all over again. Many Southern whites agreed with South Carolina's Thomas Pickney Lowndes, who wrote several years later that "for us the war is not ended. We had met the enemy in the field and lost our fight, but now we were threatened with a servile war, a war in which the negro savage backed by the U.S. and the intelligent white scoundrel as his leader was our enemy."[10]

Southern whites acted on this premise. Violent acts spread throughout the South, ranging from midnight assassinations of black and white Republicans to full-scale riots in Memphis and New Orleans in 1866 that killed forty-six and thirty-seven blacks, respectively. A shadowy organization with the ominous sounding name of Ku Klux Klan carried out many of these actions. Similar secret societies arose in other states. Louisiana experienced the worst of the violence. Hundreds of victims of guerrilla attacks met their death in Louisiana in the three years between Appomattox and Grant's nomination for president.[11]

Paramilitary groups composed mostly of Confederate veterans killed hundreds more in other states. Federal occupation troops were far too few and spread too thinly to prevent most of the killings. Little wonder that people longed for surcease from constant strife and crisis. "Let us have peace" echoed many newspapers when they published Grant's acceptance letter. If anyone could win the peace, they hoped, it was the man who had won the war.

But there would be no peace. It was not for lack of trying. In several Southern states, Republican governors organized militia companies to suppress the violence. In Tennessee, Arkansas, and other places, they enjoyed considerable success. But positive results were exceptional. In many areas, county sheriffs organized posses, but they were often outgunned by counter-reconstruction guerrillas. The sheriff of Fayette County, Alabama, put his finger on another problem: "When I gather my posse," he testified, "I could depend on them, but as soon as I get home, I meet my wife crying, saying

---

[9] Michael Perman, *Reunion without Compromise: The South and Reconstruction 1865–1868* (Cambridge, 1973), p. 82; Andrews, *The South since the War*, p. 391.

[10] Quoted in Richard Zuczek, *State of Rebellion: Reconstruction in South Carolina* (Columbia, SC, 1996), p. 47.

[11] Gilles Vandall, *Rethinking Southern Violence: Homicides in Post–Civil War Louisiana, 1866–1884* (Columbus, OH, 2000). The author classifies an estimated 4,986 homicides in Louisiana from 1866 to 1884, with peaks in 1868 and 1873–1874. Many of these were ordinary murders rather than politically motivated killings, but the latter constituted at least half of the total. See, especially, pp. 13 and 22.

that they have been there shooting at the house. When we scatter to our houses, we do not know at what time we are to be shot down; and living with our lives in our hands this way, we have become disheartened."[12]

If the militia or sheriffs did manage to apprehend Klansmen, what then? Even in Republican counties, it proved difficult to empanel a jury that would convict. Although militia and white troops might be able to protect witnesses and jurors during trials, they could not prevent retaliation on a dark night months later – and sometimes the intimidation occurred during the trial itself. To cite just one example, the district attorney in northern Mississippi saw a case fall apart when five key witnesses were murdered. The example was not lost on witnesses elsewhere.

North Carolina's Governor William W. Holden came to grief because of his attempts to stamp out the Klan. County sheriffs and civil courts proved helpless to contain a rising tide of terror that swept over the state in early 1870. The legislature authorized Holden to proclaim a state of insurrection but refused him the power to declare martial law or to suspend the writ of *habeas corpus*. Knowing that nothing short of these measures would do the job, Holden in effect declared martial law by executive order. The militia arrested scores of Klansmen while dozens of others turned state's evidence in hope of light or suspended sentences. In response to the mounting pressure, Holden dropped his plan to try offenders in military courts. As usual, the civil courts failed to convict any of those arrested. After the Democrats won control of the legislature (with the aid of Klan violence) in 1870, they impeached and convicted Holden in March 1871 for having illegally declared martial law. He was the first governor in American history to be removed from office by impeachment.[13]

As the death toll from Klan violence mounted during 1870, Southern Republicans desperately petitioned the Grant administration for help. Rigorous legislation to enforce the Fourteenth and Fifteenth Amendments became major items of congressional business. A stumbling block to such legislation was the federal system, under which the states had jurisdiction over the crimes of murder, assault, arson, and the like. In the view of the moderate Republicans, the prosecution of such crimes by federal officials would stretch the Constitution to the breaking point. Nevertheless, the clauses of the Fourteenth and the Fifteenth Amendments giving Congress power to enforce their provisions by appropriate legislation seemed to provide constitutional sanction for a departure from tradition.

Missouri's Senator Carl Schurz, a refugee from the German Revolution of 1848, a founder of the Republican Party, and a major general in the Union

---

[12] Quoted in Allen W. Trelease, *White Terror: The Ku Klux Klan Conspiracy and Southern Reconstruction* (New York, 1971), pp. 268–9.
[13] Ibid., pp. 189–225.

Army during the Civil War, eloquently supported an enforcement law. In a Senate speech, he scorned in incessant harping by the Democrats on what they euphoniously called "self-government and . . . State sovereignty. . . . In the name of liberty [they] assert the right of one man, under State law, to deprive another man of his freedom. [But] the great constitutional revolution" accomplished by the war had brought in its wake "the vindication of individual rights by the National power. The revolution found the rights of the individual at the mercy of the States . . . and placed them under the shield of national protection." And how did the Democrats respond, asked Schurz rhetorically? "As they once asserted that true liberty implied the right of one man to hold another man as his slave, they will tell you now that they are no longer true freemen in their States because . . . they can no longer deprive other men of their rights."[14]

In May 1870, Congress passed an enforcement act that made interference with voting rights a federal offense and defined as a felony any attempt by one or more persons to deprive another person of his civil or political rights. But at first, Grant, fearful of charges of Caesarism, did little to enforce the law. Klan violence continued to increase. Grant and his new attorney general, Amos Akerman, finally decided to take off the velvet glove that had cloaked the iron fist. Congress helped by passing an even stronger law at a special session in April 1871, popularly known as the Ku Klux Act. This law empowered the president to use the army to enforce the 1870 law, declare martial law, suspend the writ of *habeas corpus* in areas that he declared to be in a state of insurrection, and purge suspected Klansmen from juries by an oath backed with stiff penalties for perjury.

Under these laws, the Grant administration cracked down on the Klan. Government detectives infiltrated the order and gathered evidence of its activities. In 1871, a congressional committee conducted an investigation of the Klan that produced twelve thick volumes of testimony documenting its outrages. The president sent cavalry to the South to supplement the Federal infantry to cope with the fast-riding Klansmen. Grant also suspended the writ of *habeas corpus* in nine counties of South Carolina. There and elsewhere, federal marshals aided by the soldiers arrested thousands of Klansmen. Hundreds of others fled their homes to escape arrest. Federal grand juries handed down more than three thousand indictments. Several hundred defendants pleaded guilty in return for suspended sentences. The Justice Department (established in 1870) dropped charges against nearly two thousand others in order to clear clogged court dockets for trials of major offenders. Approximately 600 of these were convicted and 250 acquitted. Of those convicted, most received fines or light jail sentences, but sixty-five

---

[14] Frederic Bancroft, ed., *Speeches, Correspondence, and Political Papers of Carl Schurz*, 6 vols. (New York, 1913), vol. 1, pp. 487, 488, 489, 490, 495, 502.

were imprisoned for sentences of up to five (in a few cases, ten) years in the federal penitentiary at Albany, New York.[15]

The government's main purpose in this crackdown was to destroy the Klan and restore a semblance of law and order in the South rather than to secure mass convictions. Thus, the courts granted clemency to many convicted defendants and Grant liberally used his pardoning power. By 1875, all the imprisoned had served out their sentences or received pardons. The government's vigorous actions in 1871–1872 did bring at least a temporary peace to large parts of the former Confederacy. As a consequence, blacks voted in solid numbers, and the 1872 election was the fairest and most democratic presidential election in the South until 1968.

This experience confirmed a reality that had existed since 1865: While counter-Reconstruction guerrillas assaulted unarmed white and black Republicans, teachers in freedpeople's schools, sheriffs' posses, and state militias, they carefully avoided conflict with federal troops. Yet, the success of federal enforcement in 1871–1872 contained seeds of future failure. Southern whites and Northern Democrats hurled charges of "bayonet rule" against the Grant administration. Southern Democrats learned that the Klan's tactics of terrorism – midnight assassinations and whippings by disguised vigilantes operating in secret organizations – were likely to bring down the heavy hand of federal retaliation. They did not forswear violence but openly formed organizations that they described as "social clubs" – which just happened to be armed to the teeth. Professing to organize only for self-defense against black militias, "carpetbagger corruption," and other bugbears of Southern white propaganda, they named themselves White Leagues (Louisiana), White Liners or Rifle Clubs (Mississippi), or Red Shirts (South Carolina). They were, in fact, paramilitary organizations that functioned as armed auxiliaries of the Democratic Party in Southern states in their drive to "redeem" the South from "black and tan Negro-Carpetbag rule."

Most of the paramilitaries, like those who had constituted Klan membership, were Confederate veterans. A careful study of the White League in New Orleans analyzes the membership of this order and finds that 88 percent of its officers "can be positively identified as Confederate veterans who served in Louisiana during the Civil War."[16] But they were not eager to reprise the war of 1861–1865, so they too were careful to avoid conflict with the

---

[15] Everette Swinney, "Enforcing the Fifteenth Amendment," *Journal of Southern History* 27 (1962), pp. 202–18; Robert J. Kaczorowski, *The Politics of Judicial Interpretation: The Federal Courts, Department of Justice and Civil Rights, 1866–1876* (New York, 1985), pp. 79–99; and Lou Falkner Williams, *The Great South Carolina Ku Klux Klan Trials, 1871–1872* (Athens, GA, 1996).

[16] James K. Hogue, *Uncivil War: Five New Orleans Street Battles and the Rise and Fall of Radical Reconstruction* (Baton Rouge, LA, 2006), p. 130.

dwindling number of federal troops stationed in the South and portrayed their increasingly murderous attacks on blacks and Republicans as purely defensive.

The most notorious confrontation occurred in 1873 at Colfax on the Red River in the plantation country of western Louisiana. Colfax was the parish seat of Grant Parish, the population of which was almost equally divided between whites and blacks. Disputed elections had left rival claimants for control of both the state and parish governments. Simmering warfare between the White League and black militia came to a head in Colfax on Easter Sunday 1873. Claiming that "Negro rule" in the parish had produced corruption, pillage, and rape, the White League vowed to reassert white rule. Occupation of the courthouse by armed blacks provoked whites into a frenzy. On April 13, nearly three hundred armed whites rode into Colfax pulling a cannon on a farm wagon. Using tactics learned as Confederate soldiers, they attacked the courthouse from three directions. After shooting down in cold blood several blacks trying to escape, they set the courthouse on fire, burning several men alive and killing the rest as they moved out to surrender. At least seventy-one blacks (by some accounts, as many as three hundred) and three whites were killed – two of the latter by shots fired from their own side. Federal troops steaming upriver from New Orleans arrived in time only to count the dead.

A federal grand jury indicted seventy-two whites under the enforcement act of 1870 for violating black civil rights. Only nine came to trial and only three were convicted. These three went free in 1876 when the Supreme Court ruled (*U.S. v. Cruikshank*) that the enforcement act was unconstitutional because the Fourteenth Amendment prohibited only states, not individuals, from violating civil rights. "The power of Congress ... to legislate for the enforcement of such a guarantee," declared the Court, "does not extend to the passage of laws for the suppression of ordinary crime within the states. ... That duty was originally assumed by the States; and it still remains there."[17] The Court failed to say what recourse victims might have if a state did not or could not suppress such crimes.

In Louisiana and Mississippi, White Leaguers and White Liners carried on their campaigns of intimidation and murder with little regard for courts, either federal or state. Federal troops were either too few or too late to protect most targets of violence. Tensions rose in 1874 as elections approached. The White League in the Red River Parish southwest of Shreveport forced six white Republicans to resign their office on pain of death – and then brutally murdered them after they had resigned.[18]

---

[17] 25 *Fed. Cas.* 707, p. 210; 92 *U.S. Reports*, p. 542.
[18] Ted Tunnell, *Crucible of Reconstruction: War, Radicalism, and Race in Louisiana, 1862–1877* (Baton Rouge, LA, 1984), pp. 196–202.

"For many former Confederates, this was a glorious time," writes Nicholas Lemann in his history of these events.

> After years of defeat and loss of power and control, it looked as if they might be winning again.... They were taking their homeland back from what they saw as a formidable misalliance of the federal government and the Negro. The drama of it was so powerful that killing defenseless people registered in their minds as acts of bravery, and refusal to obey laws that protected other people's rights registered as acts of high principle.[19]

Two weeks after the Red River Parish murders, on September 14, New Orleans became the scene of a battle between the White League on one side and the police and state militia on the other. The commander of the state forces, which included both white and black units, was none other that former Confederate General James Longstreet, who had become a Republican after the war and was now fighting against men who had once served under him. Longstreet's little army killed twenty-one White Leaguers and wounded nineteen but suffered eleven killed and sixty wounded – including Longstreet – in the course of being routed by the White Leaguers. The latter installed their own claimant to the governorship (from the disputed election of 1872), but Grant then stepped in and put an end to the exercise. Three regiments of U.S. infantry and a battery of artillery arrived in New Orleans (then the state capital) supported by a flotilla of gunboats anchored in the river with a full complement of marines. "New Orleans became host to the largest garrison of federal troops in the United States," writes the historian of these events, "and assumed the appearance of an occupied city, much as it had during the Civil War."[20] The soldiers ensured a fair election in New Orleans. Grant also sent part of the 7th Cavalry (George Armstrong Custer's regiment) to patrol the turbulent Red River parishes.

In addition, Grant ordered to Louisiana his top field commander, General Philip H. Sheridan. This hot-headed fighter had pulled no punches in his Civil War career, nor did he now. "I think the terrorism now existing in Louisiana, Mississippi, and Arkansas could be entirely removed, and confidence and fair dealing be established, by the arrest and trial of ringleaders of the armed White Leagues," Sheridan wired the secretary of war in a dispatch that was widely published in the press:

> If Congress would pass a bill declaring them banditti, they could be tried by a military commission. The ringleaders of this banditti, who murdered men here on the 14th of September, and also more recently at Vicksburg, Miss., should, in justice to law and order, and the peace and prosperity of this southern part

---

[19] Nicholas Lemann, *Redemption: The Last Battle of the Civil War* (New York, 2006), p. 28.
[20] Hogue, *Uncivil War*, p. 145.

of the country, be punished. It is possible that if the President would issue a proclamation declaring them banditti, no further action need be taken except that which would devolve on me.[21]

We shall never know if Sheridan's approach would have worked for it was never tried. His banditti dispatch provoked a firestorm of condemnation in the North as well as the South. Instead of bringing peace, Grant's Southern policy seemed to be causing ever more turmoil. Many Northerners adopted a "plague on both your houses" attitude toward the White Leagues and the "Negro-Carpetbag" state governments. Withdraw the Federal troops, they argued, and let Southern people work out their own problems, even if that meant a solid South for the white supremacy Democratic Party and curtailment of black civil and political rights.

"People are becoming tired of . . . abstract questions, in which the overwhelming majority of them have no direct interest," declared the leading Republican newspaper in Washington in 1874. "The Negro question, with all its complications, and the reconstruction of the Southern States, with all its interminable embroilments, have lost much of the power they once wielded." A Republican politician commented even more bluntly the following year, "The truth is that our people are tired of this worn out cry of 'Southern outrages'!!! Hard times and heavy taxes make them wish the 'nigger,' 'everlasting nigger,' were in ____ or Africa."[22]

Benefitting from this sentiment as well as from an anti-Republican backlash caused by the economic depression that followed the Panic of 1873, the Democrats gained control of the House of Representatives and several Northern governorships for the first time in almost two decades. And the Supreme Court was already sending signals that it would strip the 1870–1871 enforcement laws of their teeth.

Despite the presence of Federal troops in Louisiana, the election of state legislators in 1874 produced a new round of disputed results. Democrats appeared to have won a majority in the lower house. But the returning Republican board threw out the results in several parishes on the grounds of intimidation. The board certified the election of fifty-three Republicans and fifty-three Democrats, with five cases undecided and referred to the lower house itself. When this body convened on January 4, 1875, Democrats carried out a well-planned maneuver to seat the five Democratic claimants before the befuddled Republicans could organize to prevent that action. In response, the Republican governor asked Federal troops to eject the five Democrats who had no election certificates. Soldiers marched into the House and escorted the Democrats out.

[21] Quoted in Lemann, *Redemption*, pp. 93–4.
[22] *Washington National Republican*, January 24, 1874; William B. Hesseltine, *Ulysses S. Grant, Politician* (New York, 1935), p. 358.

This affair caused an uproar in Congress as well as the country. Even a good many Republicans condemned the unprecedented military invasion of the legislature. Carl Schurz, who had spoken so powerfully for federal enforcement of reconstruction, with troops if necessary, had changed his tune by 1875. "Our system of republican government is in danger," he proclaimed in a Senate speech. "Every American who truly loves his liberty will recognize the cause of his own rights and liberties in the cause of Constitutional government in Louisiana." The "insidious advance of irresponsible power" had drawn sustenance from the argument that it was "by federal bayonets only that the colored man may be safe." Schurz conceded that "brute force" might make "every colored man safe, not only in the exercise of his franchise but in everything else.... You might have made the national government so strong that, right or wrong, nobody could resist it." That is "an effective method to keep peace and order.... It is employed with singular success in Russia." But "what has in the meantime become of the liberties and rights of all of us?," asked the Forty-eighter who had left Germany to escape just such tyranny.

> If this can be done to Louisiana... how long will it be before it can be done in Massachusetts and in Ohio? How long before the constitutional rights of all the states and the self-government of all the people may be trampled under foot?.... How long before a soldier may stalk into the National House of Representatives, and, pointing to the Speakers mace, say, "Take away that bauble"?[23]

A compromise kept the Republican administration in Louisiana afloat for two more years. In 1875, the focus of attention shifted to neighboring Mississippi, where legislative elections took place that year. Of all the Reconstruction state governments, Mississippi's was one of the most honest and efficient. And of all the "carpetbaggers," Governor Adelbert Ames was one of the most able, effective, and idealistic. Few carpetbaggers fit the nefarious stereotype of the genre, and Ames fit it least of all. Having graduated near the top of his class at West Point in 1861, this native of Maine fought in most of the battles of the Eastern theater in the Civil War, trained up the 20th Maine and its eventual commander Joshua Chamberlain, was awarded the Congressional Medal of Honor, and achieved promotion to brevet major general in the regular U.S. Army in 1865 at the age of twenty-nine. After commanding the military district of Mississippi and Arkansas and shepherding those states back into the Union, Ames was elected senator from Mississippi in 1870 and governor in 1873. His experiences in the Civil

[23] Bancroft, ed., *Speeches, Correspondence, and Political Papers of Carl Schurz*, vol. 3, pp. 111, 121, 144, 151–2, 141, 130–1, 125.

War and afterward produced a deep and genuine commitment to education and equal justice for the freed people.

To most whites in Mississippi, it mattered little that the state government under Ames was relatively honest and efficient by the standards of the time. It was not *their* government. Whites owned most of the property and thus paid most of the taxes. They resented the portion of those taxes that went to black schools. The black majority sustained Republican county and state governments for which few whites had voted. In 1875, the White Line rifle clubs determined, as they expressed it, to "carry the elections peacefully if we can, forcibly if we must." Their strategy became known as the Mississippi Plan.

Part of the plan involved economic coercion of black sharecroppers and laborers, who were informed that if they voted Republican they could expect no further work. But violence, threatened and actual, was the main component of the Mississippi Plan. White Liners discovered that their best tactic was the "riot." When Republicans held a political rally, several White Liners would attend with concealed weapons and others would lurk nearby in reserve. Someone would provoke a shoving or heckling incident. Someone else would fire a shot – always attributed to a Republican – whereupon all hell would break loose. When the shooting finally stopped, black and Republican casualties usually outnumbered White Liner casualties by about twenty to one. Then, the White Liners would ride out into the country and shoot any black man they suspected of political activism – and sometimes his family as well. Several years later, one White Liner candidly confessed that

> the question which presented itself then to the people of Hinds County was whether or not the negroes, under the reconstruction laws, should rule the county.... Throughout the countryside for several days the negro leaders, some white and some black, were hunted down and killed, until the negro population which had dominated the white people for so many years was whipped.[24]

The only way to counter this force was by equal or greater force. Ames was reluctant to mobilize the black militia – who in any case would be outnumbered and outgunned – because it would play into the hands of the white propagandists who spouted endlessly about savage Africans murdering white men and raping their women. The only solution was federal troops. Ames sent an urgent message to Washington requesting military support. Grant meant to comply. He instructed his attorney general to prepare a proclamation ordering lawless persons to cease and desist – a necessary prelude to sending troops – but also urged Ames "to strengthen his position

---

[24] Lemann, *Redemption*, p. 114.

by exhausting his own resources in restoring order before he receives govt. aid."[25]

The attorney general, a conservative Republican, goaded Ames more than Grant intended. "The whole public are tired out with these annual autumnal outbreaks in the South," wrote the nation's chief law-enforcement officer,

> and the great majority are now ready to condemn any interference on the part of the government.... Preserve the peace by the forces in your own state, and let the country see that the citizens of Mississippi, who are ... largely Republican, have the courage to *fight* for their rights.[26]

No federal troops came.

Ames did mobilize a few companies of black militia, even though he recognized that to use them in combat against the heavily armed Confederate veterans in the rifle clubs "precipitates a war of races and one to be felt over the entire South."[27] To avoid such a result, Ames negotiated an agreement with the Democratic leaders whereby the latter promised peace in return for disarmament of the militia. "No matter if they are going to carry the State," commented Ames wearily, "let them carry it, and let us be at peace and have no more killing."[28] It is not surprising that violence and intimidation continued under this "peace agreement," and on election day, black voters were conspicuous by their absense from the polls. In five counties with large black majorities, Republicans polled twelve, seven, four, two, and zero votes, respectively. In such a fashion, a Republican majority of thirty thousand at the previous election became a Democratic majority of thirty thousand in 1875.

The Mississippi Plan worked so well that other Southern states carried out their own versions of it in the national election of 1876. The last Republican state governments in the South collapsed when the new president, Rutherford B. Hayes, withdrew all federal troops in 1877. The Democrats had "redeemed" the South, which remained solid for their party and for white supremacy for almost a century. "Reconstruction, which had wound up producing a lower-intensity continuation of the Civil War, was over," writes an historian of the era. "The South had won."[29]

---

[25] Ibid., pp. 122–3.
[26] Richard N. Currant, *Three Carpetbag Governors* (Baton Rouge, 1967), p. 88.
[27] Lemann, *Redemption*, p. 120.
[28] "Mississippi in 1875: Report of the Select Committee to Inquire into the Mississippi Election of 1875," *Senate Report* no. 527, 44 Congress, 1 Session (Washington, DC, 1876), p. 1807.
[29] Lemann, *Redemption*, pp. 179–80.

CONCLUSION

This did not mean, however, that the loser of the Civil War had garnered the fruits of victory after all. In the war of the armies of 1861–1865, the North had prevailed and unequivocally achieved the principal goals of that war: preservation of the United States as one nation, indivisible, with liberty for all. A third goal, justice for all, was achieved on paper with the Fourteenth and Fifteenth Amendments. Moreover, it had come tantalizingly close to success on the ground for a few brief years. In the end, that justice was sacrificed for the unjust peace ushered in by "redemption" of the South, a peace marred by disfranchisement, Jim Crow, poverty, and lynching. Yet, the Fourteenth and Fifteenth Amendments remained in the Constitution. Exactly eighty years after Hayes withdrew Federal troops from the South, another Republican president – who also happened to be a famous general – sent them back to begin the painful processes of winning the final fruit of victory in the larger conflict of which the war of 1861–1865 had only formed a part.

MAP 5. Europe in 1871 and the making of Germany.

7

Vae victoribus: Bismarck's quest for peace in the Franco-Prussian War, 1870–1871

MARCUS JONES

Vae victoribus! Victory is a poor advisor, and nations tend to slip on the blood they have shed. Rome under its Caesers did not suspect that its *Vae victis* would apply in equal measure to Rome itself. After every victory, there's a new tomorrow. Waterloo follows Austerlitz. And so, too, our cry: Victor, beware!
"En campagne," *L'illustration*, 13 September 1870, a Parisian weekly. An admonition from *Neue Freie Presse*, a Viennese daily, addressed to Prussia.[1]

On 20 July 1870, the French ambassador to the United States, Lucien-Anatole Prevost-Paradol, shot himself in a hotel room in Washington, DC after learning that the government of Napoleon III had declared war on Prussia and its allied German states of the North German Confederation. Not from anguish over the possible fate of the Napoleonic regime did he commit suicide; indeed, as a prominent journalist and member of the liberal opposition, he had no great love for the empire. He had offered his services to Napoleon only as recently as 1869 during the brief period of liberalization that immediately preceded the outbreak of the war. Most likely, he acted out of distress at the disastrous outcome such a war, won or lost, implied for France.

Only two years before, Prevost-Paradol had published *La France nouvelle*, an extraordinarily prophetic account of the Franco-Prussian rivalry, which had depicted the two states speeding toward one another like trains on a collision course. No matter the military result, he argued, victory in such a conflict was impossible for France: A triumph would further inflame German

[1] Wolfgang Schivelbusch, *The Culture of Defeat: On National Trauma, Mourning, and Recovery* (New York, 2001), p. 125; from Michael Jeismann, *Das Vaterland der Feinde: Studien zum nationalen Feindbegriff und Selbstverständnis in Deutschland und Frankreich, 1792–1918* (Stuttgart, 1992), p. 174ff.

nationalism with dire implications later, while a French defeat would signal the end of her status as a great power.[2] With astounding clarity, Prevost-Paradol glimpsed the stakes involved in the rivalry and the realignment of strategic power in Europe that inevitably accompanied Prussia's rise.

The figure most responsible for the rise of Prussia and unification of Germany under its auspices during the Franco-Prussian War of 1871 was Otto von Bismarck, then the chancellor of the North German Confederation and minister–president of Prussia. Historians and political scientists have thoroughly picked apart the causes and course of that war, which serves as an object lesson in the importance of civil over military authority as well as the violent emotions generated by nationalist wars.[3] Much less common have been examinations of the manner in which the contending sides brought the war to an end, many months after major combat operations against the conventional army of France had ended successfully for the Germans.[4]

The successful campaign to exclude France from German affairs engineered from July 1870 to February 1871 by Bismarck ushered in one of the most enduring periods of international stability in modern European history, in part because its author understood clearly the precarious strategic underpinnings of the new German nation-state and how to safeguard them diplomatically. At the same time, that the First World War broke out forty-four years later and assumed the form that it did owed much to the popular and destructive nature of the war between Germany and France,

---

[2] See the account in Schivelbusch, *Culture of Defeat*, pp. 103–4.

[3] A brief listing includes, most notably, Michael Howard, *The Franco-Prussian War: The German Invasion of France, 1870, 1871* (London, 2001); Stéphane Audoin-Rouzeau, *1870: La France dans la guerre* (Paris, 1989); Geoffrey Wawro, *The Franco-Prussian War: The German Conquest of France in 1870–1871* (Cambridge, 2003); Francois Roth, *La Guerre de 1870* (Paris, 1990); Wolfgang von Groote and Ursula von Gersdorff, eds., *Entscheidung 1870: Der Deutsche-Französische Krieg* (Stuttgart, 1970); Henri Welschinger, *La guerre de 1870: Causes et responsibilities*, 2 vols. (Paris, 1910); Léonce Rousset, *Histoire générale de la guerre franco-allemande (1870–1871)*, 2 vols. (Paris, 1910–1912); for the official German military account in five volumes and four map addendums, see Kriegsgeschichtliche Abteilung des Großen Generalstabes, ed., *Der deutsch-französische Krieg 1870/1*, 5 vols. (Berlin, 1874).

[4] The standard analysis is Eberhard Kolb, *Der Weg aus dem Krieg: Bismarcks Politik im Krieg und die Friedensanbahnung 1870–1871* (München, 1989); idem, "Der schwierige Weg zum Frieden. Das Problem der Kriegsbeendigung 1870/71," *Historische Zeitschrift* 241 (1985) 51–79; to a more limited extent, idem, "Kriegführung und Politik 1870/71," in Theodor Scheider/Ernst Deuerlein, eds., *Reichsgründung 1870/71: Tatsachen, Kontroversen, Interpretationen* (Suttgart, 1970) 366–85; Robert I. Giesberg, *The Treaty of Frankfort: A Study in Diplomatic History, September 1870–September 1873* (Philadelphia, 1966); Léonce Rousset, *L'armistice de 1871* (Paris, 1927); Johannes Haller, *Bismarcks Friedenschlüsse* (Berlin/Stuttgart, 1917); Hans Herzfeld, *Deutschland und das geschlagene Frankreich 1871–73: Friedensschluß–Kriegsentschädigung–Besatzungszeit* (Berlin, 1924); and Fritz Richert, "Reichsgründung und Friedensschluß (Staatsaufbau, Friedensverhandlungen, Bestazungsmethode) 1871–1873," Dissertation, University of Erlangen, 1948.

which he brought about, and the enduring French hostility to its consequences, lending emphasis to the admonition of the Viennese paper quoted
at the beginning of this chapter. Bismarck understood the purpose of the
Franco-Prussian War of 1871 at its outset as the "realization of rational
political objectives in the tradition of *raison d'état.*"[5]

Although the conflict appears historically to have been among the last
of the conventional *Kabinettskrieg* among nation-states, the long and difficult process whereby Bismarck concluded it suggests how radically different
future national wars promised to be from the more limited conflicts that
dominated the European military history of the post–Napoleonic era: the
Crimean War, the War of 1859, the Danish War of 1864, the Austro-
Prussian War of 1866, the Russian-Turkish War of 1876–1878, and the
Greek-Turkish War of 1896–1897.[6] Most notably, Bismarck's making of
peace in the Franco-Prussian War typified the age-old problem of military conflict as resistant to purely military solutions, and his recognition
that because the outcomes of national conflicts depended on factors other
than rational strategic calculation, discretionary wars were to be avoided at
almost any cost.

What distinguished Otto Eduard Leopold von Bismarck-Schönhausen
from others of his time was not his uncanny grasp of the vast landscape
of European relations but rather a Machiavellian flexibility in marrying
unorthodox, even revolutionary means to strictly conservative ends. "Politics is neither arithmetic nor mathematics," he wrote on several occasions:
"To be sure, one has to reckon with given and unknown factors, but there
are no rules and formulae with which to sum up the results in advance."
Called to the minister–presidency of Prussia in September 1862 by a king
who had reached the point of virtual despair in his deadlock with parliament
over army reforms, Bismarck had the reputation of being a reactionary even
by royalist standards; nearly everyone in Berlin regarded him as too much
of a political outsider to be effective.

Early on, however, he demonstrated a willingness to traffic with those
forces viewed with the greatest suspicion by conservative interests to create effective new political constellations for furthering the interests of the
crown. In doing so, he revealed his guiding light: an unbending loyalty to the
Prussian state and its interests in Germany, a loyalty much greater than any
he felt for the specific monarch at whose pleasure he served or the abstract

---

[5] Pflanze, *Bismarck and the Development of Germany*, p. 468.
[6] The American Civil War was perhaps the most important exception, little appreciated even
   by contemporaries, a point disputed by Mark E. Neely, Jr., "Was the Civil War a Total
   War?", and James M. McPherson, "From Limited War to Total War in America," both in
   Stig Förster and Jörg Nagler, eds., *On the Road to Total War: The American Civil War and
   the German Wars of Unification, 1861–1871* (Cambridge, 1997), pp. 29–51 and 295–309.

idea of a unified German people or nation.[7] While willing to bargain with Prussian liberals as they pursued their national dream, the idea of unification was meaningful to Bismarck only insofar as it served as a vehicle for the protection of the Hohenzollern throne and its prerogatives. The complexion of the new German nation-state after 1871, wherein the Prussian King functions dually as German Kaiser and both the Prussian and imperial governments serve entirely at his pleasure, bore the unmistakable imprint of Bismarck's Prussian particularism.[8]

As the undisputed director of German affairs for nearly three decades, Bismarck proved a shrewd and imaginative statesman and daring risk-taker but always with the prudent recognition that conservative Prussia remained but one European power among several – a power the comparative vulnerability of which required strategic vigilance and imagination to survive. He demonstrated consistent moderation in defining and pursuing Prussian interests, bearing in mind that "[w]e do not live alone in Europe, but with three other powers who hate and envy us."[9] Throughout his career in politics, he seemed much influenced by a traditional vision of a poor Prussia enveloped by larger, wealthier neighbors, especially France, and warily convinced that success in military and diplomatic ventures could just as easily result in failure.

It is no exaggeration to say that the outcome of the War of 1866, which surprised many in Europe, made a conflict between Prussia and France nearly inevitable. French fear and suspicion of Prussia was long-standing and deep, and the formation in 1867 of the North German Confederation – which reduced the number of sovereign German states from thirty-nine to six – created a menacingly powerful new entity on France's northeastern frontier. The imperial ruler of France, Napoleon III, had dominated French affairs since 1852, but his regime was suffering declining popularity and a crisis of legitimacy throughout the 1860s. Indeed, one of the hallmarks of what has variously come to be known as Bonapartism is a displacement through charismatic leadership of domestic concerns into foreign adventure.

---

[7] Significantly, Bismarck selected an adaptation of a poem by Schiller for his gravestone, describing himself as a "faithful German servant of Kaiser Wilhelm I" while making no mention of his service to Wilhelm II.

[8] Bismarck's authority as minister–president of Prussia and later chancellor of the German Empire was wholly dependent on the great confidence of the Prussian King. In regard to Bismarck's capacity in 1866 to convince Wilhelm I of the essentially conservative rationale behind his support for universal suffrage in a German confederation, wits in Berlin said that Bismarck was the king's "last mistress, for only such a creature can wield so magic a power over an old man." Otto Pflanze, *Bismarck and the Development of Germany*, vol. 1, *The Period of Unification, 1815–1871* (Princeton, NJ, 1963), p. 301.

[9] Giesberg, *Treaty of Frankfort*, p. 20.

In 1866, Napoleon had sought to take advantage of the rivalry between Austria and Prussia through the threat of intervention but saw that advantage denied him through the unexpectedly rapid victory of Prussian arms. Like many in France, he interpreted the formation of the North German Confederation as an explicit challenge to traditional French influence in southern Germany and demanded territorial compensation for his country's loss of face, demands which Bismarck refused. Moreover, Bismarck successfully drew the southern German states closer to Prussia in the aftermath of the war through a series of tightly interlocking security treaties, which obligated them to defend one another in the event of war. Despite these security arrangements, he remained concerned after 1867 about the semi-independent status of southern Germany, which had fought against Prussia in the War of 1866 and which seemed ripe for manipulation by France or a vengeful Austria. He resolved to seize the opportunity, should one arise, to draw them as tightly into Prussia's embrace as he had the northern German states in 1867.

When war finally arrived, it did so largely through Bismarck's canniness and French blundering. Both sides clearly sought war, but Bismarck understood the advantages of localizing the struggle between Germany and France and ensuring the neutrality of the other European powers. He devoted careful diplomacy to isolating France and ensuring that hostilities would remain confined to their two countries, just as French bluster propelled France into a fight without similarly careful reflection on the need to secure international support against Prussia. Bismarck's management of the proximate events leading to the outbreak of war reveals him at his masterful best. In 1868, the Spanish military unseated Isabella II and began casting about Europe for a replacement of suitable stature who would also be acceptable to the Spanish parliament. The Spaniards eventually approached an obscure Catholic member of the Hohenzollern family, Prince Leopold von Hohenzollern-Sigmaringen, who turned out to have scant enthusiasm for assuming Europe's shakiest throne. He rebuffed the Spanish with the support of his higher ranking relative, William I, and the matter would have died there had it not been for the overreaching of the French emperor.

Napoleon III ordered his ambassador to demand a guarantee of the Prussian king that no Prussian prince would ever consider such an offer. In the face of such diplomatic impudence, William acquitted himself properly and promptly sent a telegram to Bismarck, which provided a favorable account of his meeting with the French ambassador. Recognizing a prime opportunity, the chancellor released the telegram to the press on 13 July but not before altering the language of the exchange to seem sharper and more insulting. The effect was to whip up German national feeling against the French and create a firestorm of indignation in France against Prussia.

Under the circumstances, with political recriminations flying both ways, the French imperial regime opted to draw on the immense popular surge of support for punishing Prussia and declared war on 19 July 1870. In doing so, they inadvertently served Bismarck's purpose of having the French appear as aggressors in international opinion and the North German Confederation as engaged in an involuntary defensive struggle; indeed, the *Neue Zürcher Zeitung* of 17 July branded France as the "oppressor of Europe." These factors proved critical to Bismarck's later efforts to end the conflict in terms favorable to Prussia and draw the southern German states into Prussia's embrace.

With hostilities under way, events rapidly deteriorated for France. French operational planning in the late 1860s for a war against Prussia involved mass offensives through Trier into the Rhineland, accompanied by diversionary naval and amphibious operations in the Baltic.[10] Such operations, assuming that the mobilization of the French Army proceeded smoothly, and French leadership in the field was competent, and might well have yielded fruit. Instead, neither assumption held. French military leaders deluded themselves into believing that the fragile North German Confederation would dissolve beneath the pressures of war and opted for a plan devised by General Charles Frossard, which called for awaiting the growth of tensions among the German states and then having the French Army march into southern Germany as liberators of the southern German states, which the French rather romantically thought to be the victims of brutal Prussian domination.[11] In the end, it seems unlikely that the French could have managed to pull off even so limited a strategy in light of their grave organizational deficiencies and the more decisive approach of their opponent. Indeed, the French Army turned out to be incapable of mounting any serious offensive challenge against German territory or even of upsetting the Prussian general staff's operational timetables.

The Prussians conducted their operations in August 1870 with an efficiency and effectiveness that has since come to stereotype their military history in the latter half of the nineteenth century. Helmuth von Moltke had headed the *Grosser Generalstab*, or Great General Staff, since 1857, transforming it through gifted leadership and an innovative vision of military operations into the most capable command organization in the world. Its exhaustive prewar planning and well-considered exercises ensured that

---

[10] On the naval war, see Alfred Schulze-Hinrichs, "Der Seekrieg 1870/71," *Marine Offizier Vereinigung (MOV) Nachrichten* (1970), pp. 127–8.

[11] Showalter moderates this view by pointing out that southern German support was uncertain until the publication of the Ems dispatch and that even the cohesion of the North German Confederation was somewhat questionable: Showalter, *Wars of German Unification*, p. 241.

by 3 August, more than 320,000 German troops stood on the French border. Swift offensive operations through the Lorraine gap led to three major French defeats in rapid succession, at Weißenburg on 4 August and at Wörth and Spichern two days later.

Reports of the setbacks dealt a grave blow to the French public's perception of the military situation and led immediately to a rash of hyperbolic media speculation in Paris that, after only a few engagements, the Germans stood poised to strike down French power in Europe permanently. German public opinion was only marginally less fervent in its expectations. Few on either side anticipated that the conflict would outlive the autumn. Indeed, even so sober an observer as Bismarck, who rarely assumed more than circumstances could bear, felt secure enough in German military fortunes to write his wife on 16 August that the campaign is "as good as ended, unless God should manifestly intervene for France, which I trust will not happen."[12]

Subsequent engagements qualified Bismarck's assessment somewhat but failed to disprove it, as local French resistance stiffened and the Prussians endured high casualties in a spate of early, brutal battles. A Prussian drive between Paris and the two main French field armies under Marshals Bazaine and MacMahon forced the former to retreat eastward and eventually hole up in the fortress at Metz on 3 September. MacMahon, accompanied by Napoleon III with a reserve army from Châlons, attempted to come to Bazaine's aid. German forces adroitly surrounded MacMahon's lumbering and exhausted army at Sedan and pummeled it with artillery fire until it capitulated on 2 September, taking into captivity 104,000 French soldiers along with the rather care-worn Bonapartist Emperor of France.[13]

In the eyes of most observers, and certainly those of Bismarck, Wilhelm I, and the Prussian military, the French defeat at Sedan and capture of Napoleon III represented a decisive battle. It should have brought hostilities to a close and, according to the standard formula of peace making in that era, led to an armistice and discussion of peace terms, culminating finally in a treaty of peace.[14] One cannot exaggerate how favorable were the circumstances under which the German states waged the war and sought peace in 1870. Bismarck had succeeded in isolating France diplomatically, no mean feat in a Europe deeply suspicious of Prussian ascendancy after 1866, and the

---

[12] Pflanze, *Bismarck and the Development of Germany*, vol. 1, p. 462.

[13] Showalter, *Wars of German Unification*, pp. 281–2.

[14] The conventional formula involved an armistice, a preliminary peace, and a final settlement: Kolb, "Der Schwierige Weg zum Frieden," pp. 54, 66; from Coleman Phillipson, *Termination of War and Treaties of Peace* (London, 1916), p. 94ff; a good discussion of the formal processes is also in Paulus Andreas Hausmann, "Friedenspräliminarien in der Völkerrechtsgeschichte," *Zeitschrift für ausländisches öffentliches Recht und Völkerrecht* 25 (1965), pp. 657–92.

French themselves had squandered much diplomatic capital by imprudently declaring war on Prussia. International opinion stood squarely on Prussia's side, making the intervention and interference of neutral powers far less likely. Mobilization and operations had proceeded smoothly, with a victory at Sedan as decisive as any optimist could have hoped for in advance. Had the French proven willing to behave as proper nineteenth-century statesmen waging limited war, they would have conceded defeat and skulked home to lick their wounds until the next opportunity arose to reassert French imperial power in Central Europe.

For the Germans, political and military objectives had developed in textbook harmony down to Sedan. The aim of German military efforts had been to bring about as rapid and decisive a defeat of French forces as possible, consistent with prewar Prussian doctrine, so as to yield the preconditions for a settlement on the basis of German strategic objectives. The object of Bismarck's political efforts had been to localize the war as much as possible and prevent the intervention of the other European powers.[15] The isolation of the conflict held tenuously into early September, with the neutrals watching the subordination of Bonapartist power with satisfaction but considering with just as much unease the growth of German power. Up to that point, Bismarck had little reason to involve himself in military strategy or operations. There he awaited that point at which matters on the battlefield bore clear fruit for the subsequent peace.[16]

Little in war conforms to expectation, however. In their wildest prewar fantasies, Bismarck and Moltke might have anticipated a rapid military victory, but neither foresaw the capture of the emperor and so sudden and complete a political turn. Before the war and in its first weeks, Bismarck had strongly preferred to negotiate a settlement with Napoleon, judging his regime to be the best guarantee against British influence on the continent, as well as against the growth of liberal and republican sentiments in Germany.[17] Basic to his thinking was his conviction that French antipathy to the growth of German power was popular and deep-seated and that no possible alternative to the empire would prove any more amenable to a unified Germany's strategic interests.[18] After deliberating at length on his options in the early, uncertain days of the war, Bismarck, therefore, recognized the importance of ensuring the continuation of the Bonapartist government.[19]

---

[15] Kolb, *Der Weg aus dem Krieg*, p. 196.
[16] Annelise Klein-Wuttig, *Politik und Kriegführung in den deutschen Einigungskriegen 1864, 1866 und 1870/71* (Berlin, 1934), p. 92.
[17] Kolb, *Der Weg aus dem Krieg*, pp. 104–5, 195–7; Giesberg, *Treaty of Frankfort*, p. 69.
[18] Ibid., pp. 158–9.
[19] Ibid., pp. 104–5.

The fall of Napoleon with the French forces at Sedan (which Bismarck referred to as a "great misfortune and embarrassment"[20]) introduced a troubling new dimension into what had seemed a straightforward strategic problem of defeating France and securing a favorable peace. Indeed, the implications of this development were as uncertain for the French as they were for Bismarck, as was suggested when Bismarck asked the French emissaries sent to negotiate the terms of the army's surrender whether Napoleon intended to surrender himself or all of France.

Taken aback, Napoleon's spokesman fumblingly replied that the surrender was personal and that Bismarck was to direct official petitions to the empress–regent in Paris.[21] Napoleon's surprising abdication of responsibility left Bismarck to contemplate the sticky process of finding somebody in France with enough weariness to accept Prussian peace terms and enough political capital to see them through, "the kind of settlement which left enough on the table to deter the loser from later attempts to reverse the situation through war."[22] This would constitute the central problem of Bismarck's efforts to end the war during the next six months, in which time no issue occupied him more urgently than the need to conclude hostilities and extricate German forces from France.

News of the French defeat at Sedan and capture of Napoleon III led to political events in Paris that brought home to the Germans the enormous implications of their victory. On 4 September, a Parisian mob disrupted an afternoon meeting of the *Corps Législatif* and joined republican delegates, led by the impetuous Leon Gambetta, in marching on the Hôtel de Ville, where he assumed the historical role of Danton in the latest iteration of the French revolutionary drama.[23] Empress Eugénie, acting as regent in Napoleon's stead, immediately fled into English exile.

A day later, the newly proclaimed Third Republic, with General Louis Trochu at the head of a self-styled "Government of National Defense," issued a *Proclamation au peuple français* to stiffen the resolve of the French citizenry and carry on the war against the German invader.[24] The tasks

---

[20] From a report of Prince Luitpold von Bayern of 11 January 1871, in Kolb, *Der Weg aus dem Krieg*, p. 196, n. 3.

[21] Herbert Geuss, *Bismarck und Napoleon III: ein Beitrag zur Geschichte der preussisch-französischen Beziehungen, 1851–1971* (Köln, 1959), p. 280; Giesberg, *Treaty of Frankfort*, p. 69; for the influence of the empress on the empire, see Elisabeth Esslinger, *Der politische Einfluß der Kaiserin Eugenie auf die Regierung Napoleons III* (Stuttgart, 1932).

[22] Showalter, *Wars of German Unification*, p. 286.

[23] See Etienne Arago, *L'Hôtel de Ville de Paris au 4 Septembre et pendant le siege* (Paris, 1874); another contemporary source is Émile Andréoli, *1870–1871: Le gouvernement du 4 septembre et la commune de Paris* (Paris, 1871).

[24] Jacques Desmarest, *La defense nationale, 1870–71* (Paris, 1949); also Pierre Hoff, "Le ministère de la Guerre à Tours et à Bordeaux en 1870–1871," *Revue historique des armées*, 135:2, 1979, pp. 70–85.

facing the new government were formidable: to bring under its control quickly those parts of France not occupied by German forces and define itself as the legitimate government of France in the midst of a desperate war. The provisional government claimed nominal authority over the nation of France but specifically disclaimed any right to negotiate a peace in the absence of a popular referendum on its legitimacy.

Republican plans provided for the raising of new conventional armies in the north and west of the country and called for an insurgency war, wherein so-called *franc-tireurs*, or irregular formations of partisans, would undertake scattered attacks on German forces and communications throughout the country.[25] Initially, such attacks were no more than a nuisance; over time, their frequency and effectiveness grew, with consequences for the ability of German forces to conduct operations and supply their forces. German units reserved a special ire for these bands of partisans, whose tactics consisted primarily of sniping and ambushing vulnerable contingents, especially foraging parties, and occasionally killing stragglers or the wounded. One cannot doubt that some took up the task spontaneously, but one should also not overlook the encouragement offered by republican officials like Leon Gambetta or the republican prefect of Côte d'Or, who pointed out that "[y]our fatherland does not ask you to gather in large numbers and oppose the enemy openly; it only expects that each morning three or four resolute men will leave their village and go to where nature has prepared a place suitable for hiding and for firing on Prussians without danger."[26]

While popular memory much exaggerated the actual military effects of the *franc-tireurs*, their activities added a troubling new dimension to the war for the Prussian General Staff, which deplored what it understood to be the coming horrors of a people's war. Egged on by the military advice offered to him by the American Union General Phillip Sheridan, who suggested the wholesale destruction of towns and villages where opposition occurred, Bismarck enthusiastically advocated a more savage response to the partisans.[27] As it was, the German military response involved a considerable degree of brutality and destruction, with a predictable decline in the discipline and morale of the troops forced to endure partisan raids and carry out reprisals. Noting the anger that irregular tactics aroused among German forces, Karl Marx mockingly remarked that "It is a real Prussian idea that a nation commits a crime when it continues to defend itself after

---

[25] Showalter, *Wars of German Unification*, p. 315, underscores the quite practical limitations on the French capacity to wage a genuine partisan war; on Gambetta in the provinces, see J. P. T. Bury, *Gambetta and the National Defense* (London, 1971).

[26] Thomas Rohkrämer, "Daily Life at the Front and the Concept of Total War," in Förster and Nagler, eds., *On the Road to Total War*, p. 506; from Geoffrey Best, *Humanity in Warfare: The Modern History of the International Law of Armed Conflicts* (London, 1980), p. 198.

[27] Howard, *Franco-Prussian War*, pp. 380–1.

its regular army has lost."[28] The rise of partisan activity underscored to the Prussian military leadership the fact that what had began as a limited war for discrete objectives had become a struggle against the French people, with no clear outcome in sight. The combatants had opened a "[p]andora's box of national feeling and the spirit of popular sacrifice."[29]

If the Prussian leadership was uncertain about the war it had to wage after Sedan, its French republican counterparts were no less so. At its inception, the government of the Third Republic seemed not to have understood the reasons for the lost war or its own vulnerable position in the ensuing political maelstrom. Wildly overestimating the likely effectiveness against German forces of the makeshift military units then being raised in the countryside, republican officials doubled-down their bets on continued resistance and inadvertently assured that when negotiations began, Bismarck would have to contend with a far more recalcitrant Prussian leadership, wholly disinclined to meet even minimal French demands.

Most important, many of the new government's senior representatives fell into the alluring trap of ascribing their country's current dilemma not primarily to military and diplomatic defeat but rather to the incompetence and even seditious behavior of the empire's leaders.[30] The foreign minister, Jules Favre (a man described by the British ambassador, Lord Lyons, as "too much led away by his feelings to be a man of business"), drafted a circular outlining the government's approach to negotiations that proclaimed in grandiose terms that France would "cede neither an inch of our territory nor a stone of our fortresses."[31]

Favre's initial communications with Bismarck, indicative in no way of a nation in the throes of a military meltdown, offered no more than a temporary armistice to allow consultation with the neutral powers about peace terms and hold elections to permit the French people to decide for peace or war, terms which Bismarck contemptuously rejected out of hand.[32] Within Paris, the sentiment took hold that European peoples would rejoice at the coming of a French republic and that the French themselves would

---

28 Karl Marx, "Brief an Ludwig Kugelmann in Hannover," 13 December 1870, in Karl Marx and Friedrich Engels, *Marx-Engels-Werke*, Institut für Marxismus-Leninismus beim ZK der SED, ed., vol. 33 (Berlin, 1956–1989), p. 163; from Rohkrämer, "Daily Life at the Front and the Concept of Total War," in Förster and Nagler, eds., *On the Road to Total War*, p. 506.

29 Pflanze, *Bismarck and the Development of Germany*, p. 469.

30 Giesberg, *Treaty of Frankfort*, p. 31.

31 Ibid., p. 18.

32 Indeed, when Bismarck pointedly rebuffed Favre's initial overtures on behalf of the Third Republic on 11 September, he described the provisional government as representing "only a part of the left of the former legislative body in Paris" and "an imperceptible minority," pointing to the imperial regime as the only one "authorized to enter into negotiations of an international character," Giesberg, *Treaty of Frankfort*, pp. 28, 32; see also the thick interpretation in Kolb, *Der Weg aus dem Krieg*, pp. 222–3.

find themselves galvanized to new heights of national sacrifice against the foreign invader, as they had in 1792.[33]

French retrenchment bode ill for Bismarck's project of securing peace. At the barest minimum, in Bismarck's estimation, a final peace settlement acceptable to Prussia fulfilled certain criteria not subject to his sole discretion. Because Bismarck firmly believed that the French would never accept a strong, unified Germany on their eastern frontier – the French, as he stated, "have not forgiven us for Königgratz and will not forgive us our victories now, no matter how generous our peace terms"[34] – he was determined that a settlement include safeguards against its ability to attack Germany. In addition to a war indemnity sufficient to hobble French irredentism for at least a few years (roughly equivalent in amount, in fact, to the first Napoleon's financial demands on Prussia sixty-three years earlier), Bismarck expected the transfer of Alsace and Lorraine, or at least that portion of the latter that included the strategic fortress of Metz, indispensable to the defense of the western German frontier: "We must have the two fortresses [Metz and Strassburg] in order to make difficult for France another aggressive war, not in order to bring Alsace and Lorraine back to Germany."[35]

This would prove the thorniest of points to resolve. As the best research on the topic underscores, a broad swath of popular German opinion, stoked aggressively by Bismarck, had since late August come to advocate forcefully and seemingly spontaneously that the German Confederation could accept no less than the annexation of the critical border regions.[36] Concurrently, a similar consensus on the necessity for annexations developed among Prussian military leaders, including Moltke, Minister of War Albrecht Roon, and King Wilhelm I, with the primary motive of closing off permanently the most strategically vulnerable western avenues of invasion into Germany.[37]

---

[33] Kolb, *Der Weg aus dem Krieg*, p. 226.

[34] Wawro, *Franco-Prussian War*, p. 300.

[35] Moritz Busch, *Bismarck: Some Secret Pages from His History*, vol. 1 (St. Claire Shores, 1971) p. 124; from Pflanze, *Bismarck*, pp. 485–5.

[36] Kolb, "Der Schwierige Weg zum Frieden," pp. 60–1; idem, "Bismarck und das Aufkommen der Annexionsforderung 1870," *Historische Zeitschrift* 209 (1969), pp. 318–56; Pflanze, *Bismarck*, pp. 484–9. The literature on the annexation question is enormous; for starters, see Lothar Gall, "Zur Frage der Annexion von Elsaß und Lothringen 1870," *Historische Zeitschrift* 206 (1968), pp. 265–326; Josef Becker, "Baden, Bismarck, und die Annexion von Elsaß und Lothringen," *Zeitschrift für die Geschichte des Oberrheins* 115 (1967), pp. 167–204; for the role of economic motives, see Eberhard Kolb, "Ökonomische Interessen und politische Entscheidungsprozeß: Zur Aktivität deutscher Wirtschaftskreis und zur Rolle wirtschaftlicher Erwägungen in der Frage von Annexion und Grenzziehung 1870/71," *Vierteljahrsschrift für Sozial- und Wirtschaftsgeschichte* 60 (1973), pp. 343–85; for the popular dimension in the regions themselves, see Fritz Bronner, *1870/71–Elsaß Lothringen. Zeitgenössische Stimmen für und wider die Eingliederung in das Deutsche Reich* (Frankfurt, 1970).

[37] Idem, "Der Kriegsrat zu Herny am 14 August 1870: Zur Entstehung des Annexionsentschlusses der preussischen Führungsspitze im Krieg von 1870," *Militärgeschichtliches Mitteilungen* 9 (1971), pp. 5–13; Howard, *Franco-Prussian War*, pp. 227–9.

Bismarck clearly hoped, perhaps unreasonably in the early days of September, that the press of events would motivate the French to part with the regions, as revealed by his role in negotiations after Sedan. On the essential point of annexations, German public and official opinion evinced a rare unanimity in outlook in 1870, a striking historical contrast to the divisions that would so bedevil the issue of war aims some forty years later.

If German opinion was unified on the questions of annexations, French opinion in the weeks after Sedan was equally adamant in its opposition. Quite apart from any moral or political considerations involved in shifting populations around on the map against their will (which would not come to dominate French discourse on the matter until years later), republican leaders fixated on the inviolable territorial integrity of the French nation, a concept that quickly became a cornerstone of their legitimacy. When confronted with Bismarck's terms for an armistice, Favre's response was to burst into tears and exclaim, "You want to destroy France!" Only somewhat less hysterically, the philosopher and critic, Ernest Renan, remarked that a "weakened and humiliated France would be incapable of survival. The loss of Alsace and Lorraine would mean the end of France."[38]

But, as time passed, and German military superiority told on an increasingly weary population, French opinion fractured. A progression of military setbacks and the presentation of German peace terms effectively divided the country starkly between the two traditionally antipathetic modalities of the French experience: Paris and all the rest. The population of the capital, especially its practiced radical element, remained adamantly opposed through spring 1871 to any territorial concessions and proved willing to fight ferociously against surrendering to German demands.

But the outlook in the remainder of France was mixed. As republican prefects, for the most part lawyers and literary figures, assumed control of local and regional governments in the weeks following the coup, they encountered a population decidedly ambivalent about the political situation in Paris and what they regarded as the larger stakes of the ongoing war. Few cared so little as not to resist German occupation, but fewer still failed to recognize that the country's military prospects were slim and that peace on German terms was preferable to continued bloodshed.[39] The fracturing of power in France, among other things, confounded Bismarck's effort to find a credible authority willing and able to meet his terms. His need to conclude peace rapidly was urgent; the neutral powers circled warily, threatening to intervene, if the utter subjugation of France meant too great an increase in Prussian power, while the ongoing war effort threatened to undo the domestic German consensus against France. Bismarck responded

---

[38] Schivelbusch, *Culture of Defeat*, p. 110; see Favre's own account of the negotiations in *Gouvernement de defense nationale du 30 juin 1870*, I (Paris, 1871), p. 156ff.

[39] Howard, *Franco-Prussian War*, pp. 235–6.

by prevaricating and holding his options for negotiation as open as possible.

The winter of 1870–1871 saw numerous political factions jockey for power in France, including Bonapartists, republicans, Bourbon legitimists, and Orleanists.[40] Despite sporadic contact and flirtation with the latter groups, Bismarck seems to have believed that a future France under a revived aristocracy would be an even more implacable threat to Germany.[41] His practical alternatives remained limited to the Bonapartists and the republicans. Initially, he held to his original preference for the government of Napoleon III, declaring that the German Confederation would recognize only the imperial regime as a legitimate negotiating partner "for the time being."[42] However, as the republicans asserted themselves successfully in Paris and unoccupied France over a period of days, he left willfully unclear any public preference for a negotiating partner and emphasized the readiness of the German authorities to negotiate with any legitimate government, provided the French nation recognized the conditions and results of a resulting peace agreement. To hedge his bets in the ensuing months, Bismarck maintained contact with the deposed Napoleon III in Wilhelmshöhe and Empress Eugénie in London.[43] It was an option Bismarck thought advisable in the light of the provisional government's questionable stability in the near term. After all, on 23-24 September, the republican authorities had indefinitely postponed elections to a national constituent assembly originally scheduled for 16 October.

The question of Bismarck's motives in flirting with virtually every political force in France during the winter of 1870–1871 finds no straightforward answer from the evidence. Did his motives stem primarily from a desire to pressure the provisional government with a Bonapartist restoration and extract greater concessions from that quarter, or did he seriously intend to achieve a settlement with Napoleon and restore the Second Empire?[44] What seems clear is that Bismarck, on this diplomatic issue like so many others, was largely devoid of prejudice in his choice of negotiating partner and took little for granted, save his complete faith in the eternal irredentism of France. He had not resolved by mid-September to favor one party or utilize

---

[40] Kolb, *Der Weg aus dem Krieg*, p. 201.

[41] Bert Böhmer, *Frankreich zwischen Republik und Monarchie in der Bismarck-Zeit: Bismarcks Antilegitimismus in Französischer Sicht, 1870–1877* (Kallmünz, 1966).

[42] Kolb, "Der Schwierige Weg zum Frieden," p. 64; Busch, *Bismarck*, vol. 1, p. 172; Giesberg, *Treaty of Frankfort*, p. 69.

[43] Joachim Kühn, "Bismarck und der Bonapartismus im Winter 1870/71," in idem, *Historische und polemische Aufsätze zur französische Politik* (Berlin, 1920), pp. 185–237; on the exile of Napoleon III in this period, see Paul Gueriot, *La captivité de Napoléon III en Allemagne (Septembre 1870–Mars 1871)* (Paris, 1926).

[44] Kolb, "Der Schwierige Weg zum Frieden," pp. 65–6, points to a credible literature that argues for Bismarck's preference for a Bonapartist empire.

either functionally to extract concessions from the other. Rather, he sought to assess realistically how well either could fulfill his two chief requirements: that the French government accept the basic German terms, and that the French partner that accepted them enjoy sufficient domestic support and power to carry the peace.

As a result of the political fallout in Paris from Sedan, Bismarck moved to deal more intensively with the republicans than the others. The facts that Napoleon III rested luxuriously in confinement and that any restoration of his government depended entirely on German collusion could not have failed to impress Bismarck's thinking.[45] A restored Bonapartist government would still require popular backing for an armistice and, therefore, would require either a plebiscite or the support of a revived *Corps Législatif* or similar conservative assembly, which essentially differed little from what the republicans demanded.

All of that made a restoration of the Bonapartist empire with German backing a riskier and more complex option when compared to dealing with the republicans, who enjoyed the great advantage, in Bismarck's view, of being in charge of Paris and having some claim to the popular sympathies. The provisional government also controlled the vast parts of France beyond the reach of German military power, had strong claim to most of France's remaining military resources, and seemed the only party able to agree to the necessary first step to a settlement: namely, an armistice. As both the republicans and Bismarck recognized, elections to a national assembly would have to occur during an armistice and lead to the formation of a government with enough popular legitimacy either to make a binding peace or decide to continue the war.

Bismarck could not but hope that war-weariness would translate into a willingness to recognize the futility of further struggle and accept German terms. Finally, German official and public opinion, to say nothing of international sentiment, strongly opposed the Bonapartist option. It seems reasonable to identify it as a plausible alternative as long as the provisional regime refused to submit the question of continuing the war to the French people and chose instead to wage a *guerre à outrance*, or total war. Bismarck could then point to the Bonapartists as the only plausible route to a peaceful resolution of the ongoing struggle, which could not but help his case in the courts of international and public opinion.

Bismarck's tasks were made no easier by the other major issues with which he was forced to deal after the fall of Sedan. With the fall of the Napoleonic empire and the stark assertion of Prussian power within the

[45] Giesberg, *Treaty of Frankfort*, pp. 69–70, remarks prosaically that "Bismarck could see no point in killing by harsh treatment the goose which might lay the much desired golden egg of a peace treaty[.]"

now-triumphant North German Confederation, relations between it and the southern German states, bound to the Confederation after 1866 by military treaties, accelerated toward unification. Intensive discussions between Bismarck and representatives of the Bavarian monarch, in particular, as well as the myriad smaller matters connected with the founding of a new nation, consumed much of his time and attention between September and January 1871, when Wilhelm I of Prussia assumed the imperial crown of Germany.[46]

Bismarck also found it necessary to build further on his earlier diplomatic initiatives to isolate the conflict and prevent the other European powers from involving themselves in the crafting of a peace settlement. His primary means of accomplishing this was to stimulate the budding strategic relationship between the three conservative monarchies of Central Europe: those of Russia, Austria, and the incipient German Empire.[47] While probably not apparent at the time, the long-term implications of his efforts would underpin a generation of stability in Europe and deprive France of any easy means of restoring her former prominence. The impressive effectiveness of German arms and rise of the republican regime in France, an unsettling development for many European leaders, simplified his task, but the weeks and months before the critical alignments between the German states hardened into a firm national entity were tense for Bismarck.

Not all obstacles to Bismarck's plans were external. The long-standing rift between political and military spheres of authority in nineteenth-century Prussia confounded him far more than any potential diplomatic complication during the winter of 1870.[48] Bismarck owed his position with the king to the issue. William had appointed him chancellor in 1862, in the thick of a constitutional conflict stemming from the Prussian parliament's challenge to the unrestricted authority of the king over military matters. Bismarck committed himself to safeguarding the crown's traditional prerogatives and eliminating the threat of parliamentary oversight in military affairs. Because he was accountable to parliament in certain ways, he agreed to give the army the right to report directly to the king without the interference or knowledge of the prime minister.

---

[46] The historiography of German unification in 1871 is vast and detailed. The best overviews remain Otto Pflanze, *Bismarck and the Development of Germany*, vol. 1, *The Period of Unification, 1815–1871* (Princeton, NJ, 1963); and Lothar Gall, *Bismarck: The White Revolutionary*, 2 vols. (London, 1986).

[47] Heinz Wolter, "Die Anfänge des Dreikaiserverhältnisses: Reichsgründung, Pariser Kommune und die internationale Mächtekonstellation 1870–1873," in Horst Bartel and Ernst Engelberg, eds., *Die großpreußisch-militaristische Reichsgründung 1871*, vol. 2 (Berlin, 1971), pp. 235–305.

[48] A good introduction is found in Stig Förster, "The Prussian Triangle of Leadership in the Face of a People's War: A Reassessment of the Conflict between Bismarck and Moltke, 1870–1871," in Förster and Nagler, *On the Road to Total War*, pp. 115–40.

By convention and practice, the king's control over the military was total, and at no point after 1848 did the Prussian monarch extend to his prime minister the same discretion in military affairs he enjoyed in other spheres. Clearly, public opinion and the financial constraints imposed by the Prussian parliament factored into the king's oversight of the military. But the practical implication of this dualism in civil and military authority was to give the chief of the general staff wide latitude in determining military policy. At the crucial junction of political and military considerations in the period 1870–1871, therefore, Bismarck had to contend with the broad authority of Moltke, who entertained a conception of his own prerogatives and competence as stridently as Bismarck himself. Between them stood William I, who had neither the ability nor the inclination to manage both realms, and who thus acted as a final arbiter of those conflicts that bubbled to the surface.

The near origins of Bismarck's conflict with the Prussian military lay in the outcome of the war against Austria in 1866.[49] For much of the conflict, relations between Bismarck and the generals were constructive; by the end, the senior military leadership had grown to resent what they took to be his meddling in affairs best left to their discretion. In his strategy against Austria, Bismarck wisely sought to restrict Prussian involvement in Austrian affairs, reassure the other European powers of Prussia's limited intentions, and negotiate terms with an intact Austrian state.[50] From the beginning, he recognized the value of a counterweight to the power of Russia in the Balkans and a lever to drive the southern German states into a closer relationship with Prussia, and his influence with the king was such as to bring the monarch around. But the longer term significance of Bismarck's strategic success did little in that crucial moment to ameliorate Prussian military opinion, and the biting and sarcastic way he had of addressing himself to the military leadership left a bitter taste in men who had accomplished the defeat of Austria in seven weeks. The result of his relationship with Moltke and the general staff in 1866 was a bitter resolution on their part to prevent him from intruding into what they took to be properly military concerns.[51]

As long as regular French forces remained a military threat in 1871, relations between Bismarck and the general staff remained cordial, although even early on, the military worked to deny him access to current intelligence on the course of military events. Until a system for providing him

---

[49] An early, scattered synthesis is found in Wilhelm von Blume, "Politik und Strategie. Bismarck und Moltke 1866 und 1870/71," *Preußische Jahrbücher*, 111, 1903, pp. 223–54.
[50] Förster, "The Prussian Triangle of Leadership," pp. 123–4.
[51] Bismarck alleged in 1895 to have overheard a general vow as much in a railcar en route to the front in 1870: Eberhard Kolb, "Strategie und Politik in den deutschen Einigungskriegen: Ein unbekanntes Bismarck-Gespräch aus dem Jahre 1895," *Militärgeschichtliches Mitteilungen*, 48, 1990, p. 131.

with current information was established in October, he had to rely on civilian news reports, never less than five days old. The dispute grew acidic after Sedan, when the easy correspondence between operations and strategy broke down under the weight of German war aims and the French resolve to carry on the war by other means. Bismarck argued for suspending military activities until the reality of defeat impressed the French and Prusso-Germany could pursue a negotiated peace, while Moltke adhered to a concept of operations that prescribed peremptorily crushing French defiance and dictating terms. In the latter's view, German war aims were straightforward and political and strategic concerns extraneous to military events irrelevant; it mattered little whether the regime receiving German terms was Bonapartist, republican, or royalist. In Moltke's view, complete destruction of the French ability to resist would provide the grounds to persuade them to submit. The intervention of the neutral European powers was of scant concern to the chief of the general staff, and he displayed little appreciation of the factor that weighed so heavily on Bismarck's thinking: the need to reassure the other powers that a strong and unified Germany at the heart of Europe was a force for stability.

Following the French surrender at Sedan, Moltke divided his forces, sending one portion to besiege Paris and another to support the siege of Metz, wherein lay the ill-fated army of Marshal Bazaine. Additional Prussian forces under Ludwig von der Tann and Edwin von Manteuffel pressed into the south as far as Orléans to deny space for the French to raise fresh units. However, at no point during the war were German forces sufficient to occupy the vast territory of France or even meet the basic operational needs of maintaining the sieges while matching standing French units in the field. Indeed, the newly raised Army of the Loire achieved an impressive, albeit rare, victory over grizzled German veterans at the Battle of Coulmiers on 9 November, a result that underscored that France's military prospects were far from depleted and inflated French hopes of eventual victory. From this point, German units had precious few opportunities to demonstrate their prowess in conventional warfare. The majority of subsequent military engagements involved exhausting pursuit marches punctuated by brief, limited encounters with improvised or irregular French forces, a form of warfare deeply demoralizing to regular troops, taxing to the German logistics and personnel-replenishment system, and rarely anticipated by Prussian training and doctrine.[52] By early December, the Bavarian I Corps, admittedly considered by the Prussian leadership to be the weakest element in the German Second Army, had virtually broken down under the weight of

[52] See Rohrkrämer, "Daily Life at the Front and the Concept of Total War," pp. 497–518.

battle casualties, sickness, collapsing logistics, and a personnel-replacement system, which failed utterly to replenishment its ranks, "... overmarched, underfed, and regularly embarrassed by an enemy whose presence was more often sensed than seen."[53]

The inability of the German military to get a firm grip on the French countryside undercut Bismarck's best efforts in autumn 1870 to force French negotiators to accept German terms. Armistice negotiations with the representatives of the republic on 19-20 September at Ferrières (with Jules Favre) and in early November (with Adolf Thiers) proved fruitless, as French negotiators insisted that the truce last two weeks and that the Germans allow them to resupply Paris, demands which Moltke rejected out of hand.[54] As for his second option, the Bonapartists, Bismarck found little more than factionalism, resignation, and indifference, as Napoleon and Eugenie proved distinctly disinterested in paying for their return to power with large sacrifices of French territory. Moreover, they believed that their unpopularity in France necessitated substantial concessions from Bismarck compared with what he was prepared to offer the republicans.[55]

A glimmer of hope appeared in mid-October when Marshall Bazaine, besieged at Metz, dispatched an emissary to Bismarck with the aim of withdrawing his army to a location somewhere in France to reconstitute a government representative of the views of the entire country. Bismarck was well disposed to the idea in general and disclaimed to Bazaine's emissary his unwillingness to dictate the future form of France's government while affirming his desire to treat with the Bonapartists rather than the republicans. He was unbending in his basic conditions, however: Bazaine's public declaration of support for the empire, prior agreement by the empress to any terms Bismarck put forth, and formation of a French parliament to ratify the resulting treaty. Specific terms of the final treaty itself, he left deliberately unstated.[56] The empress's queasiness at the thought of agreeing to Bismarck's blank check and the odious prospect of surrendering French territory outright doomed these negotiations before they began in earnest.

The surrender of Bazaine's army at Metz on 27 October, which freed the Second Army of Prince Friedrich Karl for operations against French forces in the Loire Valley, failed to bring about any greater willingness by any French faction to accept German terms. It did have the effect of relieving somewhat the disastrous overstretching of German forces and allowed Moltke to focus

---

[53] Showalter, *Wars of German Unification*, pp. 302–3; for its end as a fighting formation at Beaugency, revealing of the toll of the war on German units, see ibid., p. 306.
[54] Howard, *The Franco-Prussian War*, pp. 330–1, 337.
[55] Giesberg, *Treaty of Frankfort*, pp. 76, 78.
[56] Ibid., pp. 73–4.

on Paris (which he correctly took to be the appropriate *Schwerpunkt* of his efforts), while he detailed some forces to handle the emergent French insurgency in his rear and on his flanks.

The investment of the vast city of Paris, one of the most drastic urban sprawls in the history of modern Europe, ranks as one of the Prussian general staff's most remarkable and little-appreciated accomplishments in the nineteenth century.[57] In its prewar doctrine, the Prussian Army had not taken seriously the need for siege operations. It viewed them as diverting critical weight from the open-field engagements that played best to its strengths in organization, speed, and firepower. Nevertheless, it quickly enveloped Paris with an interlocking network of fortifications and strong points linked by lateral communication and transportation lines that proved virtually as impregnable as the city it enveloped. Unfortunately for the Germans, the siege tied down so large a proportion of their forces that much of the rest of France remained unoccupied and simmering perilously in a state of armed resistance.

The siege of Paris brought relations between Bismarck and Moltke to a new low.[58] Throughout the latter months of 1870, Bismarck recognized more than any other German figure the larger diplomatic stakes involved in the stubborn resistance of the republican government: namely, the possibility of foreign intervention, an arbitrated peace, and the consequent moderation of Prussian influence in northern Germany. Such an outcome would have rendered German efforts hollow. In running battles with the general staff chief, he emphasized continually his original priorities: rapid victory and a negotiated peace based on firm but limited war aims. Bismarck judged as quite limited the strategic and negotiating space within which the new Germany could establish a peace favorable to its postwar position.

At the outset, Bismarck had opposed any advance on Paris. He believed its internal divisions would do more to undermine the republican government and willingness of the French to resist than any military measure.[59] When Moltke made the decision to invest the city anyway, Bismarck favored an immediate and overwhelming bombardment, for he believed that only the utmost pressure would hasten French recognition of defeat and willingness

57 Wilhelm Busch, *Das deutsche Große Hauptquartier und die Bekämpfung von Paris im Feldzuge 1870/71* (Tübingen, 1905); issues then involved in siege warfare are detailed in Hans Justus Kreker, "Die französische Festungen 1870/71," *Wehrwissenschaftliche Rundschau*, 20, 1970, pp. 505–17; on the major military figures, Emil Daniels, "Roon und Moltke vor Paris," *Preußische Jahrbücher*, 121, 1905.

58 Arnold O. Meyer, "Bismarck und Moltke vor dem Fall von Paris und beim Friedensschluß," in Karl von Raumer and Theodor Schieder, eds., *Stufen und Wandlungen der deutschen Einheit* (Stuttgart, 1943), pp. 329–41; for background, see Werner Dunkel, "Die Verzögerung der Beschießung von Paris 1870/71 und ihre Literatur," *Zeitschrift für Heereskunde*, 30, 1976, pp. 113–19.

59 Pflanze, *Bismarck and the Development of Germany*, p. 478.

to deal. A prolonged siege would permit the French to chip away at the German military and precipitate a shift in opinion among European leaders, who at this point still largely favored Germany. Roon supported Bismarck, but Moltke and most of the rest of the general staff bitterly opposed him on principled and, increasingly, personal grounds. The threat of foreign intervention fazed Moltke not in the least, while he doubted the effects that even the most impressive bombardment imaginable could have against so well-defended and enormous a target and recognized that the most militarily efficient and least costly, if not quickest, way to reduce a population center was through starvation.

Events would bear out Moltke's narrowly military suppositions: By the time the Germans assembled sufficient munitions and commenced to shell Paris in late December, the results were disappointing and contributed little to the surrender of a city already reeling from starvation. But Moltke was incorrect on the larger strategic point, as he had been so often before. Operational utility and efficiency are poor criteria by which to judge prudent military action, and Moltke refused to acknowledge that a prolonged siege of Paris or the destruction of remaining French field armies would not amount to success if the other European powers involved themselves in the peace negotiations and diluted Bismarck's effort to draw the southern states into the Confederation. In working against Bismarck's subordination of military to political considerations, Moltke forever cemented his place in history as the father of German operational prowess and strategic imprudence.[60]

Critical to French prospects for extracting more favorable peace terms from Bismarck was Adolf Thiers's diplomatic counter-offensive to break the neutrality of the European powers.[61] A widening of the conflict and the outbreak of a cataclysmic pan-European war were among Bismarck's worst fears, and Thiers seemed to appreciate the significance of the threat to the German position. International circumstances and Bismarck's diplomatic ingenuity conspired to undermine him, however, and he enjoyed scant success in efforts to leaven France's problems with the interests of the other powers.

Indeed, chafing under the strategic outcome of the Crimean War, the Russians sought to exploit French weakness by repudiating the clauses of the Treaty of Paris of 1856 and reasserting themselves in the Black Sea, which led to an international crisis that threatened to entangle all of Europe. Bismarck managed to avert that calamity only by calling an international conference

---

[60] For a sensitive treatment of a problem that scholars have frequently oversimplified, see Dennis E. Showalter, "The Political Soldiers of Bismarck's Germany: Myth and Reality," *German Studies Review*, 17, 1994, pp. 59–77.

[61] John Holland Rose, "The Mission of M. Thiers to the Neutral Powers in 1870," *Transactions of the Royal Historical Society*, III:11, 1917, pp. 35–60.

to meet in January in London to reassess the standing of all interested parties.[62] As for Thiers's best hope, the French military defeat at Sedan soured the Austrians on avenging their defeat in 1866, while the Italians saw in his plight the opportunity to stoke the fires of Italian nationalism and seize Rome from its French garrison. Only the British extended a fig leaf in the form of an offer from Lord Granville to mediate an armistice between the combatants, a proposal which Bismarck could probably have afforded to reject by that point anyway.

Upon returning to Paris and presenting these bleak diplomatic prospects to the provisional authorities, Thiers found himself stunned by the sheer inability of the republican leadership, General Auguste Ducrot in particular, to acknowledge the essentially political nature of the problem confronting France and to deal with that reality in terms other than martial honor.[63] In a meeting on 5 November in a house at the Sèvres bridge, Favres insisted that the restive population of Paris was in no mood to accede to Prussian terms, no doubt thinking of the uprising, which had taken place on 31 October and shaken the republican government deeply. The radical elements within the Parisian population, while commanding limited support, enjoyed an influence far beyond their numbers and remained bitterly opposed to any line other than resistance until death.[64] Ducrot, head of the Paris defenses, added that the stain of Sedan and Metz on French military honor made further struggle essential.[65]

As if to hammer home the irrationality of their mindset, General Trochu insisted on planning a heroic and completely implausible breakout instead of creatively using the impenetrable city of Paris and its huge garrison to pin down German siege forces and win breathing space for French forces in the field. As Sir Michael Howard has pointed out, in his dealings with Ducrot and the other republican officers in Paris, Thiers faced the same problem that Bismarck confronted with Moltke:

> Both soldiers spoke in terms of honour, and of victory through attrition. The first concept was irrelevant to a sound peace; the second disastrous to it. . . . In face of such an attitude neither Thiers nor Bismarck could find anything more to say, and the situation reverted to a purely military footing.[66]

---

[62] Werner Mosse, *The Rise and Fall of the Crimean War System 1855–1871* (London, 1963), p. 346; Kurt Rheindorf, *Die Schwarze-Meer-(Pontus) Frage vom Pariser Frieden von 1856 bis zum Abschluss der Londoner Konferenz von 1871* (Berlin, 1925).

[63] On Thiers' negotiations with Bismarck and dealings with the provisional authorities, see Adolphe Thiers, *Memoirs of M. Thiers, 1870–1873* (New York, 1973), pp. 88–99.

[64] Giesberg, *Treaty of Frankfort*, pp. 60–1; Showalter argues that Trochu and Favres understood the political temper of Paris better than their critics before or since and that the former's plan for a breakout conformed to it better than any other feasible course: idem, *Wars of German Unifications*, p. 309.

[65] Auguste A. Ducrot, *La Défense de Paris, 1870–71*, 4 vols. (Paris, 1875–8).

[66] Howard, *The Franco-Prussian War*, p. 340.

As matters stood, Thiers had little choice but to shelve diplomacy for the time being. The military situation would have to deteriorate much further before the republicans would admit defeat in the face of popular intransigence. As Trochu was said to have remarked, "The people in some drawing rooms want peace; the man in the street wants war."[67]

In the meantime, the republic managed to cobble together a decidedly respectable military force in the bleak autumn of 1870, comprising the handful of regular regiments which had escaped annihilation or capture by the Germans, some fine naval infantry brigades, nearly three hundred battalions of *Garde mobile* (i.e., second-class units not drafted into the peacetime regular army), and the nearly seven hundred battalions of the poorly trained national guard, which came as close as any large units in the modern age to outright cannon fodder. The new armies had little or no effective cavalry, artillery too sparse and ineffective to be much threat to the excellent Prussian field guns, and most important, far too few schooled field officers and staff planners to undertake any but the most rudimentary of field maneuvers.[68] What the gigantic new cadres of the republic had in abundance was enthusiasm for the national cause and a passionate hatred of *les Boches*. Unfortunately, events would show that no amount of enthusiasm could make up for their dismal lack of experience and training.

All the same, their efforts created considerable anxiety among Prussian military leaders. On 27 November, one of the early, hopeful accomplishments of republican arms came against General Manteuffel, who had two corps of Prussian infantry and a cavalry division. General Louis Faidharbe, a veteran of France's colonial wars in Africa and the most gifted field commander to serve the republic, skillfully drew Manteuffel away from the main German positions around Paris and fought him to a standstill in the country near Amiens. In December and January, he mounted a pair of impressive offensive thrusts back toward Paris, hammering veteran Prussian units in well-coordinated engagements that seemed to auger well for the republic's military possibilities. But the fights strained Faidharbe's hastily raised units to the limit and underscored that if French forces were a mile wide, they were only an inch deep.

Meanwhile, as French accounts of the bloody fight at Beaune-la-Rolande on 15 November make clear, the best efforts of two French corps from the Army of the Loire proved ineffectual against the brutally effective artillery and fire discipline of Prussian regulars, even when they enjoyed substantial numerical superiority.[69] By the onset of the new year, not even the most

---

[67] D. W. Brogan, *France Under the Republic: The Development of Modern France* (New York, 1940), p. 45.
[68] Showalter, *Wars of German Unification*, pp. 288–9.
[69] Ibid., p. 301.

fervent republican enthusiasts could deny that France's military fortunes were grim and further resistance probably futile. By the same token, the unconventional turn of the war after Sedan and its continual drain on the limited military resources of the German states underscored to the Prussian leadership that it too was incapable of waging a total war over the long term.[70]

Despite his earlier failures, Bismarck retained hope that he could reach an accord with the imperial authorities and carried on negotiations with their representatives through the winter of 1870–1871. The fact that the Bonapartists had by this point fractured into three main groups espousing different settlements considerably complicated his task.[71] From his imprisonment at Wilhelmshöhe, Napoleon III proposed a new national assembly based on the old *conseils généraux* of the empire to mold a government, a scheme to which Bismarck instinctively warmed when presented with it.[72] A second group, comprising lesser Bonapartist exiles in England, involved a similar plan but based it instead on a reconvocation of the empire's senate and legislative assembly on the doubtful assumption that they would support a conservative postwar regime. The third option involved Empress Eugenie returning to France as regent without conditions for the shape of the ensuing peace, a possibility that would most probably have resulted in successful negotiations, given Bismarck's preferences. To this end, on 16 January, she dispatched a trusted adviser, Clement Duvernois, to negotiate her return with the Bonapartist exile communities and the German authorities.

In the end, each of these divergent Bonapartist initiatives failed. The republican authorities, fearing the exploitation of traditional representative organs like the *conseils généraux* to lever Napoleon III back into power, dissolved them formally on Christmas Day, 1870. The second group, the Bonapartist émigrés, for reasons that are unclear, neglected to follow up on their plans and decided that the opportunity to restore an imperial government would not arise until after the Germans had decisively defeated the republic. But the third option, which held out the greatest promise of peace on Bismarck's terms, failed for the most foolish of reasons. Bismarck awaited the arrival of the regent's representative eagerly and with increasing irritation after 15 January, while sending out telegrams in every direction seeking clarifications as to the emissary's whereabouts and instructions to have him depart forthwith for the German headquarters. Not until 28 January did he turn up,

---

[70] Wilhelm Deist, "Remarks on the Preconditions to Waging War in Prussia-Germany, 1866–1871," in Fòrster and Nagler, eds., *On the Road to Total War*, pp. 318–20.

[71] Giesberg, *Treaty of Frankfort*, pp. 76–9, details the Bonapartist alternatives; for a good overview, John Rothney, *Bonapartism after Sedan* (Ithaca, 1969).

[72] On the status of the traditional assemblies, see Louis Gerard, Antoine Prost, and Remi Gossez, *Les conseillers généroux en 1870: Etude statistique d'un personnel politique* (Paris, 1967).

"20 minutes too late," as Bismarck rather dryly put it, having just reached an understanding with Jules Favre. Instead of making for Versailles directly and seizing the moment to deal with Bismarck, Duvernois had wasted valuable time consulting with Napoleon in Wilhelmshöhe and émigré groups in Brussels before finally reaching the German headquarters. Although Bismarck maintained some degree of contact with the imperial exiles in the following months, their moment had passed, largely by virtue of their failure to act decisively and exploit the remaining strengths in their position.

Clearly, Bismarck still took seriously the possibility of achieving an accord with the Bonapartists, or at least engaging them enough to exert strong pressure on the provisional government to concede more when Paris fell, and they had to seek terms. A memorandum of 14 January intended for his king, in which he reviewed his possible negotiating partners and weighed his options, suggests how the chancellor viewed the diplomatic situation.[73] He swiftly dismissed the royalist alternatives. The provisional government had the great advantage, in Bismarck's estimation, of being readily available as a negotiating partner but seemed unlikely to concede the territory that German war aims stipulated as the irreducible minimum acceptable. As a consequence, Bismarck still preferred to deal with the Bonapartists but not at all costs. Primary was the need to secure peace in the quickest manner possible, and he was still willing to treat with all comers.

The fall of Paris led directly to general armistice negotiations between Bismarck and Favre and led indirectly to the end of the war, although the great majority of contemporary observers and historians since 1871 have taken that fact overly for granted.[74] As strongly as Bismarck had striven to end the war, other outcomes to the capitulation of the city seemed far more probable than a general armistice and peace. Gambetta desired to maintain indefinitely the struggle against German forces while Moltke envisioned breaking French resistance totally and dictating a unilateral peace. In his own memorandum to the king on 14 January, he envisioned a complete surrender of the city along lines similar to those followed at Sedan and Metz, involving formal military delegations and the observance of protocols.[75] German forces would then have waged a war of extermination against French forces in the field. Had no French authority within Paris proved willing to assume responsibility for a complete surrender or had matters compelled an armed occupation of that famously ungovernable population, then one can only speculate how the Prussian military leadership would

[73] Kolb, *Der Weg aus dem Krieg*, p. 322; idem, "Der schwierige Weg zum Frieden," pp. 68–70.
[74] Ibid., p. 327.
[75] Arnold O. Meyer, "Bismarck und Moltke vor dem Fall von Paris und beim Friedensschluß," in Karl von Raumer and Theodor Schieder, eds., *Stufen und Wandlungen der deutschen Einheit* (Stuttgart, 1943), pp. 329–41; Kolb, *Der Weg aus dem Krieg*, p. 328, n.1.

have approached the problem. Permitting the city to starve completely in the absence of a responsible government was undoubtedly not an alternative for a nineteenth-century European nation-state like Germany, and it seems doubtful whether the international community would have stood idly by. But, of course, such thoughts did not cross the mental horizons of Moltke or the other generals.

No matter how one emphasizes the centrality of Bismarck to the making of peace in the Franco-Prussian War – and he is arguably more central to that peace than any single figure for a major conflict of the modern era – one must not overlook the factors beyond his influence that factored directly into its timing and form. Easily the most important of these was the unwillingness of any significant military or political figure in France to concede defeat and accept responsibility for the aftermath of the disastrous war. With the bread supply in Paris sufficient for only two days, it fell to Jules Favre on 23 January to sally forth to Versailles and extract from Bismarck what concessions he could in surrendering the city and its defenses. Early on, he suggested that their negotiations serve as the first step to a general armistice on German terms and free elections to a new assembly. Even at this hopeful stage, Bismarck emphasized firmly to Favre that his options were several, that he saw little advantage in treating with a provisional government whose ability to speak for all of France was dubious, and that the newly crowned German emperor might well have other priorities, by which he probably meant those of the general staff.[76] If the emperor followed that advice, then the Germans would unilaterally dictate the terms of the peace. In drawing attention to other influential voices in the German camp, Bismarck revealed to Favre the internal limitations he faced in bringing about the end of the war.

Indeed, at a war council the next morning with the senior German political and military leadership, the conflict between Bismarck and Moltke reached its zenith.[77] Earlier efforts by the crown prince to patch up relations between the men had come to nothing and, by that point, the atmosphere between them was poisonous. Because no firsthand accounts of the council are available, one must speculate that Bismarck argued from his now familiar position: that the other European powers would not stand by as the fragile new German Empire destroyed French power entirely, leaving a dangerous vacuum to be filled in the zero-sum game of European strategy, and that Germany could not afford to carry on the war indefinitely. The power of the French to resist, if not prevail, was ultimately greater than the power of the Germans to overcome them. In the crucial moment of decision, Wilhelm

---

[76] Kolb, *Der Weg aus dem Krieg*, p. 321.
[77] Ibid., pp. 334–5, points out that accounts of this critical meeting must draw a wide range of peripheral sources because no direct evidence of what transpired survives.

upheld Bismarck's position and empowered him to begin general armistice negotiations as soon as the opportunity arose. The agreement signed on 28 January gave the French three weeks to elect an assembly to oversee subsequent negotiations, stipulated that Paris immediately pay a substantial indemnity and surrender its outer fortifications, and established a demarcation line between the armies throughout the country.[78]

By resolving the issues hampering the dialogue down to that point and making possible the election of a national assembly to conduct France through the preliminary and final negotiations, the general armistice was the decisive step toward reestablishing peace between Germany and France in 1871. The road to the signing of the final treaty in Frankfurt on 10 May 1871 was winding and uncertain at points, but the outcome was virtually assured by Bismarck's deft handling of the process. After ratification of the armistice by the provisional authorities, the outcome of the French elections of 8 February represented the next critical step. The returns resoundingly vindicated Bismarck's strategy, with conservative parties committed to a settlement on the basis of the indemnity and territorial surrender scoring terrific margins over those, like Gambetta, devoted to further resistance.[79] The formation of a national assembly followed shortly thereafter, with Adolf Thiers assuming the executive office and becoming head of the commission to negotiate the terms of the final peace treaty with Bismarck.[80]

With Favre's assistance, Thiers negotiated the terms of the preliminary treaty with Bismarck; the former argued vehemently until its signing on 26 February for more favorable terms of payment and a diminution of the territorial demands.[81] Later, the immense pressure Thiers faced from the political left gravely challenged the ability of his government to achieve similarly rapid results in negotiations over the final peace treaty. The growing agitation of French radicals in March and April forced the republicans to fight for revisions of specific provisions of the settlement as outlined in the preliminaries. The outbreak of the Paris Commune on 18 March called into question the legitimacy of the republican regime to negotiate, to say nothing of its very existence.[82] Even with the final signing of the treaty, the republicans were moving forces to Paris to suppress the uprising in what

---

[78] Ibid., p. 3.
[79] See Jacques Goualt, *Comment la France est devenue républicaine: Les élections générales et partielles à l'Assemblée nationale, 1870–1875* (Paris, 1954), p. 72.
[80] Pierre F. Simon, *A. Thiers, Chef du Pouvoir Executif et President de la Republique Francaise, 17 Fevrier 1871–24 Mai 1873* (Paris, 1911).
[81] Hans Goldschmidt, *Bismarck und die Friedensunterhändler 1871: die deutsch-französischen Friedenverhandlungen zu Brüssel und Frankfurt März-Dezember 1871* (Berlin, 1929).
[82] Eberhard Kolb, "Der Pariser Commune-Aufstand und die Beendigung des deutsch-französischen Krieges," *Historische Zeitschrift*, 215, 1972, pp. 265–98.

would be among the bloodiest and most violent operations against civilians in the course of the nineteenth century.[83]

CONCLUSION

The Franco-Prussian War prefigured the total wars of the twentieth century even if it did not entirely fulfill the paradigm. The conflict's status as a conventional, limited war between traditional European states did not last beyond the major battles and sieges in September and October of 1870. The provisional government's decision to draw on popular sentiments of national resistance and identity, especially in Paris, in waging a *guerre à outrance* and the extreme countermeasures of the German military demonstrated a clear tendency toward the totalization of the war, wherein victory comes not through defeating enemy forces but rather in crushing the national will to resist. Under such circumstances, accompanied frequently by waxing expectations and demands on both sides, the prosecution of rationally devised and clearly articulated war aims became nearly impossible. Had Bismarck not enjoyed the confidence of the Prussian king over the military and not been in a position to direct German affairs with restraint and foresight, it is easy to imagine the brutalization of the conflict along lines similar to those of the American Civil War or the First World War. Likewise, without the possibility of dealing with a figure like Bismarck – firm but open to a settlement that left something for the losing side – moderate republicans like Thiers and Favre would have had nobody in the German camp to approach, the uncompromising Gambettas among the French republicans would have fought to the bitter end, and the German military under Moltke would have pressed relentlessly and bloodily toward absolute victory and a dictated peace. The implications of such a war on the peoples of both sides would have been predictably disastrous. Moreover, it is possible that such action would have brought the other European powers into the conflict. Only Bismarck possessed the political fortitude and strategic insight to assert the primacy of politics over military concerns, reach out to his French counterparts, and strive unremittingly for an end to what could well have become a catastrophe for Europe.

But not even Bismarck could foresee that "Germany's magnificent and well-deserved victory was, in a profound and unforeseeable sense, a disaster: for herself, and for the entire world."[84] If the outcome of the war confirmed

---

[83] Some eighty thousand Frenchmen died in the war and another thirty thousand – nearly one in thirty Parisians – died in the suppression of the Commune. See Robert Tombs, *The War Against Paris, 1871* (Cambridge, 1981); Christian Lebrument, *Guerre de 1870 et la Commune: vie quotidienne à Colombes* (Paris, 2005).

[84] Howard, *The Franco-Prussian War*, p. 456.

Prevost-Paradol's predictions of French strategic decline and German ascendancy, the legacy was by no means an unmixed one for the victor. Defeated France would prove a perennial thorn in Germany's side. In the guise of the Third Republic, France spawned a political and social doctrine of rabid nationalism and hatred of Germany that unified monarchists, republicans, and radical socialists across the political spectrum for a program of revanchism and national preparedness.

Assuming this, Bismarck's diplomacy in the ensuing era depended less on the threat of war than on artful persuasion and persistence. He worked assiduously to convince the other European powers that the existing constellation of power was the most advantageous and that all stood to lose from war. Between the end of the Franco-Prussian War and his dismissal two decades later, he succeeded in weaving the European powers into an elaborate network of treaties, both overt and covert, "whose common denominator was that no one could count on support for aggressive behavior as defined by others."[85]

But his successors in the chancellery and foreign ministry doubted the value of such an intricate and calibrated system, preferring for a while a more aggressive approach to diplomacy and eventually a jingoistic *Weltpolitik* that emphasized cheap successes and self-indulgent claims of Germany's right to a place in the sun.[86] By 1900, few policy makers identified with Bismarck's circumspect view of a weak and vulnerable Prussian homeland sandwiched between restless and potentially hostile neighbors, constantly mindful of the need to remain on the side of three against two in European strategic affairs, and content with small gains at the expense of great risks. Moreover, virtually all of Germany's policy makers now accepted the doctrine of "military necessity" – a path that would lead to the extraordinary excesses of August–September 1914 and beyond.

The structural division between civil and military authority in Prussia, which led to such bitter conflicts between Bismarck and Moltke, persisted well after the latter's belated realization that Europe had entered a dangerous new era of technological sophistication and popular, total warfare. If Moltke himself became convinced late in his glittering career that wars of extermination were neither feasible nor desirable in the military landscape

---

85 Dennis Showalter, "From Deterrence to Doomsday Machine: The German Way of War, 1890–1914," *The Journal of Military History*, 64, 2000, p. 684; H. Rumpler and J. P. Niederkorn, *Der "Zweibund" 1879: Das deutsch-österreichisch-ungarische Bündnis und die europäische Diplomatie: Historikergespräch, Österreich-Bundesrepublik Deutschland 1994* (Wien, 1994).
86 See the essays in Annika Mombauer and Wilhelm Deist, eds., *The Kaiser: New Research on Wilhelm II's Role in Imperial Germany* (Cambridge, 2003); also Peter Winzen, *Bülows Weltmachtkonzept Untersuchungen zur Frühphase seiner Aussenpolitik 1897–1901* (Boppard am Rhein, 1977).

he helped create, his successors evinced precious little of his reserve and found themselves hampered far less in their advocacy of forceful, aggressive action by the far less capable figures who followed Bismarck.[87]

The German Army's spectacular success in the wars of 1866 and 1870–1871 brought to the military establishment of the new nation a degree of official independence and social esteem that would prove disastrous for German policy on the eve of the First World War.[88] A generation of Germans born after the great wars of unification would view them as heroic struggles waged by a heroic generation of founders and war itself the most legitimate and celebrated means of safeguarding the interests of the nation. The optimism and jingoistic chauvinism of middle-class Germany, particularly in the two decades preceding the First World War, rested on the myths of the Franco-Prussian War as well as the new economic and strategic weight of the Reich relative to its European neighbors.

Moltke, in reply to Bismarck's interference, had argued in the 1870s that military operations should begin where policy left off. In peace, according to him, the military should rest under the authority of the political leadership, but in war military leaders must dominate until the ending of hostilities again allowed the politicians to take over. At the end of his life, Moltke would come around more to the Iron Chancellor's view, but by then it was too late. By then, a new generation of German generals and theorists were arguing that military, operational concerns should dominate strategy and the making of major decisions. And so, in July 1914, on the specious grounds that war was better now than later, the German Army embarked on war with a plan, the strategic implications of which neither the civilians nor the military had considered. In every sense, operational concerns trumped strategy; by 1918, under Ludendorff, tactics were to trump operations.

Nevertheless, in the aftermath of Moltke's departure, German military power entered a period of relative decline after 1890. Russian manpower potential vastly overshadowed even the most optimistic German mobilization prospects, while France, working assiduously throughout this period to create military organizations as technocratic and professional as those of Germany, passed budgets and increased force levels in a manner that made warfare for the General Staff seem a desperate risk.[89] Under the circumstances, it is difficult not to see the miscarriage of the Bismarckian program of brief wars for limited objectives in Europe's frightening new military reality, based as it was on mass-conscript militaries, narrowly technocratic staff

[87] Stig Förster, "Facing 'People's' War: Moltke the Elder and Germany's Military Options after 1871," *Journal of Strategic Studies* 10 (1987) 209–30; Showalter, "The Political Soldiers of Imperial Germany," pp. 59–77.

[88] Friedrich-Christian Stahl, "Preussiche Armee und Reichsheer, 1871–1914," in Oswald Hauser, ed., *Zur Problematik "Preussen und das Reich"* (Köln, 1984).

[89] Showalter, "From Deterrence to Doomsday Machine," pp. 688–9.

competency, rigid mobilization timetables, and furious offensive operations culminating in brief and brutal engagements.[90] If Bismarck recognized the importance of these trends in 1871, then it was all he could manage to stave off their implications for the ensuing two decades. His successors would then proceed to wreck his creation.

[90] Ibid., p. 708; see also the fascinating study of military professionalization by Mark R. Stoneman, "Bürgerliche und adlige Krieger: Zum Verhältnis zwischen sozialer Herkunft und Berufskultur im wilhelminischen Offizierkorps," in Heinz Reif, ed., *Adel und Bürgertum in Deutschland II: Entwicklungslinien und Wendepunkte im 20. Jahrhundert* (Berlin, 2001), pp. 25–63.

MAP 6. The peace settlements in Europe.

8

Versailles: the peace without a chance

WILLIAMSON MURRAY

The Treaty of Versailles: The very words resonate with failure – a disastrous peace that supposedly enabled another catastrophic war within two decades.[1] As the French Field Marshal Ferdinand Foch morosely commented at the Treaty's signing: "This is not a peace; it is an armistice for twenty years."[2] Even more presciently he later noted: "The next time, remember, the Germans will make no mistakes. They will break through northern France and seize the Channel ports as a base of operations against England."[3] It is not surprising that historians have blamed the statesmen who negotiated and debated at Versailles for the all too obvious collapse of the European order in the 1930s.[4]

Yet, as always in history, it is the context that matters. In the end, it was not the Treaty of Versailles that made another major European war inevitable but rather the strategic, political, and military circumstances of

---

[1] For the Treaty of Versailles, Harold Nicolson's *Peacemaking 1919* (New York, 1965) still holds up remarkably well. There is also an excellent collection of articles by leading historians on the seventy-fifth anniversary of the treaty's signing. Nevertheless, it suffers from a lack of coherence of its articles, while there are few substantive references to the nature and character of the war that had just ended: See Manfred F. Boemeke, Gerald D. Feldman, and Elizabeth Glaser, *The Treaty of Versailles, A Reassessment after 75 Years* (Cambridge, 1998).

[2] Quoted in Anthony Adamthwaite, *France and the Coming of the Second World War, 1938–1939* (London, 1977), p. 17.

[3] Quoted in Margaret MacMillan, *Paris, 1919, Six Months that Changed the World* (New York, 2001), p. 459.

[4] Astonishingly, the news magazine, the *Economist*, pontificated in its millennium issue in January 2000 the following about the Treaty: "The final crime [was] the Treaty of Versailles, whose harsh terms would ensure a second [world] war." What such superficial simplicity misses are the circumstances under which the statesmen had to work as well as the contribution of events and individuals to what was to come in the two decades between the signing of the Treaty and the outbreak of the war.

the war and its sudden ending that not only drove the politicians at Versailles but largely determined the success or failure of the peace in the long term. Moreover, the policies and decisions crafted by the statesmen, politicians, diplomats, and events themselves in the aftermath of Versailles would guide Europe and the peace in very different directions from what the peacemakers of 1919 had hoped.

Historians have also tended to argue that those who framed the Treaty of Versailles had a choice among three alternatives: a liberal peace of reconciliation, a peace of revenge to pay the Germans back for their actions during the conflict, and the peace that eventually ensued, one that fell between the stools of reconciliation and *revanche*.[5] This chapter, however, charts a different course. It argues that the nature of the war, its extraordinary length, its cost in lives and damage, the fury with which the contending powers waged it, the emergence of popular opinion as a major factor in international relations, and, perhaps most important, the manner in which the conflict came to a sudden and unexpected end in November 1918 – all of these factors ensured that there could not be a satisfactory peace because the context had already largely laid out the direction of future events. In other words, the boundaries within which the immediate past encircled the leaders of the victorious powers so constrained the making of peace that the Treaty of Versailles could only enable a breather between the two great wars, much as had been the case between the Archidamean and Ionian Wars in the fifth century B.C.[6]

THE CONTEXT OF THE WAR

To understand the difficulties the peacemakers at Versailles confronted, one must begin by discussing the nature of the war as well as the German actions that contributed so much to the collapse of civilized values during the conflict's course. This is not to suggest that the Allies did not contribute some execrable acts of their own.[7] But the point here is to understand why

---

[5] One of the exceptions is Arno Mayer of Princeton, who has made the bizarre argument that the peacemakers at Versailles, including Clemenceau, were more concerned with the revolutionary movements swirling around Central and Eastern Europe – particularly in Russia with the Bolsheviks – than they were about the German problem: see Arno J. Mayer, *The Politics and Diplomacy of Peacemaking: Containment and Counterrevolution at Versailles, 1918–1919* (New York, 1967).

[6] And, unlike his contemporaries, the great historian Thucydides recognized that the period between 431 B.C. and 404 B.C. represented a single conflict, what historians today term as the Peloponnesian War. So too today, some modern historians are beginning to look at the period between 1914 and 1945 as a single great conflict.

[7] The behavior of Russian troops during their short-lived invasion of East Prussia in 1914 was hardly a model. Considerable looting and rape marked their advance in August, but those actions appear to have been more the result of the ill discipline of the troops than

the attitudes of the victorious powers at Versailles were so hostile to the Germans in the immediate aftermath of the conflict. In the postwar period, the Germans claimed that military necessity alone had driven their actions. The following analysis, however, suggests that at best that was a spurious claim and at worst, a mendacious one.

The Outbreak of War

The outbreak of war in August 1914 did not come as a surprise.[8] During the course of the previous decade and a half, a series of crises had broken over Europe, each of which had served to exacerbate a deteriorating international environment. Tensions among the powers, quarrels in far-off places like the Balkans, a rapidly accelerating arms race, and German intransigence and truculence all contributed to the explosion in late July 1914.

The clear instigator of the crisis, whatever the contribution of others, was the Kaiser's Reich. With the removal of Otto von Bismarck as Germany's chancellor in 1891, German policy began to come off the tracks. Where once the "Iron Chancellor" had manipulated Europe's strategic strings to Germany's advantage, his successors in Berlin set about kicking over Bismarck's semihegemonic system. In a matter of months, they had dispensed with the alliance with Russia in the belief that Imperial Russia and Republican France could never get together. Nevertheless, within a few years, the Czar was standing bareheaded to salute the playing of the Marseillaise in honor of the signing of the Franco-Russian alliance.

Then, in the first years of the twentieth century, the Germans began a naval race with the British in the belief they could actually maintain a great continental army at the same time as they built up a sufficiently large navy to take on the Royal Navy with some prospect of success.[9] Underlying German calculations, such as they were, was a belief that Britain could never ally itself with its traditional enemies, Russia and France.[10] In 1905, the British and

---

of deliberate policy. Moreover, the British blockade of Germany aimed at starving the populations of Imperial Germany and the Austro-Hungarian Empire to the point of either surrender or starvation.

[8] The foremost study of the outbreak of the war remains the masterful three-volume study by Luigi Albertini, *The Origins of the War of 1914*, 3 vols. (London, 1942). For Germany's responsibility, see Holger Herwig, "Germany," in *The Origins of World War I*, ed. by Richard F. Hamilton and Holger H. Herwig (Cambridge, 2003).

[9] Or at least that their fleet could cause such damage to the Royal Navy that British naval superiority would be threatened by French and Russian naval power.

[10] One of the great faults of statesmen and military leaders is to persist in courses of action despite the fact that reality underlines the faulty nature of the assumptions on which their strategic or operational policy rested at the beginning of a conflict. The Germans in the period from 1900 through 1945 exemplified this disastrous proclivity. Nevertheless, the reader's attention is drawn to Colonel H. R. McMaster's brilliant study of how American political and military leaders managed to draw the United States into a disastrous war

French established the *entente cordiale*, which settled their major differences. Two years later, an entente between Britain and Czarist Russia followed. In 1905 and then again in 1911, the Germans attempted to break out from what they believed was their growing diplomatic and strategic encirclement.

In both cases they failed. Moreover, they suffered humiliating diplomatic defeats in trying. Increasingly harnessed to the moribund Austro-Hungarian Empire, the Germans perceived themselves as being encircled in view of the ominous strategic trends in the European balance of power, as the Entente Powers strengthened their diplomatic and military connections. In addition, the rapid recovery of Russia's military power after its defeat at the hands of the Japanese in the Russo-Japanese War of 1904–1905 and Russian plans for major increases in its defense budgets caused deep worries in Berlin.[11]

To support Austrian interests, the Germans found themselves drawn into the treacherous waters of Balkan politics – an area that Bismarck had characterized as "not worth the bones of a single Pomeranian grenadier."[12] The crisis broke in early summer 1914. On June 28, Serb fanatics assassinated Archduke Franz Ferdinand, heir to the Austro-Hungarian throne, in Sarajevo. On July 5, one week after the assassination, Berlin gave Vienna a blank check to settle matters with the Serbs. In so doing, the Germans were not directly initiating hostilities in Europe as they were to do on September 1, 1939, with their invasion of Poland. But they certainly understood that they might well be unleashing a European-wide conflict.

Some, like the German chancellor, Theobold Bethmann-Hollweg, hoped Austria-Hungary could emerge peacefully from its confrontation with Serbia with its prestige enhanced. In fact, the Germans were lighting the fuse, and they understood that war was a distinct possibility. Bethmann-Hollweg readily accepted the risk of war. Others enthusiastically supported the idea of war now. General George von Waldersee, deputy chief of the great general staff, noted to his subordinates that Imperial Germany had "no reason whatever *to avoid* [a general conflict] but *quite the opposite*, [good] prospects *today* to conduct a great European war quickly and victoriously."[13]

German leaders got the war all too many of them had desired. German Army planning for war had posited a major offensive effort in the west to defeat the French as quickly as possible so that its forces could turn

---

in Southeast Asia despite the clear evidence that the United States was confronting an unwinnable quagmire: *Dereliction of Duty, Lyndon Johnson, Robert S. McNamara, the JCS, and the Lies that Led to Vietnam* (New York, 1996).

[11]   The German chancellor, Theobold Bethman-Hollweg, commented in July 1914 to his chief political advisor that Russia "grows and grows and weighs on us like a nightmare." Quoted in Holger H. Herwig, *The First World War, Germany and Austria-Hungary, 1914–1918* (London, 1997), p. 21.

[12]   Quoted in ibid., p. 19.

[13]   Quoted in ibid., pp. 20-1.

east to meet the Russian Army, which the army's planners believed would prove slower to mobilize. Thus, the Germans launched a major invasion of France in response to a crisis in the Balkans that the Austrians had initiated by mobilizing and then declaring war against Serbia, a mobilization which had then occasioned a Russian mobilization.[14] To defeat the French in time to move reserves east, the general staff had developed the so-called Schlieffen Plan, which involved a massive invasion of Belgium to outflank French fortresses as well as the difficult terrain along the Franco-German frontier.[15]

In conversation with the British ambassador to Berlin, the German chancellor dismissed the treaty – in which the great powers, including Prussia, had guaranteed Belgium's neutrality in 1839 – as a "scrap of paper," thereby providing the prowar party in Britain additional support to bring their nation into the war, a possibility that the German military had considered of little importance in its prewar planning.[16] But it was not just Germany's callous disregard for Belgium's neutrality that underlined "military necessity" as the mark of the new war. To the outrage of the Germans, the Belgians resisted the invasion of their country.

The fortresses around Liege delayed the German advance on Brussels, while the destruction of bridges, railroads, and tunnels slowed the deployment of the right wing into France.[17] From the first days of the invasion, the Germans carried out a program of executing large numbers of Belgian civilians for acts of "sabotage" and incidents such as firing on German troops. As a recent historian of the Kaiser's army argues,

> First, crimes of excess began immediately; the use of human shields in combat, the punitive destruction of buildings, and the mass execution of noncombatants began on 5 August 1914, the first day of the real shooting war. Second, they were widespread; half of all the German regiments in the western theater of operations committed such acts. In the first two months of the war there were 129 major incidents of execution (involving ten or more civilians).... Third, as

---

[14] All but the most obtuse could recognize that the train of events as well as the course of German military operations underlined Imperial Germany's decisive role in the outbreak of the war. The facts, of course, have not prevented legions of historians, and not just Germans, from arguing the opposite.

[15] A recent interesting but somewhat tendentious work has suggested that there is little evidence on which to base the existence of the Schlieffen Plan that postwar German authors claimed had driven German operations in August 1914. Whatever the actuality of German planning, there is no doubt that the Germans initiated major military operations by invading a small, neutral country. For the recent reexamination of the Schlieffen Plan, see Terence Zuber, *The Schlieffen Plan, German Military Planning before the First World War* (Oxford, 2005).

[16] Quoted in Herwig, *The First World War*, p. 30.

[17] Moreover, that destruction hindered the movement of crucial supplies forward to the German Army, as it advanced ever deeper into France.

in 1870, these acts were first committed by common soldiers or low-ranking officers, but they were swiftly approved by higher-ranking officers and systematized in orders at the army level or above.[18]

The violence the Germans inflicted on Belgian and French civilians, even by the standards of today, represented major war crimes. Proclamations plastered on the walls of Belgian towns proclaimed: "For all acts of hostility the following principles will be applied: all punishments will be executed without mercy, the whole community will be regarded as responsible, hostages will be taken in large numbers." At Aerschot, angered by tenacious resistance, the Germans shot 150 civilians; at Dinant, 664.[19]

Such actions were in express contravention of the Hague Convention, which the Germans had signed. Admittedly, compared to the atrocities the *Wehrmacht* inflicted on civilians and prisoners of war during the Second World War, these actions represented relatively small incidents.[20] But for 1914, they were egregious, inexcusable acts of violence. Overall, in August and September, German troops deliberately executed at least six thousand civilians in response to supposed acts committed by Belgian *franc-tireurs*. They destroyed between fifteen thousand and twenty thousand buildings in actions not connected with combat.[21] The Germans also managed to burn down the great medieval library at Louvain – an achievement they replicated during the opening days of their invasion of Belgium in May 1940.

While Allied propaganda shrilly overestimated the extent of German atrocities in Belgium, the record is clear enough: Against helpless civilians, German acts of ruthlessness in the war's first months were inexcusable by the standards of civilized behavior.[22] At this point, the Germans still believed

---

[18] Isabel V. Hull, *Absolute Destruction, Military Culture and the Practices of War in Imperial Germany* (Ithaca, NY, 2005), p. 207. For the approval of senior German generals for such actions after the war, see Erich von [sic] Ludendorff, *Ludendorff's Own Story*, vol. 1 (New York, 1919), pp. 34–7.

[19] Barbara W. Tuchman, *The Guns of August* (New York, 1962), pp. 226–7.

[20] The extent of the criminal behavior of the German Army – and we are talking here about the German Army and not the Waffen SS – in the Second World War is underlined by Christian Streit's work on how the Germans treated their Soviet POWs over the course of the Second World War: *Keine Kameraden, Die Wehrmacht und die sowjetischen Kriegsgefangenen, 1941–1945* (Stuttgart, 1978). Among a host of works in German and English that have appeared over the course of the past two and a half decades cataloguing the criminal behavior of German Army units, especially on the Eastern Front but elsewhere as well, see also Wolfram Wette, *The Wehrmacht: History, Myth, Reality*, trans. by Deborah Lucas Schneider (Cambridge, MA, 2006). The semi-official histories of the Militärgeschichtliche Forschungsamt have been both groundbreaking and ruthless in their criticism of the behavior of the German military toward civilians.

[21] Tuchman, *The Guns of August*, p. 210.

[22] For a more complete discussion of the issues of German atrocities in the First World War, see John Horne and Alan Kramer, *German Atrocities, 1914: A History of Denial* (New Haven, CT, 2001).

that they were going to win a quick, easy, and decisive victory. Within a month, they were to suffer defeat on the Marne. That defeat ensured the war would be long rather than short. Ironically, by their invasion of Belgium to enable a short war, the Germans had brought the British Empire with its immense resources into the conflict, a major factor in the coming long war. Moreover, their actions, including the atrocities in Belgium, led the majority of Americans to favor the Allied cause, a predisposition the Germans reinforced in succeeding months.

The Conduct of War and Military Necessity

The war on which Europe had now embarked reflected the convergence of trends associated with the French Revolution and its mobilization of the populace and the nation's resources with the Industrial Revolution which had been gathering steam – quite literally – throughout the nineteenth century.[23] The signals of what this conjunction implied for war had emerged in the American Civil War, but few in Europe paid much attention to that war, which Moltke had described as a conflict between ill-trained militia.

The consequence of those two revolutions allowed the major powers to draw on a cornucopia of manufactured goods and resources thereby keeping huge armies in the fields for an indeterminate period. Ironically, in view of the widespread belief among politicians and generals at the time, the societies of the First World War were enormously resilient in terms of both popular support and the capacity to "bear any burden, pay any price."[24]

Moreover, the forty-plus–year period between the Franco-Prussian War of 1870 and 1914 had seen a scientific and technological revolution on a scale which had never occurred before in history. It changed the face of war. Military organizations now confronted intractable and insoluble problems in adapting to the new weapons. The result, after the killing battles of late summer and early fall 1914, was a stalemate. One of the few to see the implications of that situation was the new chief of the German general staff, Eric von Falkenhyn, who suggested to Theobold von Bethmann-Hollweg, the German chancellor, that Germany should seek a compromise peace. But the chancellor displayed no interest. Nor did any one else in leadership

---

23 On the influences of systemic change on military organizations and war, see Williamson Murray and MacGregor Knox, "Thinking about Revolutions in Warfare," in *The Dynamics of Military Revolution, 1300–2050*, ed. by MacGregor Knox and Williamson Murray (Cambridge, 2000).

24 The words of John F. Kennedy in his inaugural speech, January 1961. Virtually everyone among the financial, economic, and political experts believed that Europe could not possibly bear the strain of a prolonged, major conflict for more than a few months without economic or political collapse.

positions among the major contenders; the opposing sides had shed too much blood in the war's first months to be willing or able to accept the idea of a compromise peace.

To maintain the struggle against opponents who could deploy significantly greater forces, the Germans consistently fell back on "military necessity."[25] In April 1915, they used poison gas for the first time on the Western Front, despite the warning of Crown Price Rupprecht of Bavaria, commander of the Sixth Army, that the Allies could easily replicate poison gas. Moreover, since the winds blew from west to east in France and Belgium, gas warfare would place German troops at a considerable disadvantage.[26] Urged on by other senior army commanders, despite the fact that the Hague Peace Conference had banned the use of poison gas, the Kaiser decided differently.[27] For a one-time tactical advantage which inflicted heavy casualties on one French division, the Germans provided the Allies with a major tactical and operational advantage in the fighting on the Western Front.[28] Even more disastrously, they drew considerable opprobrium on the Reich, especially in the United States.

In May 1915, after declaring a U-boat blockade around the British Isles, the Germans sank the liner *Lusitania* – an action they had predicted in an advertisement on the front pages of the *New York Times*. Of 2,000 passengers, 1,198 drowned, of whom 159 were Americans. To exacerbate the propaganda disaster, the Germans struck a medal to celebrate their "success."[29] Again, international agreements signed before the war had forbidden submarine attacks on passenger or merchant ships without providing sufficient warning time to allow crew and passengers to abandon ship.

American public opinion was so outraged that the United States almost declared war. Only President Woodrow Wilson's refusal to bend to public opinion kept the United States on the sideline. These German actions gained little except opprobrium, while they allowed the British to tighten the blockade. At least for once, a realistic appraisal of the balance led the German civilian leaders to persuade the Kaiser to halt the unrestricted U-boat war.

---

[25] On this, see particularly the extensive discussions in Hull, *Absolute Destruction*, pp. 123–6, 237–42, and 320–32.

[26] On the development of gas warfare and the arguments in favor of its use among the Germans, see Herwig, *The First World War*, pp. 169–70.

[27] Germany was a signatory.

[28] Not only did the winds in Flanders favor the Allies but also the crucial raw material in making tight-fitting gas masks was rubber, which the Allies possessed in abundance while the Germans had no access to rubber throughout the war because of the British blockade. For a discussion of the Allied advantage in gas warfare, see Albert Palazzo, *Seeking Victory on the Western Front: The British Army and Chemical Warfare in World War I* (Lincoln, NB, 2002).

[29] Sir Llewellyn Woodward, *Great Britain and the War of 1914–1918* (Boston, 1967), pp. 196–7.

The danger of an American entrance into the war receded, at least for the moment.

The year 1916 heralded a downturn in German fortunes. The British assault on the Somme followed immediately on the heels of the terrible losses the German Army suffered at Verdun. The Germans termed what occurred on the Somme the "*Materielschlacht* (battle of materiel)." An increasingly serious situation brought Field Marshal Paul von Hindenburg and Erich Ludendorff to the military and political leadership of the Reich. Their program was a renewed effort to mobilize the Reich's resources with the emphasis on military necessity; in other words, military factors would trump all other arguments. They demanded the conscription of Belgian workers to man the Reich's factories to free up Germans to serve in the army, the ruthless use of French and Belgian industrial resources in the occupied areas, and the wholesale confiscation of farm production from Poland as well as northern France and Belgium. Only extensive American relief efforts, headed by Herbert Hoover, prevented mass starvation in Belgium.

The radicalization of military policy had a number of consequences. Unrestricted submarine warfare began again in January 1917. Within three months, unrestricted submarine warfare brought the United States into the conflict.[30] In late February and March 1917, Hindenburg and Ludendorff ordered a major withdrawal in France to shorten the front and free up reserves for the hard-pressed army. The apt code name for the retreat was *Alberich*, the malicious dwarf of German myth. The *Oberste Heeres Leitung* (*OHL*) ordered that

> It is necessary to make extensive preparations for the complete destruction of all rail lines, and further, all streets, bridges, canals, locks, localities, and all equipment and buildings that we cannot take with us but that could be of any use at all to the enemy. The enemy must find a countryside completely sucked dry in which his own mobility is made as difficult as possible.[31]

[30] The "military necessity" which led to the resumption of unrestricted submarine warfare in January 1917 against shipping around the British Isles rested on fallacious numbers and assumptions which the Kriegsmarine presented to the *OHL* and which Ludendorff and Hindenburg and their staff seem not to have even bothered to examine. It is worth noting that at the end of 1916, at the same time that he was enthusiastically supporting the resumption of unrestricted warfare in the Atlantic – a decision he knew would bring the United States into the war – Ludendorff was worrying that Denmark or Holland might enter the war on the Allied side. For a discussion of these German miscalculations, see Holger H. Herwig, *The Politics of Frustration, The United States in German Naval Planning, 1889–1941* (Boston, 1976).

[31] There was considerable irony in this because the ferocious destruction of the area the Germans abandoned in 1917 placed a major stumbling block in the path of the area that the German offensives in 1918 had to cross. The quote is from Hull, *Absolute Destruction*, p. 259.

The pain inflicted on the population was somewhat mitigated by the fact that the commander responsible for the execution of the *OHL*'s orders was Field Marshal Crown Prince Rupprecht of Bavaria. Rupprecht came close to resigning. At least, he softened the worst aspects of the population's removal. However, within a vast area of northern France – more than 1,000 square miles – the Germans destroyed every building, every lock, every bridge as they retreated to new defensive positions. They tore up the roads, poisoned the wells, and cut down the orchards. The results produced "a desolate, dead desert." To carry out their demolitions, the Germans used 2,500,000 kilograms of dynamite and then, astonishingly, filmed their efforts. As the Third Army's commander noted: "We saw factories fly into the air, rows of houses fall over, bridges break in two – it was awful, an orgy of dynamite. That this is all militarily justified is unquestionable. But putting *this* on film – incomprehensible!"[32]

Admittedly, German actions made it difficult for the Allies to mount effective military operations from the areas *Alberich* had ravaged.[33] But what happened in late summer and fall 1918 was another matter. By that point, given the casualties suffered by the German Army – nearly one million soldiers in the offensives of spring 1918 – and the swelling tide of American soldiers, the war was lost. Beginning August 8, 1918, with a major British attack on Arras – according to Ludendorff, the "blackest day in the war" for the German Army – Allied attacks drove the Germans back in Belgium and northern France.[34] By early September, even the *OHL* recognized the Allies were wrecking the German Army in the west while it was dissolving in the rear. By this point, approximately 700,000 deserters were either hiding at home or wandering around in rear areas. Front-line companies were down to fewer than fifty men; platoons, where they existed, were barely larger than squad size.[35]

Nevertheless, as the Germans retreated, their troops carried out extensive acts of destruction. In some cases, such efforts aimed at slowing the

---

[32] Quoted in ibid., p. 259.
[33] With a certain amount of ironic justice, the Michael offensive of spring 1918 would find the advance of German troops as well as their resupply substantially hindered by the damage that Alberich had inflicted on the French countryside.
[34] For recent accounts of these British victories, which served to break the back of the German armies in the west and which are finally beginning to attract the attention of serious military historians, see Timothy Travers, *How the War Was Won, Command and Technology in the British Army on the Western Front 1917–1918* (London, 1992); and J. P. Harris with Niall Barr, *Amiens to the Armistice, The BEF in the Hundred Days' Campaign, 8 August–11 November 1918* (London, 1998).
[35] The Reichsstag held a series of largely unpublicized hearings in the early 1920s that underlined that the German Army in Fall 1918 was a badly beaten and defeated force with little hope of recovery. Not surprisingly, no one in Germany and few outside the Reich paid any attention to that fact, while some historians today still perpetrate the myth that the German Army was a thoroughly beaten force in the west by November 1918.

Allied advance. But much of the destruction was simply wanton. Retreating troops destroyed virtually all of the French coal mines: Forty were flooded while extensive demolitions rendered the remainder inoperative by destroying their elevators, blowers, and electrical facilities.[36] The comments of a senior officer summed up the attitude of many German officers in the war's last days:

> It will be necessary for our enemies to pay for every step ahead with streams of blood. Large areas that have so far been unaffected by war will be wrecked completely. If the enemy wants to push us out of the occupied parts of northern France, and if they want to force a retreat from Belgium, they will have to count on an extended period of bloody battles and the completely useless destruction of their own territory.[37]

The German Army in its retreat in fall 1918 made every effort to live up to that standard. The areas into which Allied armies had advanced before and after the armistice were not as badly wrecked as those devastated by *Alberich*, but only because the Germans lacked the time to execute a systematic withdrawal. But the damage was bad enough – more than 850,000 buildings in France destroyed or badly damaged.[38] Moreover, rapacious German demands for economic resources had squeezed the occupied areas of France and Belgium dry. In effect, the Germans had created an economic desert in the areas they had occupied.

The War's End: March 1918–November 1918

On March 21, 1918, the German Army came west in a stunning exhibition of the "new way of war": With combined arms tactics, modern warfare had come of age. During the succeeding three and a half months, the Germans launched five great offensives, which through the use of superior tactics had punched great holes in Allied lines. They returned tactical maneuvers to the battlefield. But these offensives were also entirely barren of operational, much less strategic, results.[39] At the strategic level, they were a catastrophe for the Germans. They bled the army white at a time when swelling numbers of Americans were arriving on the Western Front. Whatever the gains in territory – substantial compared to earlier campaigns in the west – the casualty bill was astronomical: approximately one million Germans were dead or wounded.[40]

---

36 Hull, *Absolute Destruction*, p. 260.
37 Quoted in ibid., p. 262.
38 Ibid., p. 262.
39 See the stunning new work, which draws on new documentary sources available not only in the Federal Republic but in the United States as well: David T. Zabecki, *The German 1918 Offensives, A Case Study in the Operational Level of War* (London, 2006).
40 The figure of one million is based on figures for the various German offensives in the official history, *Der Weltkrieg*. See Travers, *How the War Was Won*, p. 179.

Yet, the gains appeared impressive, and German propaganda delightedly exaggerated the successes. Even on the Allied side, there were moments when it appeared the war was lost. In March, Field Marshal Douglas Haig, commander of the British Expeditionary Force (BSF), and Marshal Phillipe Petain, commander-in-chief of the French Army, were on the brink of splitting their forces apart and opening an avenue for the Germans to drive through to the Channel. Only the appointment of a supreme commander, Marshal Foch, forced a level of cooperation that allowed Allied armies to halt the Germans.[41]

In the end, the Germans had neither the means to exploit their tactical gains nor a high command with the slightest sense of what lay beyond tactics.[42] By late summer 1918, when it was clear the offensives had failed, the *OHL* displayed no interest in seeking a compromise peace. Then, beginning in August, Allied offensives broke the back of German forces on the Western Front, while Germany's allies, recognizing the game was up, scrambled to save something from the smash-up. At this point, the Reich confronted military defeat in the west and strategic defeat elsewhere: Turkey, Bulgaria, and Austria-Hungary collapsed, the surrender of the last opening up not only Austria to Allied advance but southern Germany as well.[43] It is not surprising, given German successes in the spring, that Allied leaders found themselves astonished at the rapidity of the enemy's collapse. Indeed, virtually everything in Allied military planning had posited the continuation of the conflict into 1919.

There were two problems with the sudden collapse of German military and political power in fall 1918. First, Allied forces had yet to reach German territory.[44] Only in terms of the blockade's baleful impact on civilian society was it obvious that Germany had lost. Virtually no damage had occurred on the Reich's territory with the exception of that inflicted by a few minor air raids, while the fighting in the west had remained limited to northern France and Belgium. Thus, the palpable evidence of defeat that came in May 1945, with millions of Allied soldiers on German territory and with the blasted ruins of Germany's cities and infrastructure, simply did not exist in November 1918.

---

[41] And, of course, as a Frenchman, Foch was able to rein in Petain's pessimism.

[42] When Crown Prince Rupprecht asked what the objective of the Michael Offensive of March 1918 might be, Ludendorff had replied: "We will punch a hole into [their lines]. For the rest we shall see. We did it this way in Russia." Quoted in Herwig, "The Dynamics of Necessity," p. 40.

[43] Which is one of the reasons why the German revolution would prove to be so enthusiastically received in Bavaria, the most conservative of all the German states.

[44] A factor which would lead both Winston Churchill and Franklin Roosevelt to support strongly the strategic bombing offensive against industrial and civil targets throughout the Reich.

Equally important was the fact that Allied military forces, except in south-eastern Europe, were yet to occupy the areas over which the statesmen in Versailles would have to make crucial decisions. Mao Tse Tung may have exaggerated in his claim that political power comes out of a barrel of a gun but, in the aftermath of war, the occupation of territory by military forces represents a major factor in the establishment of peace.[45]

Exacerbating the political fallout from the war's end were the armistice terms the Allies extended to the Germans. Not until mid-October 1918 did the issue of an armistice arise in Allied councils – not surprising since virtually no one expected the war would end so soon. Thus, there was little time to debate the terms the Allies would offer to the beaten Germans. There was, in fact, considerable disagreement among Allied military commanders. General John J. Pershing, commander of American forces, urged that the Allies reject the German request for an armistice so that Allied armies could continue their advance into Germany and dictate terms in Berlin.[46]

In retrospect, that would have been the best course for it would have made clear to the Germans who had won. But with the casualties suffered thus far in the conflict, America's allies were not about to continue. Haig's proposals reflected British interests: a surrender of the German fleet and withdrawal by the German Army to the Reich's frontiers. Thus, the Germans would only have to abandon the occupied territories of France, Belgium, and Luxembourg. French terms fell somewhere between those of the British and the Americans: The Germans would surrender their heavy artillery and field guns, most of their machine guns, and a substantial number of trucks and railcars. In the end, the armistice terms demanded the Germans pull back to the Rhine and allow Allied armies to occupy territory on the Rhine's left bank. Since Foch was the Allied commander-in-chief, those were the terms the Germans received.[47] And they were terms that only a defeated and broken army and nation would have accepted.

---

[45] As U.S. forces were soon to find out in the months that followed their takedown of Saddam's regime in summer 2003.

[46] Pershing noted at the end of October to his colleagues Foch, Petain, and Haig that "I believe that complete victory can only be obtained by continuing the war until we have forced unconditional surrender on the Germans.... " Quoted in John S. D. Eisenhower, *Yanks, The Epic Story of the American Army in World War I* (New York, 2001), p. 278.

[47] According to Allied terms, the German Army was to surrender 2,500 pieces of heavy artillery, 2,500 field guns, 25,000 machine guns, 5,000 trucks, and 150,000 railroad wagons. In effect, these demands guaranteed the disarmament of the German Army. In addition, the Kriegsmarine was to surrender ten battleships, six battle cruisers, and all of its U-boats. This action, of course, guaranteed British naval superiority. In addition, the Allies would occupy all of the Rhineland with three major bridgeheads over the Rhine at Mainz, Coblenz, and Cologne. Ludendorff, who had aimed to use an armistice to reconstitute the German Army to continue the war, realized that the terms would make continued resistance impossible. He urged that the Germans continue the war. Alan Palmer, *Victory 1918* (New York, 1998), p. 281.

In retrospect, the signing of the armistice proved a serious political mistake as well. The Allies allowed the German Army's leadership to foist the onerous task of signing the armistice on the backs of the nascent Weimar Republic's socialist leaders with professions of the army's gratitude.[48] In the near future, those same military leaders would join in the chorus of howls from the political right in Germany that denounced the signing as one more indication that the politicians had failed the army. Certainly, at a minimum, the Allies should have demanded that Germany's military leaders, naval as well as army, sign the armistice.[49]

The seeming successes of the spring 1918 offensives remained indelibly impressed on the German psyche, while the series of devastating blows launched by Allied armies in the fall receded from memory.[50] The result was the creation of the myth of the *Dolchstosslegend*: supposedly, the German Army had stood unbroken and undefeated in the field, only to be stabbed in the back by the Communists and the Jews. Nothing could have been further from the truth, but the evidence of that defeat did not exist on German soil. Moreover, the Germans did everything they could to erase the memory of their defeat.[51]

THE MAKING OF THE EUROPEAN PEACE: VERSAILLES 1919

Not surprisingly, the leaders of the victorious nations meeting at Versailles in January 1919 confronted a difficult situation, one for which they were not prepared to understand, much less solve. The ending of the war, as well as the nature of the German problem, presented enormous hurdles. Moreover, the peace making itself confronted new and daunting problems. In the first place, Wilson's first point of the fourteen clearly stated: "Open covenants of peace, openly arrived at, after which there shall be no private international understandings of any kind but diplomacy shall proceed always frankly and in the public view."[52]

However strange that point may sound at the beginning of the twenty-first century to those accustomed to the efforts, even in the democracies,

---

[48] Admittedly, this appears to have been a sin of omission rather than commission.
[49] In particular, Ludendorff and Hindenburg.
[50] And not just from German memories.
[51] Gerhard Weinberg's explanation for why the German military raised no objections to Hitler's declaration of war on the United States in December 1941 is right on target. Weinberg argues that the German belief that the 1918 defeat had resulted from the Jews and Communists stabbing the unbroken and undefeated German Army in the back led them to discount almost entirely the economic and military contribution the United States had made to Allied victory in 1918. See Gerhard Weinberg, *A World at Arms, A Global History of World War II* (Cambridge, 1994), p. 262.
[52] President Woodrow Wilson's address to the Joint Session of Congress, January 8, 1918.

to shroud the business of negotiation with an impenetrable fog of secrecy, Wilson was recognizing that the framework of international diplomacy had fundamentally altered.[53] The milieu within which the Congress of Vienna had taken place no longer existed. Indeed, Wilson had recognized that public opinion and the media were now major players in the conduct of international relations. What the American president refused to recognize was that the deep, bitter feelings the war had raised, particularly in France, would represent an ever-present factor in deliberations.[54] In fact, the president would soon find much of Europe's public opinion arranged against him.

One should also not discount the fact that the beliefs and personalities of leading statesmen in the democracies themselves represented substantial stumbling blocks. Harold Nicolson, in his study on the Congress of Vienna, wonderfully sketched out the contribution that individuals make to the interminable processes of negotiations:

> Nobody who has not actually watched statesmen dealing with each other can have any real idea of the immense part played in human affairs by such unavowable and unrecognisable causes as lassitude, affability, personal affection or dislike, misunderstanding, deafness or incomplete command of a foreign language, vanity, social engagements, interruptions and momentary health. Nobody who has not watched "policy" expressing itself in day to day action can realise how seldom is the course of events determined by deliberately planned purpose or how often what in retrospect appears to have been fully conscious intention was at the time governed and directed by that most potent of all factors, – "the chain of circumstance."[55]

Those personalities, who had driven the Allies to victory, now interacted to design the peace treaty. In terms of the French contribution to the debates at Versailles, Margaret MacMillan has drawn a wonderful portrait of Clemenceau:

> Throughout his long life Clemenceau had gone his own formidable way. His enemies claimed that his slanting eyes and his cruelty were a legacy from Huns who had somehow made it to the Vendée.... [H]e made a name for himself as an incisive and witty orator and a tenacious opponent, happiest when he was attacking governments he saw as too conservative.... In his relentless attacks on authority he was prepared to do almost anything to win. "He comes from

---

[53] In regard to the point on the efforts to shroud the business of government in secrecy, one might note the recent efforts of America's intelligence agencies to reclassify documents that had already been declassified, including in one case a document that had actually been printed in the State Department's series, *The Foreign Relations of the United States*.

[54] Moreover, Lloyd George's coalition government had just won a general election in Britain on the basis that Germany should be squeezed "until the pips squeak."

[55] Harold Nicolson, *The Congress of Vienna, A Study in Allied Unity: 1812–1822* (New York, 1946), p. 19.

a family of wolves," said a man who knew him well. Clemenceau did not help himself by his contempt for convention and his profound cynicism.[56]

Like Churchill, Clemenceau was deeply mistrusted by his fellow politicians. Only the desperate situation in spring 1917 had forced them finally to call on him to rescue the Republic, a task he accomplished with ruthlessness, relish, and enthusiasm – as well as competence. No other Frenchman could have achieved what he achieved at Versailles, no matter how flawed the final settlement might have seemed from the point of view of its catastrophic collapse in the late 1930s.

David Lloyd George and Woodrow Wilson could not have been more different than the French premier in background and outlook. Lloyd George was a brilliant speaker with a mercurial and at times undisciplined mind. He often proved too clever. Wilson thought the prime minister possessed no principles but missed Lloyd George's British pragmatism. The prime minister also had a tendency to assume knowledge that he did not possess. Unlike Clemenceau and Wilson, Lloyd George had to contend with the growing force of the Empire's Dominions, which were now virtually independent states. Nevertheless, like Clemenceau, the prime minister pursued policies he believed would best guarantee British interests against an uncertain future. To do so, he brought to bear in his discussions his formidable talent as a debater. Clemenceau once sharply but accurately commented about the British prime minister: "All arguments are good to him when he wishes to make a case, and, if it is necessary, he uses the next day arguments which he had rejected or refuted the previous day."[57]

Woodrow Wilson possessed as formidable a mind as his counterparts. At times, he possessed considerable flexibility. However, he often proved deeply stubborn in refusing to yield crucial points. In the end, that stubbornness, born of a deep sense that his positions were morally right, caused the Treaty to fail in its crucial test before the U.S. Senate. This should not have been surprising to those who had followed his career as the president of Princeton and governor of New Jersey, where Wilson had found it increasingly difficult to get along with his contemporaries, particularly given his tendency to focus on the moral correctness of his arguments and positions.

Perhaps even more disastrous was Wilson's naïvete when confronting the realities of Europe, not to mention human nature. Here, he succumbed to a number of assumptions, such as the reasonableness of popular opinion, that secret diplomacy was bad, that the creation of the United States had brought a unique and morally blessed form of government into being, and

[56] MacMillan, *Paris, 1919*, pp. 29–30.
[57] Quoted in MacMillan, *Paris, 1919*, p. 41.

that popular sovereignty would be the best guarantee of lasting peace. All proved dangerously at odds with the strategic and political problems the war had only served to exacerbate.[58] In particular, Wilson and most of his advisers had little idea of the complexities involved in drawing up frontiers that could satisfy the popular sentiments of different nationalities with the economic, not to mention strategic, requirements of stability.[59]

The inherent differences of these three, who would dominate the conference, would have counted for less had the diplomats prepared themselves better for the problems that peace making would entail. But so desperate had the situation appeared for much of 1918 that few in the foreign ministries had done the necessary background work on the difficulties the peace conference would confront. Moreover, the conference opened barely two months after the signing of the armistice at Compiegne. Thus, the foreign offices were not prepared to handle anything more than their nation's immediate *desiderata*. While Austria-Hungary's collapse in October 1918 had seemingly eased the problems the Italians confronted in gaining their territorial desires,[60] that collapse simply increased the difficulties confronting the other major powers.

Yet, for all its seeming complexity, the problem of creating a stable peace boiled down to the German problem. It had been the Germans who bore so much of the responsibility for the war's outbreak. It had been the Germans who had driven deep into western Russia and conspired at setting up a Bolshevik regime in Moscow. And it had been the Germans who smashed their way across Belgium, Luxembourg, and northern France in August and early September of 1914 and then treated the occupied populations with callousness and contempt. Perhaps most alarming of all to those who took the long view was the fact that Germany had emerged from its defeat with its industrial plant largely undamaged.

Yet, it was not with an examination of Germany's fate that the peacemakers began. Instead, Wilson's most basic assumption was that creation of The League of Nations would provide a solid block against the possibility of a future repetition of the Great War: most especially because it would represent the ideals and wishes of mankind. As he commented in New York shortly before the end of the war: "The counsels of plain men have become on all hands more simple and straightforward and more unified than the

---

[58] And they certainly had no idea of the anomalies such as those that would cause 300,000 Polish Protestants to vote to remain with Germany rather than join their Catholic brethren in the new Polish state.

[59] The ethnic cleansing occasioned by the ferocious war between Nazi Germany and the Soviet Union cleared up much of the intermixing of populations in Eastern Europe but at a hideous cost that beggars imagination at the beginning of the twenty-first century.

[60] And, of course, it did nothing of the sort.

counsels of sophisticated men of affairs, who still retain the impression that they are playing a game of power and playing for high stakes."[61] Wilson's belief, quaintly American, was that in this open forum, the nations of the world, great and small, could come and settle their differences. In the largest sense, he believed that international pressures alone would obviate the need for military force.

The discussions about the form and nature of The League of Nations consumed the first weeks of the conference, as well as much energy. Even at this early date and with an issue far removed from the pain and bloodshed of the war, the big four – not yet the big three but soon to be so – found their conception of the League far apart. For Wilson, the League appeared the best means of guarantying there would be no repetition of the Great War. Such an organization, by its existence, would do away with the need for alliances, while the pressure of international public opinion expressed through the League would deter those who might consider breaking the world's peace. At least, Wilson had the realism to believe the Germans initially should not have membership in the League but rather would have to earn membership.

In the end, the American president took the Treaty of Versailles down to defeat in the United States because of the inclusion of additional clauses in the sections dealing with the League, placed by Henry Cabot Lodge, the Republican head of the Senate's Foreign Relations Committee. A number of historians have seen the failure of the Treaty in the Senate as a major factor in the eventual outbreak of the Second World War. Such a belief, however, requires acceptance of the assumption that the United States would actively have participated in supporting the League in limiting German power in the 1930s – a belief that flies in the face of American attitudes and assumptions about the world throughout the 1920s and 1930s.

Clemenceau viewed the League in different terms. To him, it might prove a useful tool in preventing the Germans from becoming a major threat to the Republic's security. And he was certainly willing to defer to the American president's desires in regard to the League if he could gain concessions in other areas. Lloyd George's attitude toward the League shifted from cynicism to idealism depending on his mood. Nevertheless, here too, he found the attitudes and the pressures of the Dominions of major importance in charting Britain's course.

Not surprisingly, it was the German problem that consumed the French. As Winston Churchill so perceptively commented later:

Worn down, doubly decimated, but undisputed masters of the hour, the French nation peered into the future in thankful wonder and haunting dread. Where

[61] Quoted in MacMillan, *Paris, 1919*, p. 87.

then was that SECURITY without which all that had been gained seemed value-
less, and life itself, even amid the rejoicings of victory, was almost unendurable?
The mortal need was Security....[62]

André Tardieu noted the following in *Foreign Affairs* in September 1922
about what France had suffered in the Great War:

> The war blooded us terribly. Out of our population of less than 38,000,000
> there were mobilized 8,500,000; 5,300,000 of them were killed or wounded
> (1,500,000 killed, 800,000 *mutilés*, 3,000,000 wounded).... Almost 4,000,000
> hectares of land were devastated, together with 4,000 towns and villages,
> 600,000 buildings were destroyed, among them 20,000 factories and work-
> shops, besides 5,000 kilometers of railroads and 53 kilometers of roads.... The
> financial consequences of the annihilation of all these resources bear down on
> us heavily today. The war cost us 150 billions of francs. The damage to property
> and persons comes to 200 billions.[63]

While there was considerable anger over the behavior of the Germans
among the British and the Americans, that anger proved a wasting asset
for the French, even during the course of negotiations at Versailles. Neither
nation, of course, had felt the impact of German atrocities. Haig, not the
most outstanding of operational commanders but possessing a fine-tuned
political antenna, underlined by his proposed armistice terms that the British
were not interested in permanently hobbling the Germans.[64] The Americans,
while for the short term willing to punish the Germans, clearly believed that
their former opponents would come around to a liberal *Weltanschauung*.
And, not surprisingly, the British would move increasingly in the direction
of the Americans.

The problem then was Germany. Given the mood in that nation, one
can wonder whether there was any conceivable peace the Germans might
have accepted except an outright peace of the victor – not exactly in the
cards after their defeat in fall 1918. For the French, the issue was how to
limit German power by restrictions the Treaty would impose on its future
potential. However, from the start, there was an inherent contradiction in
the French *desiderata*. The French had every expectation the Germans would
pay for the war's damage. Even without considering the indirect costs, such
as widows' and orphans' pensions and veterans' benefits, the bill for the
damage was going to be astronomical. How then would the Germans pay,

---

[62] Winston S. Churchill, *The Second World War*, vol. 1, *The Gathering Storm* (Boston, 1948),
p. 6.

[63] Quoted in Robert A. Doughty, *Pyrrhic Victory, French Strategy and Operations in the
Great War* (Cambridge, MA, 2005), pp. 1–2.

[64] The two crucial terms that Haig suggested were the surrender of the High Seas Fleet and a
withdrawal of the German Army to the Reich's frontier rather than back to and over the
Rhine.

unless they were to dominate Europe economically? The Americans and the British could look on such a German economic recovery in the postwar period with a certain amount of equanimity. In fact, since Germany had been Britain's largest trading partner before the war, such a recovery appeared to many in Britain as essential to the United Kingdom's economic health. But the French could not.

In terms of the territorial settlement for the new Weimar Republic, the return of Alsace-Lorraine to France was a foregone conclusion. Not only had these provinces had a long connection with France, but the population itself largely desired a return, even among the German speakers. In the case of the Saar, the rich industrial area on the new Franco-German border, the best the French could get was a League mandate and agreement on a plebiscite to take place in fifteen years.[65]

The French had hoped for more. Throughout the discussions at Versailles, French agents scoured southern Germany and the Rhineland to encourage separatist movements but had found little response. For better or worse, Bismarck had made a German *nation*, and only an overwhelming Allied victory, during which their armies occupied the entire Reich, could have made such division possible.[66] The best the French could obtain was a military occupation and demilitarization of the Rhineland to last for fifteen years. The military occupation would end in the late 1920s with a guarantee that the Rhineland would remain demilitarized thereafter. Six years later, at Hitler's direction, the German Army would cross the Rhine River bridges and remilitarize the Rhineland.

In the east, it seemed reasonable to create a corridor for the new Polish state through to the Baltic. The Polish corridor contained a majority of Poles, but a significant number of Germans remained in the area. More troublesome was the fact that Danzig, the major Hanseatic port at the end of the Vistula, contained a vociferous German population that had no desire to become a part of Poland. Here, as with the Saar, the statesmen agreed to separate Danzig from Germany under the control of the League. In the 1930s, the Nazis would gain control of Danzig's city government and utilize it as a means to harass the Poles diplomatically and politically until September 1, 1939, when the Germans chose other means.

Given the performance of German military institutions during the First World War, the victorious powers placed major restrictions on the new republic's military institutions. The *Kriegsmarine* and a potential German

---

[65] One of the clear indications of how deeply the disease of fanatical nationalism had bitten into German consciousness was that despite the fact that the majority of the Saar's population was Social Democratic, it voted for the province to rejoin a thoroughly Nazified Reich by a wide margin in the plebiscite of 1935.

[66] Which, of course, was to happen at the end of the Second World War. Nevertheless, forty-five years later, when the occupying power, which had maintained that division through armed might – namely, the Soviet Union – withdrew its support, Germany swiftly reunited.

air force presented the easier set of solutions. In the case of the latter, the Treaty simply prohibited the Germans from possessing military aircraft. With the former, the fact that the High Sea Fleet now lay anchored in Scapa Flow under the guns of the Royal Navy effectively disarmed the Reich in naval terms. The Treaty then proceeded to forbid the German Republic's navy from possessing any *Dreadnought*-class battleships, battle cruisers, or submarines, with a severe limit on the tonnage of naval shipping the Germans could maintain.

The restrictions placed on the German Army were no less onerous: It was to eliminate its famed Great General Staff. In weaponry, it was to possess neither tanks nor heavy artillery. The victors set its size at 100,000 soldiers, who were to serve twelve years, while the officer corps was to contain no more than 4,000 officers.[67] In effect, the Treaty forced Germany to disarm and placed the Reich in a position where it was incapable of defending itself against the armies of Poland and Czechoslovakia, much less the French Army. In the atmosphere of "fairness" that soon enveloped the European landscape, the Germans were to claim they had been mistreated since none of their neighbors had disarmed.

In the long run, a number of provisions in regard to German armaments and military forces were to work to the advantage of German rearmament. Moreover, an examination of innovation and the German military in the interwar period suggests that other factors were equally if not more important than the restrictions the Treaty placed on Germany's military.[68] Yet, the provisions of the Treaty helped the Germans in some ways. Clemenceau and Lloyd George had had extensive arguments about the size of the German Army. The French had favored a 140,000-man conscripted army while the British favored a 200,000-man volunteer army.

Compromise resulted in the worst of all worlds – a 100,000-man, all-volunteer force. Thus, instead of having to train new batches of recruits each year, German officers could focus almost exclusively on intellectual preparation for the next war. That factor allowed its officer corps to study the lessons of the last war and thoroughly learn them.[69] Thus, in 1933, when Hitler came to power and provided the new *Wehrmacht* with massive sums

---

[67] James S. Corum, *The Roots of Blitzkrieg, Hans von Seeckt and German Military Reform* (Lawrence, KS, 1992), p. 34.

[68] For the German Army's innovation during the interwar period, see Williamson Murray, "Armor," in *Military Innovation in the Interwar Period*, ed. by Williamson Murray and Allan R. Millett (Cambridge, 1996).

[69] One of the least perceptive myths about military organizations is the one that argues that military organizations study the last conflict and that is why they do badly in the next. Nothing could be further from the truth in the case of the German Army, which in 1920, under the direction of its commander-in-chief, General Hans von Seeckt, established no less than fifty-seven different committees to study the lessons of the First World War. For further discussion of this point, see Corum, *The Roots of Blitzkrieg*.

for rearmament, the German Army had already figured out with considerable accuracy the tactical and operational framework of the next war.[70] Consequently, the rearmament program of the 1930s took place within a thoroughly realistic context.

Nevertheless, Versailles' restrictions did have some impact on Germany's ability to support the *Wehrmacht*'s rearmament. The fact that the bulk of German tanks through 1941 consisted of the obsolete and unsatisfactory Mark I and Mark II models reflected the treaty's impact on German tank development that had really only begun in 1933.[71] Similarly, the *Luftwaffe* found its rearmament efforts considerably constrained by the impact the Treaty had on the Reich's aircraft industry. Like the French aircraft industry in 1933, German industrial capability at the time to produce modern aircraft was almost nil.[72] Only by huge expenditures did the Germans establish the industrial capacity to produce numbers of up-to-date aircraft.[73] Moreover, German aircraft engines remained constrained by the impact of Versailles' restrictions through to the midpoint of the Second World War.

The failure of Versailles lay not in the restrictions themselves but rather in the failure of the Allies to force the Germans to live up to the Treaty. Almost from the day they signed the Treaty, the Germans began a systematic program of cheating. They maneuvered around the prohibition against a general staff by renaming that organization *Truppenamt* – an action that had no impact on its actual duties. While the army could possess neither tanks nor aircraft, it made every effort to keep up to date with weapons technology – its cooperation with the Soviets the most obvious indication of that effort. Finally, in arms dumps scattered throughout the Reich, the Germans maintained outlawed weapons away from the prying eyes of French and British inspectors. Most important, the Treaty of Versailles could not prevent the Germans from thinking more seriously about the implications

---

[70] In regard to operations and strategy, the Germans did less well. In the case of the former, German contempt for logistics and intelligence would provide a major contribution to the Third Reich's defeat from 1941 on, while in the realm of strategy, the German military enthusiastically supported their Führer in repeating every strategic mistake Germany had made in the First World War in the new world war.

[71] Admittedly, the Germans had gained some knowledge about tank development in the late 1920s during the period of cooperation with the Soviets. Nevertheless, that cooperation only provided the Germans with a starting point. The Mark I weighed six tons and was equipped with machine guns as armament, while the Mark II weighed ten tons and possessed a 37 mm cannon. Only in the late 1930s did the first Mark IIIs and Mark IVs, both medium tanks, begin appearing in German armored formations.

[72] For the state of the German aircraft industry in February 1933, when the Nazis took over, see Williamson Murray, *Luftwaffe* (Baltimore, MD, 1985), ch. 1.

[73] And the French weakness in the air in 1940 had nothing to do with the obsolescence of their aircraft industry in 1933 but rather the unwillingness of the French government and its army, which to a considerable extent controlled the military budget, to provide sufficient financial support to build up the French Air Force. Here, the Blum government of 1936 was particularly responsible.

of the last war than their eventual opponents. What happened in 1940 and 1941 was a general failure of Germany's opponents to adapt to the harsh lessons of the last war, and that reality had nothing to do with the Treaty.

RUSSIAN AND EASTERN EUROPEAN PROBLEMS

One of the most disastrous acts the German government perpetrated in 1917 was in aiding and abetting Lenin's movement across the Reich to Sweden and then on to a Russia wracked by revolution. They then extended financial support to the Bolsheviks to undermine the new republic throughout summer and fall 1917. The creation of Lenin's regime represented a factor that would eventually haunt not only the Germans but the whole world. But, for the short term, Ludendorff and Hindenburg sought to take advantage of the collapse of Russia that the Bolshevik Revolution represented. The so-called October Revolution – nothing more than a *coup d'état* – brought the Bolsheviks to power and offered the Germans the possibility of peace in the east so they could focus on defeating the Western Allies before the Americans arrived.[74]

Almost immediately, the Germans discovered in their negotiations with the Bolsheviks that they were not dealing with a government which subscribed to normal patterns of international behavior. As the train with the Bolshevik negotiators pulled into Brest-Litovsk in January 1918, Karl Radek, a senior member of the Soviet delegation, was busily tossing propaganda leaflets off the train's rear car that urged German soldiers to overthrow their rulers.[75] When negotiations broke down over Bolshevik intransigence, Trotsky proclaimed a "state of neither peace nor war."[76]

While Trotsky reveled in posturing, Lenin understood that military force was not necessarily amenable to political bombast. The German reply to Trotsky's declaration was to resume their march into Russia. Everywhere,

---

[74] In fact, they did nothing of the kind. Driven by dreams of conquest almost as megalomaniacal as those of Adolf Hitler, Ludendorff pursued further conquests in the east and so left most of the German forces in Russia and the Ukraine as well as beginning moves against the Crimea and the Caucasus. The victories in the west in spring 1918 were achieved not by reinforcements from the Eastern Front but rather by major tactical adaptations – in effect, the invention of combined-arms tactics – that changed the face of war. For the ground-breaking work on this, see Timothy F. Lupfer, *The Dynamics of Doctrine: The Changes in German Tactical Doctrine During the First World War* (Leavenworth, KS, 1981).

[75] John W. Wheeler-Bennett, *Brest-Litovsk, The Forgotten Peace, March 1918* (New York, 1971, first edition published in 1938), p. 153.

[76] The negotiations at Brest-Litovsk, as well as his tenure as foreign minister of the Bolshevik regime, did not represent Trotsky's greatest moments, but he would move on to become the founder of the Red Army and the man responsible, even more than Lenin, for the Bolshevik's victory in the ensuing Russian Civil War. For a clear discussion of Trotsky's role in that conflict, see the brilliant study by Earl Ziemke, *The Red Army from 1918–1941, From Vanguard of Revolution to U.S. Ally* (London, 2003).

demoralized Russian armies gave way. Recognizing the inevitability of German *force majeure*, Lenin browbeat his party into accepting the punitive peace terms the Germans were demanding: no less than the surrender of Poland, Finland, the Baltic States, White Russia, and the Ukraine.[77]

The terms the Germans imposed on a broken Russia foreshadowed the peace they intended to impose in the west, if they had been victorious.[78] According to their plans, Belgium would have disappeared, while much of northern France would have found its way into the Reich. Such war aims, as well as the treaty of Brest-Litovsk, made a mockery of the German attacks on the Versailles Treaty's "unfairness" in the 1920s and 1930s. The larger point, however, is that events in Russia had introduced a revolutionary regime into the diplomatic and strategic equation. And there was no way that Lenin's regime would accept any settlement the victors might make in Versailles because its aim of world revolution represented no less than the overthrow of *all* non-Communist regimes.

Thus, at the end of the war, the Allies confronted a hostile, revolutionary regime in the east. They were to make halfhearted efforts to support the Whites in the Russian civil war, but nowhere did the democracies have the stomach to undertake major military operations to remove the Bolsheviks from power. Without that will, the amount of influence the major powers could exercise over Russia's acceptance of the eastern settlement was minimal. But, the fact that Russia found itself largely without influence in the resulting peace treaties also reflected how little power the Bolsheviks themselves exercised in 1919.

The problems of Eastern and Southern Europe represented an equally considerable conundrum for the peacemakers. These areas offered up no reasonable or easy solutions. The collapse, first of Czarist Russia and then the Central Powers, had resulted in the emergence, or reemergence, of a host of smaller powers, all of which followed their own national agendas, most of which were at odds with the conceptions of those in Paris attempting to mold the peace. It was fine to talk of national self-determination, but nationality patterns of Eastern Europe bore no resemblance to sensible economic or strategic frontiers. The collapse of Austria-Hungary represented an economic disaster of the first order. Whatever its political divisions or troubles, the Habsburg monarchy had made considerable economic sense, and the

---

[77] Over the course of the summer, Ludendorff would pursue further conquests in the Crimea and the Caucasus until the collapse in the west brought a certain sense of reality to the OHL. Lenin succinctly summed up his attitude toward the treaty he had signed with the Germans in the following terms: "I don't mean to read it, and I don't mean to fulfill it, except in so far as I'm forced." Quoted in Wheeler-Bennett, *Brest-Litovsk*, p. 276.

[78] For German war aims in the west, see Hans W. Gatzke, *Germany's Drive to the West: A Study of German War Aims During the First World War* (Baltimore, MD, 1950).

empire's collapse resulted in deep economic troubles in Eastern Europe that lasted throughout the interwar period.[79]

Exacerbating these economic troubles were deep political divisions among the different nationalities as they sorted out the new frontiers. What appeared reasonable in terms of national *desiderata* for one, almost invariably conflicted with the claims and traditions of others. The Poles seized Vilna to the dismay of the Lithuanians; the Czechs, Tschen, to the outrage of the Poles; the Poles, the Polish corridor at the expense of the Germans and a substantial chunk of the western Ukraine at the expense of the Russians; and the Rumanians, Transylvania, at the expense of the Hungarians – to name just a few of the semiquestionable territorial decisions that the treaty makers in Paris had no choice but to sanction. Moreover, the deep-seated rivalries, distrust, and hatreds in Eastern Europe and the Balkans made even the simplest economic – not to mention political – cooperation virtually impossible.[80]

The Germans found themselves particularly outraged by the refusal of the victors to follow through with Wilson's promise of self-determination when the Sudeten Germans and Austrians attempted to join the Reich. But how could the Allied powers allow the Sudeten districts to separate from Czechoslovakia when the mountainous areas within which the Sudeten Germans lived were essential to Czechoslovakia's strategic defense?[81] Similarly, how could they allow Austria to join the Reich when that move would significantly improve Germany's economic and political strength, while control of Austrian territory would allow the Germans to meddle in the affairs of the Balkans as well as place military pressure directly on the Italians?[82]

---

[79] Even during the war, the Allies had recognized this reality to a considerable extent and not until 1918 did they begin to push actively for the breakup of the Austro-Hungarian Empire.

[80] The French managed to create a grouping of Czechoslovakia, Yugoslavia, and Rumania, nicknamed the "Little Entente." But at the first sign of trouble in the late 1930s, the group dissolved, and the three countries went their separate ways.

[81] How far the victors' understanding of strategic issues would collapse during the period of British appeasement in the late 1930s is suggested by a letter from the British ambassador in Berlin, Sir Neville Henderson, to Lord Halifax about Nevile Chamberlain's mediator for the Czech-German confrontation in summer 1938, Lord Runciman. Henderson commented: "Personally I just sit and pray for one thing, namely that Lord Runciman will live up to the role of an impartial British liberal statesman. I cannot believe that he will allow himself to be influenced by ancient history or arguments about strategic frontiers and economics in preference to high moral principles." *Documents on British Foreign Policy*, 3rd Ser., vol. 2, doc. 590, 6.8.38., letter from Henderson to Halifax.

[82] And at least until the mid-1930s and Mussolini's disastrous turn to Hitler as a result of the Abyssinian crisis, the maintenance of Austrian independence to ensure Germany's removal from the Brenner remained a major objective of Italian foreign policy. For Italian foreign and strategic policies in the late 1930s, see MacGregor Knox, *Mussolini Unleashed, Politics and Strategy in Fascist Italy's Last War* (Cambridge, 1982).

As long as Russia and Germany remained relatively powerless, the unstable situation in Eastern Europe would last. Once, however, the two great powers regained their strength and position, Eastern Europe's smaller powers, whatever their pretensions, simply could not maintain their freedom of maneuver. Some would go under quickly – the demise of Austria and Czechoslovakia in March and October 1938 the first signs of collapse, others would follow soon after – Poland, Lithuania, Latvia, and Estonia in 1939.[83] And only Finland, admittedly at huge cost in two great wars against Stalin's Soviet Union, would maintain a modicum of independence throughout the Second World War and into the Cold War.

For the French, this proved a dismal outcome to hopes that Eastern Europe's nations could provide strategic weight on the Reich's eastern frontiers similar to that which the Russians had borne before the First World War.[84] In fact, given their history, there was never any chance the Eastern Europeans would act in concert once the Reich no longer found itself held by the chains of military defeat and Treaty provisions, and Russia had reemerged as a major power.

THE GERMAN PROBLEM

Germany's collapse in November 1918 shrouded the larger problem that would make the Versailles' settlement so untenable in the long run.[85] In effect, the Germans had been the real strategic winners of the First World War. In 1914, the Reich possessed frontiers with three major powers: France, Russia, and the Austro-Hungarian Empire.[86] Four years later, the situation had radically changed. Austria-Hungary had collapsed into a welter of

---

[83] Of course, what the Germans entirely missed was the fact that Poland represented a shield which separated the Reich from the Soviet Union.

[84] But the French themselves were to fail to recognize that the construction of major fortifications – the so-called Maginot Line – in effect represented an indication that they would be unwilling to come to the defense of their Eastern European allies should the Germans first move east rather than west – a reality that the French consistently refused to confront. In September 1939, confronted with the German invasion of Poland, the French failed to undertake any serious military operations. The year before, a distraught Colonel Charles de Gaulle had described the potential reaction of the French military to a German invasion of Czechoslovakia to Leon Blum in the following terms: "It's quite simple.... Depending on actual circumstances, we will recall the 'disponibles' or mobilize the reserves. Then looking through the loopholes of our fortifications, we will passively witness the enslavement of Europe." Quoted in Paul-Marie de la Gorce, *The French Army* (New York, 1963), p. 270.

[85] Gerhard Weinberg pointed out this reality in a seminal article in the late 1960s that for the first time emphasized that the Germans had in the long term won the war: "The Defeat of Germany in 1918 and the European Balance of Power," *Central European History*, 2/3, 1969.

[86] In fact, the French, especially Foch, had some glimmering of the latent threat that even a defeated German state represented to their nation's security.

confused and combative states. Czarist Russia's demise had stripped it of its western provinces and created a strip of weak successor states between the Russians and the Germans.

Thus, only France of the major powers, bordering on Germany in 1914, still possessed a frontier with the Reich. But the war had thoroughly exhausted both the French nation and its economy. On the other hand, the German economy, largely undamaged by the conflict, was now even more dominant in Europe. Moreover, the splintering of the Austrian and Russian Empires into successor states, all weak economically, presented the Germans with the long-term prospect of being able to dominate Eastern Europe and the Balkans in a fashion not true before the war.[87]

Yet, the Germans displayed neither capacity nor willingness to recognize their long-term prospects.[88] Here, several factors were at work. Undoubtedly, defeat tasted bitter to most Germans, particularly since even their leaders had believed the Reich had stood on the brink of victory in spring 1918 – a victory that would have allowed them to reorder the international environment completely to Germany's advantage. Almost immediately after the war, there arose the first poisonous buds of the *Dolchstosslegend*. By late 1919, Field Marshal Paul von Hindenburg, in testimony before a Reichstag committee, declared that the German Army had been "'stabbed in the back' by the home front (Jews and Marxists, pacifists and socialists)."[89] He had then concluded: "Like Siegfried, stricken down by the treacherous spear of Savage Hagen, our weary front collapsed."[90]

Unfortunately, the *Dolchstosslegend* represented the opening salvo of a massive effort by the Germans to obfuscate, distort, and cover up what had actually occurred in the years leading up to the war and during its course. Here, the foreign office led the way. It culled its documents and excised passages contradicting the official line that Germany had not been responsible for the war's outbreak, that its actions throughout the war had been reasonable, and that there was no justification for the criminal peace

---

[87] The real mark of the strategic, economic, and diplomatic long-term fallout from the war was the ease with which Hitler was able to destroy the Versailles settlement in the late 1930s. Historians have largely ascribed that success to the failures inherent in the Versailles Treaty instead of the actual strategic situation that the war and its aftermath had created. Some within the military may have recognized this reality. One of the senior German generals, Walther Reinhardt, remarked in January 1919 that Germany's goal must be restored to its former frontiers with the "strongest, most modern army with [the] newest weapons." When queried about how long it would take, he replied, "We must and will be in a position to do so in 15 years." Quoted in Holger Herwig, *The First World War, Germany and Austria-Hungary, 1914–1918* (London, 1997), p. 449.

[88] For the reaction of the Germans to their defeat, see the outstanding discussion in Knox, *To the Threshold of Power*.

[89] Ibid., pp. 447–8.

[90] Ibid., p. 448.

the victors had imposed at Versailles – the Treaty termed the Versailles *Dictat* by many more Germans than just Hitler.[91]

The largest target was the Treaty's supposed "war guilt" clause, which had formed the basis for the Allied demand for reparations.[92] The seemingly generous nature of Wilson's Fourteen Points had supposedly tricked the Germans into signing the Armistice. But the Allies had then betrayed the Germans by the vicious nature of the peace treaty. This campaign of disinformation was successful beyond their wildest expectations. Not only did it convince the German people of the evils of Versailles, but in the long run it eventually warped perceptions in both the United States and Britain as to who had been responsible for the war and the Treaty's general unfairness.[93]

As such, it contributed to the abysmal period of Anglo-American strategy in the late 1930s, known today in the former case as appeasement and in the latter case as neutrality. As Holger Herwig has suggested about the long-term impact of the campaign:

> It serves no national interest to obfuscate and derail intellectual inquiry. Miscalculated risks are rarely glossed over simply by selectively editing pertinent documents and by having paid publicists tout the desired line through government-controlled presses and publishers. "Preemptive historiography" may succeed in the short run; over time it is likely to be uncovered as the sham that it is. In the final analysis, it is nothing short of a tragedy that, in the words of Hermann Hesse, "90 or 100 prominent men" conspired in the supposed interest of the state "to deceive the people on this vital question of national interest."[94]

In the end, it was the German people themselves who suffered the most. Within twenty years, they were to launch another great world war, in which they were to repeat virtually every strategic mistake made in the First World War.[95] The results this time, however, would bring the war back directly to Germany and wreck their nation from one end to the other.

---

[91] Holger Herwig was the first to point out the extent of this disinformation campaign. See the particularly incisive article: "Clio Deceived, Patriotic Self-Censorship in Germany after the Great War," *International Security*, Fall 1987, vol. 12, no. 2.

[92] After the Second World War, the reparations issue was solved in two fashions. The Soviets simply took everything movable back to the Soviet Union. In the west, not much remained that the strategic bombing campaign had not smashed to smithereens. Quite simply, there were no pips left to squeak.

[93] Such attitudes were supported by works such as that by John Maynard Keynes, *The Carthaginian Peace* (London, 1920).

[94] Herwig, "Clio Deceived," pp. 43–4.

[95] The disinformation campaign helps to explain why the senior leadership of the German military so casually endorsed the Führer's declaration of war on the United States in December 1941. After all, since the Reich's defeat had been the result of the army's being stabbed in the back by the Jews and the Communists, then America's entrance into the war in 1917 had made no significant difference to the war's outcome.

THE FAILURE OF VERSAILLES AND THE COMING
OF THE SECOND WORLD WAR

It has been all too easy for historians to apportion the Treaty of Versailles much of the blame for the outbreak of the Second World War in September 1939, as if history were simply the unfolding of a Greek tragedy.[96] In fact, Versailles simply recognized much of the strategic realities that the ending of the First World War in November 1918 had created. The flawed settlement in Eastern Europe was the result of a distribution of population that made conflicts in that area inevitable. Only the massive ethnic cleansing that followed the Second World War would settle the deep-seated tensions of ethnic hatreds in Eastern Europe.[97]

Moreover, the temporary collapse of Germany and Russia suggested the Eastern European settlement would remain in question for the foreseeable future, especially after those two powers recovered economically and politically.[98] Yet, it hardly seems fair to blame the peacemakers for the troubles inherent in the breakup of the Austro-Hungarian Empire, as well as the collapse of Imperial Germany and Tsarist Russia in 1917 and 1918.

Similarly, the nature of the German problem ensured an uncertain and dark future for Europe. And here, the ending of the war itself, not to mention the massive efforts at self-deception mounted by the Germans themselves, was a greater contributor to the outbreak of another conflagration than the Treaty of Versailles. Moreover, the appearance of Adolf Hitler and his vicious brand of racial hatred could only have come about through other contributory factors, such as the disastrous inflation of 1923, the divisive nature of Weimar politics – especially the split that divided the left between the Social Democrats and the Communists – and, above all, the catastrophic impact of the Great Depression.

In addressing the failures of the Treaty of Versailles, historians must ask what other alternatives were available to statesmen. There was no doubt that Alsace-Lorraine would return to France. It was difficult to see how Poland could have become a viable nation were it not to possess the Polish Corridor and access to the Baltic. While the Treaty might have pared down the territory the Poles received with the Corridor, it is doubtful German nationalists would have found the existence of the Corridor in *any form* anything other than a gross insult to their national sensibilities. The other

---

[96] Thucydides would have understood the outbreak of the Second World War but for very different reasons.

[97] The troubles in the Balkans following the end of the Cold War suggest that the questions of ethnicity and population distribution remain very much alive in that area of the world.

[98] And the Soviets were to come close to overthrowing the settlement in Eastern Europe barely one year later, when the Red Army rolled all the way into central Poland and was defeated only by the most desperate measures by the Polish Army in front of Warsaw.

pieces of German territory shaved off – Memel to Lithuania, Malmedy to Belgium, a few parcels of Silesia to Poland, and northern Schleswig-Holstein to Denmark – hardly represented serious damage to the Reich. But, of course, it was not the territory the Reich lost that mattered to Germans. It was the idea of losing German territory to these "worthless, small" nations that bothered the great majority of Germans.[99]

The conference might have held back in carving off these areas, but again it is doubtful whether such forbearance would have exercised much influence on the Germans. In regard to the Sudeten Germans and the Austrians, both of whom desired inclusion within the new Weimar Republic, given the political realities of 1919, it is difficult to see how the victorious Allies could have countenanced such an aggrandizement, which would have expanded the Reich well beyond the borders of 1914. The inclusion of the Sudeten Germans would have placed the new Czech Republic at the Reich's mercy, while an *Anschluss* would not only have made Germany a net gainer in territory but also would have stretched the Reich's influence deep into the Balkans while surrounding the Czechs on three sides. Here, of course, the Allies, and especially the Americans, were hoisted on the petard of national self-determination. In this case, they dumped self-determination in favor of reasoned statesmanship – a fact that Hitler would throw back in the faces of French and British appeasers in the late 1930s.[100]

In the end, it was the "war guilt" clause, above all, that infuriated the Germans. From the vantage point of the twenty-first century, is there any doubt but that the Germans were largely responsible for the war's outbreak or that they had caused deliberate and unnecessary damage on an enormous scale? The authors of the Treaty had felt it necessary to include Article 231 as a means to establish Germany's legal responsibility to pay reparation. Unfortunately, what was legal and what was right made little economic sense. Moreover, the Allies, because they themselves could not agree, failed to establish an amount as to what the Germans were to owe in reparations. The reparation conundrum was exacerbated by the economic problem that the Germans could pay the huge sums, of which Allied statesmen were thinking, only if the Reich's economy were to dominate Europe's.

Of all the difficulties the Treaty of Versailles confronted, the greatest and most insoluble was one which Allied victory and the currents of the age had only inflamed: namely, nationalism. At the end of the Napoleonic Wars, the

---

[99] And one should not forget the kind of peace the Germans had dealt out to the Soviets at Brest-Litovsk – not to mention German plans for Western Europe had they ended up winning the war.

[100] In the disastrous year of 1938, the Western Powers would surrender not only Austria but also Czechoslovakia to the tender mercies of the Nazis. To a considerable extent, they would accomplish this act of strategic suicide not only because of fear of another war but also because they believed that reasons of expediency should not drive foreign policy.

Congress of Vienna had attempted to put that evil genie back the bottle. To a considerable extent, its statesmen succeeded, much to the dismay of liberal academic historians but equally much to the benefit of Europe's peace and tranquility after 1815.

However, at Versailles, only slightly more than a century later, the statesmen could not have put nationalism back in the bottle even had they wished to do so. And, given Wilson's idealism as well as the climate of public discourse, they certainly could not. Moreover, they were a part of the problem, for the notion of national self-determination was inherent in their most cherished beliefs. The genie was out and the limits that the Treaty of Westphalia had attempted to place on the conduct and behavior of states operating within the system had largely broken down. The ideological and racial wars that began in 1937 in Asia and in 1939 in Europe underlined that reality and brought the world back to the dark days of the wars of religion and the Thirty Years' War. In effect, the Treaty of Versailles failed because it was incapable of performing the impossible: namely, placing either a political framework or limits on the conduct of European politics, much less a future war. Thus, it was incapable of preventing a resumption of the German war. However, how and why that struggle would occur in September 1939 would be the result of the contributions of politicians, national leaders, and chance more than the Treaty itself.

9

"Building buffers and filling vacuums": Great Britain and the Middle East, 1914–1922

JOHN GOOCH

If the peace which the victorious powers imposed on the Middle East at the end of the First World War has not stood the test of time, the fault lies only partly with those who made it. How long a peace lasts is to some degree a function of the skills and foresight of its constructors, but sooner or later the currents of history, which one cannot reasonably have expected its architects to foresee, undermine every such construction.

The shape of the Middle East that emerged as a consequence of the world war, and its degree of stability, was a function of the interactions among three dimensions of peace making. The first, which was difficult to master, was circumstance. The turmoil which the war caused in the international power system made the shaping of medium- and long-term policy extremely difficult while imparting a commanding urgency to the short term.

The second dimension, which statesmen might have managed better, was process. Making policy was the business of a machine with multiple moving parts – a Rubik's cube of competing agencies and forceful individuals, whose activities never combined to show a uniform face. The third dimension, least understood by contemporaries, was local context. Peace making between warring states had once been a matter of drawing new maps of power. The maintenance of peace in a region, where religious beliefs were complex, social structures primitive by European standards, and polities in the sense familiar to the peacemakers effectively nonexistent, required a level of cultural understanding that far surpassed what European statesmen, diplomats, and soldiers had hitherto needed. It is here, in what proved to be the most important dimension of peace making, that the fundamental weaknesses in the settlement imposed in the Middle East after 1918 are to be found.

TRADITIONAL THEMES AND CHANGING CIRCUMSTANCES

The aims of Britain's policy in the Middle East were at once simple to define and difficult to achieve. During the First World War and as a consequence of it, the British sought to create a power vacuum by removing Turkish authority and control and then fill it to their best advantage. The purposes for which Britain sought to replace Ottoman rule in the region shifted as the tides of war washed over the great powers that were her partners in the struggle, and the shape that she intended it to assume changed both during and after the war as policies altered to accommodate old and new pressures. The Middle East – a term only given popular currency by the journalist Valentine Chirol in 1902 – was a part of the world "the political arrangements of which were so ramshackle, the political and social institutions so weak, so exposed to the violence of ideological adventures, and of the voracious cupidities of political and military figures whom there was little to restrain." Not surprisingly, the region was especially vulnerable to manipulation, misunderstanding, and mismanagement.[1]

The multiple goals which influenced the regional architecture the politicians and diplomats began laboriously to assemble during the war to replace Turkish rule blended traditional methods with established imperial interests. The weakening of Turkey – and the consequent strengthening of Russia – had been on the diplomatic horizon since Sir Edward Grey's pledge in 1908 to give favorable consideration to the opening of the Straits to Russia when a suitable moment presented itself. The outbreak of war created the impetus to break up the Ottoman Empire. In mid-August 1914, Grey told the Russian foreign minister that St. Petersburg could have compensation from Turkey after the war; on November 1, he offered the prospect of a free hand to dismember Turkey; and eleven days later, he specifically offered Russia Constantinople and the Straits to dissuade her from attacking Persia. The large list of claims, which Russia presented to the West on March 4, 1915, was thus not a complete surprise. Grey's acceptance of it without making any of the massive counterclaims in the Middle East which Kitchener, Churchill, and Lloyd George all urged was evidence of the fact that British war aims were still a long way away from constituting a clear and consensually agreed program. Indeed, it was not until March 1917 that Lloyd George formally declared the dismemberment of the Ottoman Empire, an operational goal from the early days of the war, as a war aim.[2]

---

[1] Elie Kedourie, *England and the Middle East: The Destruction of the Ottoman Empire 1914–1921* (Boulder, CO, 1987), p. 8c.

[2] M. G. Eckstein-Frankl, "The Development of British War Aims August 1914–March 1915," University of London Dissertation, 1969, pp. 227–8, 253; V. H. Rothwell, *British War Aims and Peace Diplomacy 1914–1918* (Oxford, 1971), p. 127.

Regional power-balancing was a traditional function of international diplomacy; thus, the possibility of a threatening Russian presence in or close to the Middle East in the foreseeable future led London to pour old wine into new bottles. A Russian advance southward into Syria and an extension of what Ronald Storrs, oriental secretary at the British Residence in Cairo, regarded as "the inevitable French Protectorate over Lebanon" threatened British interests and, therefore, gave rise to the question of whether or not England should annex Mesopotamia. The prospect of enemy control of the Ottoman khalifate, which Kitchener believed another power could use to undermine Britain's imperial grip on India, Egypt, and the Sudan, was equally worrying.[3] An imperialist *par excellence*, Kitchener wanted England to emerge from the war with a continuous line of land communications from the Mediterranean to the Persian Gulf, which meant taking Alexandretta and controlling northern Syria. Thus, the British identified some ambitious regional goals early in the war in company with more limited reformulations of the map of great power influence in the Middle East of a type long familiar in international diplomacy.

The traditional imperial preoccupation with creating buffers and barriers, and the region's function in providing them, was still dominant as the First World War came to an end and the process of peace making began. Thus, in December 1918, Curzon saw Palestine as "the strategic buffer of Egypt."[4] Now, however, the politico-military geography of the First World War was different. Russia had exited from the military scene but Germany still appeared to present a danger. In summer and early autumn 1918, as Foch's great Allied drive forced a weakened German Army back along the Western Front, London remained concerned about the threat that the Central Powers presented to the region. Germany, with Turkey, had two lines of advance on India: a northern line through the Caucasus and Turkestan, and a southern line from the east coast of the Mediterranean through Palestine, Arabia, Persia, and Afghanistan. "It is the countries comprised within these two lines that constitute the Middle East problem," Curzon told the Imperial War Cabinet on June 25, 1918.[5] The concept of a regional defense against a Turco-German *Drang nach Osten* lasted beyond the war's end in 1918 and, at least while the powers settled the future of the Middle East, London assumed the combination to be a permanent factor in international affairs.[6]

[3] David Fromkin, *A Peace to End All Peace: Creating the Modern Middle East, 1914–1922* (London, 1989), pp. 96–7, 143.
[4] John Fisher, *Curzon and British Imperialism in the Middle East 1916–19* (London, 1999), p. 212.
[5] Ibid., p. 164; Rothwell, *British War Aims and Peace Diplomacy*, pp. 188–9.
[6] Fisher, *Curzon and British Imperialism*, p. 183.

Peace making in the region – already not an easy task – grew more complex as quite different scenarios of the future developed. In one, military operations in the Middle East – and the diplomatic machinations that went alongside them – aimed at safeguarding the area against penetration by the wartime enemy and thereby "establish the essential predispositions for some subsequent single-handed show-down against Germany victorious on the continent."[7] In another, it seemed likely to form a "second tier" behind the protective shield, which in 1919 Curzon wished to establish in the republics of Georgia, Armenia, and Azerbajan before Russia revived. In the event he failed, and the Anglo-Persian Agreement of August 9, 1919, proved no defense: Nationalist-minded Persian deputies refused to ratify it and, after he seized power in a British-approved coup in February 1921, Reza Khan at once denounced the agreement. A third scenario involved the resuscitation of the Turkish military threat when Istanbul confronted a peace treaty, which required her to accept the loss of Armenia, Constantinople, Thrace, and Anatolia. Would the Turks bow once more to Kismet, Curzon asked in March 1919, "Or will they think it worth while to strike another blow...for Islam and the few remaining vestiges of their freedom?"[8] To make matters yet more complex, the question of the future of the region had by the war's end become a matter in which Arab politics now mattered at least as much as the wider interests of the great powers preparing to reshape it.

RECRUITING THE ARABS

On September 24, 1914, the secretary of state for war, Field Marshal Lord Kitchener, sounded out Sharif Hussein of Mecca about assuming a friendly attitude toward Britain in event of war with Ottoman Turkey. His purpose in doing so was simple: the cementing of imperial control. A month later, shortly after Turkey had joined the war, he promised Hussein's son, Abdullah, that if the "Arab nation" assisted Britain in the war, she would see to it that Arabia was not molested. Kitchener also tempted Hussein with the khalifate, which would be removed from Constantinople and relocated in Mecca or Medina. The next day, Kitchener spoke to Abdullah of what in Arabic read as an unqualified and general commitment to support an Arab movement not just in the Hejaz but more widely. Sir Ronald Storrs, sympathetic to the idea of an Arab khalifate but somewhat prone to giving hostages to fortune, sent out an even more sweeping declaration on

[7] Brock Millman, "A Counsel of Despair: British Strategy and War Aims, 1917–18," *Journal of Contemporary History*, vol. 36, no. 2, April 2001, p. 260.
[8] Fisher, *Curzon and British Imperialism*, p. 239.

December 4, 1914, suggesting Britain intended to possess no part of the Arabs' country either by conquest, protection, or occupation – a message that appeared to apply to Arabia, Palestine, Syria, and Mesopotamia.[9]

Kitchener's approach to the Arabs, driven by the possibility that after the war Britain might confront Russia or France or both as enemies, rested on unsafe foundations. On the one hand, he proposed as part of the arrangement that Britain give Syria to the Arabs but met objections from the Foreign Secretary, who had conceded even before the war that Syria lay within the zone of French influence in the Middle East. On the other hand, he viewed the khalifate as having purely spiritual or theological powers like the papacy, whereas to Sunni Arabs, it possessed temporal power too. The India Office realized what the secretary of state for war did not: that offering Hussein the khalifate would carry with it the expectation, if not the obligation, that Britain would help him conquer Arabo-Turkish territories. There were also fears about how Indian Moslems would react to a challenge to the Istanbul khalifate. Vaguely aware of the unsafe ground onto which Kitchener was venturing, Grey issued contradictory instructions about raising "the dangerous question of the Caliphate."[10] Kitchener's perception of how the Muslim inhabitants of the Empire would view having the Sharif of Mecca as their leader turned out to be quite wrong: After the war, the Khilafat movement in India saw Hussein as a British puppet whose goals endangered Islam.[11]

During 1915, the idea of an expanded Arab presence in the Middle East continued along the parabola that would eventually bring peacetime disputes and spatchcocked compromises. In July, Abdullah sought British acknowledgment of Arab independence in the Levant, Mesopotamia, and Arabia; a treaty making Britain responsible for its defense; and British approval of the declaration of an Arab khalifate of Islam.[12] Although initially these propositions encountered no direct encouragement, many policy makers in or around Cairo were sympathetic to the idea of an Arab khalifate; as well as Storrs, their number included Sir Henry McMahon, Sir Reginald Wingate (Governor-General of the Sudan and Sirdar of the Egyptian Army), and brigadier-general G. F. Clayton (Head of Intelligence of the Arab Bureau in Cairo). Wingate saw it as tied in with the creation of a federation of semi-independent Arab states and with Sunni Islam as a counterpoise to

---

[9] Elie Kedourie, *In the Anglo-Arab Labyrinth: The McMahon-Husayn Correspondence and Its Interpretations 1914–1939* (Cambridge, 1976), pp. 17–22; Kedourie, *England and the Middle East*, pp. 50–1, 53.

[10] Fromkin, *A Peace to End All Peace*, pp. 96–8, 140; Kedourie, *England and the Middle East*, p. 53; Kedourie, *In the Anglo-Arab Labyrinth*, p. 28.

[11] Briton C. Busch, *Mudros to Lausanne: Britain's Frontier in West Asia, 1918–1923* (Albany, NY, 1976), pp. 215–22, 247–51; Timothy J. Paris, "British Middle East Policy-Making after the First World War: The Lawrentian and Wilsonian Schools," *Historical Journal*, vol. 41, no. 3, September 1998, p. 776.

[12] Abdullah to Storrs, 14 July 1915: Kedourie, *In the Anglo-Arab Labyrinth*, p. 4.

"the aggressive Pan-Islamism of the Ottoman school."[13] Sir Ronald Storrs thought in not dissimilar terms about the role the Arabian Peninsula could play:

> If, as would seem the ideal solution, we could make this latter into a sort of Afghanistan uncontrolled and independent within, but carrying on its foreign relations through us we would be giving a maximum of satisfaction and assuming a minimum of responsibility. . . . [14]

However, like many of the schemes to make use of the region, this one carried an inescapable and complicating corollary. It was not feasible, Storrs believed, "unless we hold Syria."

As the Arab cause began to roll, the British added an ethnographic flavor to the geostrategic and propagandistic ingredients comprising the cocktail of regional policy. Sir Mark Sykes, about to negotiate one of several overlapping territorial arrangements for the region, exhorted the Arabs – a people whom he had despised as anarchic before the war – to unity. Taking forward a notion whose basis was at the least questionable, T. E. Lawrence championed the idea of Arab nationality and an Arab national movement – which, in the view of one authority, he virtually invented as an antidote to Turkish rule and in which he did not believe unless created by Britain and the Allies – as a "third force" to set against Indian imperialistic goals in Mesopotamia and French colonial greed in Syria.[15]

The McMahon–Hussein correspondence, at first shrouded in mystery and subsequently wrapped in controversy, began on July 14, 1915, with a grandiose claim by Abdullah on behalf of Sharif Hussein for virtually the whole of Syria, Mesopotamia, and Jazirah. McMahon went beyond earlier British responses, but certainly in the direction favored by Kitchener, in stating positively that London would welcome an Arab khalifate. Then, in autumn 1915, Lieutenant Muhammed Sharif al-Faruqi arrived in Cairo to report on the activities of the Arab secret societies in Syria and their contacts with the Sharif. Acting as an unofficial go-between with Clayton's backing, al-Faruqi presented the territorial demands of the Arabs: an independent Arabian peninsula; autonomous government in Palestine and Mesopotamia; and the towns of Damascus, Aleppo, Hama, and Homs to be included in the Arab federation and not occupied by France.

Clayton and the Egyptian commander-in-chief, Sir John Maxwell, were prepared to negotiate the future control of Mesopotamia above the Basra *vilayet* and of the four towns. McMahon pressed urgency of a deal. In reply, Grey favored "an assurance of Arab independence" and a subsequent

---

[13] Wingate to Hardinge, 26 August 1915; Kedourie, *In the Anglo-Italian Labyrinth*, p. 43.
[14] Storrs, February 1915: Fisher, *Curzon and British Imperialism*, p. 101.
[15] Kedourie, *England and the Middle East*, pp. 80, 87, 95–6, 101.

discussion of boundaries but gave McMahon latitude to "give something more precise," if needed.[16] Accordingly, McMahon committed the British government to "recognize and support the independence of the Arabs within the territories included in the limits and boundaries proposed by the Sherif of Mecca." The districts of Mersina and Alexandretta and "portions of Syria lying to the west of the districts of Damascus, Hama, Homs, and Aleppo" were specifically excluded as not being "purely Arab" – the latter to accommodate French interests, about the exact extent of which McMahon was ignorant. In the *vilayets* of Baghdad and Basra, Britain had to be allowed "special measures of administrative control" in order to defend them from foreign aggression, promote the welfare of the local population, and "secure our mutual economic interests." Palestine was not mentioned.[17]

This correspondence left much confusion in its wake. Terminologically inexact because of the mistakes made by McMahon and Storrs in translating Arabic words, it was so confusing to Arnold Toynbee that when he came to examine it in 1918 as part of the preparations for the peace conferences, he "struggled to make out what McMahon had meant."[18] Grey saw it as little more than a recruiting tool, telling McMahon, "Our primary and vital object is not to secure a new sphere of British influence, but to get Arabs on our side against Turks."[19] For his part, Sharif Hussein ignored the exclusion of Damascus, Hama, Homs, and Aleppo and declared himself unwilling to give up Basra and Baghdad; Britain could occupy them "for a short time" and pay him compensation. Writing to the permanent undersecretary at the Foreign Office (a former viceroy of India) in December 1915, McMahon airily dispensed with the idea that the document had any long-term meaning at all: "I do not for one moment go to the length of imagining that the present negotiations will go far to shape the future form of Arabia or to either establish our rights or to bind our hands in that country," he told Lord Hardinge. The Arabs had to be detached from the enemy and brought over to Britain's side "and to succeed we must use persuasive terms and abstain from haggling over conditions."[20] Given all of this, it is perhaps scarcely surprising that one scholar has detected in the correspondence British "attempt[s] to cheat . . . by pretending to meet Hussein's demands. . . ."[21] However, the degrees of confusion, volumes of ambiguity, and amounts of unresolved issues both within and surrounding

---

[16] Grey to McMahon, 20 October 1915: Kedourie, *In the Anglo-Italian Labyrinth*, p. 94.
[17] McMahon to Hussein, 24 October 1915; ibid., p. 97.
[18] Arnold Toynbee, "Isaiah Freedman, 'The McMahon-Hussain Correspondence': Comment and Reply," *Journal of Contemporary History*, vol. 5, no. 4, 1970, p. 188.
[19] Grey to McMahon, 6 November 1915: Kedourie, *In the Anglo-Italian Labyrinth*, p. 107.
[20] McMahon to Hardinge, 4 December 1915; ibid., p. 120.
[21] *Contra* Fromkin, *A Peace to End All Peace*, p. 186.

the correspondence make this seem highly improbable. Confusion and not conspiracy was the hallmark of British policy in the region.

The "Cairo policy" embodied in the McMahon–Hussein correspondence pleased neither the vice royalty in Simla nor the India Office in London. Austen Chamberlain, Secretary of State for India, told Grey in April 1916 that McMahon had "raised the expectations [on the part of Sharif Hussein]."[22] Grey attempted to clarify the position by authorizing Wingate to inform Sharif Hussein that the British government "will make it an essential condition, in any terms of peace, that the Arabian Peninsula and its Mohammedan Holy Places should remain in the hands of an independent Sovereign Moslem State." What the British intended as a limited pledge they first distributed in leaflet form through Arabia and then, in July 1916, after the Hashemite revolt had begun, repeated in an official communiqué.[23]

SYRIA AND THE SYKES–PICOT AGREEMENT

The postwar future of Syria, which first came into play in 1915–1916, embodied a variety of regional and international strategic, diplomatic, and political considerations. Since Grey had allowed in June 1913 that it lay within the zone of French influence, it seemed initially that there was little Britain could do there: "We cannot act as regards Syria," the Foreign Secretary minuted on a letter from Kitchener in November 1914.[24] Immediately, the position in the Arabian Peninsula had to be protected from Turkish-inspired hostile locals. Beyond that, an Arab state would represent a weak power and, therefore, one whose vulnerability had to be guarded.

Kitchener and Storrs feared that France could not be kept out of Syria, which led them to think that it would have to be incorporated into the Egyptian sultanate while the Arabian Peninsula became a kind of Afghanistan. After Delcassé told Grey in February 1915 that France claimed Syria, the Foreign Secretary rejected any idea of attaching Syria to the Egyptian sultanate. By March 1915, when Britain ceded Constantinople to Russia, the French demand for Syria had expanded to include Palestine. In the face of this threat, Kitchener wanted a continuous line of communications stretching from the Mediterranean to the Persian Gulf. He would have preferred it to start from Alexandretta but wanted southern Syria up to Haifa and Acre as a minimum gauge of postwar imperial security.[25] In this scenario,

---

[22] John Fisher, "The Rabegh Crisis, 1916–17: 'A Comparatively Trivial Question' or 'A Self-Willed Disaster'," *Middle Eastern Studies*, vol. 38, no. 3, 2002, p. 76.
[23] Isaiah Friedman, "The McMahon-Hussein Correspondence and the Question of Palestine," *Journal of Contemporary History*, vol. 5, no. 2, 1970, p. 85.
[24] Kedourie, *In the Anglo-Arab Labyrinth*, p. 53.
[25] Kedourie, *England and the Middle East*, pp. 31–3.

a British-controlled Palestine would link up with Iraq and Jazirah and keep the French out of the southern portions of the Middle East.

Other considerations were also in play in addition to the purely military and strategic ones that preoccupied Kitchener. The Foreign Office wanted to undermine the French footing in the Middle East and on the eastern seaboard of Africa. In addition, and as the now-inescapable corollary of the McMahon–Hussein agreement, Sharif Hussein's territorial ambitions had to be reconciled with France's claims to a position in Syria, as Grey acknowledged on October 21, 1915. In an attempt to reconcile some if not all of these priorities, conversations began with the French. Francois Georges-Picot, first secretary at the French Embassy in London, received the task of handling the French end of the negotiations over the future of Syria while Sir Mark Sykes acted for London.

France's objective in the Middle East, defined in an official directive by Georges-Picot himself, was the creation of a "Greater Syria" which incorporated Palestine in the south and whose eastern boundary ran along the Tigris basin. Confronting the Foreign Office's evident wish to hold out to Hussein the goal of a future Arab state and obvious British concerns about Egypt and Mesopotamia, the French objective now became "to keep the maximum amount of territory outside the Arab kingdom and obtain the maximum number of privileges within the sphere of influence that will be assigned to us." The result, embodied in an exchange of diplomatic notes between the two governments (May 9-16, 1916), permitted France to annex coastal Syria as far south as Acre and gave her a zone of influence which ran east from Aleppo and Damascus to Mosul on the upper Tigris and thence to the Persian border. Britain, for her part, would annex lower Mesopotamia and operate a sphere of influence running from the central Tigris (including the oilfields of Kirkuk) in an arc west and south to the Sinai Peninsula and the Gulf, forming a "lid" on the Arabian peninsula (Jazirah). An international regime was to be established in Palestine. The French sphere was to act as a buffer between England and Russia in a postwar Middle East.[26]

Grey's acceptance of these arrangements was conditional on two provisos: "that the co-operation of the Arabs is secured, and the Arabs fulfill the condition and obtain the towns of Homs, Hama, Damascus, and Aleppo."[27] From the British point of view, the exclusion of the four towns, the absence of any specific commitment on the future of Palestine, and the undertaking implicit in the Sykes–Picot agreement that the Allies would take into account Arab interests was what made it interlock with the McMahon–Hussein

[26] Edward Peter Fitzgerald, "France's Middle Eastern Ambitions, the Sykes–Picot Negotiations, and the Oil Fields of Mosul, 1915–1918," *Journal of Modern History*, vol. 66, no. 4, December 1994, pp. 707–15.

[27] Grey to Cambon, 16 May 1916: Kedourie, *England and the Middle East*, p. 43.

letters.[28] However, such conjointedness was far from self-apparent. Matters grew more complicated for London when on December 6, 1917, three days after Allenby's capture of Jerusalem, Jamal Pasha revealed to the Moslem world the contents of the Sykes–Picot agreement, which the Bolsheviks had just published. Sharif Hussein of Mecca declared himself king of the Arab countries that same month but did not openly contest the Sykes–Picot agreement. To some historians, this has been grounds to suggest that there was no innate or insuperable conflict in his mind between it and the McMahon–Hussein agreement – and, indeed, no conflict at all since the two documents "amount, in the end, to much the same thing."[29] Not all have agreed.[30] Certainly, while the Arabs were prepared to see Basra and southern Mesopotamia under British rule, they were totally opposed to the French occupying Aleppo, Hama, Homs, and Damascus.

MESOPOTAMIA: THE "FORWARD" IMPETUS

On November 23, 1914, Anglo-Indian forces occupied Basra, and the question immediately arose as to whether they were to push farther north up the Tigris valley. Three separate but interrelated geostrategic views now came into play. Acutely aware of the importance of the region in defending the Gulf and the Persian flank of the Indian Empire, Hardinge, Kitchener, and Crewe wanted permanent possession of Basra, though they were not in full agreement about whether Britain should extend pledges now or at the end of the war. Curzon, himself a former viceroy, agreed that going to Basra would protect Gulf and Persian oil interests but did not favor advancing up the Tigris to Baghdad. To his mind, a territorial leap of that magnitude would bring with it major defense responsibilities, including that of a frontier coterminous with Russia. Sir Edward Grey thought capturing Baghdad would bring the Arabs over to Britain's side, and Balfour thought it a gamble worth trying. The withdrawal from the Dardanelles and the siege of Kut added issues of imperial military prestige to the mix.

Overall, the pressures to advance were too strong and the gains too alluring to resist. After initial setbacks, British troops entered Baghdad on March 11, 1917. With lower Mesopotamia now firmly in their hands as a consequence of the Sykes–Picot agreement, the British could make decisions

---

28 Kedourie, *In the Anglo-Italian Labyrinth*, pp. 141–3.
29 Kedourie, *England and the Middle East*, p. 56. This view was apparently shared by the Cairo officials, who had no doubts about the compatibility of the two sets of discussions. "But then what they had said was so vague and ambiguous that it was compatible with almost anything"; Kedourie, *In the Anglo-Arab Labyrinth*, p. 126.
30 "The spirit, if not the letter, of the Sykes–Picot Agreement was clearly in conflict with the British promises to the Arabs"; Paul C. Helmreich, *The Partition of the Ottoman Empire at the Paris Peace Conference of 1919–1920* (Columbus, OH, 1974), p. 9.

about its future unilaterally. On March 29, the War Cabinet instructed that Basra was to remain permanently under British rule and Baghdad was to be "an Arab State with local ruler or government under British Protectorate in everything but name. . . . " In what was afterwards seen as a piece of blatant imperial sleight of hand, it explained that Britain would administer Baghdad "behind the Arab façade as far as possible as an Arab province by [an] indigenous agency."[31] Three days later, a report by Curzon from a subcommittee of the Imperial War Cabinet urged that Britain retain Mesopotamia and Palestine – not yet captured – at the war's end. He did not want to extend India's responsibilities but thought that once it had occupied Mesopotamia, Britain could not hand the province back as that would break promises to the local Arabs and revivify "the shattered German ambition of a great Teutonised dominion" running from Europe through Asia Minor to the Gulf.[32] Lloyd George, now prime minister, thought the committee a trifle avaricious but was ready to accept its findings as recommendations.

The India Office, under whose aegis the area came, adopted a gradualist strategy during 1917 designed to prevent the French from gaining a foothold there and, by extension, elsewhere; keeping out French consuls; and resisting attempts by French banks to establish themselves in the area. After speeches by Lloyd George and Woodrow Wilson on national self-determination made on January 11, 1918, it was evident that straightforward annexation was impossible. Now, however, new considerations came into play which demanded not merely that London exert a firm grip on the region but that she use her power and influence as a lever against an ally who was simultaneously a partner on the Western Front and a rival in the Middle East. In January 1918, Curzon was in favor of an advance up the Euphrates to Hit – against the advice of the Director of Military Intelligence, Sir George Macdonogh – "on account of the oil wells."[33] Maurice Hankey, secretary to the War Cabinet, thought the future supply of water for British-sponsored irrigation and navigation, as well as oil, justified such a move. Also, pushing up to the northern border of the Baghdad and Mosul *vilayets* would provide a jumping-off point for Syria.

Thus, by early 1918, "forward" policies began to predominate in consideration about the role of Mesopotamia at the war's end and in the peace to follow. There was a general consensus, in which India Office hands took a significant part, that Britain must maximize her presence in Mesopotamia even in defiance of the McMahon and Sykes–Picot arrangements. Sir Percy Cox, about to leave his position as civil commissioner in Baghdad for a two-year stint in Teheran, concisely summed up the forward

[31]   Kedourie, *England and the Middle East*, p. 176.
[32]   David Gilmour, *Curzon* (London: John Murray), p. 475.
[33]   Fisher, *Curzon and British Imperialism*, p. 112.

view shared now by the "old Indianists" and the "new imperialists" when he told Curzon that "[e]verything depends on full practical British control of the [Mesopotamian] administration for many years to come."[34] Denied the possibility of formal annexation, Britain aimed to establish herself in Mesopotamia by means of commercial and civil development and to rely on the principle of self-determination to win consent. In a word, postwar Mesopotamia was to be run like prewar Egypt. When the possibility of a Hashemite ruler on the throne of Mesopotamia came to be mooted, therefore, the Government of India set itself more firmly than ever against Cairo's "Arab" policy.

PALESTINE: RACIAL, FINANCIAL, AND STRATEGIC REASONING

An early whisper of what was to become the Balfour Declaration of 1917 came in November 1914 when Grey, responding to an approach by Herbert Samuel about the possibility of restoring a Jewish state in Palestine, observed that the idea "had a strong sentimental attachment for him." However, Sir Ronald Storrs's proposal in December 1914 that Palestine could become a buffer state against Russia or France fit rather better with the geostrategic paradigm of peace making applied to the region in the early stages of the First World War.[35]

Undecided because unconsidered, the future of Palestine more or less languished until David Lloyd George succeeded Asquith as British premier in December 1916. As David Fromkin has noted, the new premier viewed the Middle East "as a prize worth seeking in itself" and not just as a way station on the road to India.[36] This was a new brand of geopolitics and, to carry it out, Lloyd George donned the garb of a *conquistador,* whose soldiers would retake the Holy Land. At his first cabinet meeting, held on Saturday, December 9, 1916, he informed Sir William Robertson, chief of the imperial general staff, that he wanted operations in the Sinai accelerated in order to mount a great military offensive into Palestine and Syria. This, he believed, would encourage Arabs outside the peninsula to rebel against the Turks. Lloyd George wanted the region permanently from the start, telling Francis Bertie in April 1917, "we shall be there by conquest and shall remain."[37]

With the conclusion of the Sykes–Picot agreement, the question arose of what to do with Palestine. The prime minister evidently felt the need for a

---

[34] Cox to Curzon, 9 February 1918: ibid., p. 128.
[35] Kedourie, *In the Anglo-Arab Labyrinth,* p. 55; Storrs to Fitzgerald, 28 December 1914, ibid., p. 34.
[36] Fromkin, *A Peace to End All Peace,* p. 235.
[37] Kedourie, *In the Anglo-Arab Labyrinth,* p. 159; also p. 160.

buffer to protect his coming conquests against French incursions – and saw a way to do it. In April 1917, briefing Sir Mark Sykes before he departed to join the Egyptian Expeditionary Force, Lloyd George and Curzon stressed "the difficulty of our relations with the French in this region and the importance of not prejudicing the Zionist movement and the possibility of its development under British auspices."[38]

Zealotry, altruism, and pro-Jewish sympathy undoubtedly played their part in leading the British government to adopt the Balfour Declaration, in which it "view[ed] with favor the establishment in Palestine of a national home for the Jewish people" and undertook to "use its best endeavors to facilitate the achievement of this object" on November 2, 1917. However, entirely new considerations drove the adoption of a policy which was to have long-term repercussions in the Middle East. For one thing, the British war debt to the United States was approaching £757.3 million in 1917–1918, a fact which led Lloyd George to back the Declaration in the hope that it would win the support of American Jews for the British war effort.[39] For another, the need early on in the war to do something to undermine the actions of pro-German Jewish "spies" on the Russian front and the efforts of "[o]penly pro-German" Jewish bankers in America who were reportedly "toiling in a solid phalanx to compass our destruction" was transmuted by the second Russian Revolution into a requirement to weaken the attempts by "Jewish–Bolshevik revolutionaries" to bring about a separate peace with Germany.[40] The declaration, in other words, embodied a policy designed to resolve problems entirely extraneous to the Middle East.

In the cabinet discussion on October 4, 1917, during which Balfour defended his proposal, Curzon raised the practical question of how the present occupants were to make space for the incomers. However, by the end of the month, he was ready to set aside these problems and admit the force of Balfour's diplomatic arguments. The Foreign Secretary had won the day – with the prime minister's backing. The Balfour Declaration managed to have things both ways at once, for while the government now favored the establishment of a Jewish homeland in Palestine, it would do nothing which might "prejudice the civil and religious rights of the existing non-Jewish communities in Palestine."[41] In doing so, it may have met Balfour's high standards of balanced philosophical discourse, but it did not make the task

---

[38]   Fisher, *Curzon and British Imperialism*, pp. 82–3.
[39]   Roger Adelson, *London and the Invention of the Middle East: Money, Power, and War, 1902–1922* (New Haven, CT, 1995), pp. 134, 136.
[40]   Mark Levene, "The Balfour Declaration: A Case of Mistaken Identity," *English Historical Review*, vol. 107, no. 422, January 1992, pp. 60–3, 69–70, 72; Fromkin, *A Peace to End All Peace*, pp. 295–6.
[41]   Helmreich, *From Paris to Sevres*, p. 7; Gilmour, *Curzon*, p. 482.

any easier when it came time to shape the region anew in the wake of the Turkish defeat.

A NEW IMPERIALISM?

As the war drew on, positions on the goals of peace in the Middle East hardened. The "Indian school" grew more determined than ever that the Arabian peninsula must be an exclusively British preserve since it lay on the path of two main approach routes to India. If anyone else got a footing there, General Barrow declared in January 1917, "We shall have warring factions on our borders, the arms trade will be intensified, the peaceful development of commerce will be arrested and the 'Haj' in which, on account of our Mahommedan subjects, we are so profoundly interested may be interrupted to our detriment."[42] In April 1917, Curzon's cabinet committee adopted the report of a subcommittee on territorial changes which stated that "[t]he ultimate connection by railroad of Egypt, Palestine, Mesopotamia and the Persian Gulf is an object to be kept steadily in view."[43] The prime minister fully shared this traditional view of the strategic priority to be given to imperial communications. In August 1917, Lloyd George told Sir Reginald Wingate that if England lost its grip on the Red Sea and Persian Gulf communications, there was practically no gain in the war that could compensate for the loss.

Simultaneously, the British found themselves drawn deeper into the contradictions embedded in a policy in which Arab nationalism was to play a part alongside the "hidden hand" of great power manipulation. Curzon's position demonstrated how the two positions could be – and were – combined. He supported cutting the Hejaz railway in 1914 and landing troops at Alexandretta in 1915, but he was also skeptical about inspiring an Arab revolt and setting up a state in former Turkish territory. At the same time, he wanted to do nothing to encourage French pretensions in the Hejaz, so in July 1917, he opposed the idea of a jointly controlled Arab Legion on the grounds that it would "give them claim to employ force elsewhere in furtherance of French ambitions in Palestine or Syria...." He also believed that once given, pledges must be honored and warned the cabinet in October 1917 that Britain "must be careful that any peace program did not work to the detriment of the Arabs." Not surprisingly, then he opposed both the Sykes–Picot agreement and the Balfour Declaration.[44] In trying to secure Britain's special position, Curzon was working against the Foreign Office's policy of active Anglo-French cooperation in 1917.

[42] Fisher, *Curzon and British Imperialism*, p. 68.
[43] Ibid., p. 78.
[44] Fisher, *Curzon and British Imperialism*, p. 83; Gilmour, *Curzon*, p. 476.

Thwarting the French became a policy that appeared at once both attractive and necessary. French actions and the fear that they might presage something more unwelcome provided a powerful stimulus. In November 1916, the French put forward the unwelcome idea of a joint Anglo-French bank at Jeddah. In December, France issued a declaration of disinterest in the Arab peninsula but, a month later, there were fears the French might be planning to set up a consulate in Mecca. (The building in question turned out in the end to be a pilgrims' hostel.) Sir Reginald Wingate, not confident about the Sykes–Picot agreement, wanted to revise it to allow Britain to control Arabia and get hold of Syria. Curzon shared Wingate's stance, remarking in July 1917 that "historical connections, our geographical position, and our political interests in Arabia, render it inevitable and indeed essential . . . that a preponderant political influence should be exercised by Great Britain throughout the Arabian Peninsula."[45]

In one respect, Britain's policy in the Middle East remained fully in accord with a long-established principle. As Lloyd George of the Foreign Office noted in August 1918: "From a British strategical and political point of view a settlement which allowed a great power to establish an eastern empire right athwart of us in middle Asia would immensely add to our anxieties, to our military commitments and to our difficulties in administering Arab and local nationality."[46] However, as a guide to shaping practical policy in the region, this only pointed to an indeterminate destination. In traveling the remainder of the road, London slowly but inexorably tied itself in knots. When Baghdad fell in March 1917, the British government authorized Sir Mark Sykes to encourage all Arabs to unite, and the next month it told Cox in Mesopotamia that it intended to carry out the Sykes–Picot agreement.

By January 1918, the foreign office was speaking of a determination to realize "Arab unity" and in June, Wingate specifically disowned Sykes–Picot, telling Hussein that was not "an actual agreement." The "Declaration to the Seven" issued on June 8, 1918, gave not one but two hostages to fortune. It promised that the government of territories freed by Allied armies from the Turks would rest on the consent of the governed and put itself potentially in conflict with the Sykes–Picot agreement by stating that the British government would recognize the "complete and sovereign independence of the Arabs" in areas they themselves emancipated.[47]

The military dynamics of war played their part in exacerbating the already considerable internal contradictions in regional policy. Preparing for the third battle of Gaza, which began on October 30, 1917, General Allenby allowed T. E. Lawrence to operate in the French zone of influence in Syria

[45]   Fisher, *Curzon and British Imperialism*, p. 93.
[46]   Ibid., p. 144.
[47]   Kedourie, *England and the Middle East*, pp. 110, 112–13, 116.

without a French officer attached. He regarded operations there by Faisal's tribesmen as important "to confirm and consolidate my success in Palestine."[48] Thereafter, he ran the rest of the Palestine campaign, most notably and most symbolically the capture of Damascus on October 1, 1918, in such a way as to install Faisal's Hashemite Arabs in Syria and thus unmake part of the Sykes–Picot agreement. His policy was to recognize Arab administration and independence in the occupied territories east of the Jordan River, which included both the British and French zones of influence as defined by the Sykes–Picot agreement, while warning Faisal not to interfere in the coastal *vilayets* or Lebanon. The peace conference would settle their future when, Allenby told Faisal, the Allies would be "in honour bound to endeavour to reach [a] settlement in accordance with [the] wishes of the people concerned."[49] In the view of one leading scholar, it was Allenby's abandonment of Damascus to Sharif Faisal after the Australians got into the city first that "created the myth of an Arab Revolt."[50]

REASSEMBLING THE PIECES AND MAKING THE PEACE

As the Allies moved from war making to peace making, they made nods in the direction of the Middle East in respect of Wilsonian ideas of self-determination. In January 1918, Lloyd George declared that "Arabia, Armenia, Mesopotamia, Syria and Palestine are in our judgment entitled to a recognition of their separate national conditions." In what form he would not say, but "it would be impossible to restore [them] to their former sovereignty."[51] Three days before the armistice brought hostilities to a close, a joint Anglo-French declaration expressed the Allied wish "to encourage and assist in the establishment of indigenous Governments and Administrations in Syria and Mesopotamia." London and Paris both denied that they had any wish "to impose any particular institution on these lands," which was not entirely true, and undertook to support the governments these areas "have adopted of their own free will."[52]

These intentions may not strictly have been at cross purposes with the Sykes–Picot agreement, but the British certainly did not intend to be bound by it. On October 7, 1918, a week after Allenby's troops entered Jerusalem,

[48] Allenby to Robertson, 13 & 17 October, 15 November 1917: Matthew Hughes, ed., *Allenby in Palestine: The Middle Eastern Correspondence of Field Marshal Viscount Allenby* (London, 2004), pp. 66, 67, 85.
[49] Allenby to War Office, 30 September, 6 October 1918; Allenby to Wilson, 11 October 1918; Allenby to War Office, 17 October 1918: Hughes, *Allenby in Palestine*, pp. 191, 201–2, 205–6, 207–8. See also Matthew Hughes, *Allenby and British Strategy in the Middle East 1917–1919* (London, 1999), pp. 88–110.
[50] Kedourie, *England and the Middle East*, p. 122.
[51] Adelson, *London and the Invention of the Middle East*, p. 154.
[52] Kedourie, *England and the Middle East*, p. 132.

London officially informed Paris that it did not regard the agreement as "suitable to present conditions."[53] Later that month, Colonel T. E. Lawrence produced an "Arabist" plan for the postwar administration of the Middle East in which Faisal would preside over an autonomous Syria; Hussein's youngest son, Zaid, would rule the northern part of Mesopotamia; and his second son, Abdullah, would rule southern Mesopotamia. In a variant of it, Sir George Macdonogh proposed a single state of Iraq stretching from north of Mosul to the Gulf under Abdullah, Jezireh as a single state under British influence, and Syria as an Arab state in the hinterland with a coastal strip under a British minister.[54]

Almost everybody was now at cross purposes. Lawrence wanted to secure the Middle East for the Arabs; the foreign office wanted to keep French influence out of northern Mesopotamia; and the India Office wanted, at a minimum, to keep the Arabs out of southern Mesopotamia. The idea of self-determination for Syria, where Faisal was in possession of Damascus and where the Declaration to the Seven had promised areas liberated by the Arabs would have independence, met one of those goals but threatened another.

In December 1918, as part of the preparations for the upcoming Paris Peace Conference, the British produced an agreed list of their objectives in the Middle East. The Sykes–Picot agreement, characterized by Curzon as "a sort of fancy sketch to suit a situation that had not then arisen" incorporating divisions so "fantastic and incredible" as to lead to incessant difficulties, went by the board. Curzon took the view that the McMahon–Hussein correspondence had committed Britain to ensuring that Mesopotamia, Palestine, Acre-Haifa, and the British and French zones of influence should be "Arab and independent," while Lloyd George wanted to get control of Mosul, which was in the French sphere, and Palestine, which was mostly in the international zone. To get them, he was willing to see the French administer the Syrian coast or the interior. On December 1, Clemenceau agreed to cede Mosul and Palestine to Britain – the former not as great a concession as some have suggested since the known oil-bearing fields were already in the British zone, and France was unable either on legal or practical grounds to challenge Britain or compete with her there. London then decided "to back Faisal and the Arabs [in Syria] as far as we can, up to the point of not alienating the French," and to set up an Arab government in Mesopotamia.[55]

[53] David French, *The Strategy of the Lloyd George Coalition, 1916–1918* (Oxford, 1995), p. 263.

[54] Paris, "British Middle East Policy-Making after the First World War," p. 775; Fisher, *Curzon and British Imperialism*, p. 235.

[55] Kedourie, *In the Anglo-Arab Labyrinth*, pp. 216–7; Fitzgerald, "France's Middle Eastern Ambitions," pp. 723–4; Paris, "British Middle East Policy-Making after the First World War," p. 778.

The larger issues of Syria and Mesopotamia pushed Palestine and the Zionist question somewhat into the wings. Faisal, who had privately made positive noises to Weizmann as a possible ally but now had publicly to disavow him, indicated that he would not oppose the British line if they kept the French out of Palestine and Syria. The Palestinian population, Christian and Moslem alike, unanimously opposed Zionism. In January 1919, concerned that Zionist leaders were now calling for a "Jewish commonwealth" which would lead inevitably to clashes with Arabs, Curzon told Balfour of his worries. The Foreign Secretary airily reassured him that Weizmann had never asked for a "Jewish Government," a claim he would regard as "inadmissible." Curzon consulted his dictionaries in an attempt to find the difference.[56]

Although it was the year of the Paris Peace Conference, 1919 was in practice a year of temporary solutions and transitional arrangements. As far as Mesopotamia, Montagu at the India Office wanted representative national government, Curzon hesitated to go that far, and the "Indian" hands put up a strong defense of their position against Lawrence's designs for Hashemite rule there. Sir Percy Cox, the civil commissioner in Baghdad until March 1918, could not see "the slightest justification for introducing one of the family of the Sherif" since "King Hussein and his family carry no weight whatever in Iraq." His successor, Sir Arthur Wilson, as well as agreeing with him on this believed that the Mesopotamians were "unfit to govern themselves."[57] After a managed referendum, Wilson went his own way as acting High Commissioner, creating a veiled protectorate over the Baghdad *vilayet*, annexing the Basra *vilayet*, and running the Mosul *vilayet* from Baghdad. Agitation developed from the summer of 1919, during which Sharif Hussein and the plebiscite held at the end of 1918 encouraged the locally disaffected. A year later, Wilson was facing an intensifying local revolt supported not only by Hashemite money and propaganda but also by large quantities of arms: at the end of the disturbance in 1920, the British collected 63,046 rifles and 2,904,513 rounds of ammunition. Iraq, Wilson complained, was "a savage country where people do not argue but shoot."[58]

Faisal attempted to yoke his own family ambitions with Woodrow Wilson's known predilections. "If our independence be conceded and our local competence established," he told the Paris Peace Conference, "[then] the natural influence of race, language, and interest will soon draw us together into one people." He was immediately contradicted by the representative of the Central Syrian Committee, Chekri Ganem, who stated that

[56] Gilmour, *Curzon*, p. 520.
[57] Paris, "British Middle East Policy-Making after the First World War," pp. 777, 779.
[58] Kedourie, *England and the Middle East*, p. 195.

despite similarities in language and religion, Syria was not an Arab region.[59] One could well have said the same, perhaps with more justification, of Mesopotamia either side of Mosul, where the Turkomans, Kurds, Christians, Jews, Yezidis, Nestorians, Chaldeans, and Jacobites outnumbered the Arabs.

On April 20, 1919, at the Council of Four, Woodrow Wilson suggested an inquiry into the wishes of the inhabitants of Syria and Palestine. Deadlock between the British and French delegations – the result of Clemenceau's refusal to send a French delegation until Britain handed over control of Syria and Britain's refusal to do so – meant that the American King–Crane commission went alone. It met a well-orchestrated campaign by Faisal in Syria designed to persuade it that the Arabs would accept an American mandate first and a British mandate second. Faisal's policy failed in every respect. Britain made it clear it had no intention of accepting a Syrian mandate; the notion of an American mandate lost whatever life it might ever have possessed when the U.S. Senate rejected Wilson's proposal for an American mandate over Constantinople and Armenia on May 24, 1920; and the King–Crane commission's recommendation to preserve the unity of Greater Syria rather than creating separate states in Palestine and Lebanon foundered on the rocks of British and French interest.[60]

Force of circumstance now took over. In late summer 1919, domestic economic and social pressures forced Lloyd George to pull British troops out of Syria. The British brokered a deal with the French in September, in which the area east of the Sykes–Picot line (i.e., the four cities) went to Faisal while the area to the west, including Lebanon, went to the French. The final boundary of the frontier between Syria and Palestine remained to be settled. In delimiting this and the Palestine/Mesopotamia frontier, London was especially concerned to include all potential railway, pipeline, and air routes between Palestine and Mesopotamia via the Euphrates.[61] The British troop withdrawal started on November 1 and in the same month, a French high commissioner arrived in Beirut. Faisal found himself left to deal with the French alone. Local resistance to any deal forced him to abandon negotiations, and the situation spiraled downward in a series of incidents, which included attacks on French garrisons and Christian villagers. The Turks, who under Kamal were resisting the Sevres settlement, provided the Arabs with guns and munitions. In March 1920, resisters assembled the Syrian Congress and declared Faisal King of Syria.

In April 1920, the San Remo Conference settled Feisal's immediate fate – and the future shape of the Middle East. Gathering at what Curzon described

---

[59] Helmreich, *From Paris to Sevres*, pp. 53, 54.
[60] Kedourie, *England and the Middle East*, pp. 138–40; Fromkin, *A Peace to End All Peace*, pp. 395–8.
[61] War Office to Allenby, 23 May 1919; Hughes, *Allenby in Palestine*, pp. 263–4.

as "a second-class English watering place" against a background in which the Syrians had proclaimed Faisal as Hashemite monarch the previous month, the Palestinians had petitioned Allenby not to be separated from Syria and the Iraqis had chosen Abdullah, the European powers engaged in what Woodrow Wilson described as a "disgusting scramble" for territory.[62] As far as the Middle East, Britain received mandates over Palestine, which was to become the site of the "Jewish national home," and over Mesopotamia; France received a mandate over Syria; and the Jazirah Peninsula remained to the Arabs. The Treaty of Sevres later embodied the San Remo terms. Now free to exercise the full weight of military force in Syria, the French General Gouraud defeated the Sharifians at the battle of Khan Maisalun on July 24, 1920, and entered Damascus as its conqueror the next day. Two days later, Faisal was exiled.

What now remained to be settled was the future of strife-torn Mesopotamia. Having been thrown out of Syria, Faisal's star now began unexpectedly to rise. "If we were to offer him the Amirate [of Iraq]," Sir Arthur Wilson suggested, "not only might we re-establish our position in the eyes of the Arab world, but we might go far to wipe out [the] accusation of bad faith both with Faisal and with [the] people of this country."[63] French opposition led to a decision to postpone any decision for two years, but Lawrence; Percy Cox, who returned to Baghdad to replace Wilson in October 1920; and Gertrude Bell, who had acted from April 1917 as Cox's oriental secretary, all favored the idea. Bell, who had opposed the idea of an Arab administration in Mesopotamia in 1918, was converted to the Hashemite cause after meeting Lawrence and Faisal in Paris in 1919. Now a firm believer in Arab nationalism, she went over Wilson's head in an attempt to persuade the India Office that an autonomous Arab government could do well in Iraq.[64] Thanks to a combination of political circumstances, which included Winston Churchill's political ambitions and military optimism, as well as Cox's return to Baghdad and Bell's influential position there, Faisal would shortly triumph – if that is the right term.

Between December 1920 and February 1921, Lloyd George finally resolved the confusion among competing authorities over policy making in the Middle East. The India Office effectively bowed out of the contest and the cabinet handed control of Iraq and Palestine to the colonial office, which Churchill agreed to head. A new Middle Eastern department was set up to handle the region. Curzon was by no means happy, believing that the newly

[62] Elizabeth Monroe, *Britain's Moment in the Middle East, 1914–1936* (London, 1963), p. 66.
[63] Paris, "British Middle East Policy-Making after the First World War," p. 787.
[64] Liora Lukitz, *A Quest in the Middle East: Gertrude Bell and the Making of Modern Iraq* (New York, 2006), pp. 121–9.

arrived secretary of state for the colonies, with Palestine and Mesopotamia under his authority, wanted to be "a sort of Asiatic foreign secretary," and the two clashed over control of Arabia.[65]

Churchill's winning formula for indirect imperial control of Iraq combined Hashemite rule with economies in the defense budget to be secured by the use of air power as a replacement for troops on the ground. Cox and Bell produced the political formula the new colonial secretary needed – a middle way between Wilson's failed policy of direct British military control and Lawrence's vision of total Arab independence, which maintained British control of Iraq behind a façade of Arab sovereignty. At the Cairo Conference in February 1921, Bell found to her pleasure that this program "coincided exactly with that which the Secretary of State [Churchill] had brought with him."[66] It was duly decided to install Faisal as king of Iraq on the back of a popular "call" and to give his brother Abdullah temporary governorship of Transjordan. In London, Lawrence eulogized Faisal and Abdullah, and in Iraq, Cox and Bell worked hard to gain public support for Faisal. In the subsequent plebiscite, 96 percent of the Iraqi population voted in favor of Faisal – supposedly, because they knew the British were behind him – despite the fact that the majority of the population was illiterate. The petition by Basra for separate treatment shortly before his arrival was a sign of the difficulties to come as the British imposed a Sunni regime on a Shia society.[67]

In mid-June 1921, Churchill explained in a speech to the House of Commons how his "Cairo" policy was intended to work. Instead of copying the Turkish method of "setting up administrations of local notables in each particular province or city, and exerting an influence through the jealousies of one tribe or another," Britain was seeking to "build up around the ancient capital of Baghdad . . . an Arab state which can revive and embody the old culture and glories of the Arab race." Bell once again played her part in what was now the endgame, taking Faisal to the reconstructed palace at Ctesiphon in August 1921 and telling him the story of the Arab conquest. "It was the tale of his people . . . I don't know which of us was the more thrilled," she told her father, though the event probably left a greater impression on her than it did on the subsequent history of Iraq.[68] An attempt at nation-building may well have been of value in itself, but behind it lay more prosaic

[65] Gilmour, *Curzon*, p. 524.
[66] H. V. F. Winstone, *Gertrude Bell* (London, 1978), p. 235; see also Lukitz, *A Quest in the Middle East*, pp. 138–44.
[67] Faisal wanted his new kingdom to incorporate the Kurdish districts of southern Kurdistan to counterbalance the Shia, but at the Cairo Conference it was agreed that they would be kept under British mandatory supervision until a suitably representative body of Kurdish states chose inclusion in Iraq: Busch, *Mudros to Lausanne*, pp. 372–3.
[68] Gertrude Bell to H[ugh] B[ell], 6 August 1921: Florence Bell, ed., *The Letters of Gertrude Bell* (London, 1927), vol. 2, p. 616.

considerations of self-interest. Writing to his colonial secretary in September 1921, Lloyd George put the matter in a nutshell: "If we leave [Iraq], we may find a year or two after we have that we have handed over to the French and Americans some of the richest oilfields in the world."[69]

There remained the question of Palestine. Britain and France agreed on the Syria–Palestine border at the London Conference (February 12–April 10, 1920). The colliding goals of the regional actors became apparent in July 1921, when Chaim Weizmann challenged the restrictions on Zionist immigration – imposed on the grounds of the capacity of the country to absorb Jews – and asked that they be lifted. Simultaneously, a Palestine Arab delegation sought representative government, the reversion of the Balfour Declaration, and Palestinian membership in a confederation of Arab states. Deadlock ensued when Lloyd George, Balfour, and Churchill all refused to go back on the Declaration. It was resolved – at least for the time being – in Summer 1922, when the League of Nations approved a Palestine mandate, incorporating the British commitment to Zionism. As elsewhere in the Middle East, the terms of the settlement nourished the roots from which dark troubles would flower in the not-too-distant future.

THE CAUSES OF FAILURE

In his congratulatory address to the King on November 18, 1918, Curzon declared that "the British flag never flew over a more powerful or a more united Empire than now." For some contemporaries, the flag soon looked more than a little tattered. Writing in *The Edinburgh Review* in January 1923, Valentine Chirol declared that if Lloyd George were "to go down to history as the man whose great qualities did at any rate very much to win the war," he would also go down "as the man whose great defects went far to 'lose the peace'."[70] For at least one historian, the flag that fluttered in the Middle Eastern breezes was still bright since by the end of the first Lausanne Conference in January 1923, "Britain had regained her prestige in the Near East."[71] For another, though, it was in shreds:

> The British government had changed, British officials had changed, and in 1922 the arrangements arrived at in the Middle East did not accurately reflect what the government of the day would have wished ... *British policy-makers imposed a settlement upon the Middle East in 1922 in which, for the most part, they themselves no longer believed.*[72]

---

[69] Adelson, *London and the Invention of the Middle East*, pp. 201, 205.
[70] Gilmour, *Curzon*, p. 497; Adelson, *London and the Invention of the Middle East*, pp. 210–11.
[71] Gilmour, *Curzon*, p. 566.
[72] Fromkin, *A Peace to End All Peace*, pp. 562–3 [italics in original].

The explanation for the failure of the Middle Eastern peace settlement to fashion a lasting solution – or even to produce peace and order – lies first in the role of war as the means to an end. The First World War ended the more or less clear-cut nineteenth-century dichotomy between wartime, in which destruction reduced or eradicated the enemy's fighting power, and peacetime, in which diplomatic manipulation created a correspondingly appropriate international balance. Nor, in the broadest terms, did the military outcome correspond to what history had led the diplomats to expect – or at least for which to hope. Although Allenby won his battles, there was no "decisive victory" in the Middle East which put the conquered entirely at the mercy of the conquerors. Instead, the conquered merely withdrew, leaving the victors to fashion and impose a peace on third parties. In circumstances which were then entirely novel – but with which we are now all too familiar – peace making failed to grasp the underlying realities of what was, in essence, a new kind of problem.

The process of peace making began when the war had barely started and continued throughout its course. In dealing with the Middle East, British government committees and ministries deliberated on the *desiderata* while functional officials and representatives parceled out territories in a process which was, to say the least, poorly coordinated. While they did so, the geopolitical ground was shifting beneath their feet in ways they could not have foreseen. By 1919, neither the interim solutions to the problems of 1915 and 1916 nor the longer term imperial ambitions, which some policy makers had nursed, were what the circumstances required.[73] British peace makers were stuck with the former and tried to preserve as much of the latter as they could.

Part of the explanation for failure, therefore, lies in the process and also, to some degree, in the personalities who directed and operated it. The languorous Asquith was incapable of corralling the many competing policy-making agencies inside a combined policy, and even Lloyd George's energetic hand only managed to achieve such a solution at the end of his premiership. During the war, with so much to do, the tasks of coordinating the aims and methods of the war office, the foreign office, the India Office, Cairo, and Delhi and hammering out a joint conspectus for the region which would also satisfy the Allies were probably beyond anyone's capability. The machinery was run by the officially appointed and influenced by the externally canonized. Churchill looked for guidance not only to selected permanent officials but to T. E. Lawrence and Gertrude Bell, the "political advisers" of their day. The depth of their expertise and understanding of the region's complexities was an important contributory issue but was a difficult one to

73   See Busch, *From Paris to Sevres*, p. 51.

resolve. Curzon, for example, was able to use what was to contemporaries a masterly knowledge of the ethnography of upper Mesopotamia to fight postwar Turkish designs on the Kurdish part of the region. Yet, he ordered the eastern world according to a concept of hierarchies of civilization (in which the Egyptians came above the Arabs). According to a sympathetic biographer, he "did not understand a phenomenon he had not come across in the bazaars of Isfahan or the pages of *Hajji Baba*."[74] Lawrence's expertise remains the subject of unresolved argument.

Finally, and most important, the British politicians and soldiers whose job it was to shape the Middle East after the Turks had gone found themselves engaged in an entirely new task: that of state-building in an age of dawning nationalism. Partitioning an empire was not a familiar task: a hundred years had passed since European statesmen had last been engaged in it. On the international level, it required the jettisoning of the "old diplomacy" as embodied in the Sykes–Picot agreement and the adoption of the principles enshrined in the covenant of the League of Nations. Applying them took a lot for granted, as Balfour pointed out on August 11, 1919:

> These documents proceed on the assumption that if we supply an aggregate of human beings, more or less homogeneous in language and religion, with a little assistance and a good deal of advice, if we protect them from external aggression and discourage internal violence, they will speedily and spontaneously organize themselves into a democratic state, on modern lines.... [75]

Nowhere was such an outcome more difficult to achieve – or more unlikely – than in the Middle East, and the British never really tried to bring it about. Instead, behaving like the imperial power she was, London used the traditional implements of indirect rule and force. The Hashemites were handy instruments and Lawrence's desert Arabs appeared to be a local version of the subaltern martial races on whom British rule in India had relied ever since the Mutiny. To back them up and keep them in power, Churchill deployed the latest technological instrument of counter-insurgency warfare. Cheap and effective – for a dozen or so years, at least – the aeroplane would keep the Middle Eastern Empire going.

In reaching this solution, British diplomats and statesmen failed adequately to grapple with the most important underlying issue. Peace making in the Middle East – and peace maintenance, with which it was intimately connected – were transcultural transactions. Because they failed to perceive or to acknowledge the full depth of the cultural complexities of the region, the British failed to identify properly the problems that had to be solved and even made matters worse for themselves.

[74] Gilmour, *Curzon*, pp. 523, 518–19.
[75] Kedourie, *England and the Middle East*, p. 41.

In the Hejaz and Jazirah, British wartime activity encouraged tribal rivalries, and other Arabs saw Hussein's campaign as "an attempt to shatter the regional balance of power and gain supremacy." At the war's end, territorial division by demarcated lines imported a novel concept – and a potent ground for discontent. In peacetime, the British Empire might be in office, but it was not in control: "British authorities could determine the formal map of the region and the nominal power structure, but not the actual power dynamics, which were determined by relations among tribes and local rulers."[76]

One final cause of instability was becoming apparent by June 1919, when General Sir Edmund Allenby rang a warning bell. Muslim sectarianism in the shape of the Wahabism of Ibn Sa'ud and his followers, which he likened to the fanatical Puritanism of the Cromwellians, was a matter causing him considerable concern: "It is extremely contagious; and is attractive to the wild, illiterate Arab, who sees his opportunity of gaining a martyr's crown."[77] That bell still echoes today. By the time that a bankrupted Sharif Hussein fled Mecca and Ibn Sa'ud took the heart of Islam over in 1924, it was already evident that forces were loose in the region that the British did not control and with which the peacemakers had not reckoned.

[76] Joseph Kostiner, "Prologue of Hashemite Downfall and Saudi Ascendancy: A New Look at the Khurma Dispute, 1917–1919," in *The Hashemites in the Modern World: Essays in Honour of the Late Professor Uriel Dann*ed, ed. by Asher Susser and Aryeh Shmuelevitz (London, 1995), p. 57.

[77] Allenby to Wilson, 6 June 1919: Hughes, *Allenby in Palestine*, p. 274.

10

Mission improbable, fear, culture, and interest: peace making, 1943–1949

COLIN GRAY

> I have yet to see any problem, however complicated, which, when you looked at it the right way, did not become still more complicated.
>
> Poul Anderson

This chapter argues that the Soviet–American Cold War was overdetermined. Since human agency, not impersonal forces, drive history, no event can be literally inevitable. But, some happenings, both great and small, are the product of so many factors pushing synergistically in the same direction that their occurrence is as close to a certainty as to make no difference. So it was with the Cold War. For the purposes of this chapter, the Cold War began with the proclamation of the Truman Doctrine on March 12, 1947, and ended with the destruction of the Berlin Wall on November 9, 1989.

With only mixed success, this analysis strives to distance itself from the rather tiresome and unproductive debate about the origins of the Cold War which has become a cottage industry for scholars. There is an obvious sense in which "peace making, 1943–1949" has to be about the origins, onset, and full emergence of what came to be termed the Cold War. But, this author wishes to follow strict navigational guidance intended to reveal the reasons why it was difficult to make peace out of, and after, the Second World War. Such a contextual perspective is more likely to reveal plausible insights than would yet another foray explicitly into the dark forest of Cold War studies.

The claim here is that the Cold War, or Long Peace – an abominable retrospective concept subsequently abandoned by its author, John Gaddis – had several causes.[1] And to such familiar factors as geopolitics, ideology,

---

[1] John Lewis Gaddis, "On Starting All Over Again: A Naïve Approach to the Study of the Cold War," in *Reviewing the Cold War: Approaches, Interpretations, Theory*, ed. by Odd

and personality, one must not forget the play of accident or friction, incompetence, and downright folly. Scholars with powerful arguments based on the cunning plans and dirty or dubious deeds of Machiavellian policy makers are apt to forget the merit in the eternal truth expressed so clearly in the immortal words of Donald Rumsfeld, "Stuff happens!" Indeed, it does, and it did from 1943 to 1949. The history of those years was not significantly nonlinear from the perspective of this study, but it was so richly detailed with the evidence of fear, honor – or culture, to update Thucydides[2] – and interest that one needs to alert oneself to resist the siren calls of theory. A little international relations theory goes a long way.

It may be helpful to register now, at the outset, some hostility to scholars playing the "what if..." game. A liking for virtual history can lead them seriously astray. He or she may favor historical explanations which, explicitly or implicitly, rely critically on the belief that "if only" statesmen or politicians had followed a different policy, or even just one or two major decisions had been different, the whole course of events would inevitably have followed a different course. Not excluding plain error, folly, accident, and contingency, there were many deep-seated reasons why the key human agents, who moved world politics from 1943 to 1949, behaved as they did. Their behavior was not entirely predetermined, and they were certainly not puppets, though Soviet Foreign Minister Molotov could give that impression. But neither were they operating in anything remotely resembling a context wherein leaders could invent and then assess policy alternatives strictly by their contemporary merits. Thucydides really did say it all.

This chapter does not argue that the Cold War was literally inevitable. But, it suggests that the vital contexts for international relations in the mid and late 1940s were such that it would have required close to a miracle for Soviet–American rivalry to find itself so constrained politically and institutionally that it would resemble a latter-day variant of nineteenth-century great power politics as usual. Moreover, such a vision, or "what if," is profoundly unhistorical. America and the Soviet Union were what they were, and their leaders and – in the U.S. case – general public behaved according to their nature. This is not to deny the occurrence or importance of historical contingency. But it is to deny that an event or two, or a decision or two, might have enabled Moscow and Washington to construct a lasting political peace out of the war waged to destroy Nazi Germany.

The plan of attack here opens with a review of the debate over the origins of the Cold War and explains why that erudite and evermore archivally

Arne Westad (London, 2001), pp. 32–3; idem, *The Long Peace: Inquiries Into the History of the Cold War* (Oxford, 1987), ch. 8.
[2] Thucydides, *The Landmark Thucydides: A Comprehensive Guide to "The Peloponnesian War,"* ed. by Robert B. Strassler (New York, 1996), p. 43.

impressive range of theories is apt to mislead. That debate tends to lack historical empathy for the principals, often shows little appreciation of the salience of the several contexts within which real people had to function, and shunts aside the wisdom of Thucydides to make room for archival revelations, or appealing theory. Then, this chapter examines and explains the main structure of the argument. The text advances by providing a rather rapid assessment of the main historical narrative from 1943 to 1949 and then concludes by holistically examining geopolitics, ideology, and personality. But, first, what sense has sixty years, or three generations, of scholarship made of the peace-making story of 1943–1949?

COLD WAR STUDIES

The popular maxim which holds that people can be too clever for their own good seems to apply to some well-published, careful, and generally professionally excellent historians of the international relations of the mid to late 1940s. The more sophisticated and nuanced the studies of peace making, or however one elects to characterize non-Axis inter–great power behavior from 1943 to 1949, the more likely one is to miss the major truth. The host of minor truths, probable truths, and possible truths provide a happy hunting ground for theorists of all persuasions. They can deploy their "Riga" and "Yalta Axioms," their "extra-regional hegemonial theory," and the like,[3] and – who knows – they may have interesting, even insightful things to say.

But what they will not have to impart is a plausible story that explains why peace among the erstwhile nominal allies of East and West was so difficult to achieve. Indeed, generally they fail to explain convincingly why the Allies of 1941–1945 appeared to be on the brink of war in August 1946, in late spring and early summer 1948, and again in summer and fall 1950. There was no single problem, or even a handful of problems, that better, practicable policy making in Washington and/or Moscow could have resolved. History had loaded the multicontextual dice of Soviet–American history far too heavily in favor of East–West conflict for the Cold War to have been avoided. There were too many and too powerful reasons – fear, culture (honor), and interest – working overtime to preclude a postwar international order characterized by anything resembling a political peace. This elemental historical truth is a commonsensical judgment made in the light of recent archival revelations and confirmations.

---

[3]   See Daniel Yergin, *The Shattered Peace: The Origins of the Cold War and the National Security State* (London, 1980), p. 17; and Christopher Layne, *The Peace of Illusions: American Grand Strategy from 1940 to the Present* (Ithaca, NY, 2006).

One may object that history consists of considerable numbers of complex contexts of more or less deep antagonisms that did not result in great conflicts, the great wars that got away. Leaving aside the issue of negative evidence, this author does believe that the Cold War was not literally inevitable. In the late 1940s and well beyond, there were potent and even compelling reasons to believe the Cold War would likely conclude with an approximation of Armageddon. And, yet, it did not. So, strictly viewed, the condition, which at times approximated all but warfare and which endured for forty-two years, did not have to succeed the war that concluded in May and August 1945. But the chances of global international relations avoiding a great conflict after the great war of 1937–1945 were exceedingly small. Long odds do turn up, admittedly, but, as we know, that is not the way to bet.

There is no compelling reason to devote space to the many variations on the principal schools of thought in Cold War scholarship. We find that scholarship has proceeded from thesis, through or to antithesis, to synthesis. To those interested in such academic arcana, the schools are usually referred to as (1) orthodox, (2) revisionist, and (3) postrevisionist. There are others, but this short list will suffice.

School one, the orthodox view, insists that the post–Second World War world was blighted almost immediately with another great conflict because one of the victors was by its nature, and, therefore, consequentially its behavior, consistently aggressive and expansionist with global political and strategic pretensions. In short, the Cold War was the product of a Soviet threat to civilized values and Western security that had to be resisted, *in extremis* if necessary by nuclear war itself. End of story. This simple tale was the orthodox wisdom for many years, certainly until the mid 1960s, and it has retained a hold on a surprising number of minds through to the present. The orthodox view was by no means wholly in error or unpersuasive in many respects, as far as it went. The trouble was that it only told one side of the story. In its perspective, the Western Powers were simply the initially naïve and innocent victims of a ruthless, dedicated, and duplicitous foe. In a sense, this school airbrushed the West out of the role of being active participants in the onset of the Cold War. This was analytically convenient. For the scholar and the practitioner, would that international relations were so simple. But, they are not, and they certainly were not in the 1940s.

The second school of opinion is, in effect, a reversal of the player roles of school one. Unfortunately, but alas inevitably, the antithesis in revisionist writings was no less one-sided than was the orthodox view. This time, the principal villain is the United States. It sought global hegemony, especially through the medium of economic penetration. Backed by its unique ownership of a slowly growing atomic arsenal and the influence accruing from global dependence on U.S. economic preponderance, America aspired to be a global empire.[4] Supposedly, American policy makers believed that political transformation would follow U.S. economic penetration, the whole protected by a strategic context dominated by a latent atomic menace. There was an intellectual – really, perhaps a cultural – basis for this view of the United States as systemically and irreducibly hostile to the Soviet Union and all its works, save temporarily for its contribution in warfare from 1941 to 1945. That view traces back to the 1920s, was canonized in the so-called Riga Axioms in the 1930s devised by U.S. diplomats in the Baltics, and reappeared in full flood in the policy-crucial "Long Telegram" sent from Moscow by Charge d'Affaires George Kennan on February 22, 1946. Its implications, at least in some anxious official minds, found reflection in the containment doctrine as expressed in NSC 68 of April 14, 1950.

Undoubtedly, ideological assumptions and historical analyses which concluded that Moscow's purposes and behavior had geopolitical and economic implications permanently inimical to U.S. values and interests led these key contributions to American attitudes toward the Soviet Union. In short, school two found the United States guilty as charged of believing that the Soviet Union was its long-term enemy and of behaving on the basis of that premise, save for the brief but vital collaboration of convenience between 1941 and 1945. Although there were always a few contra-orthodox voices in the U.S. policy community and academe, the second school began to prosper in the 1960s as apparent evidence of American imperial arrogance and ambition flowed in from Vietnam. Overall, though, except among true believers on the left, school two was only a way station toward a more defensible middle ground. That predictable historical fact brings us up to date to the emergence and flowering of school three, "postrevisionism."

The message of school three is synthesis and interaction. Both East and West were responsible for the difficulties in making a political peace in the mid 1940s, though the Soviet Union was almost certainly more guilty than the United States. The rise and fall of the popularity of the distinctive arguments of schools one, two, and three tell us more about the political context in which their development nested than about the 1940s. School one flourished in a climate of anti-communism, a combination of American triumphalism, and a sense of acute anxiety and fear of the Red menace. School two enjoyed its major strategic moment when the traditional American way of war found itself confounded in Southeast Asia and the country suffered extensive domestic turmoil. School three accompanied the winding down of the Cold War, the opening of Soviet and other Warsaw Pact archives,

---

[4] The U.S. nuclear stockpile climbed from a modest total of 6 by the end of 1945, through 11 in 1946, 32 in 1947, 110 in 1948, to 236 in 1949. R. S. Norris and H. M. Kristensen, "Global Nuclear Stockpiles, 1945–2002," *Bulletin of the Atomic Scientists*, vol. 58 (2002), pp. 103–4.

the demise of the Soviet Union, and an American worldview that could not readily come to grips with the notion that Moscow might have been a truly deadly enemy. Moreover, the passing of time helped by providing perspective. Although it is inevitable that one attempts studies such as this, authors cannot help but discover the fragility of judgment because of the historical proximity of the 1940s. Scholars today, especially older ones, carry considerable emotional and political baggage concerning attitudes toward the Cold War and the purportedly Grand Alliance of the Second World War.

One can justly summarize school three as a rather obvious and unimaginative solution via conflation to the combat between orthodoxy and revision. When in doubt, simply put it all together. Argue that everybody is more or less half right. The postrevisionists, fairly convincingly, argue that it took two to make the severely troubled peace of the mid to late 1940s. The United States was responsible for behavior, which interacted with Soviet behavior, both of which drove and were driven by assumptions and interests deemed hostile or at least challenging by the other. Moreover, neither American nor Soviet leaders could perceive the world from the other's point of view. A principal reason for that unhappy shared condition was the fact that both polities were deeply ideological and, hence, strongly believed in the righteousness of their values and purposes.

Sensible though the postrevisionists are in their melding of sharply contrasting approaches and their emphasis on interaction and the working of the law of unintended consequences, they share a fallacy common to the other schools. Implicitly, all three suggest that the Cold War was avoidable, or at least capable of being far more disciplined in its dynamics, had only.... Whether one blames the Russians, the Americans, or both, the central explanation for the fractured peace of the Cold War is really the same. Errors occurred which had potentially dangerous consequences. So far, so plausible; indeed, so far, so unarguable. The fallacy lies in the belief there was another postwar 1940s and beyond in world politics that was missed. In other words, the details of Soviet and American words and behavior from 1943 to 1949 mattered greatly.

The view expressed in this chapter is that the details of Soviet–American relations did not much matter. The devil was not in the details; rather, it lay in the dynamics and the contexts of the period, which, with the deeper of their roots, shaped assumptions and policies almost regardless of the unfolding events. For a conflict as recent as the late and unlamented Cold War, it is especially improbable that the views currently most fashionable among scholars will long survive the expanding industry of Cold War studies.[5]

---

[5] Although it is aging rapidly, the best guide to the scholarly debate on the Cold War remains Westad, ed., *Reviewing the Cold War*. For a useful recent bibliographical review, see the

THE ARGUMENT

This author's principal difference with many – probably most – scholars of all the schools of thought lies not so much with their narratives or even their analyses. Instead, it reposes in his rejection of their conclusion. That is to say, this chapter advances the argument that the Cold War, the negation of a stable political peace – though fortunately not of a tolerably stable international order – was to all intents and purposes unavoidable.

This is probably the correct place to introduce the subversive thought that the important, nay vital, concern of "making peace out of war" itself has the potential to mislead. The conventional wisdom likes to quote only the first part of Basil Liddell Hart's economically expressed truism that "[t]he object in war is to attain a better peace."[6] His sentence continues thus: " . . . even if only from your point of view." And that must stand as a qualifying point for the ages. The victors of the Second World War were not making peace as a virtuous, necessary, yet somewhat abstract exercise in statecraft. Instead, they found themselves trapped inalienably in the toils of the Thucydides triptych. The malign workings of the triptych do not always promote all but inexorable further conflict, but in 1943–1949 they most assuredly did. Fear, honor/culture, and interest were functioning overtime. The statesmen of the period were far more interested in coping with the policy challenges of the triptych than in constructing anything that popular usage would recognize as peace. After all, was not peace achieved in May and August 1945? The world was at peace, was it not? Of course, it was not. As often as not, the wars that succeed "The War" are as bloody, or bloodier, than was the main event. Consider the Balkan Wars of the 1990s or the civil wars in Russia after 1917 and the wars among the new states of Eastern Europe.

The focus on "making peace" is a welcome trend in scholarship, but it risks isolating and overemphasizing the importance of dedicated peace making.[7] It suggests that the roots of the next war lie in the fashion in which states concluded the previous one and in the arrangements made for the postwar settlement. That suggestion is not wrong but it overreaches. It is apt to be a meaningless truism. Since there is always another war, with the advantage of hindsight, we know that the postwar world produced a further bloody future. So, we are able to work backwards to demonstrate how the errors and general shortsightedness of a previous generation of

---

student textbook by Martin McCauley, *The Origins of the Cold War, 1941–1949*, 3rd edn. (Harlow, UK, 2003), pp. 145–8.

[6] B. H. Liddell Hart, *Strategy: The Indirect Approach*, rev. edn. (London, 1967), p. 366.

[7] See Stephen R. Rock, *Why Peace Breaks Out: Great Power Rapprochement in Historical Perspective* (Chapel Hill, NC, 1989); and especially Matthew Hughes and Matthew S. Seligman, *Does Peace Lead to War? Peace Settlements and Conflict in the Modern Age* (Stroud, UK, 2002).

statesmen had to be at least partially responsible. Somehow, the significance of historical contingency, of decisively intervening variables, receive short shrift, if any shrift at all. Overall, the weakness in a focus on "the making of peace out of war" is that it encourages the isolation of a necessary activity both from the stream of history's course and from the true complexity of contexts that load the dice for those who attempt the peace making.

In examining the strategic and political situation in this period, there are six clear issues that demand elucidation.

1. *A political peace was not achievable in 1943–1949 between the Soviet Union on one side and the United States and Britain on the other. There were too many, too powerful, too deeply rooted reasons for rivalry, conflict, and possibly war between the United States and the Soviet Union for a true political peace to be attainable from 1943 to 1949.*

Unusually in the history of peace making, the challenge of this period was not to find terms acceptable to the defeated foe: that is, terms which it could accept with reluctance as being both preferable to a continuation of the struggle extant and not so intolerable as to require a return match in the not-too-distant future. In 1945, the problem was not how to make peace with Germany; rather, it was how to make peace about Germany and its future. But peace is a slippery concept with at least two distinctive meanings. There is the political peace, which refers to a condition wherein a rough consensus on the major terms of international political life unites the powers in signing up to a particular condition known as an international order. This is what occurred when the Cold War eventually faded, died, and was replaced by the no-name decade of the post–Cold War world of the 1990s. And then there is peace simply as the absence of actual warfare. There was peace of this character between East and West between 1945 and 1989. Should one refer to it as the Cold War or as the Long Peace?

Unfortunately for the statesmen and periodically terrified publics of those years, they could not know they were enjoying the benefits of a long peace. Occasionally, the prospects of imminent nuclear war seemed all too real. Only with the inestimable benefit of hindsight can one take a relaxed, if not actually dismissive, view of the perils of the Cold War. It is quite common today for scholars to advocate the logically impressive but, in practice, desperately unsound conviction that peace between East and West was overdetermined. The comfortable conviction that the nuclear standoff all but guaranteed the absence of a great East–West war is thoroughly unsound. Such a belief assumes a comparable process of decision making, driven by an acultural process of rational choice, firmly determined the events in Moscow and Washington for nearly forty years.

A stable international order, a condition for a lasting peace, eventually was all but achieved by the mid 1950s, but that was not a peace resting on shared norms beyond the necessity of avoiding dangerous behavior likely to raise the risks of nuclear war. The Cold War was about the future of

Germany. But it was also about Eastern Europe and Stalin's demand for a new degree of territorial security; the stability of the regime in Moscow; the Soviet messianic mission both for communism globally and the Russian Empire; revenge and repayment for damage suffered; meeting the needs of Stalin's personality; and a dozen other items on the Soviet side alone. When one adds in the United States, the British, the French, and the minor actors' concerns, as one must, it rapidly becomes apparent why the train of rivalry, antagonism, and conflict – potentially to the point of war – was moving downhill with great force and momentum in the late 1940s. There was a large and growing adverse imbalance between the factors and trends making for a political peace worthy of the title and a condition marked by evermore acute hostility.

There may well have been lost opportunities for advantageous cooperation caused primarily by Western suspicions or miscalculation, but they did not really matter. The people who attempted to construct a lasting peace out of the Second World War represented all too faithfully distinctive worldviews, and they carried in their briefcases a full load of fear, culture/honor, and interest. And history, unlike the organization of its writing, happens simultaneously. Whereas historians can isolate a dimension to Soviet–American antagonism – say, Poland, Germany, or the military-scientific race for nuclear weapons – to the policy makers of the day, such vital concerns crowded in on each other. A benign development over one issue, the limited nature of Soviet demands on formerly Axis Finland, for example, could not possibly derail the Cold War train as the principal contemporary process in the shaping the course of history.

2. *Peace was made easily with Germany – by political and military annihilation – with more difficulty with Imperial Japan – by negotiation short of annihilation – and even eventually among the erstwhile co-belligerents of the misnamed Grand Alliance.*

The victorious powers secured peace of a kind, though not until the close of the 1940s, and even that claim is challengeable as being unduly optimistic. This author prefers the immediate post-Stalin period of 1955 as the Locarno year (1925) for East–West relations and the effective institutionalization of a stable, albeit highly dangerous, international order. Paradoxically, it was the nuclear danger in the structure of that order that guaranteed its stability. The peace of the Cold War years was real enough, but it was not the normative peace of common usage. Still, it sufficed, probably more by luck than by good judgment, wise doctrines, or clever plans.

3. *The details of international relations so beloved by diplomatic historians were of only minor consequence for the course of peace making between East and West from 1943 until 1949.*

No flutter of a butterfly's wings on the White House lawn or on the veranda of one of Stalin's dachas was going to have seismic consequences for the terms of a new international order. The world stage was already far too set for conflict of one sort or another for the contingency of nearly any unexpected event to have a significantly benign impact. Scholars wedded to a rational-choice model of policy decision making need to remember that the human agents making the supposedly rational choices are distinctively encultured persons. Everyone may be rational, meaning that they purposefully attempt to connect means and ends, but the ends thus rationally selected will not necessarily be reasonable in foreign eyes. Two extraordinarily large details in the course of history marked 1945 as an unusual year. Indeed, those details had the potential to function as history-shifting nonlinearities: the defeat of the Axis powers and to the successful weaponization of nuclear physics, leading to the employment of the atomic bomb.[8] Those traumatic events had accelerator effects on Soviet–American rivalry, but they did not herald a new dawn.

To the degree to which they altered contexts, the alteration was not for the betterment of relations among the Allies. The defeat of Germany and Japan promoted no change of policy course in Moscow. The surprise effects of Hiroshima and Nagasaki on Stalin, who had up to then failed to grasp sufficiently the political and strategic implications of atomic weaponry, led him to initiate a crash program to make up for lost time. But he changed neither policy nor course. Assumptions, attitudes, and ultimately behavior were too well set to be readily revised, let alone overturned, by the details of the issues of the day. An inch of cooperation here was always more than matched by a foot of obstruction elsewhere.

4. *The difficulties impeding political peace making from 1943 to 1949 among the Grand Allies of the Second World War were so likely to result in a lethally blighted postwar order–disorder that they have to be judged as insurmountable.*

Scholars of a "what if . . . " persuasion need to remember that they should discipline their fertile imaginations by the reality check provided by actual events. Because events and processes impact on and interact with each other, often with unexpected consequences, it is unsafe to theorize about the probable results of a policy shift here or there. Events – perhaps more accurately trends in events – usually are overdetermined by many factors. This is why imaginary history – in this case, a fictional 1945, 1946, or 1947 – is unhelpful. "What might have been" could not have been because it was multicontextually all but impossible.

5. *With respect to the prospects of future great power conflict, the period 1943–1949 resembled the 1930s, not the 1920s.*

---

[8] See Vladislav Zubok and Constantine Pleshakov, *Inside the Kremlin's Cold War: From Stalin to Khrushchev* (Cambridge, MA, 1996), pp. 43–5. The early years of the Soviet nuclear story are superbly presented and analyzed in David Holloway, *Stalin and the Bomb* (New Haven, CT, 1994).

The Versailles settlement, though inherently objectively moderate, was unhelpful for international order in the medium to long terms. The reason why has been explained with admirable clarity by Michael I. Handel. "For the results of victory to endure, they must be accepted as final by the defeated side, whose interests and concerns must be taken into account."[9] In the 1920s, German discontent with the premises and terms of Versailles did not much matter. Weimar was in no position to do anything adventurous. Instead, through patient and cunning diplomacy, the decade's leading statesman, Germany's Foreign Minister, Gustav Streseman, whittled away at many of the more unwelcome features of Germany's isolation. The central truth about the interwar decades was that the order established at Versailles was only stable so long as no one could challenge it credibly.

Nevertheless, it is nearly impossible to arrive at the Second World War from the contexts of the late 1920s. But after the Great Depression gave Germany six million unemployed and, as a consequence, Adolf Hitler as Reich Chancellor and eventually Führer, it was literally impossible for a great war not to occur sometime in the near future.[10] Soviet–American rivalry, conflict, and plausibly even war itself was as unavoidable in the second half of the 1940s as had been the war with Germany in the late 1930s. That argument fully appreciates the fact that contrary to the political context of the 1930s, where Hitler both wanted and intended war, neither the United States nor Stalin's Soviet Union wanted open conflict. What came to be known as the Cold War or, by the 1980s, contestably, the "Long Peace," was not the product of an error here, a mistake there, a lack of imagination somewhere else. To believe that is to demonstrate that one has not really taken Thucydides' timeless wisdom sufficiently on board. One obvious source of difficulties was the reality of Stalin's worldview. While he certainly did not want war, neither was he seriously in the peace-making business, save on terms that the America of President Harry S. Truman and his State Department would never accept, even if it was obliged to tolerate some of them, *faute de mieux*.

6. *The Grand Alliance was a coalition of brief necessity.*

Britain and America were allies; Britain, America, and the Soviet Union were not. The concept and label of the Grand Alliance was a propaganda invention, thoroughly understandable at the time. But the trouble with deceptive concepts is that they essentially capture their inventors. If such genuinely tough-minded believers in the practice of *realpolitik* as Churchill

---

[9] Michael I. Handel, *Masters of War: Classical Strategic Thought*, 3rd edn. (London, 2001), pp. 197–8.

[10] A powerful additional nail has been driven into this particular coffin by Adam Tooze, *The Wages of Destruction: The Making and Breaking of the Nazi Economy* (London, 2006). Tooze demonstrates how foreign exchange and material resources crises helped spur Hitler to hasten the tempo of his gambles.

and Roosevelt talk often enough of a Grand Alliance that is a fiction in normative and practical ways, and praise the Soviet leader for his presumed commitment to an international order compatible with Western interests and values, even they began to believe what they were saying. As one might phrase the matter today, almost the entire Western discourse about the Grand Alliance from 1941 to 1945 was ill conceived. It was just plain wrong. However, for obvious reasons of contemporary expediency, the generally undeceived Churchill and Roosevelt could not voice their real attitudes toward their Soviet co-belligerent whose troops were doing most of the fighting and dying for the "Free World."

The point of importance here is to register in the most unambiguous way the fact that the Anglo-Americans and the Soviets were not genuine allies; they were co-belligerents. They were allies of a kind, in that all three states found themselves to be at war with Germany at the same time, and – arguably – it required the contributions of each of them to bring down the Nazi super-state. This is not to forget for a moment the disproportion among their efforts. In June 1944, for example, the *Wehrmacht* deployed 90 divisions on all fronts except the Eastern Front: in the east, the *Ostheer* deployed 250. The logic of that condition was that the Grand Alliance did not erode and break down in the 1945–1947 period because it could not. That Alliance never existed except in words. What occurred was simply the way it was and the way it had to be, given the context of the 1940s. Eventually, grand deceptions in statecraft must come to an end; a player must show his cards. Rivalry, open conflict, and then the Cold War were the logical – indeed, the necessary – consequence of the death of unwarranted expectations concerning the construction of a consensual European order.

THE COLD WAR COMETH

The Cold War was the all-but-inevitable result of two victorious super-states, albeit highly asymmetrical ones, being obliged to meet the realities of Thucydides' triptych in contexts that effectively foreclosed enduring cooperation.[11] The conflict was not avoidable, but its timing, detail, and eventual severity certainly were the products of decisions over which human agents had ultimate discretion. But, there were compelling reasons why the significant alleviation of inter-Allied tension proved impossible to realize. And that statement is to ignore the universal and ubiquitous factors of friction, accident, and sheer error committed through poor information or incompetence or both.

---

[11] For an interesting contemporary analysis by a distinguished American scholar of international relations, see William T. R. Fox, *The Super-Powers: The United States, Britain, and the Soviet Union – Their Responsibility for Peace* (New York, 1944).

For the sake of improving empathy with the Allied players of the period, one needs to remember just how large Germany loomed in the minds of decision makers, both during the war and after. It represents a difficult stretch for some historians today to "think 1940s" when they inhabit a world that contains the current post-military Germany. In 1943, even after the surrender of Field Marshal von Paulus and the ragged remainder of the Sixth Army, only 90 thousand weak at the close of January 31, Germany was far from beaten. Thus, Stalin and the West needed each other. He had made one deal of tactical expediency with Hitler on September 23, 1939, which in effect opened Germany's door to France. Who could be certain he would not make another? Despite the totality, ferocity, and barbarism of the war in the east, Stalin sanctioned secret talks – one cannot say negotiations – with Nazi Germany in 1943. Moreover, he assumed that his British and American peers would be willing to do likewise, should the incentives prove compelling. Stalin was not in any sense committed to a Grand Alliance with the purpose of destroying an evil regime and restoring a European order characterized by freedom and justice. His motives were far less lofty and abstract. First, he needed survival – personal, regime, and state – and, second, he needed to improve the Soviet security context – so that it would prosper in the ongoing competition with the capitalist–imperialist great powers.

Arguably, but not wholly incredibly, Germany might have changed the course of the war in its favor had it succeeded in dealing the Red Army the smashing blow intended by "Operation Citadel" at Kursk in July 1943. One can speculate that the *Ostheer* could just possibly have achieved a significant victory at Kursk, thus enabling Germany to stabilize the Eastern Front and switch the balance of its forces to other fronts and, more particularly, potential fronts (i.e., the Balkans, Italy, and especially France). Worthy of special mention is the opportunity that a large-scale defeat of the Red Army should have enabled the Germans to conduct a more effective air defense of the Reich. Recall that the *Luftwaffe*'s defeat was a vital prerequisite for any major Anglo-American landing on the coast of France.[12] There were many reasons why such a scenario would not have played out. Hitler would certainly have overreached in the euphoria of victory. And, with regard to a more potent possible consequence of success at Kursk, he would not have offered Stalin terms the Georgian could accept. For example, we know that Hitler would never voluntarily have handed back the Ukraine, not even in the interest of winning the war.

Nonetheless, the time line in this chapter begins in a year when Germany still might have won the war. Stalin's Soviet Union was still extensively

---

[12] The story is well told in Horst Boog, Gerhard Krebs, and Detlef Vogel, *Germany and the Second World War*, vol. 7, *The Strategic Air War in Europe and the War in the West and East Asia, 1943–1944/5* (Oxford, 2006), part 1.

occupied and the *Ostheer* had staged a rapid recovery from its losses at Stalingrad, though not from its loss of reputation for battlefield invincibility. It was the Red Army which had overreached itself. Actually, it overreached in major ways twice in 1943. In a replay of its over-optimistic continuation of the great winter offensive of December 1941 for far too long into 1943, the Red Army overreached in its efforts to exploit the victory on the Volga, and it was to repeat that mistake following victory at Kursk in July.

The importance of the narrative and analysis in the previous paragraph is that it explains the crucial importance of the context of a war yet to be won for the fashion in which the principals managed the Grand Alliance at the time. The Anglo-Americans were almost desperate to prove to Stalin they were pulling their weight. Of course, they were not, at least not with respect to the fighting and dying. They needed the Soviet Union to remain in the war and attrit German strength to the point where a genuine continental Western Front would be a practicable undertaking. And such an undertaking would not be practicable until they had won both the U-boat and air campaigns. The Allies defeated the U-boat in May 1943, but the Luftwaffe remained formidable into spring 1944. In 1943, prudent American and British statesmen could not exclude the possibility that Moscow might secure a separate peace with Berlin; after all, it had occurred twice before under duress. One might have taken Stalin's hints and menaces on the subject as bluff, but they might not have been.

The ultimately sad fate of the Grand Alliance owes more to Anglo-American duplicity and self-deception than it does to Stalin's cunning, not that that was in short supply. From 1943 at the Tehran Summit (November 28–December 1) to 1945 at Yalta (February 4-11), Roosevelt and Churchill played the cynical, expedient roles of *realpolitik* statesmen that Stalin played himself and, naturally, expected his foreign peers (only two of those) to play as well. The Grand Alliance worked well enough for Stalin in 1943–1945. His co-belligerents conveyed no serious signals of intent to thwart his near-term ambitions concerning the rewards that would accrue to a Soviet Union that had contributed the most heavily to victory over Germany. If there were a major discontinuity in East–West relations which might have marked a process of deterioration in apparent amity, it was the result of real or apparent policy change in the West, not the East.

Stalin was not guilty of dissimulation, at least not as he understood the way in which the world conducted politics among and within states. He could dismiss the high-flown sentiments of the Atlantic Charter as empty verbiage, mere words for public consumption. Stalin made the serious error at Yalta of signing the "Declaration on Liberated Europe," convinced that that was just another piece of diplomatic theater. As testimony to the potency of ethnocentrism, Stalin failed to grasp the depth of the American ideological commitment to a truly "liberated" Europe and the probable consequences of his practical disdain for Washington's expectations.[13]

Stalin knew that politics was all about power. And as the war trailed slowly to its conclusion, he had two good reasons to expect that the core and beyond of his ambitions would not meet determined opposition from Washington and London. First, the West's Big Two had conceded either explicitly, albeit informally, or implicitly his demands for preponderance in Eastern Europe. Given his robust approach to statecraft of all kinds, Stalin assumed that Churchill and Roosevelt understood well enough what he meant by "friendly governments" and by "democratic processes." He had little difficulty with the idealistic rhetoric about freedom-loving nations and, indeed, the whole package of the virtues wrapped up in the Atlantic Charter.

Difficulties would only arise if his Allies tried to insist on the practical application of their interpretation of such vague concepts as freedom, democracy, and friendship. Stalin's second reason for confidence grew in significance from the German failure at Kursk in July 1943 until the end of the war. Specifically, the course of military events increasingly placed his Red Army in a position to enforce his political demands. This meant that even if the United States and Britain proved less compliant toward Soviet postwar security demands than he expected, there would be little or nothing that they could do to resist them. Four years of unstinted Anglo-American official public admiration for the heroic sacrifices of the Soviet peoples and the inspired leadership of Uncle Joe – one of history's least charismatic warlords – not to mention four to six years of their own efforts, would preclude or neutralize any temptation to deny Stalin his territorial goals.

The Cold War that emerged full blown by 1948–1949, and defensibly by 1947, was not the result of misunderstandings. But the timing and manner of its gradual emergence after Yalta most certainly was, especially on the part of Stalin. He behaved honestly and honorably, according to his lights. With nods, winks, silence, and excuses, during the war Britain and the United States accommodated nearly all of his expressed ambitions in Europe, as well as a few in Asia. At least, those were the signals that Stalin read. No doubt, he read more compliance than he ought, and he allowed himself to be somewhat, but only somewhat, misled by the collegial style of "Big Three clubbyness," as well as by the human proclivity for hearing what one wants to hear. Allied politicians haggled and objected no more than he expected of leaders of powerful states. Moreover, Stalin accepted what amounted to British and American demands for recognized spheres of interest. At

---

[13]   See Ken Booth, *Strategy and Ethnocentrism* (London, 1979).

least, he secured explicit agreement with Churchill. Roosevelt would not explicitly endorse such an approach to international security but, in practice, he tolerated without notable objection the fiction of Allied consensus on the principles that should govern the rebuilding of international order, especially in Europe. Moreover, and probably more important, Roosevelt deceived himself into believing that he, personally, could handle "Uncle Joe." It would all come right enough on the night, courtesy of Roosevelt's friendship with Stalin and the relationship of trust that existed between them.

The Grand Alliance came apart rapidly in 1945 but not because mistakes occurred in policy by Moscow, Washington, and London – mistakes which historical hindsight suggests might well have been avoided. Rather were the problems, first, that the United States and Britain abruptly changed course both in style and their public tolerance of what Stalin believed were "done deals." And, second, there was a double, sequential, military-strategic influence on inter-Allied relations that had contrasting implications for the potency of Soviet diplomacy. The Western Allies, obligingly, had not hastened to conclude the war in 1944–1945. This meant that the Red Army was generally already in possession of what Stalin wanted, though strangely it had not advanced at high speed to occupy Germany itself. That highly material fact, when added to the moral strength behind Stalin granted by the sheer scale of the Soviet war effort and losses, translated beyond argument into primacy in East Central Europe.

The Soviet Union barely had time to bask in the glow of its dominant role in securing victory over one of the finest fighting machines in history, when the Manhattan Project upset the strategic equation – perhaps fatally – certainly, for a long time to come. Hiroshima and Nagasaki bore the unmistakable message that the United States had just outflanked the newly rebranded Soviet (formerly Red) Army, a possibly decisive scientific and technological shortfall. Coming as it did in tandem with the apparent shift in Western attitudes and policy toward noncompliance, evident even before Potsdam in July–August, the new atomic fact compelled Stalin to recognize that no longer was there an Allied consensus on sphere of interest, if there had ever been one. U.S. behavior after Potsdam translated irresistibly in Stalin's ever suspicious mind into the conviction that his erstwhile co-belligerents now – August–September 1945 – believed they had the military-strategic leverage to clarify, as one might put it, just what was and what was not tolerable Soviet international behavior. Stalin decided to proceed with his flexible agenda for East Central Europe. He moved at variable speed in different countries, suborning what he was able and what he had been led, perhaps misled, into believing would be his by right of Soviet power and interest.

When historians discern a malign interaction between East and West in 1945, 1946, and 1947, they are correct. But where they stray is when they come to believe the Cold War to be was the result of that interaction: It was not. Save only in a secondary sense, the Cold War was not the result of a lethal spiral of steps and missteps, misunderstandings, and errors. Instead, the defeat of Germany, the abrupt changes in Western leadership and diplomatic style, and the atomic bomb in lethal combination radically altered the contexts of inter-Allied diplomacy. The disagreements that had always lurked beneath the surface of public Grand Alliance amity quite suddenly surfaced. They were not the creations of the years 1945 to 1947. The necessities of their own contemporary details of fear, honor, and interest had trapped both east and west. During the war, Churchill and Roosevelt needed to keep Stalin on their side lest he should decide to leave the game. Stalin spoke and behaved as his anxieties for the present and future (fear), his ideology (honor/culture), and the interests of Soviet – which meant personal – power (interest) commanded. The result, as the saying goes, is history.

In 1945, it was the case not so much that the gloves came off in the relations among the Allies but rather that the veils were partly, though still only partly, lifted. Both sides had grounds for believing malfeasance on the part of the other. Stalin discerned accurately that Western words and behavior toward the Soviet Union had just registered close to a sea change that now privileged nontoleration of many Soviet interpretations of previously uncontested formulae. Truman and Attlee, especially the utterly inexperienced former, did not understand well enough that they were behaving toward the Soviet Union in a way that Stalin must regard as hostile. They had never signed on for and probably never really appreciated that their immediate predecessors in office appeared to have conceded in wartime a large measure of postwar continental preponderance to the then-vital Soviet ally.

Is this argument overdrawn? It fits the known facts, but several theories can make the same claim. The year 1945 was when many of the difficulties in East–West political relations had to be confronted, if not adequately comprehended. But, were those difficulties so severe that more adept statecraft in the 1945–1947 and perhaps 1943–1947 periods might not have alleviated or resolved the more poisonous among them? How serious were the difficulties that underlay what became the Cold War? And, just what were those difficulties?

It is necessary to be clear about the basic course of East–West relations from 1943 to 1949 (i.e., the plot line). Thus far, this chapter has endeavored, possibly with undue success, to eschew the pleasure of storytelling, particularly of a narrative history that is little disputed today. Nonetheless, chronology matters. The Cold War did emerge slowly from 1945 until 1949, while its more immediate causes had flourished mightily under the joint impact of expedient inter-Allied wartime diplomacy and the contingency of unfolding events. What follows is recognition of the most relevant pieces in the story arc of the years 1943 to 1949.

THE HISTORICAL CONTEXT

- *1943:* German defeats at Stalingrad, Kursk, Tunisia, and at sea constituted a true turning point in the war. German victory was now highly
improbable. The First Big Three summit was held at Tehran (November 28–December 1). Uncertainty over the future course of the war
encouraged diplomatic vagueness. Whose armies would be where on
VE Day?

- *1944:* The Red Army entered non-Soviet territory and demonstrated
brutally the meaning of Stalin's insistence on friendly polities on his
Western borders. On September 12, the Allies signed the London Protocol on occupation zones in Germany and on a multinational administration for Berlin. None of the Allies favored a partitioning of Germany. Neither the Red Army nor the Western Allied Armies exactly
raced to the heart of the Reich. The Soviets held for months on the Vistula and swung to the southwest into the Balkans and the north rather
than straight on for Berlin. General Eisenhower's broad-front strategy guaranteed an absence of overwhelming force everywhere, with
the inevitable consequence that the *Wehrmacht* achieved an impressive
recovery on its national frontier. The Soviet Union did not endorse the
Bretton Woods solution to world monetary and economic problems:
the creation of an International Monetary Fund and a World Bank.
After all, Stalin wanted to bury capitalism, not to save it.

- *1945:* The second Big Three summit at Yalta (February 4-11) had almost
wholly unfortunate consequences. Roosevelt was at death's door but
believed that his personal relationship with Stalin was vital for the future
of inter-Allied cooperation. As a result, the conference settled nothing
of much substance; platitudes and postponement ruled the day. Tough
issues like reparations, Germany's political future, and the advancement
of Poland's western frontier far into erstwhile Germany (to compensate
for Soviet gains in the east of Poland) remained on the table for discussion at some later date. Crucially, Roosevelt had been a member of
Woodrow Wilson's administration and had been scarred by Wilson's
failure to bring the Senate on board for U.S. membership in the League
of Nations. Roosevelt determined that his administration would not
repeat that sorry episode. For good reasons, he attached extraordinary
significance to securing Stalin's agreement to Soviet membership and
key principles and structures of the new United Nations (UN). With the
prospective UN dominating his none-too-alert mind at Yalta, Roosevelt
was not an effective negotiator on most issues important to Western
security. Roosevelt died on April 23. This elevated an ill-informed but
tough, if personally uncertain, Harry S. Truman to deal with Stalin and

Churchill. With Germany defeated, it was or should have been decision time for negotiation on the terms of the peace. The Germans were not to be players in this protracted drama. It is well worth noting that Truman's lack of grasp and grip on, let alone prudent empathy for, Stalin's point of view was almost matched by his difficulty understanding the positions and condition of his British ally.

It was time for serious peace making among the leaders of the Grand Alliance. At Potsdam (July 17–August 2), U.S. diplomacy displayed a harsh tone toward the Soviet Union for the first time, as Truman behaved like a leader who had an atomic ace up his sleeve. The three leaders failed to settle in detail the most important issue of the hour: the administration and future of occupied Germany, as well as reparations from Germany. Soviet behavior in occupied, or liberated, Eastern Europe, most especially in Poland, persuaded many leading Americans that Stalin had lied at Yalta and before. He had signed the impressively liberal-sounding Declaration on Liberated Europe with no intention of adhering to its plain meaning, for example. The military reality of the atomic bomb had a dramatic effect on Soviet policy, but that was not immediately evident in Washington. Truman and Secretary of State James F. Byrnes found themselves puzzled by the increasing truculence of a Soviet Union that ought to have felt decisively outgunned in the strategic arena.

Each side was genuinely uncertain about the intentions of the other in the closing months of 1945. From Stalin's perspective, was the West attempting to renege on what it appeared to have agreed to, at least through Yalta? If it were, just how far would it go in opposing Soviet designs to improve its territorial security in Europe? Washington was no less baffled. Had yesterday's ally and apparent friend become an enemy? If so, how dangerous a one, and was there still time to interdict the contemporary trend of antagonism, suspicion, and outright hostility?

- *1946:* For the United States, diplomat George F. Kennan provided a satisfactory solution to its Soviet conundrum with his "Long Telegram" from Moscow of February 22.[14] In essence, Kennan told his readers that by its nature, Stalin's Soviet Union was a permanent enemy of the United States, and that it could not be bribed, persuaded, or even threatened into friendship. For the first time, Washington had to hand a well-argued comprehensive explanation of its growing Soviet problem. And the timing of Kennan's all-too-clear message was critical. He did not

---

14   "The Long Telegram" is reprinted accessibly in Thomas H. Etzold and John Lewis Gaddis, eds., *Containment: Documents on American Policy and Strategy, 1945–1950* (New York, 1978), pp. 50–63.

anticipate war, hot or cold, but he did his best to demolish any illusions still extant about Soviet–American cooperation in the reconstruction of a European order compatible with U.S. values and aspirations.

Stalin's bafflement was of a different kind. He believed he understood the United States. Indeed, how could he not with Marx and Lenin as guides? He knew that America was a permanent enemy. But, he did not know how that enemy would behave in the near term. Moreover, Stalin needed to make plain to his realm that the days of apparent affability among allies were now past. In his first public postwar speech, on February 9, 1946, he poured the coldest of water over those at home and abroad who had wanted to believe the deterioration in East–West relations was likely to be only temporary. On February 18, Stalin flatly rejected the ill-conceived U.S. "Baruch Plan" for the international control of atomic fission. That rejection formed a pattern with his demand for what would have amounted to the creation of a new military-technological complex capable of competing with that of the United States.[15]

Later in the year, on August 8, Stalin overreached diplomatically by behaving threateningly toward Turkey over the issue of Soviet bases at the Dardanelles, a démarche that prompted a sharp American response, both diplomatic and naval. The intellectual basis for the course of and public turn in Soviet policy in 1946 was provided, to order, by its nominal equivalent to Kennan's "Long Telegram." On September 27, the Soviet ambassador to the United States, Nikolai Novikov, dispatched to Moscow a telegram which explained "U.S. Foreign Policy in the Postwar Period."[16] Not surprisingly, it amounted to a fairly sophisticated appreciation of the enemy. By late 1946, the Soviet Union was preparing for an unavoidable long struggle with a formidable American foe. The conflict was a go.

- *1947:* There is good reason to select 1947 as the date for the Cold War's beginning, but to do so risks misunderstanding the complexity, duration, and depth of the difficulties that confounded peacemakers and strategists. After all, it takes two or more to make political peace and, by 1947, even 1946, Stalin had made it plain enough that he was not dancing. His ideological convictions precluded the acceptance of a

---

[15] To appreciate just how severe was the physical and economic challenge to the Soviet Union posed by the U.S. atomic program, it is worth noting that adjusted for inflation into 2006 dollars, the Manhattan Project cost approximately $24.1 billion. To compete with maximum urgency, Beria, with Stalin's full backing, had to create an entire new industry. The opportunity cost to Soviet society of the dash to build an atomic bomb was truly immense.

[16] For the text of the "Novikov Telegram," see Kenneth M. Jensen, ed., *Origins of the Cold War: The Novikov, Kennan and Roberts "Long Telegrams" of 1946* (Washington, DC, 1991), pp. 3–16.

political peace, no matter how flexible he might prove over tactical matters. Whatever doubts about American policy intentions that lingered in Stalin's devious mind into 1947 soon disappeared in a direction that brooked ill for the future of cooperative East–West relations.

Two American policy initiatives settled the matter definitively. On March 12, Truman accepted responsibility for the maintenance of security in the Eastern Mediterranean, most especially over Greece and Turkey, from the bankrupt British. In character, with his famous Doctrine, Truman globally threw down the gauntlet to the Communist menace. The Doctrine was, of course, astrategic at the time and largely impractical, but that did not much matter. What Truman did, in effect, was declare a U.S. global guardianship against further Communist (read Soviet) expansion. In the highly unlikely event that Stalin retained hope that the United States might yet accept accommodation, the surprise announcement by Secretary of State George C. Marshall on June 5 of his European Recovery Plan (ERP) provided the conclusive answer in the negative.

The United States intended the so-called Marshall Plan, designed to revitalize Europe's currently dead economic boilers, to play a vital role in the immunization of societies against communist subversion. Stalin understood, correctly, that although he had much to gain from joining the ERP or from permitting his new "friends" in Eastern Europe to join, he had much more to lose. The ERP carried mandatory baggage concerning capitalist practices and open markets that posed potentially deadly risks to the political health of Stalin's growing imperium. He interpreted the ERP as constituting a declaration of war. Despite some embarrassed wobbling among the East Europeans, Foreign Minister Molotov, as ever his master's faithful voice, rejected the ERP out of hand at the Foreign Ministers' Conference in Paris June 27–July 1. By the end of the year, continued deadlock over implementing the Potsdam agreements on the governance of Germany obliged the Western allies to seek a nonconsensual solution. Plans for what became the new West German state were set in motion.

- *1948:* The slide in East–West relations grew ever more slippery. A Communist coup in Prague on February 19–25 shocked Western public opinion and even surprised governments. Nearly simultaneously, the three principal Western Allies moved rapidly toward state-building in their zones in occupied Germany. On June 20, they took the fateful step of introducing a new currency for those zones, the Deutsche mark. In prompt albeit dangerous and inept reply, on June 24. Stalin began a blockade of all access to Berlin by road, rail, and water. The Soviets maintained the blockade until May 12, 1949. By late 1948, the Cold War was a fact. How long it would remain cold was profoundly uncertain. Indeed, whether it could be kept cold was a question that attracted increasing attention. The United States and the Soviet Union were not at war but neither could they be said to be at peace, at least not in the normative sense of that ambiguous concept.

- *1949:* This year set what one might term the Cold War paradigm for what were decades to come. Soviet misbehavior in 1948 in Czechoslovakia had prompted Europeans to found the Western European Union (WEU) in February. That was a necessary step on the hard road to persuade the U.S. Congress to agree to a permanent peacetime alliance. Americans needed to believe that Europeans were willing to act seriously on their own behalf. In other words, the WEU aimed at telling the United States that Western Europe was worthy of American protection. 1949 saw the WEU augmented and, naturally, overshadowed by the creation of NATO on April 4. A Federal Republic of Germany soon emerged from the three Western zones of occupation on September 20. Stalin replied with his own German Democratic Republic on October 7. There was a new international order in Europe. Europe was where the Cold War began, most directly that was what it was about, and that was where it had to conclude, one way or another.

DIFFICULTIES: THUCYDIDES WAS RIGHT

So much for the bare narrative. But why did the story just told deny world order a political peace for forty-two years? What was the plot? Did the Allies fall out once the glue provided by the common commitment to defeat Germany was removed? How much agreement had there ever been among Moscow, London, and Washington? Perhaps the end of the war simply revealed the scope and depth of inter-Allied disagreement that had always been extant. Scholars continue to struggle to understand how the Cold War came about. Monocausality is out of fashion, so most explanations strive to emphasize the mutual reinforcement of the geopolitical and ideological. And then there was the critical factor of personality. If one can understand the Second World War as "Hitler's War," was the Cold War, in like manner, Stalin's?[17] The scholar is in danger of losing his or her way amidst the still growing richness of emerging historical details, the range of alternative theories, and the sheer complexity of the relevant contexts. Moreover, there is the lurking anxiety that when an event or process such as the Cold War

---

[17]   The doyen of American Cold War historians, John Gaddis, now argues that "the Cold War – like the American Civil War – was a necessary contest that settled fundamental issues once and for all. We have no reason to miss it. But given the alternatives, we have little reason either to regret its having occurred," *The Cold War* (London, 2005), p. ix. Such is the current state of play on the frontier of postrevisionist thought.

seems to have been so generously overdetermined, it is easy to confuse contingency with necessity.

The Cold War was a great event. It could have concluded with an event of such grimness that few would have survived to debate the merits of the military strategies employed. It should be the case that such great events have deep origins, great causes, and probably dramatic precipitating happenings. But what if history does not always move like that? Is it possible, even probable, that the difficulties that impeded peace making from 1945 to 1947 were not significantly systemic or irresistibly contextual? Instead, they may well have been the result of erroneous assumptions, quirks of personality, and poor decisions based on imprudent judgments. These speculative thoughts are important because they pertain to the matter which lies at the heart of this study. Why was it so difficult to make political peace out of the Second World War? Was it a case of mission impossible? Or, did statecraft fail world order?

Earlier, this chapter boldly proclaimed the view that the difficulties that impeded constructive peace making from 1943 to 1949 were all but insurmountable within the contexts of the times. The "all but" reflects only out of academic habit, not scholarly conviction. The challenge is to find a concept or, more grandly, a conceptual framework, which binds together convincingly the separate strands of the historical plot. The literature is replete with explanations which privilege geopolitical, ideological, and personality explanations for the troubles of the peacemakers. Each has merit. So also do the rival theories which assign blame unequally between East and West. To make sense of this apparent redundancy of explanation, this chapter finds that only one conceptual framework suffices to capture, grasp, and interrelate the often separate-seeming plot lines: the Thucydidean triptych. Fear, honor/culture, and interest collectively explain why statesmen in 1943–1949 were unable to construct a political peace. More happily, the triptych also explains why they were able by trial and error to manufacture a minimal but workable and stable peace.

No matter how skillfully one performs the analysis, distinctively geopolitical or ideological treatment of Soviet–American relations in 1945 cannot help but risk misleading both analyst and reader. Geopolitical and ideological antagonisms poisoned those relations. Only two great powers remained standing over, or approaching, the prostrate wreck of a defeated enemy whose territory lay at the heart of Europe. There was a vacuum of power. On the one side, Stalin's continentalist Soviet Union approached security issues territorially. On the other, insular America, with its frontiers historically long unchallenged, believed that the road to security, order, and peace lay through norms, principles, treaties, and institutions. Two sharply contrasting mindsets toward order and security ruled in Washington and

Moscow.[18] One can explain them adequately in geopolitical terms. It is not difficult to develop a wholly geopolitical explanation for the difficulties of peace making. How could two victorious states, alone in their joint if asymmetrical and unequal preeminence, not be rivals? And it is only a few short steps from rivalry and suspicion to antagonism and actual conflict. At least, the steps proved few, given the malign workings of contingency, chance, friction, and ineptitude.

As if the geopolitical strand in this tale were not potent enough, the addition of ideology and culture, as well as their synergistic effects, made for an explosive brew. Both the new Bolshevik Republic and the United States were polities wedded to – indeed, claiming legitimacy from – ideologies which claimed to enjoy global authority. Threat is not only a question of capability; it also requires the addition of the fuel of intention. The "superpowers" of 1945 had plausible reasons of *realpolitik* to be suspicious of each other. But also each possessed an ideology which recognized the other was an evil enemy. It would be a grave mistake to dismiss ideology, on either side, as mere decoration on a body of hardnosed geopolitical logic. The policies of the United States and the Soviet Union were influenced – in some cases, driven – by ideological assumptions that rendered successful political peace making improbable.

Stalin knew that the United States, the leading capitalist–imperialist state, was an enemy. In fact, Soviet ideology did not distinguish sharply between conditions of war and peace. Stalin expected the capitalist victors of the Second World War to fight among themselves over trade and control of markets. Correctly, though, he appreciated that America's policy drive to spread democracy and an open economic door posed a potentially lethal menace to his closed territorial imperium. From the other side, Stalin's determination to impose tight control on his new security buffer zone in Eastern Europe was unmistakable. And the greatest prize in the clash of ideological approaches was, of course, Germany. Neither Moscow nor Washington wanted a divided Germany. But such a result was the default option, when the alternative could be a united country leaning politically toward one side or the other of the great European divide.

The Cold War was not about ideology or about geopolitics alone. It was about both, and any attempt to separate the two must mislead. The ideological assumptions of American and Soviet leaders had geopolitical consequences.[19] In addition, policy and strategy adopted for narrowly geopolitical

---

[18]   The sharp contrast between Soviet and American strategic cultures is well explained in John Lewis Gaddis, *Russia, the Soviet Union, and the United States: An Interpretive History* (New York, 1978), esp. p. 176.
[19]   The use of the plural for leaders in the Soviet as well as the American context should not be allowed to mislead. In this period, there was only one leader, one voice, in Moscow: Stalin's. Only Molotov, the Foreign Minister, was trusted to speak for his master. He was

reasons confirmed the wisdom of prior ideological worldviews. One might easily fall into the trap of arguing that it was only the directly antagonistic ideologies of the superpowers that caused constructive peace making to founder in 1945–1947. After all, absent the near axiomatic ideological hostility, the United States and the Soviet Union should have been able to negotiate terms for a tolerable postwar order, as great powers had in the past. This thought is best retired. In 1945, even with ideology in abeyance, the two superpowers simply were too outstanding, too open to temptation, too prone to mutual anxiety to behave after the fashion of their predecessors in 1814–1815.

Did personality matter? Of course! It always matters, albeit variably and unpredictably. Stalin's paranoid character, reinforced by an ideology that told him why Americans were his enemies, certainly was unhelpful for peace making. Similarly, an untried U.S. leader, culturally faithful to his Midwestern roots, was not well equipped to see nuance or discern underlying anxieties when presented with evidence of Soviet wrongdoing. But neither Stalin nor Truman precluded the making of a political peace in these years. Anxiety, rivalry, suspicion, antagonism, conflict, and just possibly hot war itself were contextually determined (that fatal word).

When one stands back from the narrative history and the somewhat competing explanations, it is only Thucydides who comes close to providing a toolkit to aid in comprehension. As with Clausewitz's trinitarian theory of war, the Greek's trinitarian summary of the principal motives in statecraft is almost breathtaking for its insight and its perceptive inclusiveness. The sum of the three – adapted to fear, honor/culture/ideology, and interest – considered in unison is infinitely more powerful than a perspective that favors only one. It is relevant to observe that Thucydides' "honor" plays a role in policy determination almost identical to the first element in Clausewitz's "trinity": primordial violence, hatred, and enmity. In other words, Stalin's misdeeds eventually aroused Western publics and obliged politicians to reflect that popular sentiment. The Soviet Union was trampling on Western values and in democracies, the publics are wont to express their dislike of that phenomenon.

CONCLUSION: THE COLD WAR PEACE

Despite the potent reasons for antagonism and conflict that have preoccupied this chapter, the statesmen of 1943–1949 did make peace out of a great war. Furthermore, they made, or perhaps stumbled into, a condition of long-lasting peace. At least, that peace endured sufficiently long to outlast

---

not quite a ventriloquist's dummy, but if one assumed that he was, one would not err far from the truth.

the actual demise of one of the superpowers. The peace of the Cold War was good enough, especially when one considers the leading, much worse alternative. What the peacemakers of the 1940s could not achieve was a political peace. They could not build an international order founded on shared political assumptions and values. Moscow and Washington did not share vital assumptions and values except with respect to those that bore directly on the prospects for national survival in the face of nuclear risk. That would have to suffice, and it did. Just how great was the margin of safety, we cannot know today, any more than leaders knew at the time. Most probably, the contestants were more fortunate than clever in their peace making and subsequent efforts to maintain international order through fear.

The Cold War did not conclude geopolitically but rather ideologically. A Soviet Union claiming its legitimacy from the presumed authority of the canonical texts was politically incapable of making peace with the West. But once it discarded the doctrine which mandated more or less permanent hostility, all things became possible. The political peace that Europe needed in 1945 was not secured until 1989–1990. In reality, in 1945 political peace was mission impossible, though softened in the title to "improbable." Recall the malign combination of great power geopolitics, ideology/culture, and personality, not to mention the normal friction and contingencies of the course of history, including human incompetence. Those factors all but guaranteed that the difficulties challenging would-be peacemakers must prove insurmountable.

In the end, it is a mistake to think of Stalin and Truman as peacemakers. They were, admittedly, jockeying and pushing and pulling to construct some approximation to an "order" to their liking. But from 1945 to 1949, each found himself increasingly engaged more in a quest for competitive advantage than in the search for a lasting political peace. By spring 1946, there was little room for doubt either in Moscow or Washington that a political peace by local cultural definition was not attainable.

One might even suggest that the details of the historical narrative of 1943–1949 did not really matter for postwar peace making.[20] One cannot deny that the sheer double novelty of a bipolar antagonism combined with a

---

[20] For the contrary view, that the details of policy did matter, see Marc Trachtenberg, "The Myth of Potsdam," in *Haunted by History: Myths in International Relations*, ed. by Cyril Buffet and Beatrice Heuser (Providence, RI, 1998). Trachtenberg rejects a metahistorical view which sees the Cold War as "flowing from the basic nature of the two systems, and not as a secular conflict shaped by specific policies and concrete decisions that could easily have been different," p. 102. Trachtenberg, an historian whom I hold in high regard, errs by posing a false opposition. The view that he rejects, which is to say the view that runs through this study, does not rest its case simply on the antagonistic nature of the two political systems. My argument in the text explains the difficulty of making a political peace in terms of the malign combined effects of geopolitics, ideology, and personality.

nuclear dimension translated into diplomacy in an unknown country. However, it is plausible to claim that problems of peace making in that period were deeply and multiply contextual. Particular events did not blight the prospects for achievement of a stable international order. The nonpolitical peace that became the Cold War was unhealthily overdetermined. How was stability to be maintained? What kind of peace, which is to say what character of order, was invented? Sir Michael Howard reminds us that "new world orders... need to be policed."[21] Among the elements of Thucydides' triptych, the powerful synergistic influence of fear and interest proved sufficient to offset the danger inherent in honor, ideology, and culture.

[21] Michael Howard, *The Invention of Peace and the Reinvention of War* (London, 2001), p. 124.

MAP 7. Territorial adjustments after the Second World War.

11

The economic making of peace

JIM LACEY

In December 2006, sixty-one years after the end of the Second World War, Britain sent a final payment of $87 million to the U.S. Treasury and thereby closed out its Second World War debt. Clearly, in the decades following the war, Britain had repaired its war-torn economy and even regained much of its former wealth. This happy circumstance periodically led to parliamentary discussions about using some of Britain's new wealth to pay off the loan early. However, the loan terms were so absurdly easy that the usual response mirrored that given by Lord McIntosh of Haringey to the House of Lords in 2001, "The basis of the loan is that interest is paid at two percent. Therefore, we are currently receiving a greater return on our dollar assets then we are paying in interest to pay off the loan. It is a very advantageous loan for us." In other words, as early as the 1960s, the loan was more than paying for itself. In effect, it was even adding cash to the British Treasury.

A Britain prosperous enough to even consider early repayment of its war loans, which constituted a significant portion of the United Kingdom's gross domestic product when they were made, was by no means a foregone conclusion in 1945. In fact, as the war ended, Britain was bankrupt, while the remainder of war-ravaged Europe was in even worse condition. Moreover, as the war drew to a close, a global pessimism about the likelihood of a rapid economic recovery that would follow in the wake of peace was pervasive. Polls at the time revealed that an overwhelming number of the British and Americans thought the war's end would bring a return of the Great Depression. This was not surprising given that for most of the soldiers returning from the war, a depression economy was all they had known since early childhood. For most of the world, economic deprivation had been the natural state of affairs prior to the war and few were hopeful of postwar change.

Moreover, historical experience gave little reason for cheer. There had never been a major war that severe postconflict economic dislocation and often a crippling deflation had not followed hard on its end. It is difficult today to understand the impact of deflation and the fear its potential return aroused among not only the general population but the experts as well. In recent decades, the bane of central banks and national economic policy makers has been the war against inflation, and everyone understands the pernicious effects of that economic condition. However, most in modern society have forgotten the damage that inflation's cousin – deflation – had wreaked on the international community. Historians do not exaggerate when they suggest that a crucial cause for the Second World War was the world's last major bout of global deflation: the Great Depression.

That another round of general economic failure and collapse did not take place after the Second World War was more by accident than design. In 1944, some of the best economic minds in the world had gathered in the small New Hampshire town of Bretton Woods with the intent of establishing a new global economic system. What they came up with, contrary to later mythology, was rather ineffectual. The reasons lying behind this failure were threefold. First and most important, the economic technocrats worked in virtual isolation from their political systems. Therefore, the institutions they created at Bretton Woods never developed the political and popular support required to be effective. Second, these economists were familiar with and had long worked to solve the problems of the Great Depression. So, in many ways, the institutions they created were admirably suited to solve the economic problems of the period from 1929 to 1938. They were, however, woefully unprepared to address the problems a war-ravaged world confronted in 1945. Finally, because most of their work remained divorced from political oversight, there was considerable opportunity for a single individual to cause great damage. Unfortunately, such an individual existed in the person of America's chief negotiator, Harry Dexter White.

If the postwar economic boom, for which *miracle* is not too strong a word, was not an outcome of Bretton Woods, what was its cause? The simple answer is that the postwar economic resurgence was a direct result of the Cold War, which forced politicians in both the United States and Western Europe to reengage in global economic matters. While only a few key individuals propelled and guided certain crucial policies, such as the Marshall Plan, everyone involved understood that without subjecting economic plans to debate and compromise within their political system, they had little hope of success. However, such a course was not without risks and several times the global economy teetered on the brink of collapse due to political intransigence either in the United States or Western Europe. It took the emergence of a malevolent Soviet Union to focus energies on solutions to the looming global economic crisis. Without the need for a strong Europe as a partner against the looming Soviet threat, it is doubtful the U.S. Congress would have approved the Marshall Plan or remained silent in the face of huge trade imbalances for more than three decades.

The history of the creation of the postwar economic settlement requires one to trace its development through several key individuals uniquely placed to oversee and influence events. Like any good story, this one has both heroes and villains. In the early phases of economic restructuring, two names stand out: John Maynard Keynes and Harry Dexter White. When dealing with these two men and the global economic system they had an outsized role in creating, this chapter addresses two misconceptions which have gained acceptance over the years. The first is that both men are heroes in this story. Nothing could be further from the truth. Only John Maynard Keynes was a hero, while Harry Dexter White played a malicious and dishonest role. The second misconception is that in the battle between the plans of Keynes and White, White won out while Keynes failed. Such a view is both wrong in particulars and, by focusing on only the Bretton Woods technical agreements, it has limited understanding of the wider scope of the global economic settlement to an unwarranted degree.

Before examining the story of the economic settlement, there is a critical point which clarifies the driving force behind many of the economic proposals and decisions made between 1942 and 1950. Harry Dexter White, the number-two man in the U.S. Treasury Department, was a traitor. While one should never discount the role of incompetence in human affairs, the evidence indicates that White was superbly competent in his job. It also overwhelming demonstrates that White consistently advocated policies that favored the Soviet Union and was in constant contact with his Soviet handlers. Early biographies of White spent considerable effort in casting doubts on the evidence of his activities as a Soviet agent but remain largely unconvincing.[1] As late as 2004, one historian was still trying to cast doubt on the evidence and, failing that, to make excuses for White's inexcusable actions.[2] As recently as 2006, several monographs by International Monetary Fund (IMF) historian, James M. Boughton, extolled the virtues and contributions of White over Keynes while excusing or failing to address White's treason.[3]

However, whatever limited doubt once existed as to White's pro-Soviet activities vanished with the release of the Venona Transcripts in the

---

[1] See David Rees, *Harry Dexter White: A Study in Paradox* (New York, 1973), p. 350.
[2] See R. Bruce Craig, *Treasonable Doubt: The Harry Dexter White Spy Case* (Lawrence, KS, 2004).
[3] See "Why White, Not Keynes? Inventing the Postwar International Monetary System," IMF Working Paper, 2002; and "American in the Shadows: Harry Dexter White and the Design of the International Monetary Fund," IMF Working Paper, January 2006, p. 6.

mid-1990s.[4] The transcripts clearly identified White as a Soviet spy with the code name "jurist." They include discussions on the best way for him to meet with his handler (i.e., half-hour conversations in a moving automobile) and how to accept payments and other gifts (e.g., for his daughter's private-school education) from his Soviet masters. This last puts to rest claims that while he may have been a spy, only the "noblest purposes" motivated his actions.

One must balance White's accomplishments, fewer than recent historians have suggested, against the damage caused by his actions. To assess the extent of this damage as well as to grasp the magnitude of the postwar economic settlement, this chapter moves beyond the Bretton Woods agreements and the Marshall Plan, which tend to dominate most economic discussions of the period. A complete understanding must also include China, Japan, Germany, and the postwar U.S. loans (particularly to Britain), as well as the long-term effects of Lend Lease. In all of these areas, White had an impact, the results of which were uniformly pernicious – caused either by imbecility or malicious-ness. While the demise of the British Empire may have been inevitable, anyone looking to discover which American was most enthusiastically pushing it off the cliff at the end of the war needs look no further than Harry Dexter White.

LEND LEASE

To comprehend the post–Second World War economic settlement, one must begin with the effects Lend Lease had on the economic landscape. What Winston Churchill once called "the most unsordid act" on closer examination may not qualify as such. While the amount of equipment America supplied, mostly free of charge, made it possible for Britain to remain in the war, Lend Lease was not an act of unrequited generosity since the United States had strong strategic interests in supporting a military ally, which for more than a year had been the only bulwark standing against Nazi Germany. For example, no one refers to the proportionally similar sums Britain paid to keep the Prussians in the field against Napoleon as an "unsordid act." Those payments were clearly seen for what they were – expenditures to further Britain's self-interest.

---

[4] In 1995, the U.S. National Security Agency broke a half century of silence by releasing translations of Soviet cables decrypted back in the 1940s by the Venona Project. Venona was a top-secret U.S. effort to gather and decrypt messages sent in the 1940s by agents of what is now called the KGB and the GRU, the Soviet military intelligence agency. The cables revealed the identities of numerous Americans who were spies for the Soviet Union. To see the complete set of Venona documents released so far, go to the NSA's Venona Documents page at www.nsa.gov/docs/venona/venona_docs.html.

Furthermore, Lend Lease did not come without conditions. The first and most damaging of these was that it forced Britain to bankrupt itself before Lend Lease would go into action. At White's instigation, Treasury Secretary Henry Morgenthau convinced President Roosevelt that Congress would not embrace Lend Lease until Britain was down to its last farthing. In practical terms, Britain had to sell off, at fire-sale prices, virtually all of its overseas investments. Moreover, the U.S. Treasury insisted that Britain exhaust its foreign currency reserves and borrow heavily from creditors within the sterling area before it presented Lend Lease to Congress.

An attempt to add injury to injury came with a final condition which Roosevelt almost forced on Churchill during the Arcadia Conference. The American president insisted that Churchill agree to dismantle the imperial preference system for international trade. While an open global-trading system generally benefits all concerned, it can, given certain economic conditions, cause considerable economic dislocation – conditions surely present in post–Second World War Britain. The Americans quietly dropped this requirement from the final Arcadia agreements, but it remained a key goal of U.S. diplomats and treasury officials, who were ideologically wedded to the view that free-trade always remains a net positive under any circumstances.

In his masterful multivolume biography of Keynes, Robert Skidelsky claims that the Americans purposely tried to destroy Britain's prewar financial position, based on "the sterling area and imperial preference." Furthermore, he argues that "White's pro-Soviet stance led him to advocate policies designed to boost the international position of the Soviet Union at the expense of Britain and Western Europe."[5] A number of economists have attacked Skidelsky's view of White's efforts. They argue that White was a gifted public servant, whose clear-sighted formulations were both idealistic and designed to enhance postwar global prosperity greatly. Such arguments have some validity, but White's policy initiatives also aimed at ensuring a Soviet–American partnership, which had no room for Britain, would dominate this new world. Moreover, White strongly advocated Lend Lease programs for the Soviet Union free of any of the conditions that he insisted Britain accept. Further evidence of White's animus to Britain lies in the negotiations for a postwar loan for the British, which White opposed, though he advocated a massive (i.e., three to four times what Britain was requesting) low- (or no-) interest loan for the Soviets.

The second argument economists and historians have used to defend White's policy proposals is that, in any event, the British Empire was

---

[5] Robert Skidelsky, *John Maynard Keynes: Fighting for Britain 1937–1946* (London, 2000), p. 22.

doomed. They are correct, but White's uneven treatment of Britain as compared to the Soviet Union made an orderly retreat from the empire impossible. Throughout the war, White worked to ensure Britain's postwar bankruptcy, which made it financially impossible to maintain the empire. For instance, as the British worked assiduously through 1943–1944 to accumulate sufficient currency reserves to offset their sterling debt and pay for much-needed postwar imports (particularly food), White, working closely with his Soviet handlers, manipulated the Lend Lease list to draw down those reserves.

It is a common fallacy that Lend Lease supplied the British with everything they needed without charge. In truth, the United States modified the list of Lend Lease items available to Britain throughout the war based on its ability to pay. It was White who controlled those decisions. So, though Keynes and other British officials repeatedly stated that Britain required approximately $5 billion in reserves at the end of the war, White consistently removed items available through Lend Lease to keep British reserves under $1 billion. Significantly, he never advocated encumbering the Russians in a similar fashion. In summary, though Lend Lease was critical to Britain's salvation and the Allied war effort, its misuse at the behest of a single individual damaged Britain's postwar economic prospects and, by extension, hindered the recovery of all of Western Europe.

BRETTON WOODS

For many historians, the agreements reached at the small New Hampshire town of Bretton Woods in 1944 represent the lynchpin of the postwar economic settlement. This fallacy probably results from the fact that the two institutions created by the conference – the International Monetary Fund (IMF) and the International Bank for Reconstruction and Development (IBRD, or World Bank) – still survive today. This centrality, which the Bretton Woods Conference plays in most analyses of the postconflict economic settlement, is surprising given the historic ineffectualness of both organizations. Although at present the IMF and World Bank play important but not critical roles in the current global economic system, their influence in the years immediately after the Second World War was negligible.

In fact, the IMF's first real test (i.e., sterling convertibility) was a dismal failure. In 1947, after receiving a considerable stabilization loan from the United States, Britain attempted to make sterling convertible into gold and dollars, as mandated in the Bretton Woods agreements, despite Keynes's and the U.S. Treasury's warnings of disaster. An immediate run on the pound, which Britain futilely tried to defend until it had exhausted the entire multibillion-dollar loan, greeted the convertibility announcement. When the loan ran out, the British had to suspend the convertibility of the pound, and no other European country would make a similar attempt until 1958. From beginning to end, this Sterling crisis lasted only eight weeks.

This sterling crisis exposed the IMF's *raison d'etre* – currency stabilization – as nothing but pretense. How could this have happened? Both White and Keynes agreed that one of the primary causes of the Great Depression had been competitive devaluations of national currencies, coupled with protective tariffs to keep out cheap exports. The end result was that international trade seized up and deflation took hold. Both men came to Bretton Woods intent on establishing an institution that could focus on currency stability and do away with unrestricted, competitive devaluations. Convertibility was the lynchpin idea that supposedly would make the system work. Without the tedium of analyzing the specifics of both plans and the ensuing technical debates, one can summarize them as follows:[6]

- Keynes wanted a currency union capitalized with a massive $26 billion fund, which would have had access to even greater funds on demand. He wanted to allow countries facing economic disequilibrium to borrow from this fund liberally, freely, and without conditions.
- White wanted a stability fund with a much lower capitalization ($5 billion) with limited access to additional funds. Furthermore, the new system would discourage nations from borrowing from the fund, and those that did so would be able to draw funds only after agreeing to meet stringent conditions.

White won the argument; Keynes, however, was right. In the end, the IMF found itself undercapitalized for the immense task that it was supposed to undertake. Moreover, no government could agree, except under the direst straits, to its conditions, which were always deflationary and certain to throw millions of people out of work.[7]

Any pretense that the IMF could stabilize currencies and eliminate competitive devaluations, which had ruined the prewar global economy, died in 1949, when Britain undertook a massive devaluation of sterling to make its exports more competitive and write down wartime debts. The IMF thereby failed in its primary responsibility. Although it was to reinvent itself (several times) as it followed its bureaucratic imperative to survive, its contributions to postwar economic activity were nil.

As for the World Bank, that institution never received much of White's attention. In fact, Keynes headed up the subcommittee at Bretton Woods

---

[6] Anyone interested in all of the technical details of the competing plans is encouraged to read J. H. Riddle, "British and American Plans for International Currency Stabilization," National Bureau of Economic Research, New York, 1943.

[7] Readers interested in the Bretton Woods debates are referred to Raymond F. Mikesell, *The Bretton Woods Debates: A Memoir* (Princeton, NJ, 1994); and Georg Schild, *Bretton Woods and Dumbarton Oaks* (New York, 1995).

that wrote most of the rules for the new organization, which definitely reflected a British worldview of what the post–Second World War era would require. Some historians and many Bretton Woods participants concluded that White diverted both Keynes and the U.S. State Department from the IMF negotiations by giving them responsibility for designing the World Bank. Dean Acheson, who headed the state department team, complained that White had shortchanged him when it came to staff. He also considered the experts whom White had provided the state department to be ill-informed and disorganized, particularly when compared to the efficient team White had assembled for the IMF negotiations.[8]

In the end, the World Bank found itself capitalized with $9.1 billion, a remarkably inadequate sum given the task it confronted. After all, by this point in the war, the Allies alone were spending $15 billion a month to blow large segments of the globe to pieces; it would take many times that amount to put it back together. Worse, the Bank's original charter called for it to underwrite or guarantee private investment in wartorn countries. Nevertheless, it had no plans or authority to loan out its capital for projects. In effect, any country, which needed a loan to rebuild a dam, a bridge, or a port would first have to convince a private bank, usually in New York, to supply the funds. The two parties would then ask the World Bank for a guarantee. If the loan met rather strict guidelines and was judged to contribute to a nation's general economic health, the guarantee would receive approval.

If the World Bank had received the authority to operate like a private bank, its small capitalization would not have mattered. For instance, banks today have to keep approximately 8 percent of their loan portfolios in cash (or approved equivalents) reserves. Therefore, a bank with $9 billion of paid-in capital could actually loan out more than ten times that amount. In fact, if the World Bank had adopted current international banking reserve rules, it could have loaned an unlimited amount of cash since nation-states are absurdly considered risk-free borrowers and do not require lenders to reserve capital against defaults. However, the United States could not consider what private banks consider sound banking principles safe for the World Bank, mostly because White feared presenting a bank plan to Congress that might appear to place U.S. taxpayers in a position of unlimited liability to provide ever greater funds on demand.

In the end, the bank found itself limited to committing just its paid-in capital and forbidden to underwrite any loans in excess of that figure. Still, $9 billion was not an insignificant amount, and the bank could have made substantial postwar contributions if its directors had acted aggressively

---

[8] Randall Woods, *A Changing of the Guard: Anglo-American Relations, 1941–1946* (Chapel Hill, NC, 1990), p. 136.

within the limits of their charter. They did not. Feeling restricted by their charter, the bank's directors emphasized the soundness of projects and their bankability in terms of a country's ability to repay. It was not until late in 1947, two years after its creation and the war's end, that the bank made its first loan, which was a relatively paltry $200 million to France.

In summary, the Bretton Woods negotiators had not designed their institutions to operate effectively in conditions of growing political and economic disequilibrium, which was precisely what the world experienced in the immediate postwar years.[9] One would have to search long and hard to unearth any significant contributions that either the IMF or the World Bank made to economic growth or stability in the decade immediately after the war. In fact, positive action would not come until the United States adopted new economic policies in reaction to the Cold War and the advent of the Marshall Plan.

Finally, many historians who suggest that White won many of the arguments on the design of the Bretton Woods institutions have missed the elephant in the room. The entire framework undergirding Bretton Woods rested on a common understanding among professional economists of what economic structures the postwar world would require. This understanding derived from a common perception of what went wrong in the 1930s, as well as which policies helped nations overcome internal economic problems – most of which rested on Keynesian concepts. Everyone involved in the Bretton Woods negotiations worked on the following three common concepts:

- the belief that currency stability and convertibility was desirable
- the need for a stabilization fund to assist governments with short-term liquidity concerns
- the need to devise techniques of international economic management to manage capital flows, trade, and policies to promote full national employment[10]

In short, the Bretton Woods parties agreed to institute what amounted to a wide spectrum of Keynesian economic theory on a global basis rather than only on their national economies. White may have gotten his way on some details, but the grand edifice was a triumph of Keynesian economics. Some historians have advanced the claim that since there is no proof White read any of Keynes's work, that he came to the three economic prescriptions on his own – a bizarre argument. From the time Keynes published his famous

---

[9] Richard Gardner, *Sterling-Dollar Diplomacy* (New York, 1969), pp. 380–5.
[10] John Ikenberry, "A World Economy Restored: Expert Consensus and the Anglo-American Postwar Settlement," International Organization 46, 46, 1, Massachusetts Institute of Technology, Winter 1992.

The General Theory of Employment, Interest and Money in 1936, it was impossible for any professional economist to function without a thorough familiarity with Keynes, his concepts, and his writings. Every developed nation in the world, including the United States, was employing his advice in an attempt to break the grip of the Great Depression. It would have been astonishing, indeed, for White not to have had a thorough grounding in Keynes's work and yet have kept his job.[11]

WHAT OF GERMANY?

As the Bretton Woods discussions progressed, the Allies began considering options for postwar Germany. In August 1944, both the British Foreign Office and the U.S. State Department were completing their first draft on how they expected to treat Germany after the war. While differing in the details, both plans eventually foresaw the reintegration of Germany into the community of nations after a period of political and economic rehabilitation. Neither plan was easy on Germany. Both advocated a prolonged period of harsh occupation, with the Germans paying sizable reparations. Furthermore, both plans wanted stringent restrictions placed on German industry to ensure that that country's productive potential could never again threaten world peace.

White handed the state department plan to his boss, Treasury Secretary Henry Morgenthau, while both were en route to England. Knowing that Morgenthau would find the plan insufficiently harsh, White had purposefully not included a treasury statement on the plan.[12] White was right. Morgenthau wanted far more than a hard peace; he desired a Carthaginian peace. During the flight and in discussions with Eisenhower and leading British officials, Morgenthau laid out a plan that would bear his name. Simply put, The Secretary of the Treasury advocated that the Allies raze or remove all German industry and turn the country into a giant pasture. By the time he left England, Morgenthau wrongly believed that both Eisenhower and most British politicians supported his plan. White, who had strongly supported Morgenthau's efforts, received the task of preparing a written plan for the president.[13] As one British politician later commented, "It fell to White to clothe a bad thesis with an appearance of intellectual respectability."[14]

On September 1, 1944, White had completed his assignment and presented Morgenthau with a detailed and comprehensive scheme to reduce German

---

[11] James Boughton, "American in the Shadows: Harry Dexter White and the Design of the International Monetary Fund," IMF Working Paper, 2006.

[12] Rees, *Harry Dexter White*, p. 243.

[13] White only demurred over the flooding of the Ruhr/Saar coal mines, which he wanted to hand over to Britain or, preferably, France.

[14] Rees, *Harry Dexter White*, p. 248.

power permanently. One can gain some insight into White's approach from knowing that at one point, during the writing of the plan, he told treasury economist Edward Bernstein to prepare a study on how much steel-production capacity the Allies should allow Germany to keep after the war. Bernstein's study argued that Germany should keep sufficient capacity to aid in the rebuilding of Europe. White, however, did not want Germany to have any capacity at all, even if it deprived other nations of badly needed steel for their own reconstruction. He then commented to Bernstein, "We're not interested in having any German steel production. We want you to give us economic reasons to remove all of their capacity."[15]

Morgenthau, using his close personal relationship with the president, secured a cabinet meeting in which he pushed for approval of his plan over that of Secretary of State Hull's. He was confident the president would approve his plan. Based on private conversations with Hull, he believed the Secretary of State was willing to support him. Morgenthau also knew that his plan had one implacable foe: Secretary of War Henry Stimson. Stimson, a former U.S. District Attorney, Secretary of State, and twice Secretary of War, had mastered the ways of Washington and was a vicious and accomplished political infighter, when required. He was also a humane man possessed of deep guiding principles. For instance, when the Allies gained the upper hand in 1944, Stimson became a vocal opponent of what he believed to be needless attacks on Germany; he particularly opposed the terror-bombing of Japanese cities. Immediately before the cabinet meeting, Stimson wrote to Morganthau:

> Nor can I agree that it should be one of your purposes to hold the German population "to a subsistence level" if this means the edge of poverty. This would mean condemning the German people to a condition of servitude in which, no matter how hard or how effectively a man worked, he could not materially improve his economic condition in the world. Such a program would, I believe, create tension and resentments far outweighing any immediate advantage of security and would tend to obscure the guilt of the Nazis and the viciousness of their doctrines and acts.
>
> By such economic mistakes I cannot but feel that you would be poisoning the springs out of which we hope that the future peace of the world can be maintained.... Such methods, in my opinion, do not prevent war; they breed it.[16]

The cabinet debate swung back and forth, and Stimson became dejected when Roosevelt began a long monologue about how pleasant life was in 1810 when everyone wore homespun wool and cares were few and far

[15] Georg Schild, *Bretton Woods and Dumbarton Oaks* (New York, 1995), p. 133.
[16] Henry Stimson and McGeorge Bundy, *On Active Service in Peace and War* (New York, 1971), p. 573.

between. His clear implication was that the Germans would love leading what he pictured as a carefree, idyllic life. Nevertheless, Stimson persisted in his arguments and, much to Morgenthau's surprise, Secretary of State Hull supported the Secretary of War. By meeting's end, Stimson thought he had gained ground with the president, who seemed ready to find a middle way. Morgenthau also knew he was losing the policy debate and requested and received another meeting, this time private, with the president a few days later. By the end of that meeting, the president was firmly behind the plan and had invited Morgenthau to the Quebec Conference on September 11, 1944, to convince Churchill.

Hull and Stimson did not receive invitations and the latter was clearly worried. He confided in his diary that he was much troubled by the president's physical condition and that he was distinctly not himself prior to the departure for Canada. Stimson also worried that the president was not properly prepared to discuss the ramifications of the postwar German question. He later considered that Roosevelt was so weakened from sickness that he was easy prey for "evil men with evil intent," by whom he meant Harry Dexter White, who had assumed Hull's place on the trip to Quebec. He further noted in his diary, "He takes a man [White] who really represents the minority and is so biased that he really is a dangerous adviser to the President at this time."[17]

As the point man for the Morgenthau Plan, it is hard to underestimate how dangerous White's implementation plans had become. Keynes, after discussing the Plan with White, wrote the following note to Sir John Anderson, Britain's Chancellor of the Exchequer:

> I asked White how the inhabitants of the Ruhr were to be kept from starvation; he said that there would have to be bread lines, but at a very low subsistence level. When I asked if the British, as being responsible for the area, would also be responsible for the bread, he said that the US Treasury would if necessary pay for the bread provided always that it was at a very low level of subsistence. So whilst the hills are being turned into sheep run, and the valleys are filled for years to come with closely packed bread lines on a very low subsistence level at American expense – How am I to keep a straight face when asked to talk about this plan I cannot imagine.[18]

It got worse. When asked if there were anything that might be done to reduce the number of Germans who would require feeding by soup kitchens, White proposed moving millions of German men to Africa to work as slave labor on massive construction projects. At another point, when told that

---

[17] Ibid., p. 582.
[18] Schild, *Bretton Woods and Dumbarton Oaks*, p. 137.

thirty million people would starve to death if the Allies enacted his plans, he replied that he had done his own calculations and the figure was closer to eighteen million dead, which he found acceptable.[19]

It is doubtful Morgenthau was aware of these calculations, but there is no doubt he knew his plan would cause vast suffering among the Germans. Still, he determined to see his plan through and took his briefing to Churchill at Quebec. He was taken aback by the response. Churchill, aghast, lashed out at the plan, as well as Morgenthau personally. As Morgenthau later recalled:

> After I finished my piece he turned loose on me the full flood of his rhetoric, sarcasm, and violence. He looked on the Treasury Plan, he said as he would on chaining himself to a dead German. He [Churchill] was slumped in his chair, his language biting, his flow incessant, his manner merciless. I have never had such a verbal lashing in my life.[20]

However, by the next morning, the prime minister had a change of heart and eventually signed on. White later claimed that Churchill's staff had convinced him to agree to the plan to obtain an extension of Lend Lease and a sizeable low-interest postwar loan as a quid pro quo.

Whatever Churchill's reasons for agreement, he soon had a change of heart. On his return to Britain, the prime minister became a vigorous opponent of the plan. More troubling for Morgenthau and White, who was now the plan's point man, Stimson now turned his formidable political skills to wrecking their plan. After Stimson had finished mobilizing the press, Congressional allies, and even army field commanders to oppose the Morgenthau Plan, Roosevelt had by mid-October begun to backpedal furiously. By the end of the month, the plan was as good as dead.

In the end, a number of factors came together to determine Germany's economic fate. First and foremost, Roosevelt died and Truman became president. Truman was no fan of Morgenthau and had a strong sense of order. He believed the fate of Germany was the state department's business and not the treasury's responsibility. He was also a vocal opponent of the Morgenthau Plan and had been one even while in the Senate. Sidelined by Truman, White's and Morgenthau's abilities to influence Germany's future became nil almost overnight. The facts on the ground also strongly influenced the fate of Germany. The army, with a war in Japan still to attend to, had no interest in pushing Germany into chaos. The occupation authority ended up in the capable hands of General Lucius Clay, who, despite some

[19] Rees, *Harry Dexter White*, p. 260.
[20] John Blum, *From the Morgenthau Diaries: Years of War 1941–1945* (Boston, 1967), p. 369.

interagency bickering with the state department, quickly took charge and began to stabilize German politics and economics in the immediate aftermath of the war.

Unfortunately, despite his many good qualities as an administrator and problem solver, Clay had no idea how to rebuild a wartorn economy. Clay's professional economic advisers were just as unprepared. The German economic miracle did not really get under way until 1947, when the German economic chief, Ludwig Erhardt, decided to free all prices. In one bold stroke, Erhardt reinstituted a market economy. At the time, all price changes of market goods had to be approved by U.S. military authorities, but there was no rule against scrapping the entire price-control regime, which is precisely what Erhardt did. His actions met a storm of disapproval, particularly from professional economists. Clay called Erhardt to his office and told him that all of his economic advisers were telling him that freeing prices was lunacy. Erhardt replied, "General, my advisers say the same thing. We must ignore them." Clay had the good sense to ignore the naysayers. Within a week, previously scarce commodities began to appear on store shelves and the German economy began its revival.[21]

The final and, in many ways, most critical factor influencing German economic recovery was the advent of the Cold War. Almost overnight, Germany found itself transformed from a defeated enemy into a frontline ally in the battle with communism. All talk of reparations and punishment disappeared to be replaced by discussions on how best to strengthen the German economy and reintegrate it into global trade. A weak Germany was no longer in the interest of the West, which now foresaw a need for Germany's economic strength to help deter and possibly fight an encroaching Soviet Union. It was also obvious that Germany could only be useful in the long Cold War struggle if its power and influence rested on a firm economic base. The advent of the Cold War had a number of other beneficial consequences relating to the economic reconstruction of the world, including the birth of the Marshall Plan and America's acceptance of terms of trade, which were clearly destructive to its own economic competitiveness.

JAPAN'S ECONOMIC REBIRTH

Considering the energy spent on determining Germany's postwar economic fate, it is remarkable that Japan's postwar fate received little attention. By the time Washington policy makers considered the problem, General Douglas MacArthur had firmly entrenched himself as Japan's de facto ruler

---

[21] Daniel Yergin, *The Commanding Heights: The Battle for the World Economy* (New York, 2002), p. 8.

with veto authority over every proposal. Ironically, the Japanese economy benefited greatly from his official neglect. It was also to benefit from the fact that while the Allies had plenty of economic "experts" and overseers who spoke German, they had few who spoke Japanese. Thus, the Japanese were often able to continue to do what they thought best, against the wishes of occupation authorities, simply because there was no one to keep an eye on them. Most obviously, this took place with the re-creation of the banned Zaibatsu conglomerates into the just as powerful Keiretsu conglomerates.

Still, the Japanese economy was in a state of near collapse at the end of the war. At least ten million Japanese were out of work, at least a third of its national wealth was in ruins, its economy was suffering from runaway inflation and, since almost half of the rice crop had failed, famine stalked the land. The impetus of an impending humanitarian crisis and MacArthur's political weight propelled the United States into immediate action. For three years, America sent vast emergency shipments of food and raw materials to Japan free of charge.

By 1948, with the advent of the Cold War, American policy shifted from sending aid to helping Japan become self-reliant. Occupation authorities assisted the government in implementing harsh anti-inflation measures it could not have undertaken without the cover of American orders. The occupation authority also pushed Japan to adopt extensive land reform, which broke up the massive feudal holdings and gave the land to the tenants at minimal charge. Almost overnight, this action created millions of landowners, who almost always voted conservative. The new landowners provided Japan with a stable conservative government for more than a generation while also producing sufficient food not only to feed the country but also to bring in significant agricultural income from exports. At this time, America switched from sending raw materials to straight capital infusions coupled with transfers of advanced technology. Thus, U.S. capital began providing the seed money to rebuild, modernize, and expand Japanese industry.

Times were still hard in Japan throughout the second half of the 1940s, but they were improving at a noticeable pace. Until 1950, though, American policy makers did not consider Japan of great strategic or economic importance. That, coupled with a residual antipathy much greater than that against Germany, kept the United States from creating a grand reconstruction plan for Japan. However, in 1950, the Korean War broke out. Overnight, Japan became the main staging ground for the UN war effort, as well as a crucial supplier of war materiel. With the victory of Mao's Communists in China, the effect of Japan's key strategic position on its economic prospects would be difficult to underestimate. One example suffices to tell the story. Before the Korean War, Toyota was producing three hundred trucks a month and was on the verge of bankruptcy; after receiving an initial American military order for more than five thousand vehicles, it rebuilt its fortunes.[22]

Toyota's good fortune represented a microcosm of what took place throughout the economy as Japan absorbed cash infusions far larger than any European country had received under the Marshall Plan. The Korean War brought hundreds of millions of dollars to fund infrastructure and pay the Japanese for services, along with billions more in industrial orders. Moreover, America pushed other Asian nations to conclude treaties with Japan and normalize trade relations, which provided Japan with huge export and capital-investment opportunities. With almost blinding speed, Japan altered its status from conquered enemy to indispensable ally, thereby altering the bedrock premises of the occupation.

Occupation authorities now stopped trying to remake Japan and began to accept that there was a Japanese method of doing things, which, if supported, would greatly help America meet its new geopolitical goals. Rather than trying to stop Japan from rebuilding its business conglomerates under the new bank-centered Keiretsu system or impeding the growing centralization of economic decision making – led first by the economic stabilization board and later by the Ministry of international trade and industry (MITI) – occupation authorities assisted or turned a blind eye to those developments. This represented a major switch from the first time Japan headed down that route in 1947. Then, occupation reformers had purged Japan's economic head and most of his staff. By 1950, no one cared. All that American authorities were interested in was increasing Japanese production to support the Korean War and creating a dynamic Japanese economy that would help the Japanese become a key U.S. ally in the Cold War. How the Japanese accomplished that was a matter best left to them.[23]

By 1955, just ten years after the war, Japan Inc. was up and running at full steam, with MITI providing capital to favored industries and making them world-class competitors. Once outlawed by the Americans, cartels formed with government encouragement, or what was called "administrative guidance," to allocate production quotas and share raw materials. However, much of what Japan was doing both charged growth and violated the iron laws of economics. It could not last forever, but it lasted long enough to make Japan the second largest economy on the globe within the life span of a generation.[24]

---

[22] W. G. Beasley, *The Rise of Modern Japan* (London, 2000), p. 216.
[23] Ibid.
[24] The author remembers sitting in a graduate economics class in which the professor was extolling the virtues of the Japanese method. At one point, he was asked how Japan could violate all of the economic laws he had beaten into our brains the previous semester. He thought about it a long while and finally said, "It can't. I need to sell my Japanese-based

WHO LOST CHINA?

In the years immediately following the Communist takeover in China, one question haunted American policy makers: Who lost China? While there is much blame to be spread around, one individual did more to destabilize the Nationalist government than anyone else: Harry Dexter White again. As one sympathetic biographer has admitted, White declared a one-man embargo on gold the United States had promised China as part of a 1942 agreement.[25]

In the closing months of the Pacific war, inflation in China, high since the Sino-Japanese War had begun in 1937, was progressing to hyperinflation. To stabilize its currency, China asked for an immediate shipment of $200 million in gold that the United States had promised under Secretary Morgenthau's signature. The gold was part of a larger pledge of $400 million, the first half of which the United States had delivered at a time when both the Soviets and White supported the Nationalist government's efforts against a common foe. The Chinese had exhausted these funds in the war against Japan. Now, with the war waning, the Chinese government's first priority was to stabilize its economy in order to provide a strong economic base to support the coming civil war against the Communists.

By now, though, the Soviet Union's support of the Nationalist government had moved from ambivalent to hostile. As the Soviets went, so went White. Despite his clear knowledge that the president had approved the funds, White unilaterally withheld them. At first, he offered the excuse that sending the funds would be a mistake and waste of money. White hid his own leanings on the matter behind a barrage of memoranda written by Treasury department employee Frank Coe, who used information from another Treasury department employee, Solomon Adler, stationed by White in China. Adler's information and Coe's memos argued that the gold already sent had done nothing but enrich speculators, mostly Nationalist government officials. None of it, they claimed, was going to any useful purpose. This proved false. Both Coe and Adler later defected to the People's Republic of China after White's death, where they were to spend succeeding years contributing to the revolution by translating Chairman Mao's works into English.[26]

When Morgenthau learned of this deception, he exploded and issued severe reprimands to a number of Treasury officials. When a Chinese representative later reminded him that he had approved the gold transfer under his

---

mutual fund." He did and was spared the decade-long crushing deflation, out of which Japan is only now beginning to crawl.

[25] Rees, *Harry Dexter White*, p. 341.

[26] Ibid., pp. 232–6.

signature, he went from anger to mortification. Morgenthau had forgotten that he personally approved the transfer and was livid with his staff for not, in their voluminous presentations on the topic, reminding him. He viewed them, and particularly White, as having been culpable in besmirching his personal honor, a concept with infinitely more meaning for his generation than today's. He later claimed that this was the first time he had reason to doubt White's veracity and integrity.[27] In early May 1945, Morgenthau summarily ordered his subordinates to send the gold immediately.

White made one last stand and in mid-May asked Coe to cable Adler to forward to him every scrap of evidence or rumor that the Chinese has misused previous gold shipments. He sent a memorandum on the topic to the state department, then brought it to Morgenthau, and asked that it be sent to the president. Morgenthau reacted strongly and ordered the memo's recall from State and forbade anyone from forwarding it to the White House. White continued to argue that Morgenthau could honorably wriggle out from the commitment based on Coe and Adler's proof of Chinese duplicity. The next day, Morgenthau had a final meeting with White, Coe, and Adler, at which he called them all on the carpet for repeatedly lying to him. He informed them he was going to ask for a presidential order to transfer the gold.

On May 15, Morgenthau got a presidential signature on the transfer order, which Truman signed in White's presence. Unable to delay further, White transferred $100 million during the next few months and made plans for shipping the remainder before the end of the year. Unfortunately, it was too late to help China. Inflation, which had reached an annual rate of 100 percent when the gold transfers became an issue, had by spring 1945 reached 1,000 percent by the time the gold was shipped. The spot price of gold had skyrocketed in China and, though there was a two-month respite when Japan surrendered, hyperinflation soon reignited. Two hundred million dollars was no longer nearly enough to stabilize the Chinese economy. It probably would have taken ten times that, and there was real doubt that the wartorn economy could have absorbed that amount, even if forthcoming.

In the end, the Chinese economy went from bad to wretched in less than eighteen months, and White deserves considerable credit for the disaster. The Nationalist government, unable to stabilize China's economy, soon discovered it did not have the financial resources to undertake a civil war against the Communists, as peasants, whose future economic prospects the inflation had destroyed along with the economy, swelled the Communist ranks. There were many, most in Chaing's clique, who had some part in

27 Ibid., p. 238.

losing China to the Communists, but there is ample justification for reserving a special place of honor for the American, Harry Dexter White.

THE BRITISH LOAN

As the Second World War drew to an end, Britain's financial position was in crisis. By any practical measure, London was bankrupt or, to use an economic euphemism, it was facing a liquidity crisis of massive proportions. To meet the crisis, the British examined the following four options:

1. Persuade creditors to reduce the amount owed or modify payment terms unilaterally.
2. Obtain a new low-interest loan of suitable size and on easy terms that would see the country through the crisis and beyond.
3. Undertake severe and economically contracting measures to bring the economy back into balance with its international position.
4. Default.[28]

Within the newly elected Labour government, there was strong and growing interest for a general default on all outstanding war debt. However, the idea failed to achieve a critical mass, in no small measure due to Keynes's strong objections. For a country which continues to this day to pay interest on the consols issued to fund the war against Napoleon, a default would have proven catastrophic to its reputation. Moreover, it would have made Britain's reintegration into global financial markets both problematic and costly for decades to come. Two of the other options never gained traction. Most of Britain's creditors were also facing severe postwar financial difficulties and had no appetite for reducing the amounts owed them by Britain. Finally, tightening British belts and adopting a deflationary postwar economic policy was never in the cards. The newly elected Labour government was not going to ruin its popularity and lose its parliamentary majority by reinitiating the Great Depression.

Keynes was able to convince the Labour cabinet that he could negotiate a large loan from the United States on terms that reflected Britain's shouldering of the war's military burden alone for more than a year. He sincerely believed the United States had a moral responsibility to compensate Britain for its disproportionate wartime sacrifices. He told the cabinet that the United States would be willing to deliver $3 billion as a gift and open a credit line for $5 billion more at token interest and with easy repayment terms.

---

[28] Gardner, *Sterling-Dollar Diplomacy*, pp. 224–35.

When Keynes arrived in Washington to begin negotiations for the loan, the Americans quickly disabused him of the notion there were many in the United States who looked favorably on the idea of compensating Britain for past sacrifices. In fact, polls at the time rated Britain as America's most untrustworthy ally. Most Americans recognized the new Labour government as socialist, while many argued that aid to Britain would either be wasted or incompatible with American principles of free enterprise.[29] Whatever chance Keynes had of getting cash on the terms he hoped for had ended with Roosevelt's death and Churchill and the Conservative Party's defeat in the July 1945 British elections. The Truman administration was not particularly friendly to the new Labour government, and Keynes found that the fund of American goodwill toward Britain centered largely on the person of Winston Churchill.

Furthermore, there was a sizable segment of Americans, including many representatives and senators in Congress, who did not believe Britain needed a loan. Foremost among this crowd was Harry Dexter White, whose power had diminished but who still possessed considerable influence. While the Bretton Woods debates were ongoing in Congress, White testified that Britain's financial position was not as dire as claimed. Moreover, he could see no reason why the British needed a loan from the United States. This was a remarkable assertion since he, better than anyone, knew the grim truth about Britain's finances because he had worked so industriously to ruin them. While White was doing everything he could to throw cold water on the idea of a British loan, he was strongly advocating a $10-billion grant to the Soviet Union.

In fact, the fashion in which the treasury, under White's direction, treated British loan negotiators as compared to how they treated Soviet negotiators is instructive. As one commentator has noted,

> A British Representative ventilated a question of major interest. Why, he asked, were we subjected to these inquisitions from which the Russians were entirely free? The Americans admitted that the Russian attitude would be to refuse to answer any of our questions.[30]

One can forgive British officials if they sometimes thought a show of Soviet truculence would have served them better than bending over backwards to be forthcoming.

As the negotiations continued without much progress, Morgenthau's successor, Frederick Vinson, leaned toward giving Britain the loan. Vinson, a former member of Congress and later Chief Justice of the United States,

[29] Ibid., p. 194.
[30] R. S. Sayers, *Financial Policy 1939–45* (London, 1956), p. 435.

possessed a keen political ear. He was one of the few in Washington who could read the public and congressional mood and determine the fine line between the possible and impossible. As 1945 drew to an end, Vinson saw that the loan was politically possible but could not approach the level the British desired and would be somewhat less than even the state department advocated. To determine the actual extent of British needs, Vinson ordered the creation of an internal Treasury committee to study the problem.

White saw this as his last chance to forestall the loan and undertook to form the committee. His opposition to the loan had already caused a rift between him and two of his key subordinates, Edward Bernstein and Ansel Luxford, both of whom were intimately familiar with Britain's finances and who favored a large loan on easy terms. They were experts on the British economy, but White personally ensured they were not members of the committee.[31] When the committee returned a startlingly low estimate of British requirements, Bernstein and Luxford immediately went over White's head and sent a memorandum directly to Vinson to alert him of their opinion about Britain's plight. So armed, Vinson, who by now was no fan of White, advised the president to ask Congress for authorization to loan $3.5 billion to Britain.[32]

In the meantime, state department officials, led by William L. Clayton, had completed their own proposal. Clayton, a self-made man, had raised himself from poverty to riches as a cotton broker. He abhorred all government interference in economic life but was also a deep humanitarian, whose firsthand reports of starving women and children in Europe were instrumental in securing public support and congressional approval for the Marshall Plan. He was keenly aware of and sympathetic to Britain's plight. At the same time, he never allowed himself to forget what was in America's interest. Clayton saw the loan as both alleviating a potential humanitarian crisis as well as being good for America. For him, the more quickly Britain was economically back on its feet, the faster it could start buying U.S. exports. He also saw the loan as a way to force Britain to abandon imperial trading preferences and open its economy to U.S. exports.[33]

In the end, Truman asked Congress for and received a $3.75 billion loan for Britain. The amount was less than the British had desired and the strings (i.e., open trading) attached to the loan were not popular among either the British people or many in the Labour government. Most in Britain watched

[31] Raymond Mikesell, *The Bretton Woods Debate: A Memoir* (Princeton, NJ, 1994), p. 46.
[32] Ibid., p. 49.
[33] Gregory A. Fossedal, *Our Finest Hour: Will Clayton, the Marshall Plan, and the Triumph of Democracy* (Palo Alto, CA, 1993), p. 212.

in horror as the U.S. Congress debated the loan and asked themselves how they could put themselves in financial obligation to a legislative body filled with so many "ill natured and ignorant members."[34]

For a considerable time, it appeared as if the loan would fail until Clayton gave up on selling the loan's economic merits and began warning House members about the growing Soviet threat. The debate finally ended when House Speaker Sam Rayburn took the floor and argued,

> I do not want Western Europe, England, and all the rest pushed toward an ideology that I despise. I fear that if we do not cooperate with our great natural ally that is what will happen. If we are not allied with the great British democracy, I fear somebody will be and God pity us when we have no ally across the Atlantic.[35]

After acrimonious debate, parliament soon followed suit and approved the terms. As Clement Atlee noted, "We had no choice."[36]

The loan was critical to seeing Britain through the immediate postwar years, which, while distressing for the majority of the British population, would have been much harsher without the loan and other smaller ones which followed. While the terms (i.e., fifty years at 2 percent with a right to postpone payment in times of financial crisis) were not as soft as those for which the British had hoped, they were generous by any fair measure. What was unfortunate was the unseemliness of the debate, which demonstrated a renewed and growing friction between the wartime allies.

The biggest problem with the loan agreement lay in its insistence that Britain undertake Sterling convertibility, as laid out in the Bretton Woods agreements, at the earliest possible date. The British were reluctant to enact this particular facet of the agreement until assured of a sizeable American loan. Originally, they had claimed they would need $8 billion and then a minimum of $5 billion to undertake the measure, which was sure to cause an immediate run on their reserves. The loan was for far less than they thought necessary, but the need for an immediate cash infusion was so great that they agreed to hasten plans to enact Sterling convertibility. The result was the 1947 Sterling Crisis, which wiped out Britain's foreign currency reserves in a few months and came close to destroying the British economy.

MARSHALL PLAN: THE GENESIS

By this time, though, there were new players on the diplomatic scene. Truman and Vinson had removed White from the Treasury. The latter would

---

[34] Richard Gardner, *Sterling-Dollar Diplomacy* (New York, 1969), p. 253.
[35] Congressional Record, 82nd Congress, 2nd Session, p. 681.
[36] Gardner, *Sterling-Dollar Diplomacy*, p. 251.

soon find himself under investigation as a Soviet agent. He would die (an apparent suicide) in 1948, the day before he was to appear before a congressional committee investigating Soviet spying in the United States. Keynes, in ill health for some time, had used up his last reserves of strength in securing the best terms possible for the British loan. He died in April 1946. It was now time for an unlikely new hero to step onto the stage: William L. Clayton.

As discussed previously, Clayton had played a major role in achieving the British loan. It was definitely not a role to which he was born. In fact, Clayton, a Mississippi native, was born into poverty in 1880. By dint of his own brilliance and a capacity for hard work, he had become a self-made millionaire before the First World War and even richer by the time he had gone to work in the state department for a dollar a year during the Second World War. During the war, his principal job had been to keep critical commodities away from the Axis powers. Deploying all the tricks he had learned in commodities trading, he directed the "Warehouse War," a major American effort to locate and stockpile key raw materials, thereby denying their access to Germany and Japan. Clayton and a cadre of young aides from the financial world borrowed, cajoled, and stole graphite, rubber, and tungsten from sources close to the enemy.[37]

As the war entered its closing days, Clayton redirected his energies to peace. In this regard, he worked under two bedrock principles that he considered a requirement for future global and American prosperity: free trade and the rapid reconstruction of Europe. What made his plans possible was that by 1947, the state department was under the dynamic leadership of the former Army Chief of Staff, General George C. Marshall. Thus, State had again taken a firm hold over foreign policy, which Morgenthau's treasury had so long dominated. More important, the state department and the country in general were awakening to the growing Soviet threat to international peace and stability. Making full use of the state department's renewed status and the high regard in which Marshall held him, Clayton became the catalyst for both the Marshall Plan and the General Agreement on Tariffs and Trade (GATT).

In the early months of 1947, Clayton turned his duties of coordinating the Truman Doctrine's military aid to Greece and Turkey over to Dean Acheson and began planning for what the Truman Doctrine meant to the broader European context. In a memorandum to Marshall aimed at providing an oral briefing for the president, Clayton argued that military aid was only a start. It was an essential stopgap to halt Soviet encroachment in Greece and Turkey. Nevertheless, the United States would have to broaden it into

---

[37] Gregory Fossedal, "A Modest Magician: Will Clayton and the Rebuilding of Europe," *Foreign Affairs*, May/June 1997.

a more ambitious program to spark a general European economic recovery. This memorandum also outlined the two critical principles that made the Marshall Plan acceptable to Europe and accounted for its success: (1) any country desiring aid would have to set its internal economic affairs in order; and (2) the Europeans would have to develop plans for how they were going to use the U.S. funds provided.[38]

Soon after the memorandum's completion, Truman sent Clayton to Europe to begin negotiations for the GATT as well as to assess the continent's economic condition and financial needs. This led to a second memorandum in May that galvanized Marshall and the president. Two paragraphs provide a taste of the whole:

The European Crisis

It is now obvious that we grossly underestimated the destruction to the European economy by the war. We understood the physical destruction, but we failed to take fully into account the effects of economic dislocation on production – nationalization of industries, drastic land reform, severance of long-standing commercial ties, disappearance of private commercial firms through death or loss of capital, etc., etc. . . .

Europe is steadily deteriorating. The political position reflects the economic. One political crisis after another merely denotes the existence of grave economic distress. Millions of people in the cities are slowly starving. More consumer goods and restored confidence in the local currency are absolutely essential if the peasant is again to supply food in normal quantities to the cities. (French grain acreage running 20–25% under prewar, collection of production very unsatisfactory – much of the grain is fed to cattle. The modern system of division of labor has almost broken down in Europe.)

Furthermore, Clayton noted, "Without further prompt and substantial aid from the United States, economic, social, and political disintegration will overwhelm Europe."[39]

On his return to the United States, Clayton became the catalyst behind the planning group that formulated the basic ideas Marshall was to announce to the world in his famous speech at Harvard. Though Marshall gave just the briefest outline of the plan that would bear his name, he had thrown into the political arena the basic concept for the most far-reaching and important element of the postwar economic settlement. It was now up to the Europeans to seize the moment.

---

[38]   David Reynolds, "The European Response: Primacy of Politics," *Foreign Affairs*, May/June 1997.

[39]   Fossedal, "A Modest Magician: Will Clayton and the Rebuilding of Europe."

EUROPE IN NEED

By the time Marshall gave his Harvard speech, Europe was quite different than what it had been shortly before and not at all what America expected in the war's immediate aftermath. The continent was just beginning to dig out from the worst winter in a century. Because rail lines had frozen, coal piled up at mine heads as most of Britain shivered, while General Lucius Clay announced that Germany's situation was "truly appalling." Economically, there was one great deficiency of which American diplomats were slow to take note. Europe was suffering from a severe dollar shortage and, unless diminished, this dollar gap would prevent the continental nations from purchasing raw materials and other American goods necessary for their own reconstruction. Put another way, the Marshall Plan would not only help save Europe, it would also be good for American business.

By 1947, the United States was also coming to grips with the emergence of the Cold War. Particularly disturbing was the leftward tilt of politics in many Western nations. Almost all of Europe was under the pervasive influence of socialist ideology, while the Communist parties had made serious inroads in both France and Italy. As one commentator noted, "No one in Washington in May 1947 feared the imminent arrival of Soviet tanks in Paris or Rome. But, as George Kennan's Policy Planning Staff had pointed out, 'economic maladjustment . . . makes European society vulnerable to exploitation by any and all totalitarian movements.'"[40] In other words, a hungry, suffering electorate might vote Communist governments into power. The Marshall Plan, wrote Kennan in December 1947, "would be an effective tool in the strategy of containment."[41]

Besides the real possibility of losing France and Italy to the Communists, American European diplomacy found itself plagued by the fact that the "special relationship with Britain had reached a low ebb." As Roy Jenkins has noted,

> To American leaders, the British appeared tiresomely sensitive as they clung, with increasing difficulty, to their status as a great power. Britain refused to fall in line with American foreign policy, and the rift between the countries grew over relations with the Soviet Union. First Franklin Roosevelt and then Harry Truman sought to avoid appearing closer to Winston Churchill than to Joseph Stalin. Although the American government's position would soon change, it was initially more hopeful of Soviet cooperation than were either Tory or Labour leaders. When Churchill delivered his "iron curtain" speech in

---

[40] Diane B. Kunz, "The Marshall Plan Reconsidered: A Complex of Motives," *Foreign Affairs*, May/June 1997.
[41] Ibid.

March 1946, Truman was less enthusiastic about it than were the Labour Prime Minister Clement Attlee and Foreign Secretary Ernest Bevin. And a week later, Secretary of State James Byrnes offered the hardly heartwarming comment that the United States was no more interested in an alliance with Britain against the Soviet Union than in an alliance with the Soviet Union against Britain. Such an even-handed approach would have been unthinkable under the team of Marshall and Dean Acheson.[42]

In fact, Washington had dealt Britain's new Labour government three severe blows in the war's immediate aftermath. First was Truman's halt of Lend Lease only a week after Japan's surrender – a measure undertaken without prior consultation with the British. This was almost immediately followed by British disappointment over not being able to secure the terms or size of the postwar loan they desired. Finally, the United States ceased to share information with the British on nuclear-weapons development. The only reason there were no public recriminations over the latter, which could easily have ruptured cordial relations, was that Britain was too dependent on America. As David Reynolds reminds us, "Atlee was not the kind of prime minister to indulge in luxuries he could not afford." Thus, the Marshall Plan represented a first and major step to transforming the Anglo-American relationship while also reversing the tide of communism throughout Western Europe.

It had been Clayton's idea that the actual implementation of the Marshall Plan had to come from Europe and not America. It was Marshall, however, who added an important political refinement: America would offer aid to all of Europe, not just Western Europe. If Europe were to become divided, it must be done – and seen to be done – by Moscow and not Washington. The Soviets came to the initial Paris meeting and allowed their satellites to attend as well. But, once there, they made it clear they would delightedly receive American money but only on a bilateral basis and without any commitment to economic coordination. When the Americans refused those terms, the Soviets withdrew and took their seven Eastern European satellites with them. Marshall's calculated risk had come off.[43]

EUROPE REACTS

British Foreign Secretary Bevin was the first to realize the importance of Marshall's Harvard speech. Because it had been deliberately vague so as not to attract immediate criticism from Truman's political opponents, most cabinet members had not thought the speech amounted to much. Bevin, ignoring the reluctance of his fellow Labour politicians, went to the floor of

---

[42] Reynolds, "The European Response: Primacy of Politics."
[43] Ibid.

Parliament and explained, "It is up to us to tell them what we want; it is up to us to produce a plan."[44]

Almost immediately afterwards, Bevin flew to France to meet with the French Foreign Minister, Georges Bidault. Together, Britain and France called for a grand meeting with their counterparts throughout Europe, to be held in Paris. Both countries knew that to satisfy American requirements, they needed an integrated European plan. Nevertheless, they determined to stay in charge of the process. To assist them, Marshall dispatched Clayton as his representative and, though the latter stayed well in the background, he was a constant guiding influence on the final plan.

When the Europeans finally came together, Britain's and France's bid to remain in control of the process inevitably led to friction with several other nations, each of which wanted their own objectives firmly integrated into the final plan. It soon became apparent that among the sixteen nations present, there were sixteen ideas on how to implement the plan. Furthermore, the economic information required to judge Europe's financial requirements did not exist. The big nations found it extremely difficult to analyze their own economies, but the small countries found the task almost impossible. Reynolds relates the following story:

> Sophisticated governments found the questions challenging; for the others, the task was pure guesswork. A British official, Eric Roll, remembered finding a Greek delegate still at his desk one night at 2 a.m., laboriously filling out the questionnaires. Roll told him that these should have been sent home. "You don't really think that anybody in Athens will know anything about this," the Greek official replied scornfully. "I can just invent the figures myself."[45]

Despite these difficulties, the Europeans met their early-September deadline and produced a requirements document, which asked the Americans for $28 billion over four years. It fell to Clayton to tell them that there was no chance that Congress would approve such an astronomical figure and that Washington would not be happy with what amounted to sixteen separate shopping lists. When the Europeans remained stubborn and refused to alter their report, Clayton stormed out of a meeting, leaving a clear message for the Europeans: fix it or lose it. Realizing that Clayton was serious, the Europeans engaged in a series of frantic negotiations that reduced their requirements to $19.2 billion while also offering up platitudes on reducing trade barriers and establishing a permanent organization to further European economic integration. The Europeans had done their part. The ball was back in America's court.

---

[44] Kunz, "The Marshall Plan Reconsidered: A Complex of Motives."
[45] Reynolds, "The European Response: Primacy of Politics."

At first, there was scant support in Congress for such a massive grant. For Americans today, used to astronomical budgets, $19 billion to rescue Western Europe seems a trivial amount. To understand the magnitude of the commitment, one needs to understand that as a percent of gross national product, it would take $400 billion in today's money to equal the Marshall Plan. As a percentage of the then-federal budget, the number is even greater: $850 billion. For months, the bill languished, despite ferocious debate. And then the Soviet-supported coup in Prague by Communist stooges resulted in a rapid and radical shift in American public opinion. Eleven months after the Marshall Plan's first proposal, Congress approved a grant of more than $17 billion, with a first year tranche of $5.4 billion.

THE MARSHALL PLAN RESULTS

The first impact of the Marshall Plan was political and not economic. Almost immediately, the Communist tide in France and Italy receded and, though socialist policies remained popular for decades to come, the Marshall Plan helped to curb some socialist excesses. As Reynolds again recounts:

> The primary impact of Marshall [Plan] aid was not economic or institutional but political. Europe's economies would have recovered from the war regardless. But to cover the dollar gap, imports would have been reduced and deflationary pressures imposed. The Marshall Plan was, therefore, vital politically because it promoted growth without depressing wages. All such reasoning is necessarily counterfactual, but it is reasonable to posit that continued austerity and dislocation would have increased alienation and the appeal of extremism. In the early 1930s the right had benefited from Europe's economic troubles; in 1947 it would be the communist left which benefited, particularly in the key countries of France and Italy. From this standpoint, the Marshall Plan was more important than Marshall aid. The promise of American aid helped persuade the center-left in both of these countries to break with the communists and, in France's case, with Soviet foreign policy. Given America's isolationist record before 1939, a dramatic offer was necessary before the cautious and skeptical Europeans would embark on a gamble that went against their postwar swing to the left.[46]

While Reynolds is right in his focus on the political effects of the Marshall Plan, he shortchanges the economic impact. The years of the Marshall Plan (1948–1952) saw the fastest period of economic growth in European history. In just four years, industrial production increased by more than a third and agricultural production grew by almost a half. By the plan's midpoint, Western European nations had surpassed their prewar levels. With the dollar gap removed, Europeans could buy American agricultural products in

[46] Ibid.

1948 and 1949 that in one stroke eliminated food shortages, which had persisted through wide swathes of Western Europe after the war. For the first time, German workers could purchase sufficient food to rise above star-vation levels. This jumpstart provided the catalyst for almost a generation of unparalleled economic growth throughout Western Europe.

It has become commonplace for historians to claim that the Marshall Plan's economic impact was insignificant. The basic claim is that a Euro-pean recovery was already under way and it could probably have sustained itself even without American aid. Like many plausible theories, there is a grain of truth in the argument because economies do possess a considerable ability to repair themselves over time. After all, Eastern European economies eventually repaired themselves and began to grow, despite COMCON (the Soviet answer to the Marshall Plan) being just one more way for the Soviet Union to appropriate the wealth of those nations it had conquered. One needs to understand, however, that without the Marshall Plan, Western Europe's rate of growth would have been closer to its Eastern European neighbors, with all that would have entailed for the standard of living.

> In the first two years of the program, American aid provided a major share of German and Italian gross capital formation; then it fell, as in Britain and France, to a much smaller share. In quantitative terms, Europeans were soon accumulating their own capital. Nonetheless, Washington's assistance satisfied key needs and was targeted to eliminate critical shortages. Assistance in dollars allowed Europeans to invest without trying to remedy their balance of payments drastically through deflation and austerity. This meant that economic recovery did not have to be financed out of general wage levels. Working-class voters (at least outside France and Italy, where strong Communist political cultures still thrived) could thus be rallied by politicians who offered gradualist social-democratic alternatives and remained friendly to the West.[47]

In addition to its direct economic impact, the Marshall Plan acted on West-ern Europe's economic psychology. It assured Europeans that America was behind them and made it possible for them to take economic risks they would never have been willing to undertake if they had had only their own resources on which to rely. In effect, America provided a form of economic insurance for Western Europe, which allowed the Europeans to take risks that, if they paid off, would accelerate economic growth. Marshall Plan aid was, in fact, seed money for the expansion of the European economy. It paid for many of the infrastructure projects, which governments worrying about finding cash for food to feed their populations could not have funded. The

---

[47] Charles Maier, "From Plan to Practice: From an address presented at Harvard University," found at http://209.85.165.104/search?q=cache:pvK2QiiTfKQJ:www.harvardmag.com/mj97/marshall.plan.html+,+American+aid+provided+a+major+share+of+German+and+Italian+gross+capital+formation&hl=en&ct=clnk&cd=1&gl=us.

massive American commitment embodied in the plan did not only affect European psychology. It also worked on Wall Street. The Marshall Plan convinced American bankers that Europe would recover and was likely to do so more quickly. Almost overnight, Europeans and European firms went from being doubtful credit risks to investment-grade risks. In an instant, the floodgates opened and Europe was awash with private investment capital.

Churchill may have called Lend Lease the "most unsordid act," but any fair observer would agree that the Marshall Plan more truly lived up to this title. Marshall later received the Nobel Peace Prize for his part in the endeavor. However, Clayton resigned from the state department and quietly slid out of the limelight. He was to go on earning millions in private business but, unlike so many of his contemporaries, he never called attention to his own part in the economic rebuilding of the postwar world. The man's anonymity barely cloaks the figure of a courageous individual's contribution to Europe's recovery.

12

Ending the Cold War

FREDERICK W. KAGAN

The end of the Cold War was a miraculous event. The struggle had lasted for forty-five years, embraced every continent, and seen the mobilization of tens of millions of soldiers, tens of thousands of nuclear weapons, and uncountable billions of dollars. Nevertheless, it concluded swiftly, peacefully, and, most important, without direct military conflict between the two principal belligerents. Such a denouement is virtually unprecedented in the history of great power rivalries. Athens and Sparta, France and England, the Habsburgs and the Bourbons, Austria and Prussia, Germany and France (and Britain and Russia) – all of these long-standing rivalries and many more led to major military conflict at least once and often many times. The peaceful resolution of the Cold War was amazing and unique.[1]

The leaders of the two belligerent states deserve the praise of history for bringing about such an improbable ending. Yet, the resulting peace, thus far, has suited neither side well. The United States, of course, benefited economically and socially from the end of the Cold War on a grand scale, but American foreign policy rapidly spiraled into confusion and disarray. New threats came to the fore as the Soviet Union left the scene, and the

---

[1] One could quibble about its uniqueness, of course. The Anglo-American rivalry saw no military conflict after the War of 1812 and ended peacefully at the close of the nineteenth century. The Franco-British rivalry continued peacefully but earnestly after the Napoleonic Wars and it, too, saw no direct military conflict after 1815. It is a fact, however, that France and Britain had fought many times over the centuries before finding a means of peaceful coexistence (in nearly the Leninist sense) and that Britain and the United States fought two significant conflicts (at least from the American perspective) before coming to their senses. American and Soviet conventional forces tangled directly only once: when the United States sent troops to Russia at the close of the First World War as part of an allied effort to shore up the failing Provisional Government of Alexander Kerenskii, and in Vietnam, that trivial encounter can hardly be called a war.

United States found itself unprepared to think about them coherently or to deal with them effectively.

The post–Cold War peace has proven even more unsatisfactory for the Russians. They have seen political benefits in the form of democracy and economic benefits, admittedly spread unevenly across the country. But they have also watched the nearly complete collapse of Russia's traditional position as a great power, the breakup not only of the Soviet Empire but even of the historic Russian state, the destruction of many Soviet and Russian allies around the world, and now the unraveling of the democratic process that was their major reward for such sacrifices. Why has the peaceful conclusion of a conflict that had seemed destined to destroy the world proven so unsatisfying to the states that brought it about? Why has it led to yet another period of conflict, war, and death that bids fair to last as long and to be as destructive as the Cold War itself? As the United States contemplates the best way of ending the current struggle, both globally and regionally, its statesmen would do well to ponder the reasons for the failure of its last such effort.

The post–Cold War peace has proven unsatisfactory for four main reasons. First, it ended when the Soviet Union unexpectedly collapsed from its own internal problems rather than because the United States had seized control of the situation either militarily or politically. Second, the Cold War delayed the final denouement of the Second World War. The leaders who ended it, therefore, became preoccupied with resolving past conflicts rather than with shaping the future. Third, the Cold War had trained two generations of leaders to see the world in a simplistic manner not well suited to the challenges of the post–Cold War world. And, finally, the apparent simplicity of the conflict's end concealed the deeper complexities involved in building a new international order.

EVALUATING THE COLD WAR'S END

It is not yet possible to write the definitive history of the Cold War's end. The collapse of the Soviet Union occurred only sixteen years ago, and the future of the Russian state remains in doubt. If Vladimir Putin succeeds in his apparent aim of destroying Russian democracy, then the end of the Cold War will come to seem a transition from one set of hostilities to another between Russia and the West. There is much evidence that this process is already under way.[2] If Putin somehow fails, however, and democracy finally triumphs in Russia, then the end of the Cold War will appear historically as an epochal turning point. In either case, historians a century from now will

---

[2] Leon Aron, "What Does Putin Want?" *Commentary Magazine,* December 2006.

trace the roots of the future development of Russia and the world back to the fashion in which the Cold War ended, often by focusing on developments that now seem unimportant while ignoring factors that seem critical to us. This is the fate of any major historical event, but it is particularly apropos in this case study.

There is, nevertheless, already scholarly consensus about the most salient aspects of the Cold War's end, and most of the remaining academic controversy is of little importance to this chapter. Scholars now argue about the relative importance of structural factors, such as economic stagnation or social mobilization, and individual leaders, ideologies, or events. A flood of data from Russian and Western archives and memoirs makes possible endless scholarly debate over the precise course and significance of many particular events, ranging from the important to the inconsequential.[3]

Since the debate between structuralists and particularists in Soviet history reflects a fundamental division within the academic community, it is unlikely ever to find resolution. And since to an observer outside that debate it seems clear that the end resulted from structural *as well as* contingent circumstances, continued academic arguments about the primacy of one or the other seems unlikely to help in understanding the actual course of events. The flood of data and the ensuing controversies, moreover, represent a mixed blessing.[4] We have infinitely more accuracy about minor events of the Cold War than we ever had before – but that does not make them any more significant. Historians working diligently through this mass of data may add resolution but are unlikely to change the overall view of events substantially.[5]

---

[3] Two solid overviews of the basic history of the collapse of the Soviet Union are Don Oberdorfer, *The Turn: From the Cold War to a New Era, the United States and the Soviet Union 1983–1990* (New York, 1991); and Raymond Garthoff, *The Great Transition: American-Soviet Relations and the End of the Cold War* (Washington, DC, 1994). Olav Njølstad, ed., *The Last Decade of the Cold War: From Conflict Escalation to Conflict Transformation* (New York, 2004), provides an excellent survey of the various efforts at explaining the process. Leon Aron, "The 'Mystery' of the Soviet Collapse," *Journal of Democracy*, April 2006, considers the structuralist explanations for the failure of the Soviet state and their limitations. Extensive information from the Soviet archives has been reproduced by the Cold War International History Project (http://cwihp.si.edu), and information from American archives is now available at the Digital National Security Archive project (https://nsarchive.chadwyck.com) as well as at the Mt. Holyoke College collection (http://www.mtholyoke.edu/acad/intrel/coldwar.htm). Many of the key players on both sides have published memoirs.
[4] Njølstad, *The Last Decade of the Cold War*, p. 22, citing Westad, *Reviewing the Cold War*.
[5] We must also keep in mind that the Russians have never completely opened the Soviet archives. Although the Cold War International History Project and other similar efforts have produced amazing and valuable information from what the Russians have released, important gaps and distortions remain. Given Putin's attitudes toward both freedom of information and the West, moreover, it is unlikely that these gaps will be filled any time soon. Our understanding of the Soviet Union, though far better than it ever has been before,

WHY THE COLD WAR ENDED

Of great importance in considering why the Cold War has resulted in an unsatisfactory peace is the fact that the struggle ended because the Soviet Union collapsed unexpectedly. Presidents Ronald Reagan and George H. W. Bush both pursued policies designed to conclude the Cold War quickly and on their terms – but those terms always included a strong Soviet Union on the other side. American policy makers did not think about or prepare for a world of unipolarity because the collapse of the Soviet Union was unthinkable until it happened. By then, the United States had launched into management of an increasingly chaotic world, which it had little intellectual basis for comprehending.

The end of the Cold War began the day after Christmas 1979 when Soviet troops invaded Afghanistan. The event did not seem at the time to betoken a rapid end of hostilities. The Soviet invasion demolished President Jimmy Carter's policy of détente, which had aimed at reducing tensions by negotiating with the Soviets rather than confronting them. The Carter administration, humiliated by the first overt act of Soviet aggression since the end of the Second World War, immediately launched a major expansion of the American military.[6] This military buildup was already well under way by the time Reagan took office in January 1981, and Reagan only continued and deepened it. Reagan's first term saw the height of Cold War tensions – a period some historians have dubbed "the second Cold War" – and the moments when East and West came closest to war. In the early 1980s, nothing seemed less likely than that the Cold War would end before the decade was out.[7]

The American military buildup was a critical turning point in the Cold War because of the internal dynamics within the Soviet Union. Sharp American observers had long recognized the inherent weaknesses of the Soviet economic system. As early as the late 1940s, George Kennan, author of the containment doctrine that effectively guided American grand strategy through 1981, argued that the internal contradictions of the Soviet state would lead to its collapse if the West applied constant pressure without driving the Soviets to war.[8] By 1981, the Soviet leadership was realizing how right he had been.

---

is and will remain far less complete than our understanding of the West during the Cold War.

[6] Afghanistan was the first time Soviet troops went to war since 1945. They had been used, of course, in the suppression of uprisings in the Warsaw Pact countries many times, but those undertakings saw virtually no major combat and were, in any event, confined to a sphere that the Soviets already clearly controlled.

[7] For the Carter and Reagan buildups, see Frederick W. Kagan, *Finding the Target: The Transformation of American Military Policy* (New York, 2006).

[8] John Lewis Gaddis, *Strategies of Containment, A Critical Appraisal of Postwar National Security* (Oxford, 1982), provides an excellent encapsulation of Kennan's thinking.

The Soviet economic system rested on the rejection of private property. Instead, a "command economy," in which a central planning agency (called GOSPLAN) developed production targets for each industry and even for each factory, attempted to run the economy. There were no market incentives to drive workers, factory managers, or the bureaucrats who oversaw them to be productive, so the Soviet state had to find ways to incentivize them. Joseph Stalin (General Secretary from 1922 to 1953) used mass murder to encourage his subordinates to fulfill their quotas. Deliberately random killing ensured that no one could trust anyone else, which in turn ensured that most people attempted to perform their jobs and reported on their results reasonably accurately.[9]

When Stalin died in 1953, the Politburo (the ruling body of the Communist Party of the Soviet Union and, hence, of the USSR itself) resolved on one thing: There would be no more blood purges. Stalin's successor, Nikita Khrushchev (General Secretary from 1953 to 1964), adopted a different approach. He continually moved mid-level bureaucrats from one part of the Soviet Union's vast territory to another. In this way, he sought to ensure that no cohesive groups developed that would allow managers to make deals with one another at the expense of the state. The bureaucrats who were being shuffled around naturally disliked this system and, when Khrushchev fell from power in 1964, his successor, Leonid Brezhnev (General Secretary from 1964 to 1982), introduced the doctrine of "stability of cadres." His promise to leave bureaucrats in place pleased them to no end while securing his power base. But it destroyed their motivation for honesty and productivity. As a result, Soviet economic performance declined precipitously in the Brezhnev era, which became known as the "era of stagnation," a period marked by outrageous corruption.[10]

In the 1970s, American weakness masked the weaknesses of the Soviet state. In the wake of the Vietnam War and Watergate, the United States retreated into a reactive posture, of which Brezhnev and others took advantage. By the end of the decade, Soviet-backed revolutionaries had seized power in Afghanistan, Nicaragua, and Ethiopia while Cuban fighters were supporting a Communist movement in Angola. The Shah of Iran, America's key Muslim ally in the Middle East, had fallen from power to be replaced by Ayatollah Khomeini, whose followers promptly seized every American in Teheran on whom they could get their hands. American foreign policy seemed in ruins while Soviet foreign policy rose triumphantly.

---

[9] The basic structure and flaws of the Soviet state and attempts to remedy them are condensed cogently in William E. Odom, "The Sources of 'New Thinking' in Soviet Politics," in Njølstad, *The Last Decade of the Cold War*.

[10] See Stephen G. Brooks and William C. Wohlforth, "Economic Constraints and the Turn Towards Superpower Cooperation in the 1980s," in Njølstad, *The Last Decade of the Cold War*, for a fine recent summary of Soviet economic trends and their significance.

Economically, the 1970s also appeared to validate Marx's prediction that capitalism would ultimately collapse under the weight of its own injustice. The Arab oil embargo of 1973 and the consequences of the Vietnam War helped throw the American economy into turmoil. The situation had not improved as the decade closed, and a terrible economic problem, dubbed "stagflation," saw prices rising without economic growth. Jimmy Carter reacted weakly, declaring that America was suffering from "malaise," but seemed unable to develop an alternative.

Even so, a small movement within the Communist Party, nourished by the relative openness of the Khrushchev period, was coming to the conviction that change was necessary. Spearheaded by Yurii Andropov (Chairman of the KGB from 1967 to 1982, then General Secretary from 1982 to 1984), this movement aimed at reforming the Soviet state structure in order to strengthen and perfect communism.[11] As long as America appeared weak and Soviet power seemed to wax, this movement gained little traction. The aftermath of the invasion of Afghanistan, however, tipped the scale.

The Soviets had not sought to install a Communist puppet regime in Kabul in the 1970s, but local Communist leaders had taken the initiative in the Saur (April) Revolution of 1978.[12] Soviet advisers actually worked to slow down the communization that the Afghan government, initially controlled by Nur M. Taraki, wished to impose on the backward and traditionalist country. By 1979, it was clear that the situation was spinning out of control. The Afghan Communist government was fracturing, and Taraki's deputy, Hafizullah Amin, seized power in September, killed Taraki, and even made overtures to the United States (which Carter rebuffed because of Amin's horrific human rights record). Meanwhile, a widespread rebellion against the Afghan Communists and their policies had broken out across the country. Rightly, the Soviets became convinced that Amin's government could not hold the country and, faced with the option of chaos on their border or an attempt to enforce order, they chose the latter.

---

[11] Frederick W. Kagan, "The Secret History of Perestroika," *The National Interest*, Spring 1991.
[12] There are now numerous excellent studies of the Soviet-Afghan War and a great many Soviet documents available from the Cold War International History Project. The most interesting documents showing the Soviet reluctance to become involved militarily and some of the reasons for that involvement include transcripts of Politburo meetings and conversations between Soviet leaders and members of the Afghan Communist government, which may be found at http://www.wilsoncenter.org/index.cfm?topic_id=1409&fuseaction= va2.browse&sort=Collection&item=Soviet%20Invasion%20of%20Afghanistan. Excellent studies of the Soviet-Afghan War are Barnett Rubin, *The Fragmentation of Afghanistan: State Formation and Collapse in the International System* (New Haven, CT, 2002); Antonio Giustozzi, *War, Politics, and Society in Afghanistan, 1978–1992* (London, 2000); and Henry S. Bradsher, *Afghan Communism and Soviet Intervention* (Oxford, 2000).

When Soviet troops invaded Afghanistan at the end of 1979, they did so in the name of a new puppet government headed by Babrak Karmal. The USSR intended to install Karmal, ensure public order, encourage its new puppet to behave more moderately, and withdraw its forces rapidly. Soviet troops did, indeed, capture and kill Amin and install Karmal, but they proved unable to rein in the growing revolutionary movement that had already begun attacking Taraki's and Amin's Communist governments. By 1982, it was brutally clear the invasion had failed. Karmal's government was wildly unpopular, his armed forces ineffective, and the Soviets trapped in a counter-insurgency they had not expected.

At the same time, America had begun to recover. Its economy emerged from the slump of the 1970s while the Carter–Reagan arms buildup started to show results. Reagan immediately began to pursue a more aggressive foreign policy and promised to deploy new nuclear missiles in Europe despite major European and Soviet resistance. The world situation had changed completely in just a couple of years, and the Soviet Union's problems with its economy came once again to the fore.[13] The U.S. arms buildup, the growing American economy, Reagan's aggressive foreign policy, and the failing war in Afghanistan forced Soviet leaders to reflect on their weaknesses. When Brezhnev died in 1982, the Politburo chose Andropov to succeed him with a mandate for change. Andropov began immediately attacking the most obvious problems in Soviet society, beginning with an anti-alcoholism campaign. However, he quickly fell ill and had little chance to carry through any coherent program.[14]

Nevertheless, his tenure as General Secretary saw the height of Cold War danger. Reagan proceeded with the deployment of missiles in Europe in the face of a determined Soviet diplomatic effort to stop him – and America's success seemed a clear Soviet defeat. The American invasion of Grenada in 1983 (largely a hostage-rescue operation that almost incidentally overthrew the Communist regime) was yet another Reagan triumph over Andropov. Reagan's announcement that he would develop an antiballistic missile (ABM) system, finally, threatened the Soviet advantage in strategic nuclear warheads obtained only recently and at great cost. The crisis came when a Korean Airlines 747 accidentally crossed into Soviet airspace on August 31, 1983. The Soviet air defense network launched an interceptor jet to observe the 747 and, ultimately, shoot it down, killing all 269 aboard. Reagan's reaction was, in the end, moderate, but Andropov panicked. Apparently, the Soviets feared the "renegade" American president would launch a nuclear strike in retaliation for the atrocity (which the Soviets denied having

---

[13] Oberdorfer, *The Turn*; and Garthoff, *The Great Transition*.
[14] Kagan, "The Secret History of Perestroika."

committed, making the crisis even worse). The Kremlin, therefore, appears to have started preparations for a preemptive strike on its own. Reason ultimately prevailed, but both sides were shaken.[15]

Andropov died the following year and his successor, Konstantin Chernenko (General Secretary from 1984 to 1985), was old, ill, and almost senile. It is still not clear why the leadership selected Chernenko at such a critical moment, but it seems likely to have resulted from factional Politburo politics. Chernenko had close connections to Brezhnev and the "Brezhnev mafia," his most loyal servants and associates. Andropov's chosen successor, Mikhail Gorbachev, was not part of that mafia any more than Andropov had been, and it seems that the mafia retained sufficient strength in 1984 to see their last aged leader to the throne. However that may be, Chernenko died the following year, and the Politburo chose Gorbachev (General Secretary from 1985 to 1991) by a single vote.

Gorbachev had been part of Andropov's circle and immediately surrounded himself with Andropov's most reform-minded associates. He began his tenure somewhat tentatively, appropriately enough with another anti-alcoholism campaign that generated more amusing stories than progress.[16] But he soon moved on to more dramatic efforts at reform.[17] Gorbachev, like Andropov and his circle before him, recognized the dilemma that Brezhnev's doctrine of "stability of cadres" had caused. Bureaucrats at all levels had come to know and trust their counterparts and come to terms with them. Since there was no market incentive for them to be productive or honest, they were neither. The Soviet economy continued its collapse. Worse still, because the unproductive managers had made deals with those who had

---

[15]   This event is narrated vividly in Oberdorfer, *The Turn*, pp. 49ff. It is told from the perspective of the Soviet double-agent who helped avert an escalation of the conflict in Oleg Gordievsky and Christopher Andrew, *KGB: The Inside Story of Its Foreign Operations from Lenin to Gorbachev* (New York, 1990).

[16]   Russians, who love a good tale, claim that as Gorbachev restricted the sale of vodka in Soviet stores, supplies of sugar immediately disappeared – enterprising Soviets were distilling their own alcohol. Gorbachev began to ration sugar, whereupon supplies of jam and preserves started to disappear, Russians being endlessly inventive in the pursuit of alcohol. Whatever the truth of these stories, the anti-alcoholism campaign made little dent on the Soviet economy or Russian drinking habits.

[17]   The literature on Gorbachev and his associates is voluminous. The events of his accession and immediate actions are narrated accurately in Oberdorfer, *The Turn: From the Cold War to a New Era*, and from various perspectives in Njølstad, *The Last Decade of the Cold War*. A critical compilation of the thoughts of the reformers is Iu. N. Afans'ev, ed., *Inogo ne dano* (Moscow, 1988). Gorbachev's original exposition of his aims and programs is laid out in *Perestroika: New Thinking for Our Country and the World* (London, 1988). He has also published his memoirs and additional commentary on the period of his premiership. Among the most important revealing memoirs about the roots of perestroika are Georgii Arbatov, *The System: An Insider's Life in Soviet Politics* (New York, 1992); and Fedor Burlatskii, *Novoe myshleniia: Dielogi I suzhdeniia o technologicheskoi revoliutsii I nashikh reformakh* (Moscow, 1989) and *Vozhdi I sovetniki: o Khrushcheve, Andropove, I ne tol'ko o nick* (Moscow, 1990).

the responsibility to check and report on their productivity, the central state apparatus could not even obtain accurate records of what was happening in the economy. A centralized planning system cannot long survive if most of the reports from the factories are fiction. Gorbachev could not even find out reliably whom to fire.

He hit upon a two-pronged solution. He would conduct a reorganization (*perestroika*) of the Russian state that would make the bottom more responsive and responsible to the top. To do so, he would reintroduce the Leninist concept of openness (*glasnost'*). By granting greater freedom to the Soviet media, Gorbachev believed that the public and the press would report on the scandalous behavior of bureaucrats and managers. He would then not only be able to discover whom to fire but would also have created a socially acceptable way to incentivize key economic players.

It is clear Gorbachev did not foresee the consequences. The media did, indeed, at first report on economic malfeasance, but it rapidly turned its attention elsewhere. The war in Afghanistan attracted increasing scrutiny and even outright opposition – something almost unheard of in previous decades. Determined to maintain the reform momentum, Gorbachev handled the opposition more gently than previous leaders would have done. He also permitted the media to continue its reporting on the war, which became more scathing and detailed every year.[18] He may not have been too displeased with this coverage since he had decided, virtually on taking office, to extricate the Soviet Union from its quagmire, but the coverage and the opposition turned a defeat into an abject humiliation at home and abroad.[19]

Another unintended consequence of *glasnost'* was the collapse of the Soviet empire in Eastern Europe. The collapse began early in the 1980s when the Solidarity trade union challenged the Polish Communist regime. Brezhnev had naturally supported his client, and General Wojchiech Jaruzelski ultimately put down the troubles. But a watershed had passed as the Soviet leadership decided that it would not use its forces against the Polish opposition, even if things started to get out of hand.[20] The increasing openness of Soviet society in the late 1980s, the defeat in Afghanistan (Gorbachev announced the beginning of the Soviet withdrawal in 1988 and its completion in 1989, well ahead of schedule), and, above all, the general

---

[18] This media scrutiny produced some impressive journalistic accounts of Soviet combat and Soviet soldiers, including Artem Borovik, *The Hidden War: A Russian Journalist's Account of the Soviet War in Afghanistan* (London, 1991).

[19] The process of disengagement is described in great and fascinating detail by the Soviet military commander who led the "limited contingent" of Soviet forces in Afghanistan (the Soviet name for their occupation army) out of the country in 1989: Boris Gromov, *Ogranichennyi kontingent* (Moscow, 1994). It is also described in Tom Rogers, *The Soviet Withdrawal from Afghanistan: Analysis and Chronology* (Westport, 1992).

[20] Brooks and Wohlforth, "Economic Constraints," in Njølstad, *The Last Decade of the Cold War*, p. 99.

introversion of the Soviet state, encouraged a renewal of separatist movements in Eastern Europe. Starting in 1988, the Communist-client governments of Poland, Czechoslovakia, Hungary, East Germany, Bulgaria, and
Rumania came under increasing pressure to reform. They were less skillful
at adapting to the new realities than Gorbachev and his team and, by 1989,
all had fallen. And the Germans had torn down the Berlin Wall, symbol of
the Iron Curtain and their division.

Gorbachev took virtually no significant action as all this was going on,
partly because he wanted the East European clients to reform themselves,
partly because of his preoccupation with internal Russian issues, partly
for fear of jeopardizing his relationship with the West, but mostly because
the idea of using military force to suppress the peaceful revolutions was
unthinkable. For one thing, we must give Gorbachev his due. Almost every
time he confronted the choice between losing control and committing some
military atrocity, he chose the humane course. His rhetoric about changing
Soviet values was more than just rhetoric.

But Gorbachev had already overseen a fundamental change in Soviet attitudes toward war and the use of force by 1989 as well, which would have
made large-scale military suppression of Eastern European separatist movements extraordinarily difficult. Soviet military strategy from the foundation
of the state had proceeded from an ideological premise. Since the aim of communism was the destruction of private property and the capitalist states that
relied on it, those states would necessarily oppose and attempt to destroy
the Soviet Union. The encircling capitalist powers would probably concert
their attacks, moreover, since they all actively engaged in a conspiracy to
oppress the working classes. The USSR, therefore, had to be prepared to
fight the entire capitalist world all at once, and its military policy reflected
that determination.[21]

The age of nuclear weapons did little to change this attitude. Stalin and
his military leaders saw little difference between the atomic weapons of their
day and the effects of thousand-bomber conventional raids (most probably
because they did not understand the consequences of nuclear fallout and
radiation effects). However, as weapons became more powerful and then
it became possible to mount nuclear warheads on intercontinental ballistic
missiles, the Soviets were impressed not with the danger of nuclear war
but with the prospect of achieving a victory over the capitalist states in a
single apocalyptic strike. Western confidence in the 1960s that the Soviets
accepted the "unwinnability" of nuclear war was misplaced. Throughout
the 1960s and 1970s, the Soviets pursued a nuclear advantage with the
expectation that attaining it would allow them to triumph in a global war, if

---

[21]   An excellent and brief overview of Soviet strategic thinking is in Andrei Kokoshin, *Soviet
       Strategic Thought, 1917–1991* (Cambridge, MA, 1998).

one became necessary. They also maintained a massive conventional-forces establishment designed to repel and destroy every potential threat to the Soviet Union – all at the same time. It was this requirement that led to the massive military expenditures that ultimately bankrupted the inefficient Soviet economy.

By the late 1970s, however, Soviet military leaders had begun to question the validity of their various strategies.[22] The conviction that the Soviet Union could win a full nuclear exchange in a meaningful way began to erode, and support for the continued dramatic expansion of the nuclear arsenal started to wane. By the time Gorbachev took power, top Soviet military leaders widely accepted his assertion that nuclear war was not a usable tool of any rational policy. They also understood that the Soviet economy in its current condition could no longer support armed forces designed to defeat the entire world – but apparently unable to defeat even the *mujahideen* in Afghanistan.

In this sense, Gorbachev's announcement of a new military strategy in 1988 was the culmination of a line of thinking within the military that had been germinating for some time. The Soviet Union, he declared, would no longer prepare to overwhelm all potential enemies but rather would seek instead "reasonable sufficiency" designed to protect itself against likely combinations of foes.[23] The initial public focus of reasonable sufficiency was on the Soviet nuclear forces. Gorbachev, like his predecessors, deeply feared the development of an American ABM system. Such a system would require the Soviets to invest massively either to match it or build sufficiently numerous nuclear-attack systems to overwhelm it. Preoccupied with the inability of the Soviet economy to do either, Gorbachev made every effort to stop the American system.[24]

He therefore began to propose a series of nuclear-reduction agreements, all of which favored the United States heavily – but all of which required the abandonment of the American A.B.M. system. "Reasonable sufficiency" was the doctrinal justification for this approach, but the threat of the U.S. defensive system was the real catalyst. Reagan and Bush consistently refused to trade the ABM system even for dramatic arms-control agreements, and Gorbachev ultimately surrendered. By the end of the 1980s, saving money and maintaining a positive relationship with the United States was more important to him than winning the ABM battle.

But, by 1988, Gorbachev had extended reasonable sufficiency to cover the Soviet conventional forces as well. Given the state of the Soviet economy, this

---

[22] Ibid.
[23] The concept of "reasonable sufficiency" is described in R. Hyland Phillips and Jeffrey Sands, "Reasonable Sufficiency and Soviet Conventional Defense," *International Security*, vol. 13, no. 2 (Autumn, 1988), pp. 164–78.
[24] Oberdorfer, *The Turn: From the Cold War to a New Era*, narrates these negotiations accurately and in great detail.

was an inevitable step. Conventional forces are considerably more expensive than nuclear forces and represent the area of defense where the Soviet Union could make real savings most rapidly. Applying his new military doctrine in the name of saving the Soviet economy, Gorbachev announced a series of unilateral reductions in the Soviet troop deployment in Eastern Europe beginning in 1989.

These actions naturally destroyed Soviet leverage in Eastern Europe and complicated any thought about using military force to support the Communist satellite states. Any such action would have destroyed relations with the West, led to large-scale military conflict within the failing Soviet Empire, and cost a fortune that Gorbachev was not prepared to spend. Nor was it clear that the Soviet Union could prevail except by a massive mobilization that was, in the context, unthinkable. Finally, Gorbachev did not want to reimpose Communist dictators on the people of Eastern Europe. The originator of "reform communism" at home, he wanted the Communist states of Eastern Europe to reform as well. If they did not, and the Soviet Union allowed them to persist unreformed supported by Russian bayonets, then the USSR would have to take on full responsibility for maintaining them indefinitely. The military burden would have been exorbitant but the economic burden incalculable. As the Soviets pointed out to one another in the late 1980s, the Soviet Union could not take responsibility for Eastern Europe's massive debt or for the continued inefficiencies of its satellite economies.[25] Military suppression and political tutelage were not real policy options for Moscow in 1989.

Gorbachev had not expected to face this dilemma because he had not understood the secondary and tertiary effects of his programs in the satellite states. The peaceful revolutions in those states occurred rapidly and with little warning. They quickly reached a stage at which only the use of massive Soviet military force could have reversed them. The dynamics of the situation within the USSR and between the Soviet Union and the West, however, ruled out any such use of force. That is how the Soviet Union lost its Empire without firing a shot forty-five years after it had seized it in bloody battle.

UNFINISHED BUSINESS

Since Gorbachev lost his empire and the Cold War unintentionally, it is not surprising that the Soviet Union failed to set the terms of the ensuing peace to its advantage. But American strategy in the 1980s had aimed at inducing precisely such a peaceful collapse. The success of that strategy came as something of a surprise, but the Bush administration reacted reasonably

---

[25] Brooks and Wohlforth, "Economic Constraints," in Njølstad, *The Last Decade of the Cold War*, p. 100.

well to the changes of 1988 and 1989, including the Warsaw Pact's collapse. Western policy then became confused, however. Before the conclusion of the Cold War, it was necessary to conclude the Second World War. That process was inherently backward-looking, requiring resolution of disputes which in some cases were fifty years old and distracted attention from developing a clear vision of the post–Cold War world.

The Second World War did not end in 1945. The fighting may have ceased then, to be sure, and the belligerents demobilized their armies (to greater or lesser degrees), but no formal set of peace treaties normalized international relations or even established fixed borders for the European states. The Soviets held informal command over the countries their armed forces occupied at the end of hostilities: Poland, Czechoslovakia, Hungary, Bulgaria, and Rumania.[26] The victors initially divided Germany into four occupation zones (i.e., American, Soviet, British, and French). With no formal peace treaty in sight, the Western Powers amalgamated their zones into the Federal Republic of Germany (West Germany), which they occupied, now as protectors. They formed the North Atlantic Treaty Organization (NATO) in 1948, and the Federal Republic became a member in 1955. The Soviets, for their part, continued to occupy East Germany, which they rechristened the German Democratic Republic. In 1955, as a response to NATO, they formed the Warsaw Treaty Organization (commonly known as the Warsaw Pact), with East Germany as a prominent member of that alliance.[27]

No power recognized the formal division of Germany, even though NATO troops occupied one part and Soviet troops the other. The United States even refused to recognize the Soviet Union's incorporation of Lithuania, Latvia, and Estonia – the result of the Molotov–Ribbentrop Pact of 1939 that led to the German invasion of Poland and the start of the Second World War. Still less did it formally recognize Soviet control of Eastern Europe, although every American administration faced with the dilemma of supporting an Eastern European uprising against the Soviets responded by allowing the Soviets to crush their rebellious satellites.[28]

The collapse of the Soviet empire in Eastern Europe led immediately to the question: Would Germany reunite? In retrospect, the answer was obvious. The Germans insisted on it, and the use of force could only have prevented it, which neither the Soviets nor the Western Powers were willing to contemplate. The details of unification were nevertheless contentious. American

---

[26] Soviet armies also occupied most of Austria, but that country was first divided into occupation zones and then granted its formal independence in 1955 on the basis of strict neutrality between East and West.

[27] See Gaddis, *Strategies of Containment*, for a discussion of the debates about the formation of NATO and Germany's role in it.

[28] As they did: East Germany in 1953; Hungary in 1956; Czechoslovakia in 1968; and Poland in 1981.

troops remained on West German soil and West Germany remained part of NATO. What would happen to East Germany? Would NATO advance to the Oder? Would the Western Powers occupy military positions on the Polish frontier?[29]

Many Soviet leaders, particularly in the military, were aghast at such prospects. West Germany was a powerful state in its own right. Reunited with East Germany, it would be still more powerful. Marshal Sergei Akhromeev, Chief of the Soviet General Staff until 1988 and thereafter Gorbachev's principal military adviser, was sufficiently old to have fought the Germans in the Second World War, a conflict that had cost the Soviets upwards of 20 million dead and had ravaged every major Soviet city west of Stalingrad. The prospect of re-creating the German state that had launched that war was distressing – the idea of seeing such a state entirely within NATO was terrifying. Some Soviet leaders saw in Gorbachev's acceptance of reunification the ultimate betrayal.

The problem of reunification was no less complex in the West. The French and the British had also suffered immensely from German aggression in both world wars and remained uncomfortable about the idea of a revived German state. They believed that a continued American military presence in Germany was an important guarantor of European peace, and they lobbied vigorously for inclusion of the unified German state into the NATO alliance.

Since that result was also the preference of German leaders and since the Soviets were unwilling to contemplate using force, the outcome was never really in doubt. But the diplomatic complexities of the situation consumed much of Bush's time and energy, distracting him from developing a real understanding of what was going on within the Soviet Union or from thinking about what the postwar world would look like. Thus, the great powers of 1990 found themselves preoccupied with resolving the problems of 1945.

AMERICA'S WAR AIMS

The distraction of resolving fifty-year-old conflicts was, in some respects, welcome to the Bush administration because it had developed no clear idea of how it aimed to shape the post–Cold War world. That failure of imagination stemmed in part from a failure of American strategists ever to develop a coherent image of what the postwar world should be – in other words, a failure to establish clear and meaningful war aims.

America's aims in the Cold War, such as they were, remained remarkably stable from start to finish. The principal grand strategists of the 1940s – George Kennan, Paul Nitze, and others – agreed that the ideal ending would

---

[29]   Oberdorfer, *The Turn*; Garthoff, *The Great Transition*. See also George H. W. Bush and Brent Scowcroft, *A World Transformed* (New York: Knopf, 1998).

be the collapse of communism and the return of the Soviet Union and its satellite states to the fold of Western liberal capitalism. The United States never had territorial *desiderata* in this conflict and remained content to allow the European states to retain their 1945 borders (with the exception of Germany, which would be reunited, and the Baltic States, whose independence from the Soviet Union was a consistent, if minor, war aim).[30]

Conservative as they were, these aims did not constitute support for any *status quo ante* settlement. The Second World War had dramatically changed the power relationships among the United States, the Soviet Union, Japan, and Europe. The two superpowers on Europe's fringes had gained enormous strength relative to the traditional great powers of Central and Western Europe, and American war aims would not have restored that balance (although Kennan argued unsuccessfully that the United States should help the Europeans try to do so).[31] The transformation of the Soviet Union into a liberal capitalist state, moreover, would almost certainly have reduced its relative military power as well: Soviet military strength, after all, flowed primarily from distortions in the Soviet economy, which depended on totalitarian government and central economic control. The net result of American war aims from the start of the Cold War, therefore, was likely to be American global hegemony of one sort or another.

However, few American thinkers took that prospect seriously before 1990 because it seemed so unattainable. Hardened by civil war, purges, and the Nazi invasion, the Soviets seemed unlikely to collapse on their own accord. Nor was any responsible American leader willing to contemplate a military attack on the Soviets or their allies as a way of hastening that collapse. The West, therefore, adopted a doctrine known as "containment." Spelled out most articulately by Kennan, this doctrine presumed that if the West simply prevented the Soviets from expanding their sphere of control and applied the appropriate nonmilitary pressures to the inherently weak Soviet state, that state would ultimately fail through its own dysfunctional nature. Containment defined American grand strategy from about 1947 to 1981, when Reagan took office.[32]

In contrast to the stability of its grand strategy overall, the military policy of the United States during the Cold War suffered from considerable incoherence. The Soviet Union was consistently willing to spend a considerably higher proportion of its national wealth and demand greater sacrifices for military purposes than was the United States. At the same time,

---

[30] The best narrative of American strategy during the Cold War remains Gaddis, *Strategies of Containment*. Essential documents about American strategy in this period are Kennan's speeches and NSC-68.

[31] See Gaddis, *Strategies of Containment*, for a detailed exposition of Kennan's arguments about the need for an independent Europe.

[32] X [Kennan], "Sources of Soviet Conduct," and NSC-68.

although basic Soviet scientific research was sometimes outstanding, Soviet engineering was generally years and often decades behind that of the West. The resulting balance of military force was predictable: The Soviets maintained vast conventional armed forces, including a multimillion-man conscript army, while they built tens of thousands of technically unimpressive aircraft, tanks, and nuclear delivery systems. The West, by contrast, maintained much smaller conventional forces armed with increasingly sophisticated weapons and relied on its nuclear deterrent to keep the peace.

U.S. nuclear strategy went through many iterations between the development of the first atomic weapons and the 1960s, when it finally settled into a consistent line of thought.[33] At first, many both within and outside the military regarded the use of atomic weapons in war as appropriate and even necessary – General Douglas MacArthur strongly urged their use against China during the Korean War, for example. But nuclear theorists, mostly civilians, who developed America's nuclear strategy in the 1950s and 1960s, came to a different conclusion. They believed nuclear war was inherently unwinnable because of the enormous casualties both sides would inevitably sustain. The purpose of nuclear weapons, in their view, was to deter America's opponents from their use: thus, the doctrine of Mutual Assured Destruction (or MAD).

The idea behind MAD was simple. If both sides knew the use of nuclear weapons would lead to annihilation, then neither side would ever use them. Under no circumstances, the MAD theorists argued, should either side seek an "advantage" in nuclear weapons that might theoretically permit a "successful" strike – the mere belief on either side in such an advantage would lead to Armageddon. From this conviction sprang the corollary that defensive systems meant to disrupt an enemy's attack were destabilizing – the enemy confronting such systems would come to fear that he would lose the deterrent value of his strategic nuclear forces and so be tempted to strike preemptively before that happened. The nuclear theorists imagined that these conclusions were obvious to any sane person examining this situation and, consequently, that the Soviets must share them. The soundness of the MAD doctrine, in fact, rested on that conviction.

If the Soviets had accepted the premise that nuclear war was inherently unwinnable (as they did not into the 1980s), then this doctrine was appropriate for the limited aim of preventing nuclear war. The trouble was that the West always relied on its nuclear systems to do more than prevent nuclear war. It also relied on nuclear weapons to prevent conventional war.

Because the Western states refused to devote sufficient resources to their conventional militaries to have confidence in defeating the Warsaw Pact

---

[33] Marc Trachtenberg, "The First Generation of Nuclear Theorists," in *War and Politics*; Lawrence Freedman, *The Evolution of Nuclear Strategy* (New York, 2003).

in conventional war, they relied on the threat of an overwhelming nuclear strike to deter the Soviets from contemplating a conventional attack. For this reason, no American president ever accepted the doctrine of "no first use" of nuclear weapons, despite the emotional and political appeal of such a doctrine. "No first use" meant the West would possess no ability to deter Soviet aggression in Europe without a drastic increase in conventional forces. The reliance on the American strategic nuclear umbrella was also one of the primary factors for the nervousness which many European leaders exhibited with Gorbachev's initial arms-control proposals in the 1980s. American military strategy during the Cold War was thus schizophrenic. The United States relied on its strategic nuclear weapons to deter conventional war but adopted a nuclear strategy based on the premise that neither side would ever use nuclear weapons – and that both sides were aware of that fact.

Ronald Reagan revolutionized American Cold War grand strategy and military policy.[34] He rejected the fundamental premise of containment. Rather than seeking to prevent the Soviets from expanding their power further, Reagan sought to undermine their control of regions already in their sphere, particularly Afghanistan. At the same time, the prospect of nuclear war and America's reliance on its nuclear arsenal to keep the peace horrified him. He resolved to work toward both the elimination of nuclear weapons and the development of conventional armed forces that could stand up to the Soviets on their own. These beliefs led Reagan to continue the conventional military buildup Carter had begun while ordering work on an ABM system (which he called the Strategic Defense Initiative, or SDI, and his critics immediately dubbed Star Wars).

Both undertakings came under major attacks in the West and the Soviet Union as being destabilizing – in the Soviet Union for reasons we have already seen, and in the West on the grounds that an ABM system would disrupt what Albert Wohlstetter called the delicate balance of terror.[35] Reagan not only persevered but worked more aggressively than any previous American president to attack the Soviet Union directly. He ordered American naval vessels to violate Soviet territorial waters. He sent arms and supplies to the Contra rebels fighting the Soviet-backed Sandinista regime in Nicaragua. And he sent weapons and clandestine CIA agents into Afghanistan to help the *mujahideen* fight the Soviet armies themselves. He also undertook a series of military actions against Soviet client states such as Libya (whose capital he bombed in 1986 in retaliation for a terrorist attack), Grenada (whose

---

[34] Peter Schweizer, *Reagan's War: The Epic Story of His Forty-Year Struggle and Final Triumph over Communism* (New York, 2002); Reagan National Security Strategies (from DNSA); Gaddis, *Strategies of Containment.*

[35] Albert Wohlstetter, "The Delicate Balance of Terror," RAND Report, 1958 (available online at http://www.rand.org/publications/classics/wohlstetter/P1472/P1472.html).

pro-Communist government he overthrew in 1983), and Syria (U.S. forces sent on a peacekeeping mission to Lebanon in 1982–1983, were seen as supporting the Israelis against Syrian-backed Lebanese groups). The deployment of American nuclear missiles to Europe was another bold move in this context. Reagan's rhetoric underlined the change in Washington's basic strategic approach to the Cold War. In 1983, he referred to the Soviet Union as an "evil empire," and in 1984 he joked (into a microphone he supposedly thought was dead), "My fellow Americans, I am pleased to tell you today that I've signed legislation that will outlaw Russia forever. We begin bombing in five minutes."[36] The American counter-offensive was well under way.[37]

Reagan's approach to the Cold War did not extend to a fundamental change in America's war aims, however. He did not mean at any time to attack the Soviet Union directly. He believed rather that the Soviet Union was entering a period of terminal economic decline and that the additional military pressure would hasten its collapse. However, he did not clearly think through what that collapse would look like beyond assuming the Soviets would generally recognize the value of Western-style liberal capitalism and adopt it in some form. He developed no clear vision of what the postwar world would look like and appears to have believed that the reformed Soviet Union would play a large role as the second liberal democratic superpower.

In the early 1980s, all that seemed far off. By the time Gorbachev came to power and convinced the president and some of his advisers that he was serious about transforming the Soviet system, Reagan had focused on the prospect of reducing the threat of nuclear war rather than on creating the conditions for post–Cold War peace. The challenges involved in reducing nuclear arsenals were daunting enough to command the full attention of the president and his advisers. To begin with, Reagan's cabinet was not in accord on the desirability of negotiating for nuclear arms reductions with the Soviets. Secretary of State George Schultz was won over fairly quickly, but Secretary of Defense Casper Weinberger was extremely resistant. In addition, the president was adamant he would not abandon his SDI program, while Gorbachev was adamant he must. This issue disrupted many otherwise cordial meetings and threatened to derail summits and even the disarmament process as a whole. Meanwhile, the European allies were deeply worried by some of Reagan's more radical proposals. Keeping his own team together, in both the cabinet and the alliance, while working with Gorbachev despite the thorny problem of the ABM system represented an enormous

[36]   Oberdorfer, *The Turn: From the Cold War to a New Era*, p. 85.
[37]   Kagan, *Finding the Target*; Daniel P. Bolger, *Americans at War: 1975–1986: An Era of Violent Peace* (Novato, CA, 1988); Benjamin Lambeth, *The Transformation of American Airpower* (Ithaca, NY, 2000).

undertaking. All of this occupied the president fully and distracted him from thinking clearly about what would happen if and when the United States actually won the Cold War, as he had set out to do at the beginning of his term.

THE FALL OF THE SOVIET UNION

The fall of the USSR was as unexpected as the collapse of the Soviet Empire in Eastern Europe. It resulted from a series of unintended consequences of Gorbachev's reforms and from their partial failure. The purpose of *perestroika* had been to revitalize a flagging Soviet economy. Gorbachev meant to use the more open media to reform the political system and thereby break the stranglehold on power and the corruption of the Soviet bureaucracy. By 1989, however, his reforms had only served to lose the Soviet Union its empire without improving the economy. In fact, the Soviet economy began to falter in 1989, and its decline accelerated steadily during the next two years.[38]

Considering the enormous blow to Soviet prestige (and, in the minds of some old-style Soviet leaders, security) and the failure of the reforms to improve the economy, it was not surprising that opposition arose. Gorbachev's erstwhile supporter, Yegor Ligachev, led a conservative group that began to resist further reforms and even attempted a rollback. Worse still from Gorbachev's standpoint, a liberal opposition began to arise as well, which accused him of moving too slowly and having been either captured or bought by the conservatives.

Caught between these two, Gorbachev had little room to maneuver in the face of the challenges that ultimately destroyed the Soviet Union. The nationalist stirrings in Eastern Europe had spread like a cancer to the Soviet Union itself. The USSR was an artificial state formed in 1922 after the Bolsheviks had seized control of most of the territories of the former Russian Empire.[39] It consisted until 1990 of fifteen nominally autonomous republics under the overall guidance of the Soviet Union's Communist Party. The Russian Soviet Federated Socialist Republic (so named because it was itself a conglomerate of different nationalities, some organized into nominally autonomous regions) was by far the largest and most powerful, followed by the Ukrainian, Kazakh, and Belorussian republics. Some republics, like the Baltic states, had been independent before the Second World War. Others, like Ukraine and Belorussia, had never enjoyed statehood. Still others, like

---

[38] Brooks and Wohlforth, "Economic Constraints," in Njølstad, *Last Decade*; Garthoff, *Grand Transition*; Oberdorfer, *The Turn*; Bush and Scowcroft, *World Transformed.*
[39] See Richard Pipes, *The Formation of the Soviet Union*, for a detailed history of how the USSR came into being.

Georgia, Armenia, and Kazakhstan, could look back to more distant periods of autonomy. As the Eastern European empires collapsed and Gorbachev's reforms began to falter, nationalist stirrings grew.

The first clashes between Soviet power and the independence movements naturally arose in those republics with the most vivid memories of their autonomous past. The Soviet military brutally put down a rebellion in the Georgian Republic in 1989. Peaceful movements toward independence in the Baltic states led to tentative Soviet moves toward repression in 1989 and 1990 – and then a significant military occupation, including confrontations with civilians and civilian casualties, in early 1991.

The trajectory of this process was by no means clear. By 1990, it was obvious that the Baltic states would sooner or later regain their independence, and Moldavia (which renamed itself Moldova in a sign of linguistic autonomy) showed a similar if slightly weaker determination to abandon the union. But most other areas of the empire, including Ukraine, Belorussia (soon renamed Belarus), Armenia, and the Muslim republics (the Kazakh, Kirgiz, Tajik, Uzbek, and Turkmen Republics), initially preferred to remain integrated in some sort of federated state.

The key figure in destroying Lenin's state was Boris Yel'tsin. Gorbachev had expelled Yel'tsin from his positions in the Communist Party of the Soviet Union in the winter of 1987–1988 for his too-ferocious attack on the conservative opposition's leader, Yegor Ligachev.[40] By 1989, however, Yel'tsin had emerged as a key figure in the Russian Republic and in 1990 he became its president.[41] From the outset of his second rise to power, Yel'tsin had naturally challenged Gorbachev, championed the rights of the breakaway Baltic Republics, and worked to establish an independent power base in Russia even as Gorbachev attempted to retain centralized Soviet control. Conflict between the two was inevitable. Gorbachev had first to weaken the Soviet Communist Party and then remove it from power entirely in order to secure his own position against conservatives within the party. Gorbachev thereby placed himself increasingly at the mercy of a normalizing democratic process. Since his economic reforms were clearly failing, while Yel'tsin promised a more aggressive program of marketization, Gorbachev was nearly certain to lose the struggle unless he was willing to use force to maintain his position – something he steadfastly refused to do.

But the collapse came quickly and unexpectedly as a result of the old guard's last effort to reverse Gorbachev's reforms. In August 1991, a group of leading Soviet officials, including the War Minister, the heads of the KGB and MVD (i.e., internal security services), and other senior leaders attempted to force Gorbachev to seize or grant them emergency powers

---

[40]   Garthoff, *The Great Transition*, p. 324.
[41]   See Leon Aron's biography of Yel'tsin.

during his annual vacation in the Crimea. When he refused, they confined him to house arrest and announced a seizure of power in the name of an emergency committee. A dangerous standoff ensued, as troops initially loyal to the conspirators surrounded Yel'tsin's government in the Moscow parliament building (known as the White House). But the troops lost their will as their leaders dithered, and the siege dissolved. Yel'tsin's deputy, Alexander Rutskoi, led an armed team down to the Crimea and rescued Gorbachev.[42]

In the process, Yel'tsin moved quickly to seize the levers of power in Moscow, in the name of the Russian Federation. Initially, his justification was the need to preserve the Soviet people from conservatives who were attempting to seize power, but his own seizure of power continued even after the coup had collapsed and its leaders were under arrest. When Gorbachev arrived back in Moscow, he found Yel'tsin firmly in control. By the end of the year, the Communist Party had been banned, the Russian Federation had declared its independence, and the Soviet Union had ceased to exist.

The process of reorganizing the states of what became known as the "former Soviet Union" continued over the next several years. An experiment occurred to form some of the newly independent republics into a loose federation called the Commonwealth of Independent States. Conservatives in Moscow made one last attempt at a coup which proved an even greater failure than the first. By the mid-1990s, all meaningful experiments at maintaining a formal confederation of the former Soviet states ended, and the world had accepted the emergence of fifteen new sovereign and independent states, most of them democratic to a greater or lesser degree.

The transitions from Soviet Union to a union treaty among autonomous republics to the Commonwealth of Independent States to a set of completely independent entities occupied the attention of the Bush administration between 1990 and its departure from office in January 1993. Efforts to encourage market reforms and democracy in Russia and the newly independent states continued under Clinton's presidency, although with less emphasis and attention. From the vantage point of sixteen years, the results have proven deeply mixed. Russia's initial promising movement toward democracy and free-market capitalism has been stunted. Yel'tsin's successor, Vladimir Putin, worked assiduously to undermine most aspects, not only of Russia's democratic system but also of the media opening Gorbachev had implemented.[43] Russia's economy is now functioning better than at any time in the last several decades, but corruption remains rampant and market reforms are far from complete. The vision of bringing Russia smoothly into the family of Western-style liberal democracies is clearly faltering.

[42]   Garthoff, *The Great Transition.*
[43]   Aron, "What Does Putin Want?"

The situation in the other republics has proven even more mixed. The Baltic states moved readily to democracy and free-market systems and have now joined NATO. The 2006 NATO summit, in fact, occurred in Riga, the capital of independent Latvia. The Muslim republics have seen more tentative movement toward democracy and market reforms, with Kazakhstan doing fairly well, Turkmenistan poorly, and Kyrgyzstan and Tajikistan unstable. Promising reforms in the Caucasus have also collapsed, in that case into regional conflict made more worrisome because of its spillover into the Russian Caucasus and the vicious war Putin waged against Chechen separatists. Ukraine made its first clear move toward real democracy and a Western orientation during the "Orange Revolution" of 2004, but the subsequent unraveling of that experiment leaves the Ukraine's future in doubt. Belarus remains in the grip of a vicious dictator, who has crushed opposition and is now an international pariah.

The strategic threat of Russia for the United States has virtually ceased. Russia's borders have retreated hundreds of miles from the center of Europe, and Russia's armies can threaten NATO only because of the steady advance of NATO's borders to the East. However, Putin's Russia aspired to the international role of spoiler, resisting American initiatives and derailing them whenever possible, but neither allying with America's enemies nor supporting them in any meaningful way. In this regard, the Cold War was an unqualified victory for the West. Even that victory may evaporate, however, as Russia moves steadily in the direction of an authoritarian and anti-Western state, as Putin appeared to prefer. In that case, it is possible that within a few years or a few decades, a worrisome tension between the West and Russia will again arise.

The United States deserves only partial credit for these successes. The key actors at all times were Russian – primarily Gorbachev and Yel'tsin. They chose policies that led to the collapse of the Soviet Union and the elimination of Russia as a major military player on the international scene. The United States did not force them to make those choices, and American involvement throughout the actual process had only a limited impact. Bush's critics alternately accused him of moving too quickly or too slowly to accept the changes, but in truth it did not matter because he could hardly have affected those changes. The main focus for Reagan and Bush until the Soviet Union's collapse was on not derailing Gorbachev's reforms, not weakening the First Secretary's hold on power, and completing the series of conventional and nuclear arms-control negotiations that were America's primary *desiderata*. These goals aligned reasonably well with Gorbachev's own goals and so contributed to the continuation of his reforms. On the other hand, it is difficult to imagine any American president behaving much differently in the circumstances.

If Russia does, in fact, return to a position of both great power and great hostility toward the West, then the details of its transition to and then subversion of democracy will take on a new significance. The story of the Bush and Clinton administrations' participation in those processes will then require closer examination. From the vantage point of 2007, however, that story is secondary in importance to a more fundamental failure of those administrations to set the conditions of peace: the failure to develop and act on a clear vision of America's role in the post–Cold War world.

NEW WORLD DISORDER

George Bush declared in September 1990 that a "new world order" was dawning, but his administration remained confused about what that new order required of the United States.[44] Statements supporting democratic transitions and gaining "strategic depth" contrasted sharply with steep reductions in American military power and attempts to remain uninvolved in the major crises of the day. Before long, American leaders were declaring that the United States could not be the "world's policeman," and the idea of a "new world order" resting on American strength steadily evaporated.[45]

If the post–Cold War world had been inherently stable or self-regulating, this confusion about American policy would not have mattered so much. But the international configuration of the 1990s was anything but stable. The Cold War had frozen a number of tensions, and Soviet power and desires had kept some rogue states on a leash. The end of East–West tension led, ironically, to a rise in conflict globally, and the American military in the 1990s found itself far busier than it had been since the end of the Vietnam War.

The problem of German unification was only one of the issues the Cold War had submerged and the easiest to resolve, as it turned out. East–West tension had also controlled a number of potential crises around the world. As the Soviet Union collapsed, a number of these crises sprang unexpectedly to life, presenting the United States and its allies with unanticipated challenges for which they were unprepared. The first major crisis of the post–Cold War era actually had relatively little to do with the Soviet Union's collapse. Moscow might have attempted to prevent Saddam Hussein's invasion of Kuwait, had it still been in a position to do so – the invasion and its aftermath would certainly have created an undesirable crisis in East–West relations, if

---

44 Bush's September 1990 speech.
45 See Donald Kagan and Frederick W. Kagan, *While America Sleeps: Self-Delusion, Military Weakness, and the Threat to Peace Today* (New York, 2000) for a discussion of the development of American grand strategy during the Bush and Clinton years.

nothing else. But even at its height in 1980, the Soviet Union either could not or did not wish to prevent the Iran–Iraq war from breaking out. In 1990, it might not have been either willing or able to intercede with its erstwhile client in Baghdad in 1990.[46] The first Gulf War of 1991 is thus more properly considered in the context of the general crisis of the Muslim world that forms the subject of this chapter's final section.

The collapse of Yugoslavia, on the other hand, did result more directly from the end of East–West tensions.[47] The causes of the conflict lay buried in ethnic tensions dating back to the formation of the Yugoslav state after the First World War. The numerically dominant Serbs had always seen Yugoslavia as an expression of their historical ideal of a "greater Serbia." The Second World War, however, had seen the rise to power of a Croat, Josip Broz Tito, who had created a Communist dictatorship that deprived the Serbs of ruling status. His death in 1980 saw the release of pent-up ethnic tensions, which flared in 1989 when a Serb nationalist, Slobodan Milosevic, encouraged attacks on the autonomy of non-Serbian parts of the country. The Yugoslav regions held multiparty elections in 1990, and Milosevic became the Communist leader of Serbia while non-Communists took power in Slovenia and Croatia. In 1991, Yugoslavia's president, a Serb, was due to step down in favor of a Croat, which he refused to do so, sparking the secession of Slovenia and Croatia and Yugoslavia's collapse.

Many of Yugoslavia's regions, however, were ethnically mixed, and the rise in ethnic tensions led to war. The Serbs under Milosevic's guidance undertook large-scale "ethnic cleansing" – campaigns incorporating mass murder and rape designed to drive non-Serbs out of areas Milosevic wanted to control. The other nationalities soon followed with attacks and brutality of their own, though nothing on the same scale.

The rising ethnic violence challenged the United States and its European allies, but no one had a clear idea of how to respond. NATO's founders had not designed that organization for peace-making or peace-keeping operations, and no one had yet developed a clear purpose for the alliance in the post–Cold War world. European leaders, heady with the arrival of peace after five decades of hot and cold war, sought to take the lead in handling the Balkan crisis but discovered they had no tools. There was no European military alliance separate from NATO, and NATO relied on heavy American participation and leadership. On the other hand, Bush and his advisers determined not to be drawn into what promised to be a long and

---

[46]   Gorbachev tried repeatedly to do so, in fact, but he had lost all leverage with Saddam Hussein and his efforts came to nothing.

[47]   See Kagan and Kagan, *While America Sleeps*, for a brief summary and references; also Kagan, *Finding the Target*.

bloody conflict that reminded many of Vietnam. They were eager to let the Europeans take the lead and frustrated when the Europeans found they could not.

Three years of savage ethnic violence ensued. European and UN personnel deployed to mitigate some of the worst suffering, but by 1995 they had become targets and victims of the rising violence. President Bill Clinton became convinced that only American military power could save the UN representatives – as well as the organization's credibility. He decided that if he had to use force, he would not do so defensively, and determined instead to launch an air campaign followed by a land-based peace-keeping mission to put an end to the violence in Bosnia-Herzegovina. By the end of the year, he had done so, and a large joint American–European ground force remained in Bosnia under UN auspices until 2005, when the Europeans assumed control.[48]

A similar reluctance to involve the United States in a humanitarian disaster delayed Bush's response to the politically managed famine that gripped Somalia during his term. By 1992, however, he finally bent to overwhelming political pressure and deployed American forces to that ravaged land, solely for the purpose of relieving the suffering of Somalia's people. However, because some of the Somali warring factions were deliberately managing that suffering for political purposes, American forces quickly came under attack. The response to one such attack in early 1993 led to the disastrous "Black Hawk Down" operation, which culminated with pictures of dead American soldiers being dragged through the streets of Mogadishu broadcast around the world and around the clock. The American forces withdrew and Somalia descended once again into chaos.[49]

These crises epitomized salient facts of the post–Cold War world. The Western states had looked to the United States for leadership and military might for so long that they were unwilling or unable to control the collapse of regions kept peaceful only by the artificial constraints of the Cold War. George Kennan had argued in the 1940s that America should not seek to create a bipolar world, in which a strong United States dominated Western Europe while a powerful Soviet Union controlled the East. Instead, he argued, America should nurture independent centers of power in Europe and Japan, tolerating, even encouraging, their periodic obstruction of American policies in order to support their own confidence and independence. Whether or not this approach was feasible when Kennan proposed it, the United States had taken the opposite tack. America was the dominant

[48] Kagan, *Finding the Target*, for a discussion of the military operation and references.
[49] Mark Bowden, *Black Hawk Down: A Story of Modern War* (New York, 1999), is now the classic narrative.

power in its web of alliances and provided the essential motive force in the Western reaction during almost every crisis.[50] The Soviet Union performed the same role within its alliances. As a result, the end of the Cold War left only one effective prime mover on the scene, but the United States was reluctant to accept that role while the Europeans were reluctant to grant it. As a result, a number of crises emerged and grew into catastrophes before the United States unwillingly and sometimes ineffectively intervened, and the "new world order" began to shift away from America's desired form.

Elements of this shift were predictable. European dependence on the United States was a constant feature of the Cold War – American leaders alternately railed against it and relied on it. For Bush to expect the Europeans suddenly to acquire the will and ability to act decisively without the United States in a conflict that differentially involved the interests of various European states was folly. Nor should it have been a surprise to see Yugoslavia disintegrate and other conflicts, deadened by the Cold War, emerge. The spontaneous uprising of Eastern Europeans was evidence the Cold War settlements imposed there and elsewhere were not stable. Failure to foresee problems in Yugoslavia and around the world reflected a poverty of imagination.

On the other hand, it is important to keep in mind the matter of scale. The collapse of Yugoslavia was dramatic because it occurred in Europe – it was the first sustained, large-scale military conflict on that continent since 1945. But humanitarian crises of greater scales had occurred in Africa and Southeast Asia; India and Pakistan and Israel and the Arabs had fought a series of high- and low-intensity wars; and attempts at genocide had occurred in Nigeria and elsewhere. In almost every case, the Cold War had preoccupied the world's attention and the superpowers had done little except to restrain the winning side from pushing too far, thus destabilizing a delicate balance. That was the world Bush and his advisers had grown up in and the one to which they were accustomed. They were not prepared for a world that expected the United States to use its own force unilaterally to stop crises of this variety. And if the Cold War had still been going strong in 1992–1995, the Bosnian crisis would not have seemed quite so important.

This fact helps explain why the Bush administration either refused to manage the chaotic transition from Cold War to post–Cold War or did so only grudgingly. These inadequate reactions were nevertheless a mistake, and they reflected a deeper problem with America's understanding of the significance of the Cold War's end. For many Americans, the collapse of the Soviet Union and the apparent triumph of democracy across the former Communist lands reflected what Francis Fukuyama called "the end of

---

[50] The Suez Crisis of 1956 being one of the few exceptions.

history." Americans from common folk to congressmen expected the Cold War's demise to usher in a period of peace and prosperity, the maintenance of which would require few sacrifices. The United States reduced its military rapidly and dramatically in the name of a series of "peace dividends." Military planners and analysts spoke of a "strategic pause," in which the United States would face no enemies or major military challenges. An era of irresponsibility had dawned.[51]

The Bush administration attempted to combat this tendency, outlining a new basis for American global strategy in 1992 and 1993. These efforts, overseen primarily by Secretary of Defense Dick Cheney and his staff, aimed at taking advantage of America's uniquely powerful position to gain greater strategic depth. The Regional Defense Strategy, developed in the final months of the administration, foresaw America as a regional balancer, which would defend stability and peace in areas of vital concern to the United States.[52] Cheney resisted excessive cuts in American military power (partly out of a mistrust of the Soviet Union and Russia that proved, at least in the short run, unfounded) but to no avail.

Bush lost the 1992 election because of the apparently parlous state of the economy, and Clinton selected as his first secretary of defense Congressman Les Aspin. Aspin had been Cheney's nemesis as chairman of the House Armed Services Committee with persistent demands for dramatically reduced defense expenditures. Clinton's campaign promise to focus "like a laser beam" on the economy (along with his famous slogan, "It's the Economy, Stupid") boded ill for a proactive American role in the international system. The United States did not, therefore, manage the transition from Cold War to post–Cold War effectively and failed to take advantage of whatever strategic pause there might have been.[53] This failure was not unique. The British had made a similar set of mistakes following the First World War. It was, however, a missed opportunity to create the preconditions for a prolonged peace worthy of the effort America had put into winning the Cold War.

THE THREAT AMERICA MISSED

In the long run, however, it was not the failure to manage the transition from Cold War to peace in Europe that proved so harmful to the United States but rather the failure to recognize the development during the Cold War of a new and potent threat not directly related to the Soviet Union. This failure was understandable, perhaps even inevitable, in the circumstances of

[51] Kagan and Kagan, *While America Sleeps*; Kagan, *Finding the Target*.
[52] Department of Defense, *Regional Defense Strategy*, 1993.
[53] Kagan and Kagan, *While America Sleeps*.

the 1980s, but it nevertheless contributed powerfully to the collapse of the postwar peace that followed the September 11, 2001, attacks against the United States.

America had undertaken a wide variety of military operations during the 1980s: Operation Eagle Claw (Desert One) – the failed hostage-rescue operation in 1980 helped seal Jimmy Carter's electoral fate. The introduction of marine peacekeepers in 1982 into Lebanon led to disaster the following year when a terrorist truck bomb killed 241. American naval aircraft launched a punitive strike against positions in Lebanon and Syria later that year, but it was not terribly successful. The same year saw the spectacular if small-scale invasion of Grenada. In 1985, U.S. naval aircraft forced down an Egyptian airliner carrying the terrorists who had hijacked the cruise ship *Achille Lauro* and killed a wheelchair-bound American citizen. In 1981, American naval aircraft shot down two Libyan fighters over the Gulf of Sidra – the Libyans had attacked after American ships persisted in patrolling within the Gulf of Sidra, which Libyan leader Moammar Qaddafi claimed as Libyan territorial waters.

In 1986, Reagan struck Qaddafi again, this time destroying government targets in downtown Tripoli in retaliation for Qaddafi's support of anti-American terrorism – particularly the bombing of a discotheque in Germany, which U.S. soldiers frequented. The U.S. military was also drawn into the Iran–Iraq war when that conflict expanded to include attacks on oil tankers in the Persian Gulf. The U.S. Navy established patrols (one of which shot down an Iranian airliner by accident) and ultimately reflagged and then escorted Kuwaiti tankers. American support was also essential to the Afghan *mujahideen* and the Nicaraguan Contras. In 1989, American airborne units removed the corrupt government of druglord Manuel Noriega in Panama and arrested Noriega himself. In 1990, U.S. forces deployed to Saudi Arabia in response to Saddam Hussein's invasion of Kuwait.[54]

Almost all of these activities occurred in the Muslim world. Many represented direct responses to anti-American Muslim terrorism or the rise of a theocratic state in Iran (which led to the Iran–Iraq war and U.S. interventions related to that conflict). American support to the *mujahideen* in Afghanistan included assistance to groups like that of Gulbuddin Hekmatyar, a radical Islamist currently leading one of the major revolutionary movements based in Pakistan, seeking to destroy secular democracy in Afghanistan. It strengthened the role of Pakistan's intelligence arm, the ISI, in Afghanistan, which in turn led to increased Pakistani support for the radical Islamist Pashtun movements that would ultimately take power in Afghanistan in 1996. The anti-Soviet coalition in Afghanistan, cobbled together with American

---

[54] Bolger, *Americans at War*; Lambeth, *Transformation of American Airpower*; Kagan, *Finding the Target*.

assistance, included Saudi Arabia and other Arab states, which sent both money and fighters to drive the infidels from Muslim soil – in the process, creating a cadre of experienced and trained radical Islamists, who would prove key to the export of Islamist violence around the world in the 1990s.

The Cold War itself masked the real significance of some of these developments. Libya, Iraq, and Syria (as well as Cuba and Nicaragua) were all Soviet clients. It was easy to see in their actions Soviet efforts to rattle the West rather than autonomous initiatives with a purpose that transcended the Cold War. This effect was particularly pernicious in the area of terrorism because of the fashion in which Americans perceived it in the 1970s and 1980s.

Terrorism is not a phenomenon of the post–Cold War world. American official reports about terrorism in the early 1980s declare that each successive year saw the highest level of terrorist activity yet recorded.[55] Reagan took office with the same sort of harsh rhetoric against terrorism that he aimed at the Soviets, and he reaffirmed that commitment in 1985 and 1986 in dramatic form in both word and deed. But the terrorist threat of that period was quite different from the terrorist threat of today.

In the first place, Muslim terrorism was by no means the only or even the primary terrorist threat. For much of the 1970s and 1980s, there were more terrorist attacks against Americans in Latin America than the Middle East. The threat of Red Brigades in Europe, as well as right-wing groups both at home and abroad, seemed at least as significant as the threat from the Middle East. In particular, the Provisional Irish Republican Army received support from Libya but focused its efforts on attacking British targets. The Basque revolutionary movement ETA attacked the Spanish government on a broad scale. Indigenous terrorist groups attacked France and Germany. Terrorism as a concept had not yet come to be associated with any particular geographical region or group. Still less did it seem the province of radical religious groups since most of the terrorist organizations of the 1980s focused on politics or ideology.[56]

The Reagan administration, therefore, saw them primarily as arms of a revolutionary movement, since their aims seemed to be overthrowing or at least delegitimizing Western governments. Kidnapping was seen to be the most dangerous threat because it was a preferred tool of the terrorists. Kidnapping is ideal for terrorists hoping to embarrass governments because it places tremendous pressure on leaders to act rapidly. The time pressure increases the likelihood that governments will overreact or make

---

[55] For example, CIA, National Foreign Assessment Center, "International Terrorism in 1979" (DNSA, doc. 632) and "Patterns of International Terrorism, 1980" (DNSA).

[56] CIA, National Foreign Assessment Center, "International Terrorism in 1979" (DNSA, doc. 632) and "Patterns of International Terrorism, 1980" (DNSA).

some mistake on which the terrorists can capitalize. Kidnapping also has the advantage of minimizing the loss of life, something that terrorists of the 1970s and early 1980s seemed to prefer.[57] The Reagan administration recognized that airplanes were a likely target for terrorists but at first assumed the method would be a variation on kidnapping: hijacking. It was not until the end of the decade that it became clear that terrorist groups were changing and pursuing the destruction of aircraft as spectacular demonstrations of their power.

The political nature of the terrorists' aims and targets, their apparent self-restraint in methods, and the notion that they were radical arms of revolutionary movements fit easily into a Cold War mindset, which laid the blame for all such activities at the feet of the Soviet Union. The Soviets, after all, maintained training camps in their own territory and elsewhere at which would-be revolutionaries perfected their skills. Some of these skills transferred easily to the execution of terrorist schemes, and so it seemed the Soviets were deliberately fostering a regime of anti-Western terrorism. Others disagreed, noting that the Soviets explicitly rejected terrorism and claimed to oppose it and that there was rarely, if ever, direct evidence the Soviets had knowingly encouraged or assisted with terrorist acts.[58] It was all too easy, nevertheless, to see the broad anti-Western terrorism campaign of the 1980s as a part of the Cold War rather than as a prelude to an entirely different sort of struggle.[59]

This view gained strength from the fact that the Reagan administration saw terrorism as a state-sponsored activity rather than an undertaking of nonstate actors. There was some understanding that terrorist groups themselves were transnational and nonstate actors, and U.S. leaders gave some consideration to identifying and destroying the terror cells themselves, probably with special forces.[60] Reagan, however, did not adopt that approach. He and his advisers preferred to focus on the nation-state support network that sustained such groups. This focus made more sense in light of the nature of the attacks seen as most dangerous: kidnappings. The kidnappers must take their victims somewhere, after all, and that somewhere must be in the territory of some state – often the one that supported them in the first place.

Reagan preferred to simplify the problem of dealing with nebulous enemies by attacking the states that sheltered them. His efforts were not without success – the raid on Tripoli in 1986 led to a dramatic reduction in Libyan support for terrorism. Such an approach did, however, preclude the

---

[57] Brian Michael Jenkins, "Terrorism in the 1980s," DNSA, doc. 646; Allan S. Nanes, "International Terrorism, Updated 6/26/1985," CRS, DNSA doc. 769.
[58] Ibid.
[59] Ibid.; Allan S. Nanes, "International Terrorism, Updated 6/26/1985," CRS, DNSA doc. 769.
[60] "Some Thoughts on Negating Terrorist Organizations," 1985, DNSA, doc. 774.

development of a coherent body of thought about how to deal with the terrorist networks themselves, independent of the states which supported them. It also prevented the Reagan and Bush administrations from understanding the dangers that would arise when terrorists took root in areas with weak or no government, such as in Afghanistan in the 1990s. This trend, combined with a failure to see the significance of the rise in Muslim terrorism and a tendency to identify most Muslim terrorism as having political rather than religious motivation, prevented the Bush administration from developing a clear understanding of the dangers the United States would face in the 1990s.

These problems came home to roost most dramatically in Afghanistan. The last Soviet soldier left Afghanistan in 1989. Most expected the Communist government of Mohammed Najibullah to fall almost immediately, particularly since the Soviets had promised to cut off its aid. In fact, Najibullah hung on until 1992, when his government fell and the country plunged into chaotic civil war. The Bush administration had largely ceased supporting the *mujahideen* factions in Afghanistan when the Soviets left. When Najibullah fell, the United States lost all interest in Afghanistan. In retrospect, this was a terrible mistake. In 1996, a radical Pashtun religious movement, the Taliban, supported by Pakistan and calling for the establishment of a fundamentalist theocracy on the Iranian model, seized power in Kabul and began extending its control of the country. Its principal adversary was a group of northern, mostly Tajik, tribes led by Ahmad Shah Masoud, one of America's key allies in the war against the Soviets. But the United States failed to support Masoud, who lost control of most of the country. By September 2001, his "northern alliance" controlled only a small portion of the north, and the Taliban assassinated him the day before the September 11 attacks.

The Bush administration would have been hard-pressed to aid the *mujahideen* significantly after 1989, let alone to manipulate their factional politics in the face of large-scale Pakistani efforts to do so. Gorbachev had repeatedly attempted to extract a promise that Bush would not aid the Afghan rebels if the Soviets withdrew, and even though Bush steadfastly refused to give such a commitment, continuing large-scale aid would have undermined the East–West relationship. By 1992, however, the Soviet Union had fallen, and Russia no longer had a border with Afghanistan or any basis to claim direct interest.[61] If the United States had understood the growing and changing nature of the threat of radical Islam in the 1980s, it would have been clear that America had a large stake in who won the ensuing civil war. The fact that U.S. leaders had entirely missed the development of this threat, largely through a series of category errors, meant that the Bush

---

[61] Afghanistan now borders the three independent former Soviet states of Turkmenistan, Tajikistan, and Kyrgyzstan.

and Clinton administrations missed a critical series of opportunities to prevent the establishment of conditions that would facilitate the September 11, attacks. In other words, in this critical area, the fashion in which the United States concluded the Cold War dramatically increased the likelihood that a rising new threat would shatter the postwar peace.

CONCLUSION

This chapter emphasized the degree to which America's victory in the Cold War resulted from Soviet mistakes rather than from deliberate U.S. actions. That fact helps explain the unsatisfactory nature of the ensuing peace. Such conclusions to major wars are not all that common in modern history. Some conflicts end when all of the major belligerents become too exhausted to continue the fight (e.g., the Thirty Years' War, the War of the Spanish Succession, the Frederician Wars). They are normally followed by lengthy pauses, often decades-long, during which no power feels strong enough to attempt again to solve the unresolved tensions and conflicts. Other wars end with the victor physically in control of the territory of the defeated (e.g., the Napoleonic Wars, the Wars of German Unification, the American Civil War, and the Second World War). Such resolutions are often stable because the triumphant state must decide clearly what it wants and then impose that solution on its defeated foe.

The only modern war whose ending parallels that of the Cold War in any meaningful way was the First World War. Although by 1918 the Allies had demonstrated the will and the ability to dictate the peace, the German Empire surrendered before they were in a position to do so. The inter-allied tensions and general exhaustion that gripped the Allies after 1918 prevented them from developing a clear vision of what the postwar world should look like and, even more, from attempting to impose and maintain it. As a result, they handled the chaos that developed around the world after 1918 badly, and even the peace with Germany (along with German democracy) soon collapsed.

Like British Prime Minister David Lloyd George in 1918, George H. W. Bush and Bill Clinton sought to make America "a land fit for heroes to live in." The end of the Cold War seemed to them and to many others to have ushered in a prolonged period of peace and democratic triumph, which most thought would proceed with little or no active assistance from the United States and its allies. But the almost accidental ending of the Cold War left the United States in positive control of little of the international situation. America had not dictated a peace in Moscow but rather had steadily accepted a series of *de facto* steps the Russians proposed. The United States attempted to give control of Europe to the Europeans and only grudgingly took up the obligations of leadership when the Europeans failed to exercise any responsibility even in their own backyard. America developed no coherent program for the Middle East, despite the fact that the first Gulf War had fundamentally changed the situation in that vital region. And Iraq in 1991 reflected all of the flaws of the larger global settlement reflected in miniature: The end of the war came at a point when coalition forces had accomplished only some of Bush's objectives, the United States was not physically in control of Iraq, and the United States and its allies could only maintain the ensuing peace through continued, active engagement over a sustained period of time.

American presidents from Reagan through Clinton did not behave particularly badly. They reacted as democratically elected politicians would normally respond to such circumstances. That reflection is not comforting in light of the events of September 11, and what followed, however. Democratic leaders faced with incomplete successes often fail to think through the longer term consequences of establishing an inadequate peace. Pressures to return to an internal focus, to pull back from international engagements, and to reallocate resources to domestic priorities often overwhelm deeper grand strategic calculations. Such pressures can be even greater after major foreign-policy failures, as America's experience in the 1970s shows. The end of the Cold War, therefore, merits study not simply because it laid the foundation for the crisis facing the United States in the aftermath of September 11, 2001. It is also an object lesson in the perils of allowing events to guide policies rather than insisting on policies that can guide events.

13

Conclusion: history and the making of peace

RICHARD HART SINNREICH

In a fascinating book, first published in 1973, that received too little attention, Australian economic historian, Geoffrey Blainey, examined various theories advanced in the past to explain how wars begin and why they end. Most, he found, fail historical confirmation. The one consistent pattern emerging from his research was that armed conflict ensued when antagonists disagreed about their relative strength and ended only with the resolution of that disagreement. "War," he concluded wryly, "is a dispute about measurement."[1]

Of course, it is much more than that. The timeless motives of "fear, honor, and interest" described so eloquently by Professor Gray's analysis of the Cold War also animated in differing measure every other conflict discussed in this book. But in one way, at least, those conflicts also tend to verify Blainey's conclusion, for they suggest that a settlement that fails in a convincing way to resolve the question of relative power tends merely to invite another war. The well-known Clausewitzian admonition that statesmen and generals should never allow war to dictate its own logic must thus be reconciled with the need to achieve a settlement that is not only politically acceptable but strategically durable as well.

The issue of durability, however, inevitably introduces definitional problems. What does it mean to speak of a durable peace? How peaceful must it be? How long must it endure? To these questions there can be no unqualified answer, but any reasonable operational definition certainly would exclude continuous war and might even go so far as to insist that the same generation not confront the same enemy twice. The century of relative European peace that followed Napoleon's defeat in 1815 satisfied those conditions.

---

[1] Geoffrey Blainey, *The Causes of War* (third edition) (New York, 1988), p. 114.

The bare twenty years that followed the defeat of Germany in 1918 did not. Historians have often unfavorably contrasted the respective settlements by suggesting by implication that the statesmen who assembled at Versailles in 1919 missed something obvious, at least to their predecessors a century earlier in Vienna.[2]

But the undoubted difference in outcomes may have been less attributable to the terms of settlement than to the military circumstances in which they were reached. As the chapter on the Congress of Vienna suggests, in 1815, the allies were poised to destroy the French state utterly and evinced every intention of doing so unless the perceived agent of their distress was permanently removed. In contrast, as the chapter on Versailles suggests, the armistice of 1918 found German armies still on French soil, and the subsequent settlement did nothing to diminish German military arrogance and its pernicious influence on their ambitions.

So too was the situation with the Iraqi Army in 1991, permitted to retain significant offensive power, physically humiliated but morally unimpaired, and retaining undiminished loyalty to a despot who already had demonstrated more than once his contempt of Western resolve. Nor, until 2003, did events offer Saddam Hussein any real reason to believe his contempt was misplaced. On the contrary, the intervening twelve years saw the Gulf coalition collapse, support of continued economic and military sanctions against Iraq evaporate, and, until the attacks of September 11, 2001, American domestic support for further military action Iraq erode.

All of which simply confirms that the challenge of forging an enduring peace is, or at least should be, a central ingredient of the business of planning, fighting, and winning a war. Given that in post medieval Europe alone, war somewhere on some scale has erupted on average every fifteen years or so, it is apparent that not many belligerents throughout history have successfully reconciled these clearly interdependent requirements.

Indeed, perhaps the most disturbing possibility suggested by the cases discussed in this book, and by the historical record generally, is that, as Professor Murray proposes in his introductory chapter, disciplining the conduct of war by the peace it is intended to secure tends to be foreclosed by the modern propensity to view war as an extraordinary event and peace the secular condition. As Professor Rahe explains in his discussion of the Peace of Nicias, the ancients labored under no such misapprehension. "War for the Greeks," he notes, "was a constant presence, an ineluctable brute fact,

---

[2] In fact, the British government, at least, made a deliberate effort to consult the Vienna settlement, commissioning one of its senior diplomats to research it. Eventually published as *The Congress of Vienna* (cited fully in chapter 4), the result since has become one of the standard references on the settlement, although it appears to have had little if any impact on Britain's negotiating posture at Versailles.

one they simply took for granted.... Greek cities, when they made a treaty
of peace, ordinarily confined it to a limited span of years. They knew better
than to think that it would last much more than a generation, and they
usually recognized that even this was a pious hope."

There certainly have been periods in the past when for portions of humanity, at least, something approaching enduring peace prevailed: in the Roman
and Ottoman empires at apogee, in China during the middle dynasties, perhaps in India under the Mughals in the seventeenth and early eighteenth
centuries. As Professor Murray points out, in each case, the prerequisite was
a ruling power so predominant militarily that challenging it was literally
unthinkable.

Absent imperial hegemony, however, mankind's recorded history reveals
nearly continuous violent conflict, interrupted only episodically by military
peace and quiet. Even Americans, who flatter themselves that they are a
peace-loving people, might be astonished to be reminded that the United
States has found itself at war during roughly 60 of its 232 years, or a little
more than one year out of every four. Over time, moreover, the frequency
of U.S. military engagement has increased. During its first 115 years of
independence, America endured only 24 years of war. During the second
115, that number nearly doubled, even excluding such largely forgotten
episodes as the suppression of China's Boxer Rebellion; the turn-of-the-
century "banana" wars in Central and South America; and more recent
military interventions in the Dominican Republic, Grenada, and Panama.

Notwithstanding that bellicose experience, Americans today almost uniformly reject the possibility that war might be more than an unwelcome
and too often unnecessary interruption of normality. In former Secretary of
State Henry Kissinger's words, "Trusting in the rule of law, [America] has
found it difficult to reconcile its faith in peaceful change with the historical
fact that almost all significant changes in history have involved violence and
upheaval."[3]

That refusal to acknowledge peace as an extraordinary condition powerfully influences not only America's but also virtually all other Western
societies' approach to the making of peace and its maintenance. To suggest
only one implication, no Western government maintains a peace department
or ministry. None develops, formally at least, a peace budget. And while virtually all governments educate and train professional warriors, none makes
a concerted effort to educate or train professional peacemakers.

The view that war is an aberration also strongly influences the settlement
process. As several of the cases discussed in this book reveal, postwar settlements tend more often than not to focus on preventing recurrence of the

---

[3] Henry Kissinger, *Diplomacy* (New York, 1994), p. 55.

condition or conditions that prompted the late war rather than on regulating the new challenges presented by its outcome. One can overstate this problem, as Professor Gray rightly warns. Not all postwar challenges are foreseeable, let alone preventable. "The focus on 'making peace,'" he notes, "risks isolating and overemphasizing the importance of dedicated peacemaking. It suggests that the roots of the next war lie in the fashion in which states concluded the previous one and in the arrangements made for the postwar settlement. That suggestion is not wrong, but it overreaches." Moreover, as Professor Gooch reminds us in his dissection of Great Britain's efforts to stabilize the Middle East in the wake of the Ottoman Empire's dissolution, "[S]ooner or later the currents of history . . . undermine every such construction."

Both limited foresight and history's inherent contingency certainly are valid obstacles to even the most conscientious statesmen's ability to achieve an enduring peace. That acknowledged, however, the fact remains that treating peace as a self-evidently desirable and thus largely self-sustaining condition virtually invites the sort of disappointment and disillusionment that has afflicted so many postwar settlements.

Finally, one other result of viewing peace as "normal" – and the central justification for this volume – is the persistent failure to accord the business of making and keeping peace the same rigorous scholarly attention as the unhappily more absorbing business of war making. Diplomatic historians, it is true, have described, often with great perspicacity, the decisions and actions by which governments through the centuries have attempted to avoid, defer, or, at worst, confine the effects of war, efforts that have informed many of the chapters in this book. But no Clausewitz has ever dissected the strategy and tactics of peace making. No Jomini has advanced peace-making principles analogous to the time-honored Principles of War. No Mahan has ever catalogued the influence of peace making on history.

When, therefore, Professor Murray comments that "the vast differences in the context within which wars have ended make it almost impossible to develop a realistic theory [of peace making]," he no more than reflects the historical record. Indeed, as Sir Michael Howard points out in the preface, there is not even uniform agreement on how one might define peace: whether simply as the momentary absence of war, as the by-product of an international order satisfying some normative theological or ideological criterion, or as a sociologically unnatural condition, which thus requires deliberate creation and can survive only through constant and painstaking attention.

Perhaps reflecting to some extent that intellectual indecision, however, one can infer the outlines of at least three distinguishable theories concerning the ingredients of enduring peace from the cases described in this book. These do not necessarily conflate comfortably with the "realist/idealist" bifurcation beloved of students of international relations. On the contrary, each in its own way claims to reflect a realistic appraisal of human behavior. Each, however, grounds the maintenance of peace in different prerequisite conditions. Each approaches the peace-making processes differently. And each is vulnerable to different intrinsic dangers. As a rough shorthand, one might label these competing theories *universal governance, strategic equilibrium,* and *progressive democratization.*

The first has been, by far, the most enduring. Explaining in Chapter 3 why the Peace of Westphalia in 1648 represented such a revolutionary diplomatic departure, Professors Croxton and Parker note that "Traditionally, those who wrote on international relations in Europe viewed the existence of multiple, competing powers as undesirable. Their ideal was a single, unified empire ruled by a Christian monarch, who maintained peace and justice in all of Christendom." Not surprisingly, given France's central role in forging that settlement, some continued to doubt her own willingness to relinquish that ideal as late as a century later. Thus, writing of the 1763 Peace of Paris, Professor Anderson notes that in the view of at least some Britons, "[B]ecause the roots of [France's] power had not been destroyed, nothing could prevent it from resuming its quest for universal monarchy."

But even if among most European statesmen the Christian ideal of a single imperial sovereign perished at Westphalia, a more secular vision of universal governance informed by an agreed conception of how the world should be ordered certainly did not and, for many, still has not. Instead, resigning itself to a world of fragmented sovereignty, that vision has reemerged in repeated attempts to regulate international – and, occasionally, even domestic – political violence collectively. In the nineteenth century, it took the form first of Czar Alexander's Holy Alliance, which helped Europe evade great power conflict for four decades, and later, of Bismarck's *Drei–Kaiser Bund,* to which Professor Jones in Chapter 7 attributes similar influence following the Franco-Prussian War of 1870–1871. In the twentieth century, it reappeared first in the League of Nations and subsequently in the United Nations, the latter chartered not just to prevent war but also "to reaffirm faith in fundamental human rights, in the dignity and worth of the human person, in the equal rights of men and women and of nations large and small."[4]

Like its imperial antecedents, collective governance sought to impose some form of universal discipline on an international community believed in its absence to be incurably anarchic. Lacking the unchallenged dominion of an Augustan Rome or Ming China, however, efforts through concerted international action to approximate universal governance presumed the existence

[4] Preamble to the Charter of the United Nations (http://www.un.org/aboutun/charter/). One can imagine how nineteenth-century diplomats such as Metternich, Castlereagh, and Talleyrand would have reacted to this language.

of a sociopolitical value system sufficiently uniform, at least among the major military powers, to override competing particular interests in favor of suppressing more fundamental threats to the prevailing order.

As the chapter on the Congress of Vienna explains, in early nineteenth-century Europe, fears of a resurgent France and autocratic resistance to emerging political pluralism furnished just such a common cause. The former disappeared with Bonaparte's death and France's reintegration into Europe's cabinet diplomacy, however, while the latter survived only until exploding nationalism, Britain's retreat into "splendid isolation," and fading memories of the evils of total war demolished the political consensus that had restrained, if not altogether suppressed, continental military ambitions for nearly a century.

In the twentieth century, attempts to enforce collective universal governance collapsed much more abruptly. As Professor Murray points out, by the time the First World War's victorious Allies assembled at Versailles in January 1919, "the framework of international diplomacy had fundamentally altered. The milieu within which the Congress of Vienna had taken place no longer existed." Lacking the broadly similar cultural attitudes and political perceptions on which Vienna's negotiators could rely, even when they disagreed about practical modalities, Allied leaders approached the construction of the League of Nations from widely divergent perspectives. That was particularly true of Woodrow Wilson, whose singular faith in the disciplining power of international public opinion discounted equally both the lingering effects of the war itself and the new challenges generated by a settlement that, as Murray shows, either failed to resolve or actually exacerbated the most likely sources of renewed conflict. If, therefore, the Versailles settlement was "the peace without a chance," the collective approach to universal governance embodied in the League of Nations was similarly foredoomed.

The same would prove true a quarter century later when the representatives of fifty nations met in San Francisco to draw up the United Nations Charter. By then, no one any longer imagined that peace could be enforced by the pressure of popular disapproval alone. Instead, however, an equally optimistic premise prevailed: that an international collegium similar to the nineteenth-century's Concert of Europe, and with similar interest in the maintenance of peace, could be contrived among states as differing in political ideology, economic strength, and military exposure as those comprising the permanent membership of the UN's Security Council.

As Professor Gray explains in discussing the world after the catastrophe of 1945, that illusion vanished almost immediately as the latent contest between liberal capitalism and totalitarian communism intensified and expanded from Europe to Asia and the Third World. Victory over the Axis had in no way diminished the sociopolitical fissures among the victorious powers – fissures that predated the outbreak of war and that its conclusion swiftly enlarged. "[T]he Anglo-Americans and the Soviets were not genuine allies," Gray rightly points out. "[T]hey were co-belligerents." Similar albeit far less profound disagreements separated anticolonial America from its prewar colonialist allies such as Britain, France, and Holland.

Hence, far from underwriting the international harmony for which the UN's designers had hoped, the settlement of 1945 merely replaced one struggle with another. Peace in the sense of an absence of armed conflict endured, in Europe at least, but it owed little to universal governance. Instead, it survived precariously as the by-product of a new and even more terrifying threat than the one it had replaced. In Gray's words, it was not "a peace resting on shared norms beyond the necessity of avoiding dangerous behavior likely to raise the risks of nuclear war." Indeed, its effect, compounded by nativist revolutions, was merely to shift the locus of violent conflict from Europe to Asia.

As these cases attest, the value consensus essential to collective governance has proven impossible to sustain on anything resembling a universal scale and of limited application even when applied more narrowly to a limited geographic region in which all share a reasonably common sociopolitical heritage. Thus, today, while the European Union, for example, certainly contributes in some measure to sustaining continental peace, continued unrest in southeast Europe, the uncertain future of relations with a resurgent Russia, and, above all, the growing challenge of militant Islam all confirm its limitations as an effective peace-keeping alternative to classical imperium.

The second peace-making theory reflected in the preceding pages – the maintenance of strategic equilibrium or, more familiarly, the balance of power – is virtually the antithesis of universal governance. Far from viewing fragmented sovereignty as a threat to peace, those committed to equilibrium instead view it as peace's most reliable guarantor, provided only that no nation or coalition can grow so strong that no countervailing power can restrain it. Such a view takes for granted the persistent conflict of values and interests and makes no effort to superimpose a universal resolution beyond assuring that no single state achieves military dominance sufficient to threaten the integrity of the system overall.

Satisfying that requirement, however, has proved no easy task. As Kissinger notes, "the balance of power should be quite calculable; in practice, it has proved extremely difficult to work out realistically.... Consensus on the nature of the equilibrium is usually established by periodic conflict." As several of our chapters reveal, the settlements most closely associated with equilibrium maintenance tend to verify that appraisal.

Thus, after an all-too-brief period of military quiescence, post–Westphalia Europe was wracked in succession by a series of limited conflicts launched by European monarchs to adjust what they perceived as defects in the balance of power: the War of the Grand Alliance from 1689 to 1697, the Spanish Succession from 1701 to 1714, the Polish Succession from 1733 to 1738, the War of Jenkins' Ear from 1739 to 1742, the War of Austrian Succession from 1740 to 1748, and, finally, the Seven Years' War – perhaps the first truly global war – from 1756 to 1763.

Similarly, while the Vienna settlement of 1815 succeeded for nearly a century in preventing total continental war, it could not prevent the series of more limited military contests that began in 1848 with the wars of Italian independence and culminated in the Franco-Prussian War of 1870–1871.

Given that checkered history, it is little wonder that scholars such as Paul Schroeder dismiss as fanciful the very notion of maintaining peace through equilibrium, insisting that it would require in practice an unattainably uniform distribution of strategic advantages. An alternative and perhaps more reasonable interpretation is that strategic equilibrium is less a prescription for preventing war altogether – an objective viewed by equilibrium theorists as unachievable – than for limiting its frequency, scale, and consequences.

Even that more modest achievement, moreover, historically has presumed the existence of an effective strategic balancer, a nation sufficiently immune from threat to maintain political freedom of action in relation to its neighbors, sufficiently powerful to confer decisive strategic advantage on the weaker side of any threatened confrontation among them, and, above all, sufficiently committed to stability to be willing to do so. Throughout the late eighteenth and well into the nineteenth century, Britain fulfilled that role. Later, as the Concert of Europe foundered in exploding nationalism and Britain withdrew from routine continental involvement, Bismarck's Prussia assumed a growing share of the balancing responsibility. As Professor Jones notes, Bismarck himself "worked assiduously to convince the other European powers that the existing constellation of power was the most advantageous and that all stood to lose from war."

In doing so, moreover, Bismarck was careful never to threaten the key ingredient of Britain's power: the predominance of the Royal Navy. His successors were less prudent. Bowing to the ambitions of a monarch whose resentments overmatched his judgment, Germany after Bismarck challenged Britain in the one arena in which challenge was intolerable.[5] As a result, at the very moment when long-suppressed antagonisms were beginning to resurface and intensify among the continent's great powers, Britain under the pressure of Germany's ill-thought-out naval buildup abandoned the "splendid isolation" that had contributed materially to a half century of strategic equilibrium. The subsequent hardening of the European balance into two

---

[5] For a comprehensive treatment, see Robert K. Massie, *Dreadnought: Britain, Germany, and the Coming of the Great War* (New York, 1991).

opposed alliances progressively eroded the diplomatic flexibility on which the preservation of peace depended. What followed was, indeed, a dispute about measurement, the more terrible for permitting no resolution short of exhaustion.

One more such war would elapse and the threat of one still more terrible would arise before another deliberate attempt to construct a strategic equilibrium, this time with the United States as the putative balancer between a Soviet Union and Communist China that, by the mid-1970s, had become more threatening to each other than either toward the West. The Nixon Doctrine and "triangulation" were successful in extricating the United States from military over-commitment in Asia and in negotiating a less dangerous *modus vivendi* in Central Europe. But, much as its nineteenth-century predecessor had, the Nixon Doctrine soon came under fire for prioritizing strategic stability over political liberalization and social justice.

Meanwhile, efforts by the Soviet Union to exploit perceived American weakness in the wake of defeat in Vietnam cast doubt on its ability even to guarantee stability. As Professor Kagan points out, Soviet adventurism in the 1980s reflected a mistaken appraisal of America's strategic resilience and masked the growing weaknesses in the Soviet Empire itself. But it was sufficiently threatening to undermine America's confidence, at least among major segments of its political élite, that the United States could safely regulate relations with the Communist powers by continued balance-of-power diplomacy.

Instead, with the election of President Ronald Reagan, Kagan argues, the United States effectively abandoned equilibrium in favor of a deliberate effort to aggravate the Soviet Union's economic and military overextension. When, however, that effort – augmented by the success of Soviet reformers – produced the very implosion that diplomat George Kennan had forecast forty years earlier, the shocking abruptness of the Soviet collapse found the United States and its allies wholly unprepared for the resulting international disorder and bereft of any coherent strategy with which to manage it.

In sum, if the weakness of collective universal governance lay in its inability to achieve and sustain the necessary value consensus among an increasingly diverse range of political actors, that of strategic equilibrium has proven to be its military precariousness and, more recently, as widening information transparency increasingly has foreclosed cabinet diplomacy, the perceived amorality of its policy prescriptions. Above all, however, strategic equilibrium has proved unsatisfactory, especially to Americans, in failing to promote the progressive elimination of armed conflict entirely as a means of resolving international disputes.

Instead, confronting an international system that, freed of the disciplining embrace of rival superpowers, seems to be reverting to nearly pre-Westphalian ethnic, religious, and tribal enmities, the United States under its current leadership has revived still a third theory of peace keeping, one that at least nominally rejects the moral expedience and tolerance of episodic violence associated with balance-of-power diplomacy, and instead rests on an almost theological confidence in the intrinsically pacific impulses of popularly elected governments. Such governments, so this theory holds, almost never fight each other and can be induced to fight even autocratic states only under great provocation. Hence, the only realistic avenue to enduring peaceful change is the progressive expansion of democracy.

As historian Joseph Ellis points out, one can find expressions of that optimistic belief as early as the late eighteenth century in the conviction of revolutionaries like Paine and Jefferson that, with monarchy abolished, "the latent potential for self-government inside all human beings would flow forward to create a perfectly harmonious society requiring only a minimum of supervision."[6] The same conviction would reemerge in the next century as a central theme in emerging socialist theories. But not until after the carnage of the First World War would any statesman attempt to apply it as a practical diplomatic prescription.

For Woodrow Wilson, only the self-regulating power of popular government could be counted on to resist the selfish rivalries otherwise intrinsic to a world of independent nation-states. Wilson's "Fourteen Points" rested, in his own words, on "the principle of justice to all peoples and nationalities, and their right to live on equal terms of liberty and safety with one another, whether they be strong or weak."[7] If the great object of American involvement in the First World War was to "make the world safe for democracy," the means by which Wilson envisioned doing so was through the enlargement of democracy itself.[8] Essentially, the same view underwrites contemporary U.S. foreign policy.

As the unhappy denouement of the Versailles settlement revealed and recent events seem to confirm, however, democratization as a mechanism to achieve peace confronts thus far insuperable obstacles. For starters, paraphrasing Edmund Burke, before counting on democracy to diminish the incidence of war, we might at least pause to consider what its putative adopters are likely to do with it. Wilson himself managed blithely to ignore the eagerness with which the British and French populations marched to war in 1914, and, as the unhappy experience of dealing with popular elected leaders from Adolph Hitler to Mahmoud Ahmadinejad and Hugo Chavez reveals, more recent evidence of the intrinsic peacefulness of elected governments is anything but uniform.

---

[6] Joseph J. Ellis, *American Creation* (New York, 2007), p. 44.
[7] Woodrow Wilson, "Program for Peace," Message to Congress, January 8, 1918.
[8] Not all his allies shared his confidence. France's Georges Clemenceau commented mordantly in relation to the Fourteen Points that "God Himself had only ten."

Even were that not so, the relative influence on the acceptability of war of political process versus other competing social impulses – religious fervor, tribal or ethnic identity, historical grudges – remains unclear. Indeed, one might argue that far from suppressing such impulses, democracy instead enlarges their potential sway. There certainly is reason to doubt whether the democratization of such currently autocratic states as Egypt and Saudi Arabia would materially improve the chance of lasting peace in the Middle East.

Finally, there is the awkward problem – only too pertinent as this book goes to press – that promotion of democracy, absent agreement about the sort of society it is intended to produce, is itself a potentially destabilizing process. That such promotion can succeed is not in doubt, as the political evolution of Germany and Japan since 1945 confirms. But the prerequisite was a war to the knife that left both those societies and others in ruins. Given developments since in the means of waging war, one does not like to contemplate what a contemporary replay would resemble.

Civil wars present a peculiarly troublesome challenge to peace making since in such conflicts, the very shape and legitimacy of the sociopolitical relationship is at stake. All wars are zero-sum to a degree – if a nonzero-sum solution to the prompting dispute were obvious to both contestants, there likely would be no war in the first place – but civil wars most of all. In such conflicts, at least one and often both (or all) contending parties are seen by their adversaries as having no legitimate standing whatsoever, either to fight or to negotiate. Such conflicts historically have been especially brutal. China's mid-nineteenth-century Tai Ping rebellion, for example, may have inflicted as many as thirty million direct and indirect deaths, more than half the number suffered during the Second World War by all the warring nations added together.

For both reasons, civil wars tend to end either in the collapse of the warring state and its fragmentation into two or more geographically separated political entities or else the virtual annihilation of the losing parties or party. Where neither of these outcomes results, one commentator has noted: "The evidence across several studies suggests that such conflicts will not end in decisive military victory; they will simply continue on interminably, resulting in more deaths and more economic destruction, which makes that nation even more susceptible to a recurrence of civil war, should the current war ever end."[9]

Indeed, even apparently decisive victory in a civil war may well be incomplete and the prompting struggle may continue for many years, albeit less

[9] T. David Mason, *Sustaining the Peace after Civil War* (Carlisle, PA, 2007), p. 70.

violently. As Professor McPherson demonstrates in his chapter, the American Civil War fits that pattern. Defeat and occupation of the South preserved the Union and ended slavery but by no means assured the "justice for all" for which the war had been fought. Rather, they inaugurated a century of nonmilitary but no less pervasive resistance, the effects of which still linger today.

In other civil wars, no settlement at all may be possible without external intervention, and the latter is itself likely to be prolonged and exhausting. In Northern Ireland, for example, thirty years of violence intervened between the onset of "The Troubles" and 1998's Belfast Agreement. NATO forces remain today in the former Yugoslavia more than ten years after the signing of the Dayton Accords. And in Iraq, one government spokesman recently estimated that his country would require foreign forces for another ten years.[10] Needless to say, none of the theories described previously offers up a convincing solution to this problem.

In sum, if there is a consistent pattern among the settlements described in the preceding pages, it is that successful peace making, like successful war making, is obdurately resistant to preconceived notions about how it should be conducted and toward what end. Like war making, peace making is heavily contextual. Like war making, it is vulnerable to fog, friction, and the unforeseen and often unforeseeable consequences of apparently innocuous decisions. And, like war making, peace making is hostage to clear objectives, focused effort, the balancing of energy with patience, and the resilience to survive and overcome the disappointments it inevitably will encounter.

Above all, like war making, peace making remains a fundamentally human enterprise, in which cold calculation invariably will be filtered through the passions, perceptions, and idiosyncrasies of powerful personalities. It is altogether impossible to imagine Westphalia absent Richelieu and Oxenstierna; Vienna absent Metternich, Castlereagh, and Talleyrand; Versailles absent Wilson, Balfour, and Clemenceau. Nor, as James Lacey's compelling indictment of Henry Dexter White demonstrates, has the modern bureaucratization of diplomacy succeeded in insulating the peace-making process from such influences.

Because it is a human endeavor, finally, perfection and finality are equally unlikely. We may aspire to permanent peace as we aspire to heaven but, here on earth, are compelled to accept, with Santayana, that "Only the dead have seen the end of war." As Sir Michael Howard advises, we would be wiser, like our Greek ancestors, to acknowledge conflict as mankind's

---

[10] "All eyes are on the Iraqi Army," *Los Angeles Times*, January 7, 2008.

"default condition" and bend our peace-making – and war-making – efforts to minimize the occasions when conflict must be resolved by force. Finally, and perhaps most important, we should seek to ensure that when only a trial by arms will satisfy political ends, it is conducted in a way calculated to improve the odds that the verdict, if not permanent, is at least as enduring as ingenuity and foresight can make it.

Index

DATE DUE
